One True Life

One True Life

The Stoics and Early Christians as Rival Traditions

C. Kavin Rowe

Yale
UNIVERSITY
PRESS
New Haven & London

Published with assistance from the Ronald and Betty Miller Turner Publication Fund.

Yale University Press books may be purchased in quantity for educational, business, or promotional use. For information, please e-mail sales.press@yale.edu (U.S. office) or sales@yaleup.co.uk (U.K. office).

Set in PostScript Electra and Trajan types by IDS Infotech, Ltd.
Printed in the United States of America.

Library of Congress Control Number: 2015937657
ISBN 978-0-300-18012-1 (cloth : alk. paper)

A catalogue record for this book is available from the British Library.

This paper meets the requirements of ANSI/NISO Z39.48-1992 (Permanence of Paper).

10 9 8 7 6 5 4 3 2 1

For William Thomas and Betty Bullard Rowe
In memory of my father and in honor of my mother

Contents

Preface

We often forget that Christianity's entrance into the world was a surprise. My previous book, *World Upside Down*, was an attempt to repaint something of this surprise according to the only first-century narrative we have about it, the Acts of the Apostles. In *World Upside Down* I explored the strangeness, explosiveness, and potential for reconfiguration of human life that was initially part of the Christian way of being in a world that had never seen it. The principal focus was on what we could call common pagan culture—the central strands of the web that made being a pagan in the Mediterranean world. What happens when these strands encounter the Christian mission? Trying to answer this question according to Acts directed my attention by and large to questions of "religiousness," "politics," and, because of Paul's lengthy trial, "jurisprudence." In particular, the scenes that displayed pagan resistance to the coming of the Christians illuminated fundamental features of Christianity's surprise: businessmen discerned the danger to their livelihood (Philippi, Ephesus), politicians found themselves in a pickle (Felix, Festus), local religious authorities saw their celebrations stop (Lystra), and so on. The modes of resistance varied, but they were all eventually intertwined with a sort of violence—the type that was based on the truth that the repentance and cultural reconstitution required by the Christians amounted to a devastation of constitutive patterns of a long-established, normal way of life.

But there would have been another mode of resistance as well, strong philosophical traditions that would claim truth for their particular ways of life. As a whole I did not treat philosophy in *World Upside Down* because I was thinking more about everyday pagan life than about specific strong traditions. And of course most people were not philosophers. Yet considering the questions raised by pagan philosophical life is strictly and foundationally necessary to understanding the kind of truth that Christianity claimed. This book is thus an extension of the sort of thinking begun in *World Upside Down;* it is the second necessary part of a larger trajectory of sketching the surprise of emergent Christianity in a world that did not know what it was and—in some highly significant ways—did not want it.

There are many people to thank for all that goes into writing a book like this. Chief among them must be Al McDonald and the McDonald Agape Foundation. Al generously provided the time for me to complete this manuscript during a period of life in which I could write almost nothing without such support. Al also spoke and corresponded with me about the book's substance. I am and will remain grateful for his investment and can only hope that the future will show it to have been worthwhile. There are, of course, many others. I will simply mention some names that come to mind as the human sine qua non for the book's existence: Joe and Pam Ponzi, Richard Hays, Greg Jones, Stanley Hauerwas, Paul Griffiths, Allan Poole, the Tonns, Gini Osborne, W. Mallard, J/M Winn, M/J Dube, S. Dod, the Leims, Nathan Eubank, T. J. Lang, Chris Blumhofer, Dustin Ellington, and—yet again—Susan Bond. My colleagues at Duke, especially in New Testament, are sources of inspiration in many different ways, and I thank them. The book is dedicated to my parents because of their love. My father did not live to see the book finished, but my mother will be delighted enough for both of them.

My son Isaac knew not of my first book and cared not about the second. He has shown a little interest in this third book and wonders aloud whether ol' Dad may finally get something right. He reminds me that even if the chances for this are not so good, the bass will still bite in the summer. Gabrielle—what can really be said in public? There is only one life now.

My editor, Jennifer Banks, has carefully read this manuscript and offered wise advice and thoughtful, serious critique. Dozens of emails and many phone calls later, the book is finally finished. Dan Heaton's editing was swift and sagacious (the fact that Dan is a serious baseball fan explains this latter quality). Two anonymous readers for Yale University Press offered helpful criticism, some of which I took and some of which I did not—but the latter only with real questions and even doubts about the wisdom of my choices. But that is, after all, the base of any book: a willingness to take the chance on one's choices about what to say and how to say it. I could be wrong, but I have said what I mean to say and must now let it go . . .

One True Life

INTRODUCTION

At its heart, this book is about the fact that we can live only one life. The track from birth to death can be run—or walked, or crawled, or held in the arms of others—only once. However much we speak metaphorically of aging as an eventual return to the dependence of childhood, no human being has ever grown from an adult to an infant. We all go only one way, toward death.

How we should travel this one-way road—if in fact there is a *should*—is a question as old as human reflection on the journey itself. Is there a best or right or true way to live? To what should we entrust ourselves? Can we find healing for what ails us? Can we make it up as we go? Can we waste our lives? The remarkable thing—and it really is *very* remarkable once you contemplate it—is that there are mutually incompatible and competing answers. The human condition is such that you have to choose how to live from among options that rule one another out.[1] The path from birth to death is simultaneously, therefore, a path of lived affirmation and of negation, and not one without the other. It is this intersection between the existential necessity of lived affirmation/negation and the claim to a true way of life that lies at the center of the conflict among rival traditions.[2]

Since by training, however, I am a scholar of the New Testament and its environs, I'm most interested in pursuing the existential demands of rival traditions vis-à-vis a historically rich and important juxtaposition—that of the Roman Stoics and the early Christians. Because both Roman Stoicism and early Christianity are too vast to treat in their entirety, I made some choices. These choices create the architecture of the book.

ARCHITECTURE AND RATIONALE

The book is divided into three main parts of three chapters each. The focus of Part I is exposition of the literature of the Roman Stoics: the texts of Seneca, Epictetus, and Marcus Aurelius. Part II carries the same burden for the early

Christian saints: Paul, Luke, and Justin Martyr. In Part III I construe the relation of Part I to Part II as a juxtaposition of rival traditions of life, and reflect on the implications of the rivalry for our reasoning about incommensurable forms of life. My basic critical contention is that we cannot hope to understand the Stoic/Christian relation if we continue to read them in the way we usually have. Encyclopedic inquiry—the name for the epistemic assumptions of the vast majority of modern scholarly work on the Stoics and the New Testament—is dead and gone. We should take notice.

Stoicism and Christianity are traditions of life, and thinking their relation involves considerable difficulties that cut to the core of how we can think lived difference at all. As I will argue in Chapter 7, a tradition of life is a morally grained, historically situated rationality, a way of asking and answering questions that is inescapably tied to the inculcation of habits in the life of the knower and to the community that originates and stewards the craft of inquiry through time. *Tradition*, in this sense, is the word that best describes the forms of life that were ancient Christianity and Stoicism.[3]

In contrast to the long-dominant and dichotomous way of conceiving the work that thought is, the ancients did not sever intellection from life but instead believed that ordered, correct thought was the work of a well-lived life. The pattern of life itself was that which tutored thought in its proper work even as true thinking shaped the life that was being lived. To study the Christians and the Stoics is thus to realize that relating their traditions must take account of the fact that difference in the meaning of words is tied to difference in life. As Jonathan Barnes has shown, there was logic chopping in the imperial period, as there always will be in one place or another.[4] But as whole, for the ancients true thinking was living in the right pattern of life.

Precisely because we must deal with lived thought, the analysis does not compare our chosen early Christians with this or that item on a reconstructed philosophical smorgasbord. Smorgasbord comparison prohibits the examination of a philosophical tradition as a tradition and replaces the textual home of particular words with generalized scholarly reconstruction; the smorgasbord therefore hinders rather than aids understanding. I shall instead, then, focus on particular people, complete philosophical texts—in short, on actual philosophers.[5]

The rationale for my selection of the Stoics Seneca, Epictetus, and Marcus Aurelius is not particularly complex. It is motivated by several interdependent judgments.[6] First, as most historians realize, philosophy by the imperial period was more diffuse or, in Pierre Hadot's word, "democratized," and less concentrated in independent, opposing schemes. Witness the debate in Cicero's slightly earlier *On the Nature of the Gods*, for example, in which the competition among three friends—a Stoic, an Epicurean, and a Skeptic—invariably involves substantial agreement on many points. Yet it is also well known that to the degree that the philosophical mélange had a dominant flavor, it was Stoicism. Focusing on these three Stoics thus helps to sharpen our historical perception in that it situates our reflection within the dominant philosophical currents that surround early Christianity.

Second, as John Sellars's recent book has confirmed, it was the Stoics who were primarily known in the ancient world for focusing explicitly on philosophy as a way of life. Indeed, in the second century AD, the Skeptic Sextus Empiricus wrote against the Stoics on just this point: philosophy as the art of living was nonsensical, thought Sextus, and the Stoics quite confused.[7] Moreover, of the surviving philosophical works whose grammar displays the tendency toward lived thought, none are more important than those of Seneca, Epictetus, and Marcus Aurelius. Seneca's *Letters*, for example, have recently been called "the greatest body of surviving Stoic therapeutic writing."[8] And Epictetus's *Enchiridion* and Marcus's *Meditations* have been judged as "perhaps the most important surviving texts relating to Stoic *askēsis*."[9] When it comes to literary remains, we can do no better. Fragments of Musonius, or reported comments from Rusticus, or someone else in this text or that, do no more philosophically than fill in what we're able to see of Roman Stoicism in the works of the big three.[10]

Third, in a way that simply is not true for, say, Epicureanism or Cynicism—which are prima facie incompatible with much of the New Testament—the Stoicism of these three figures is sufficiently complex to make for an interesting juxtaposition. That is, reading Seneca, Epictetus, and Marcus Aurelius together with Paul, Luke, and Justin requires a suppleness and discrimination in judgment that takes account of the potentially puzzling phenomenon in which similarity and disagreement seem to intertwine and coexist. We cannot, therefore, simply think about overlap or divergence between Seneca and Paul, for example, but must think in terms of more complex patterns that would allow the simultaneous existence of similarity and disagreement within an overall different style of being. This, I think, is both far more interesting and illuminating than tracing this or that Platonic or Aristotelian theme or noting after a long discussion the obvious fact that the Epicureans and early Christians—though both were eventually dubbed "atheists" by those who scorned them—had virtually nothing in common.

Finally, Stoicism has long been an explicit and even close conversation partner for Christian thinkers and saints and therefore provides a stronger impetus for reflection on the final differences that keep them apart.[11] To think only of the reception of Seneca's works among Christians: not only did someone invent a collection of correspondence between Paul and Seneca, Tertullian went so far as to call Seneca *saepe noster*, "frequently ours." Only a century later Jerome went even farther. Seneca, said Jerome, was simply *noster*, "ours," and thus earned his place in a work *On Illustrious Men*. Though he is not without severe criticism, Augustine, too, in his magisterial *City of God*, approvingly cites passages from Seneca's lost work *On Superstition*. In the Middle Ages, Dante made him the ethicist in the palace of virtuous pagans. Boccaccio, Petrarch, Erasmus, and others turned to Seneca for one reason or another. Even among the Reformers, who tended to emphasize the unadulterated message of the Bible, admiration existed; as a young man John Calvin, for example, wrote a commentary on Seneca's *On Clemency*. And the list goes on and on. While Epictetus and Marcus Aurelius may not have enjoyed quite the same level of attention, they also were received as important sources both for and against Christian thinking. Epictetus's *Enchiridion*, for example, circulated in antiquity under Christian auspices. And, from the other side of the argument, when in the nineteenth century Ernest Renan developed his principal attack against Christianity, he did it via the *Meditations* of Marcus Aurelius. From there, the debate over the (in)compatibility of New Testament Christianity and Stoicism raged on through the Enlightenment, and it continues even today. This long history of reception—in which scholars attempt both to separate and to unite Stoicism and Christianity—suggests that juxtaposing Christian and Stoic traditions is a particularly promising way of eliciting creative thought about complex cases in which rival traditions negotiate each other's claims to truth through time.

My chosen Christians are virtually self-explanatory. Of the writers in the New Testament who are most aware of larger Greco-Roman philosophical currents, Paul and Luke stand out above the rest (with the possible exception of the author of Hebrews). It has also long been noted that Paul's letters constitute an attempt to shape community identity in a way that is analogically similar to Seneca's attempt to work on Lucilius (hence the early creation of a correspondence between Paul and Seneca). Moreover, Paul is a vibrant and distinctive religious thinker who speaks in his own voice and whose letters exhibit direct, vigorous argument and instruction about a pattern of life that proves particularly interesting when juxtaposed with Stoic norms for achieving wisdom. Focusing on Paul is thus a way to work inside the theology of weakness and foolishness that characterizes the way in which the "first Christian theologian" constructs the engagement with the wise. Can one live, for example, toward wisdom in the way Seneca's letters advise us while simultaneously living in light of Paul's arguments in 1 Corinthians? Or do the *Epistulae* and 1 Corinthians project mutually incompatible styles of existence that in practice cannot be merged into a single human life simultaneously? In short, do the arguments of Seneca and Paul require two different kinds of lives such that to live them both would require a conversion from one to the other, a turning away from one pattern of existence toward another, fundamentally different pattern? Such important questions, it would seem, can be answered only by developing a richly textured historical imagination, one that can look past our inherited text/life dichotomy toward the way in which a devotee of Seneca might in fact rub shoulders with a Pauline Christian. Could this happen in the same body?

Luke is the first Christian to present Paul in a dialogue with the philosophical currents of the day. The many echoes of Stoicism in Paul's famous speech in Athens are loud enough to hear for all but the most philosophically tone deaf. The Areopagus speech, however, is only one piece of Luke's larger theological program vis-à-vis pagan culture more generally. From the start of his Gospel to the end of the Acts of the Apostles, Luke narrates Christian beginnings as God's revelation to the non-Jewish world. Luke does not say that the Gentiles knew God imperfectly but something much more difficult for modern comparative sensibilities, that is, that the pagans reasoned in darkness (Acts 26:18). The need was not to reach up to God a little higher in ever-clearer knowledge but for God to make himself known to them from entirely beyond what they were in principle able to know. Despite the fact that the Lukan writings have been the subject of extensive exploration in search of philosophical influence, they plainly raise the question of reason's clarity and even viability apart from its directedness inside the movement Luke knows as the Christians. Can human beings think our way to God apart from the repentance that takes us inside the Christian community's pattern of life, where we learn what the apostles teach and how to live?

Of the early Christians who explicitly treated the relation between philosophia and Christianity, Justin Martyr was the first to speak explicitly of Christianity as a philosophy. Justin, moreover, continued to wear his philosopher's cloak after his turn to Christianity and thus argued with his life-practice for both a deep similarity between philosophical schemes and Christian life and a necessity for conversion from one to the other. Justin's was a deeply practical reason with a theoretical and exegetical flare. Other Christians were obviously interested in this relation between Christianity and philosophy, but Justin's argument that Christianity is true philosophia maintains deep continuity with the Stoic understanding of philosophy as lived wisdom and in the same breath, as it were, calls for conversion out of particular forms of the philosophical life and into the Christian pattern of being. In short, Justin raises the question of philosophical truth in its most acute form: what is the true way of life?

I explore the complexity of this question through the three chapters of Part III. The chapters' order displays the requisite pattern for serious engagement with rival traditions that claim the true life comes in the living out of their tradition. In Chapter 7 I describe the brokenness of the comparative model that underlies much work on rival traditions and subsequently articulate a more intellectually satisfying way to think their relation. In Chapter 8 I construct the narratives that are the necessary stuff of any juxtaposition between traditions of life, and subsequently demonstrate the untranslatability of one tradition's terms into the other's. Finally, in Chapter 9 I discuss Jeffrey Stout's version of bricolage and Alasdair MacIntyre's account of an "epistemological crisis" as ways to conceive the (im)possibilities of traditions that can(not) be translated. Contra both Stout and MacIntyre, it is the "wager" or "leap" stream of reflection on humanity's reasoning power that sees most deeply when it comes to our ability to reason about incommensurable patterns of life.[12]

ARGUMENT

The argument of this book is that in order to deal seriously with the relation of Stoicism to Christianity we have to deal with it as a relation of rival traditions of life. Both the Roman Stoics and the early Christians claimed that their pattern of life was the truth of all things but also that such truth could be known only through the time it took to live the tradition that was the truth. Trust, induction, discipline, instruction, formation, apprenticeship, care, healing—these were the ways the truth of all things was known and thought. Not this or that piece of information about the human condition, not this or that view of the *pneuma* (spirit/air), not this or that take on the passions, but an existentially structuring pattern, a trajectory of living the one and only life we can live in the midst of time; this was the way truth was contested. No amount of overlap in the treatment of, say, wrath or anger, no amount of agreement about the necessity of breaking with daily (pagan) life, no amount of commonality in condemnation of wayward living can erase or even blunt the fact that Stoicism and Christianity stand face to face as competing traditions of true lives. That, in fact, is exactly what they compete for: human lives in devotion to their way of truth.

Only in recent decades has the study of Stoicism become a "mainstream scholarly interest," and consideration of Stoicism's relation to early Christianity "is no more than at its very beginning."[13] It is therefore perhaps unsurprising that we lack, to my knowledge, a systematic reconsideration of what it is that we are studying and/or how to study it. To be sure, experts in ancient Stoicism—Max Pohlenz, A. A. Long, Brad Inwood, and others—have seen its claim to be the "spiritual movement" of truth for human life. And scholars of early Christianity would be all but blind—indeed, they would forfeit the designation "scholar"—were they to miss the Christian claim to truth. But construing their relation as rival traditions of true lives is missing in modern discourse.[14] And yet it is precisely this that makes their relation a real question in the first place.

The difference the names Stoic and Christian represent is thus lived truth. It is a much more difficult—and ultimately more interesting and significant—sort of difference to think about than the difference that occurs over topic X or Y within broader agreements on how to live. In fact, the book's argument is that we can think the difference itself but we cannot think inside it. We therefore cannot resolve it. Incommensurable difference in this case turns out to be rooted most deeply in the finitude of a human life and hence cannot be rationally overcome apart from the sort of reason that emerges only after the choice has been made to live in one way rather than another. Scholarly inquiry does not open all doors; without the life it takes to open them, some doors remain closed. The book's argument is thus not only about what sorts of things Stoicism and Christianity are, not only about the way we should think their relation if they are what they are, but also about how thinking lived difference is itself inseparably intertwined with the differences we ourselves live.

STYLE AND RATIONALE

The style of a book seldom requires comment, not least because style can be discerned simply through reading the book itself. In this case, however, there are two distinct styles within one argument. Parts I and II are one sort of thing, Part III another.

Parts I and II are exposition of the primary sources. *Mutatis mutandis,* what Stout said about *Ethics After Babel* is true of my argument, too: "Much of what I wanted to say . . . could only be said in close readings of particular works."[15] There is simply no way to think historically about rival traditions apart from rich and prolonged engagement with the texts that constitute the main streams of the traditions. The style of exposition in this book, however, is not that of the modern commentary in which the apparatus criticus threatens to overwhelm the primary text. Far too often exegetical notes on minutiae, discussion of the views of scholars X, Y, and Z, lexical data, and so on fill the pages of what is supposed to be an interpretation of the texts in question. By stark contrast, the reading of the texts in this book is more like what Paul Ricoeur would have called second-naïveté exposition. I am well aware, of course, of the bazillions of linguistic, textual, and critical problems for almost every passage of each text of our six authors. Still, for projects of *interpretation* at some point we have to get on with trying to say what they were trying to say.[16]

Dialogue was the most stimulating form of philosophical reasoning in the ancient world from Plato on, and I make liberal use of its advantages.[17] In my exposition I quite consciously interweave my understanding of what Justin, for example, is saying with what I hope is a creative way of using the texts to speak for him/me. It will frequently be difficult to disentangle my words about Justin from my words in Justin's mouth. Far from being an obstacle to interpretation, this, I take it, is the very point of genuine exegetical reflection—a "thinking after" as a "thinking with." We try to speak with the language of the texts as if the texts themselves speak.[18] I do not, therefore, always distinguish between my elaboration of, for example, Justin's point and Justin's point itself and am entirely unconcerned with the back-and-forth between descriptive analysis and dialogue with the texts.[19] The dialogues I construct just *are* my interpretative comments on what the ancients are doing.

I liberally quote the primary texts.[20] As Hadot put it in his commentary on Marcus's *Meditations*, "I have chosen to quote the Meditations abundantly. I thoroughly dislike those monographs which, instead of letting the author speak and staying close to the text, engage in obscure elucubrations which claim to carry out an act of decoding and reveal the 'unsaid' of the thinker, without the reader's having the slightest idea of what that thinker really 'said.'"[21] Hadot may underestimate the difficulty in knowing the "said" of the text in question, but his disdain for "obscure elucubrations" and desire to display the actual words of the texts as a way to think, describe well my basic commitment in this book. When it comes to style, Parts I and II are textually elaborate dialogical reflections on the writings of each tradition.

The style of Part III is the less creative—but no less intellectually difficult—direct engagement with contemporary scholars and thinkers. The attempt is to think both with and against those who, on the one hand, exemplify the best scholarship on the Stoics and the early Christians and, on the other, who think most powerfully about the problem of relating rival traditions.

Taken together, the two distinct styles make a unified argument about reading ancient texts of rival traditions: textually mediated thinking is necessarily intertwined with contemporary judgments about how to relate different traditions and, conversely, contemporary judgments about ancient traditions are inescapably exegetical positions of one sort or another; readers of ancient texts cannot escape the way we read. Neither, however, can self-consciousness about the complexities of reading rivalry relieve us of the need to exegete the texts as a way to think the rivalry.[22]

HOPE

My hope for this book is to renew our thinking and clarify our reasoning about the study of the ancient world so that we may once again take the ancients' claims to the truth about human life as constitutive for the way we think about the traditions their texts represent. The study of emergent Christianity within wider Greco-Roman philosophical culture has become a field of minutiae: we pick and choose this or that little theme from the Roman world, showing how it may relate to this or that small part of one New Testament document or author and miss entirely the significance of the questions that animated the sources we're reading.[23] Both the New Testament and the ancient philosophical texts are inconceivable—*tout court* inconceivable—as documents of minutiae. To study them as if matters of life and death were not on the table is not to conceive their finer grained points in moments of scholarly repose. It is, rather, to miss the point altogether.

Seneca, that thinker on death par excellence, would doubtless agree. To him we thus turn first.

Part One

1

SENECA

Philosophy . . . moulds and constructs the soul.
—*Seneca,* Ad Lucilium epistulae morales

A half-century or so before Seneca was born, no less a person than Cicero described a complete man as one who was "at once senator, man of letters, and philosopher."[1] That, indeed, was not only Cicero himself, but exactly what Seneca became. A reading of his remaining work is an encounter with one of the most remarkable and influential Romans history can remember. In retrospect, other than old Caesar Augustus himself, no Roman in Seneca's century can hold a candle to him.

LETTERS

Lucius Annaeus Seneca was a statesman and Stoic philosopher who, along with the praetorian prefect Burrus, ran the empire for the first several years of Nero's reign. Seneca tutored Nero, advised him, wrote for him, conspired against him, and was eventually forced to commit suicide because of him. Seneca is remembered in pagan and Christian literature with an ample measure of both praise and critique.

His literary output was significant in scope and content. Not only did he write theatrical tragedies and essays on a variety of topics ranging from mercy to leisure, he also composed considerable reflections on things "natural"—the Nile River, for example—and kept up what could be called a literary correspondence. The letters he wrote during the last two years of his life to his friend Lucilius were highly polished, for example, and number just shy of 125. Some of Seneca's works were lost, and there were some spurious attributions, but the remaining pieces of Seneca's oeuvre are outstanding exemplars of a Stoic philosopher and real human being at work.

We will focus on Seneca's letters to Lucilius because of his works these offer the clearest example of Seneca's attempt to shape a human life in accordance with Stoic philosophical *regulae* for true practical knowledge.[2] Indeed, as Martha Nussbaum has observed, Seneca's letters are not isolated notes to a friend but instead constitute "one long rich *exemplum*" of what the Stoic way of life has to offer.[3] We shall, of course, freely draw on his other writings where they help to illuminate the point under discussion. But by and large, the texts in the spotlight are his extant letters, "the masterpiece of the dramatic final three years of Seneca's life."[4]

A careful reading of these letters discloses a remarkably wide array of issues on which Seneca sought to offer his advice, or better, a trajectory of care. Still, there are recurrent emphases, some of which provide illuminating points of continuity and/or juxtaposition with our other two Stoics and our chosen Christians. We will focus on five such areas: death, Fortuna, God, the passions, and philosophy. We begin with death for the simple reason that for Seneca it is death above all else that requires philosophical response. Treating death first will thus provide a richer sense of how Seneca speaks about Fortuna, God, the passions, and philosophy. After our treatment of death, we may move more easily through the other four areas.

DEATH

Readers shaped by a contemporary Western culture with its emphasis on staying young and healthy may be rather surprised upon reading Seneca's letters at the frequency with which he talks about death. Of course, the ancients did not have the benefits of modern Western medicine. They suffered and died from conditions that are no longer a threat. Thus in general pain and death were more constant companions. Seneca was afflicted with an asthmatic condition that placed him in regular peril. It would be easy to attribute Seneca's focus on death to first-century realities.

But in truth this would be to misread Seneca on death. For his focus upon death is born not solely of a consciousness of the dying around him but of a sense of what the human being actually is. Our lot is to die. Seneca's language about death arises from what we would call (though he does not) the ontology of the human being. In principle, that is, in every single actual case, the kind of thing that the human being is, is the kind of thing that will die. In this way, Seneca's admonitions to Lucilius about how to practice dying are no more distant from us than we are from ourselves. Death is not closer to him than to us precisely because it is our end no less than his. Our interest in his discussion should be perennial, therefore, precisely because of the anthropologically unlimited reach of death itself.

There are many ways in which Seneca speaks about death in his letters. Yet there is a remarkable consistency that runs through his language and forms his basic analysis of death: death, so Seneca says again and again, is nothing less than the greatest cause of our dread and unhappiness. Going through a list of things people fear—the loss of children, health, reputation, and so on—Seneca writes that by far the largest number of miserable people are those "whom the expectation of death, which threatens them on every hand, drives to despair. For there is no quarter from which death does not approach" (*Ep.* 74.3). It is "everywhere near at hand" (*Ep.* 49). With a wide variety of images, Seneca develops for Lucilius the experience of the human fear of death: death is the "abyss into which everything slips" (*Ep.* 49.3) or the "precipice over which we all must fall," the end toward which "every hour thrusts us" more closely (*Ep.* 120.17). Indeed, the fear of the last hour makes all previous hours uneasy (*Ep.* 4.9). So great is humanity's fear that we consistently attempt not only to avoid pain, the most dramatic physical presentiment of death, but also to lengthen our lives by whatever means are available (*Ep.* 4). Never mind that we know that there are no degrees of death—being dead is the universal outcome regardless of the actual manner of our dying (*Ep.* 66.43)—or that we all must die. Seneca argues that we still treat death as that which happens to someone else. Like Tolstoy almost two millennia later, who knew that war can happen only because of our capacity to believe someone else will get killed in the battle, Seneca says that "we never think of death except as it affects our neighbor" (*Ep.* 101.6). Seneca's psychological point here is that human beings know they will die, but nevertheless deny their deathward existence by projecting it onto their fellows. In short, Seneca's letters repeatedly display his concern to grasp the widespread human condition vis-à-vis death as a self-destructive denial of the way things are and must be: we know that we are mortal and must die, and yet out of a fear of our death we organize our lives to a stunning degree in an attempt to avoid it. For Seneca, this is a sickness from which we need to be healed.

The heart of Seneca's therapeutic recommendations is easy to discern: old and young alike, we must look our death directly in the face, acknowledge its reality, and embrace it (*Ep.* 12 et passim). Yet, as Seneca grants, this is by no means an easy matter. Our fear of death has resulted in a set of habits that shape us to shun it. To be healed, therefore, human beings need to counter such habits with another: the practice of dying daily (*Ep.* 1, 4, et passim).

Since Plato philosophers had of course spoken about their work as training for death; indeed, Seneca even chastises the worried Lucilius by reminding him that Lucilius himself has once written eloquently about the commonplace *cotidie morimur*, "daily we die" (*Ep.* 24.19–21). Surely, says Seneca, "you meant this for yourself no less than for others" (*Ep.* 24.19). Death, Seneca reminds Lucilius, is not an event that happens only once, at the end of his life; it is, rather, something that happens to us all the time. "Every day a little of our life is taken from us; even when we are growing, our life is on the wane. We lose our childhood, then our boyhood, and then our youth. Counting even yesterday, all past time is lost time; the very day which we are now spending is shared with death." It is not "the last drop," he continues, "that empties the water clock, but all that which has previously flowed out; similarly, the final hour when we cease to exist does not of itself bring death but only consummates it. We reach death at that moment, but we have been a long time on the way" (*Ep.* 24.19–20). Each day, therefore, can be seen as a kind of schooling in death, a foretaste of the last day.

And well might it be, says Seneca, for we never know which drop is the last to empty the clock. We cannot see the span of our lives in relation to its patterns (*Ep.* 101.1). "You are younger," Seneca admonishes Lucilius, "but what does that matter? There is no fixed count of our years." Some die in infancy, others in youth, still others in middle or old age. "You do not know where death awaits you. So be ready for it everywhere" (*Ep.* 34.7). You should imitate me, Seneca implies with his counsel, for "I have looked on every day as if it were my last" (*Ep.* 93.6). With this perspective on each day, we can "order our souls as if we have come to the very end" (*Ep.* 101.8), thereby acquiring a life that is shaped by the daily recognition of death.

But how, Lucilius might wonder in his more anxious moments, does one actually do that? Fortunately, Seneca does not leave Lucilius to worry; nor does he (pointlessly) recommend dying daily as a general attitude or possible existential awareness. Instead, Seneca attempts to order well Lucilius's soul by speaking of a range of inseparable practices that bring him into a life of daily dying.

We must, for example, learn to despise death. In response to Lucilius's letter about his frequent illness, Seneca prescribes a medicine quite unlike what the *medicus* himself would give. Recalling his own recurrent bouts with a similar problem, Seneca speaks first of the importance of attentive human presence (his Stoic *amici*), and then moves to his own specific advice in contrast to that of the physician. "The doctor," says Seneca, "will prescribe for you some walks and some exercise; he will warn you not to indulge in idleness, as is the tendency of the inactive invalid; he will order you to read in a louder voice and to exercise your lungs; . . . he will recommend the proper food, and the suitable time for aiding your strength with wine or refraining from it in order to keep your cough from becoming irritated and hacking." All reasonable instructions. Seneca, however, offers different advice: "But as for me, my counsel to you is this: *despise death!*" Indeed, such scorning is not only the proper cure of your disease, Lucilius, it is the remedy for "the whole of your life" (*Ep.* 78.5). Thus where the physician's remedies tend entirely toward the preservation of physical life, Seneca seeks instead to shape the soul toward death as a way to deal with suffering and disease. "It is your body that is hampered by ill-health, not your soul" (*Ep.* 78.20).[5]

We would misunderstand Seneca were we to think that he was merely offering a coping mechanism for sickness. Much to the contrary, Seneca himself knows that we can emerge from certain illnesses physically stronger, that in a biologically important sense "disease has often postponed death" (*Ep.* 78.6). His point against the doctors, rather, is that pain and disease can serve as the occasion for clear-sighted vision of the human lot and, therefore, as the occasion to reckon with our natural end. "You will not die," he tells Lucilius in a startling turn of phrase, "because you are ill, but because you are alive." He continues: "Even when you have been restored to health, the same end awaits you; when you have convalesced, it will not be death that you have escaped—only ill-health" (*Ep.* 78.6). The fear and worry brought on by pain and disease are thus not, in Seneca's view, finally about these phenomena themselves but about our natural end in the grave. See that clearly, Seneca argues, and our worry can cease (see *Ep.* 24.12).

Like any good psychoanalyst, therefore, Seneca knows that distraction from that which worries us only increases our anxieties,[6] while facing directly their deepest source can (paradoxically) release them. He thus argues that the anxiety brought by Lucilius's sickness is not testimony to the problems of disease and pain itself but is instead the manifestation of the fact that Lucilius still fears death.[7] Caring philosophically for Lucilius in the midst of illness thus requires the treatment of anxiety by the redirection of the soul toward death. "No man," says Seneca, "can have a peaceful life who thinks about lengthening it" (*Ep.* 4.4).

No less does our ability to die daily depend upon a rigorous contemplation of death's consequences. Of the things upon which Lucilius should concentrate his attention, Seneca continually returns to four central points. First is the unpredictability of the moment of death. Focusing on the fact that death comes without consulting us about its timing should, Seneca argues, release us from anxiety about our future plans. Your plans, dear Lucilius, become obsolete because you are no longer there to live them out. In addition to a variety of images used to make this point, Seneca reminds Lucilius of the case of

Cornelius Senecio. The exemplum is particularly well chosen: Lucilius once knew Senecio, a fellow Equestrian on the rise and headed for fame and fortune. Senecio, however, did not live to see his plans materialize, for he was suddenly snuffed out by an allergic reaction to something he ate (that is, anaphylactic shock). To what substance we do not know, but the description is clear enough: one minute, on the way to riches, the next, dead and gone. One minute, a comfortable dinner; the next, a swelling of the throat, the loss of breath, and death (*Ep.* 101). Why be anxious for the future, Seneca's logic runs, when you could just as well die today from doing nothing more than eating a nut? Anxiety about the arc of a career or about the proper shape of retirement years, says Seneca to Lucilius, all presuppose our continued existence. Presuppose our death instead, and the fruitlessness of all the planning that goes with worry can appear in plain sight. There is no need to worry and frantically plan "to eternity," says Seneca, when in fact death could be directly over our shoulders (*Ep.* 101.1).

Yet Lucilius might point out that the unpredictability of death could only bring release from his anxiety were his death to mean nothing worse was going to happen to him thereafter. Indeed, differing views about what happens after death would lead to differing attitudes and practices toward unpredictable death. By no means, for example, was sudden death seen as a good thing in the Christian Middle Ages: a period of dying, so thought the medievals, gave time to prepare one's soul for the encounter with God.[8] Seneca, of course, anticipates this worry about the shape of things after death, and he is ready with an answer. So, second, the contemplation of death should show us that we really have nothing to dread. What did we dread before we were born? Seneca asks. Nothing, of course, since we did not exist prior to our birth. It will be no different with death, for death is "whatever condition existed before our birth" (*Ep.* 54.5).

Elsewhere Seneca assures Lucilius of his divine *anima:* "The divine soul, when it is about to issue forth from a man, regards the destination of its earthly vessel"—the disposal of the body—"as being of no more concern to itself than is the afterbirth to a child just born" (*Ep.* 92.34; cf. esp. *Ep.* 102.28–29). Of course, for the Stoics the totality of the cosmos is itself divine and eternal—and therefore, in their view, synonymous with *deus/theos*—so we should be careful about reading a doctrine of a distinct postmortem personhood into Seneca's psychagogic language. The "birthday of your eternity" (*Ep.* 102.26), for example, does not mean that you-as-you-and-others-know-you-in-life will henceforth exist after death as the same "you" but rather that the "you-who-you-were" becomes part of the larger, divine cosmos the day you die. In Seneca's thought, that is, the refusal to rule out altogether the possibility of postmortem life performs no positive work. It does only the work of negation: we don't know for sure that our rational souls won't live on, argues Seneca, but that does not actually matter in the least. If the soul lives on, it is obviously eternal and, therefore, cannot suffer. As all philosophers ought to know, suffering of the immortal soul would plainly violate the "rule of immortality": "Nothing can harm that which is everlasting" (*Ep.* 57.9). Don't worry, Seneca thus says to Lucilius, death either frees us or annihilates us (*Ep.* 24.18)—either way, there's nothing to fear.

Third, the contemplation of death destroys human pretension. Peacocks may well strut: they were made, in a sense, to do so. It is in accord with their nature, for they are more beautiful than the other birds. Human beings often mimic such animals, but we are fools to do so. In good Stoic fashion, Seneca argues that regardless of achievement or beauty or wealth—Seneca himself was lavishly rich—one man is not actually better than another. Focusing on death each and every day, Seneca enjoins his pupil, curtails the sense that we are better than our brothers, works against the habits that push us along in the race for recognition, and requires us to acknowledge the fundamental equality of humankind: in death, we are one. "Death alone is the equal privilege of humankind," the one thing that truly is no respecter of persons (*Ep.* 123.16). "Death has its fixed rule—equitable and unavoidable." Seneca continues, "Who can complain when he is governed by terms which include everyone?" (*Ep.* 30.11). Of course, Seneca has no foolish illusions about the lack of importance of birth and rank, but he hopes to train Lucilius to see beyond such contingencies to the deeper reality of our common mortality: "We are unequal at birth," admits Seneca, "but are equal in death." When it comes to death, there are "no distinctions between us on the basis of high lineage or of illustrious names. . . . To all creatures that burden the earth let one and the same law apply!" (*Ep.* 91.16). Yes, a "few great men" will raise their heads above "the deep flood of time that will roll over us," battling against oblivion and "maintaining their ground for long"; but even they "are destined at the last to depart into the same realms of silence" (*Ep.* 21.5).[9] All human posturing, Seneca implies, distracts us from the fact that we shall die. Focusing daily on our coming death, he reminds Lucilius, helps to overcome the distractions from death that human pretension requires to sustain its silliness and illusions. Even the emperor himself will meet the same fate as his slaves. Our end is a common one.

Finally, the contemplation of the consequences of death offers an unrivaled view onto the quality of our current life. "I'll leave it to death," Seneca writes, "to determine what [philosophical] progress I have made" (*Ep.* 26.5). Because dying discloses in a final sense the kind of life we have lived—we cannot decide to do things differently after we are dead—thinking about our coming death implicitly forces us to examine the life we are currently living in order to see what verdict death will render upon it. Such scrutiny may well uncover areas of our existence that call for deeper philosophical transformation. No matter, says Seneca: "My dear Lucilius, begin at once to live, and count each day as a separate life" (*Ep.* 101.10). Living each day as a full life—the perspective created by looking at the day as if we've died—exercises bit by bit a kind of quality control over the entire thing, regardless of when we actually expire. Life, Seneca tells Lucilius, is like a play—it matters not how long the action runs or at what precise point it ends. What matters is "how good the acting is," the philosophical quality of the life played out on the earthly stage (*Ep.* 77.20).

Seneca's repeated emphasis on these four themes as ways to reckon with death's consequences reveals a remarkably coherent and rigorous intellectual program that is intended to push Lucilius more deeply into a consistent practice of "dying daily." But, Lucilius might ask, toward what fundamental end shall I practice this art? Quite apart from the fact that it is both a commonplace and ontologically true—I grant, he evidently says, that we "advance toward death by slight degrees" each day we yet live (*Ep.* 24.19)—what is the philosophical point of the *practice* of daily dying? I will die whether I will or not: why practice it?

Seneca's answer to this question shows the heart of his philosophical therapy in the face of death. We practice dying each day, Seneca would say, because that is the only way to be free. Thinking on death simply is thinking on freedom, as even Epicurus himself knew. Epicurus, says Seneca, once admonished his pupils to "think on death"; by this he bids us to "think on freedom" (*Ep.* 26.10).[10] Were Lucilius to underestimate the connection between freedom and death, Seneca would teach him otherwise: no progress toward freedom can be made while the fear of death is in place. The very first step to freedom is to cast off the yoke of this fear (*Ep.* 80.5).[11] The consequence of remaining under the yoke of fear is not a diminished or relative freedom but slavery: "If the courage to die is lacking," Seneca bluntly says, "life is slavery" (*Ep.* 77.15). "He who has learned to die has unlearned slavery." Such a person is "above any external power or, at any rate, beyond it. What terrors have prisons and bonds and bars for him?" (*Ep.* 26.10). Indeed, "we are in the power of nothing when once we have death in our power!" (*Ep.* 91.21). If such freedom is what we would today call "negative freedom," it is nevertheless the correlative—or perhaps even precondition—in Seneca's thought to a genuine philosophical life.

But Lucilius, we could easily imagine, might object: "This is all good and well, O Director of my Soul, but even if I cast off the yoke of fear, face my coming death, and look for freedom to arrive, it never will. Death is still the master. Indeed, my freedom is radically limited precisely for the simple reason that I cannot exercise it over death: death's power is the greater, and I must serve it. Don't you see, my mortality itself is a form of service, a restriction of my freedom." Seneca obviously never had the chance to know Sartre, Camus, or any of the other existentialists or analysts of the absurd in the mid-twentieth century; still, he would recognize an argumentative similarity in their ranting against death as a fundamental conditioning of human freedom. Yet Seneca's answer to the question of freedom and death was unburdened by the complex moral considerations that later surrounded the question of suicide.[12] No, says Seneca, our freedom is guaranteed simply by the fact that we can always take our own lives. It is true, Seneca tells Lucilius, that "you can find those who have gone so far as to profess wisdom and yet maintain that one should not offer violence to one's own life. . . . We should wait, say they, for the end decreed by nature. But the one who says this does not see that he is shutting off the path to freedom" (*Ep.* 69.14). Indeed, says Seneca a little earlier in the same letter, "a wise man should live as long as he ought, not as long as he can" (*Ep.* 69.4). When sickness or pain impair our reasons for living (*Ep.* 58.36), or when troubling events make the danger to live poorly too great, we should get out (*Ep.* 70.5). Suicide is "an open space in which Nature guards us." Our freedom is thus protected: "When our plight is such as to permit it, we may look about us for an easy exit. If you have many opportunities ready to hand, by means of which you may liberate yourself, you may make a selection and think over the best way of gaining freedom; but if a chance is hard to find, instead of the best, snatch the next-best, even though it be something unheard of, something new. If you do not lack the courage, you will not lack the cleverness to die" (*Ep.* 70.24).[13] You see, says Seneca, not only do we need not fear death, we may even make it our own, and thus bring it into the realm of human freedom.[14] Thus is Lucilius amply counseled in the face of death.

Seneca's overall attempt to shape Lucilius vis-à-vis the human condition of death remains easily discernible. Before philosophical therapy we are caught in a set of habits that teach us to fear and shun death. Stoic philosophy can teach us to counter these damaging habits with another, fundamentally different set of habits that are cultivated through the practice of dying daily and intended to produce a radical acceptance of death and its consequences. Such acceptance would lead to existential peace: despise death each and every day and "you will be able to depart from life contentedly" (*Ep.* 4.4). In short, Seneca's practical philosophy of death was directed toward the art of life: it was meant to shape Lucilius's daily existence so that his performance—the "acting" Lucilius was to do before his play ended—was in accordance with the way things are and must be. And this, so Seneca teaches, is the only way to true happiness.

FORTUNA

If we were to search for Seneca's language that at one and the same time captured the nature of the world and human experience within it, the main word upon which we would land would doubtless be *Fortuna.* Fortuna and all that it invokes provide the organizing grammar of Seneca's world. It is the overarching cosmological context in which all human life is lived, the way the world's power exceeds the human attempt to live in it or mold it toward our ends. Its character is menacing or good or indifferent in turns. Is it, then, a proper goddess, divine? Only in its power. Fortuna, for Seneca, is not personal, does not operate according to intention or plan, has no mind of its own. It is, quite simply, the name for the world in all its excess—all that which touches and shapes our lives for good or for ill from somewhere beyond the reach of our control.

As with death, there are multiple ways in which Seneca speaks of Fortuna. Indeed, hardly a letter is penned without some reference to it. Amid the frequency of the theme, however, Seneca's most basic posture toward Fortune is easy to discern. Human beings, argues Seneca, are at war with Fortune. "Fortuna is fighting against me," he tells Lucilius (*Ep.* 51.8). We must gird our loins and put on our armor, for Fortune's arrows come with remarkable ingenuity, variety, and power—and they never cease (*Ep.* 45.9). In this war, no truce is possible. "Fortuna," as Seneca puts it in another work geared toward life in the face of her power, "conquers us unless we conquer her" (*De const.* 15.3).

Taken as a whole, Seneca's letters teach Lucilius about Fortuna's arrows—or the way she can conquer us—in two central ways. First, and most obvious, Fortuna assaults us through calamities that are entirely beyond the reach of any human preparation or effective response—earthquakes, tsunamis, floods, raging fire, and the like—and through unnecessary accidents of time and place, such as stepping in a deep hole in the dark and breaking one's leg, or "the cutting of the throat by a highway robber" (*Ep.* 4.8). All such things are easily named: Fortuna.

But, says Seneca, it is not only in the remarkable and freakish events of our world that we meet Fortuna's attacks; it is also in the ordinary suffering of life: the death of loved ones, the loss of a business, the failure to get a coveted position, illness and pain, and countless other matters of perennial human concern. These things, too, he names Fortuna.

Nowhere in his letters does Seneca make light of the horrible and frustrating things of the world; indeed, he sees that the work of Fortuna in large-scale disasters, accidents, and daily life can demoralize and destroy us, rendering all our hope of setting a good sail in life again rather pointless: "Fortune does not capsize us—she plunges our bows under and dashes us on the rocks" (*Ep.* 8.4). Through the course of his correspondence, however, Seneca mentions so many ways in which Fortuna would threaten us, and his overall point is so obvious—what human being has not known the touch of fortune?—that we do not need to dwell any further on this aspect of Fortuna's work. Where Seneca's counsel is perhaps less intuitive is when he repeatedly admonishes Lucilius to beware the good things of life.

Second, then, Fortuna seeks to conquer us by giving us gifts. And, indeed, there are many who spread "their arms to gather in that which Fortuna tosses abroad." Seneca continues, "Picture now to yourself that Fortune is holding a festival and is showering down honors, riches, and influence among a group of mortals." What happens? Fortune's gifts are "torn to pieces in the hands of those who try to snatch them." Even if certain gifts survive the initial stampede to grab them, "there is not a man among them—even he who has been lucky in the booty which has fallen to him—whose joy in his spoil has lasted until the next day" (*Ep.* 74.6–7). Lucilius might object that it is the group's conduct that is the problem, not the gifts themselves. But Seneca holds no such hope in the intrinsic goodness of Fortune's gifts. To the contrary, he would say, such a picture paints for Lucilius exactly the response that we should expect when Fortune campaigns among men.

Indeed, Seneca goes even further. The "gifts" of Fortune are not gifts in any sense at all. "I point other men to the right path," Seneca tells Lucilius. "I cry out to them, 'Avoid whatever pleases the mob: avoid the gifts of chance! Halt in a spirit of doubt and fear before every good that chance brings to you; for it is the dumb animals and fish that are deceived by tempting hopes. Do you call these things the "gifts of Fortuna?!?" They are snares! And anyone among you who wishes to live a life of safety will avoid, to the utmost of his power, these limed twigs of her favor by which we mortals . . . are deceived; for we think that we hold them in our grasp. But they hold us in theirs!'" (*Ep.* 8.3).

Here Seneca sees the surprising, almost self-assertive, power that gifts can come to have over those who receive them. Beware, says Seneca, for gifts can possess you. Seneca's claim here is more subtle than the typical Stoic injunction to avoid attachment to "externals" (though of course this is assumed).[15] Indeed, his warning to "other men" is that gifts draw us in and accustom us to their presence, thus creating a set of dependencies that fundamentally determine us away from the happy life. Through our fear of the gift's potential absence or the experience of grief at its departure—the loss of a fleet of grain ships, say, or a crash in the stock market—our lives reveal a basic conditioning by the presence of the gift and the existential vulnerability that is its direct result. We fear, we grieve, we damage our chance to live well. Over time, Seneca's logic suggests, our dependency on the gift is deepened, and we have learned to move within the gift's ambit. We have thus been ensnared by Fortuna, and we now belong to her. By giving us what we believed was a gift, Fortuna has in the end come to possess us. While we thought we held the gifts in our hands, she was holding us in her grasp. Fortuna's gifts, says Seneca, make us vulnerable to defeat precisely because they are not gifts. Remember your own line, Lucilius, "What Fortune has made yours is not really yours" (*Ep.* 8.10).[16] Don't be fooled, my friend, it's still the ol' bait and switch.

But what holds the sufferings of life and the gift/snares together such that they are both named as the work of Fortuna? What gives Fortuna the power to make even the gifts into snares? Seneca's answer here is Time. Time is Fortuna's real strength, the medium through which she exercises her power, and the way she exploits the chief epistemological condition of human finitude—the utter impenetrability of the future. Precisely because Fortuna's actions are always hidden behind the veil of time, they are never open to anticipation. Were we to know that her "gifts" were permanent, we would neither fear their loss nor have the ability to experience their absence. But we do not and cannot know. Only time can tell. "Nothing, whether public or private, is stable. . . . Amid the greatest tranquility terror arises, and though no external agencies stir up commotion, evils nevertheless burst forth from sources where they were least expected" (*Ep.* 91.7). "No man," Seneca reminds his pupil, "has ever been so far advanced by Fortune that she did not threaten him as greatly as she had previously indulged him. Do not trust her seeming calm; in a moment the sea is moved to its depths" (*Ep.* 4.7). Such advice is possible, of course, only with the recognition that the future is inscrutable. Fortuna is always one move ahead, hidden from us, and on the attack. The correlative is obvious: we can play only defense, and even this will inevitably be played blind.

If we are caught in a posture of permanent defense, Lucilius might ask, how can we possibly ever win in our battle with Fortuna? Has not the reality of Time already granted Fortune the victory? Seneca, after all, wrote "conquer or be conquered." How can we conquer?

Seneca's strategy in the face of attempted conquest entails two essential moves. The first could be called the turn inward. Let us admit, Seneca writes, that Fortuna has full sway not only over grand-scale phenomena (earthquakes and the like) but also over a vast range of more personal territory: the amount of money we have, our bodies, our social position and career—in short, all the things that because of Fortune's influence are "weak, shifting, prone to perish, and of uncertain duration" (*Ep.* 66.23). When it comes to matters such as these,

Seneca reminds Lucilius, "no wall can be erected against Fortune which she cannot take by storm" (*Ep.* 74.19). If, therefore, we try to construct our defenses in the world outside ourselves, we will inevitably become hostages to Fortune (*Ep.* 9.14–15). We must thus defend ourselves from behind the only wall that cannot be breached—the internal wall of a soul shaped by virtue. "Let us strengthen our inner defenses," Seneca admonishes. "If the inner part be safe, man can be attacked, but never captured" (*Ep.* 9.14–15). As he puts it in his work on Providence, Fortuna may well strike your body, but she has "no weapon with which she may strike your soul" (*De prov.* 6.6). Why not? Lucilius might wonder. Seneca's answer is clear: because Fortuna cannot take away what she did not give (*Ep.* 59.18; cf. *De const.* 5.4). Turning inward to cultivate virtue creates an impregnable fortress precisely because virtue is beyond the reach of Fortuna. She did not give it, and she cannot take it away.

The second move in Seneca's defensive strategy against Fortuna is to focus our attention on the present.[17] It is true that Seneca frequently tells Lucilius to dwell on the works of Fortune—"the torture of disease, war, shipwreck"—in order to prepare himself for what might come (see *Ep.* 91.8). So, too, Seneca recommends specific preparatory practices to combat the terrors and strikes of Fortune. "Set aside a certain number of days," he advises, "during which you shall be content with the scantiest and cheapest fare, with coarse and rough dress, saying to yourself 'Is this the condition that I feared?' . . . Let the pallet be a real one, and the cloak coarse; let the bread be hard and grimy . . . so that it may be a test of yourself instead of a mere hobby"; thus will we become "intimate with poverty, so that Fortune may not catch us off our guard" (*Ep.* 18.5–8). But contemplation and practice such as this, thinks Seneca, should be clearly distinguished from fearing the future. Indeed, the purpose of learning the texture of poverty and of calling to mind "the very greatest injustice that can possibly happen" is to eliminate fear of coming hardships precisely as a way to live in the present (*Ep.* 91.8).

Focusing on the present also naturally requires a specific stance toward the past: we are to let the past be past. The reason is obvious: remembering Fortuna's past work can inspire dread and fear. In contrast to the animals, who "avoid the dangers which they see, and when they have escaped them are free from care," human beings "torment ourselves over that which is to come as well as over that which is past." "Many of our blessings," Seneca continues, "bring bane to us; for memory recalls the tortures of fear, while foresight anticipates them" (*Ep.* 5.9). We are thus hemmed in from before and behind. We have only one space in which to live free of fear in the face of Fortuna's power: it is "the present alone" that "makes no man wretched" (*Ep.* 5.9).[18]

But, Lucilius might ask his teacher, have you not taught that "externals" are neither good nor bad in themselves—isn't that a pivotal point of Stoic doctrine? Aren't externals only what we make of them? Don't you say again and again that we're not troubled by loss itself, only the *notion* of loss—and other such things? (*Ep.* 42.10). And, if so, wouldn't this position create serious difficulties for all your talk about Fortune's terrors and gifts?

Yes, of course, Seneca might respond, were I to intend for you to take me literally. But speaking of Fortuna's terrors and gifts is simply a way to get at the world's power, Lucilius—the character of the overall environment in which we have to live. "My dear Lucilius," you're quite right, "people make a mistake if they hold that anything good, or evil either, is bestowed upon us by Fortune. It is simply the raw materials of Goods or Ills that she gives to us—the sources of things which in our keeping will develop into good or ill" (*Ep.* 98.2).

For Seneca, therefore, Fortuna does not actually afflict us or bless us but only puts things into play in human life. Our soul's response is what determines these factors for good or for ill—hence the importance of the inward turn. Constructing an impenetrable inner fortress is the necessary precondition to preserving our sovereignty in the face of "externals"—the world as it comes to us—and simultaneously makes disaster into "virtue's opportunity" (*De prov.* 4.6; cf. *De const.* 5.4).[19] If the good and bad of life are dependent upon our soul's response, then the world that is uncontrollable in itself can nevertheless be managed by us. We can deal with the world on our terms from behind our inner wall and "make" it appear good in the concrete existence of daily life: "For a happy existence one needs only a sound and upright soul, one that despises Fortune" (*Ep.* 9.13).[20] Despite the permanency of our defensive posture, we are still the more powerful party. The decision to conquer or be conquered thus ultimately rests with us: "The soul is more powerful than any sort of Fortuna," Seneca tells Lucilius; "by its own agency it guides its affairs in either direction, and of its own power it can produce a happy life or a wretched one" (*Ep.* 98.2).

In Seneca's letters, then, the language of Fortuna is used not only to speak of cosmological reality—the world in all its wild excess—but also to name an existential reality: fragility. Fortuna describes our terror at our own fragility, the fact that we can come to grief and ruin in no more time than it takes to finish reading this sentence. The arrival of a scroll from Nero's messengers, the knife of a jealous senator, an earthquake, a sharp pain in the chest, a text message from the emergency room, or a phone call with the results of the blood tests: all these betoken the same strange and terrifying sense that things are far, far beyond human control. Fortuna, that is, is a grammar of frank talk about human fragility as an inescapable and defining condition of our present existence. In a deep sense, we are simply at the mercy of the world we inhabit.

Such a clear-eyed look at the wildness of the cosmos and our fragility within it does not, of course, prevent Seneca from casting a profound vote of confidence in the human spirit: with a rightly formed soul we can triumph over fortune. Yet such confidence does not result from a kind of naïve liberalism that believes in the inherent resilience of humanity in the face of all that assails us. It comes instead from a sense that the cosmos is more complex than the language of Fortuna alone can allow and from a belief in the ability to train our souls toward virtue. We shall take these in turn.

GOD AND NATURE

Seneca's counsel to Lucilius about life in the world shaped by Fortuna requires further thought precisely because Seneca is not content to talk about the deep (dis)order of the world with the grammar of fortune alone. To the contrary, in his effort to guide Lucilius toward a well-lived life, Seneca frequently speaks about God, or a god, or the gods, or the divine, or divinity, and so forth. Because his language about theological matters is varied and complex, it is difficult to arrange into a simple or even entirely coherent picture. Seneca was no systematic theologian. Still, it is possible to discern in the complexity three central kinds of speech that can clarify the shape of the theological wisdom Seneca offers Lucilius.

First, though Seneca frequently refers to the gods, it is clear that for him the traditional gods of the Roman pantheon (Jupiter, Venus, Mars, and so on) are not personal, sentient entities. It is true that Seneca will sometimes speak of "the gods" in ways that might make modern (Western) scholars think of distinct beings. For example, in speaking of the nature of the human mind and soul, he draws an analogy between the virtually boundless quality of the mind and soul and the gods: "Tell me how closely in accord with nature it is to let one's mind (*mens*) reach out into the boundless universe. The human soul (*animus*) is a great and generous thing; it permits of no limits except those which can be shared even by the gods" (*Ep.* 102.21). But language such as this should not be pressed farther than Seneca's wider thought would allow: his basic point, as the rest of the letter shows, is that the reasonable part of the human soul is divine (by virtue of its *ratio*). In Seneca's letters, the use of the term *the gods* cannot be read simplistically, as if by counting their names on his fingers Seneca would have enumerated particular divine beings with distinct minds, wills, abilities to act, and so forth (see, for example, *Ep.* 110.2).[21]

And though Seneca would no more think of abolishing traditional cultic practice than would Cicero, it is equally clear that, like Cicero, Seneca saw such practice as rife with superstition.[22] "We do not need to uplift our hands toward heaven, or to beg the keeper of a temple to let us approach his idol's ear, as if in this way our prayers were more likely to be heard" (*Ep.* 41.1). For Seneca, worshiping the gods as if they were present in their images, when taken at face value, was profoundly problematic. Such religiously superstitious people, he would say, have not yet learned even the first bit of philosophy (see *Ep.* 115.5). In contrast to today's antireligious crusaders, however, by no means does Seneca abandon a religious vocabulary, as if by excising the words *God(s)* and *divinity* from his language he would have cured all latent superstitious tendencies in Lucilius (or his readers thereafter). Indeed, Seneca's philosophical language is itself inseparable from his theological grammar.

Analyzing Seneca's God-talk in his letters reveals two primary types of speech: personal and impersonal. Taking these two types of speech together creates an apparent tension in Seneca's theology. Whether or not Lucilius should question the coherence of this tension—or whether the tension can be resolved—is an issue to which we shall return after listening to Seneca counsel Lucilius about theological matters in both these types of speech.

Second, then, Seneca speaks of God in remarkably personal terms. In reminding Lucilius about the benefits of philosophy for life, for example, Seneca says that philosophy "will encourage us to obey God cheerfully but Fortune defiantly; she will teach us to follow God and endure chance" (*Ep.* 16.5). Or even earlier in their correspondence, when counseling Lucilius on how and what to pray, Seneca tells him to "call boldly upon God" (*Ep.* 10.4). And much later, when admonishing him to distinguish between what is necessary and what is superfluous, Seneca instructs Lucilius that God has provided all that we could ever need: "Now God, who is the Father of us all, has placed ready to our hands those things which he intended for our own good; he did not wait for any search on our part, and he gave them to us voluntarily" (*Ep.* 110.10). Whether Seneca means anything more, however, than that the human good is living according to the natural order of the cosmos is made difficult by the other primary way in which Seneca speaks of God.[23]

So, third, Seneca also speaks of God in a nonpersonal manner. Such speech is frequent in his letters, and it displays well the truth in the common view that the Stoics were basically pantheists. In this way of speaking about God, that is, there is no room for a categorical difference between the referent of the words *god* and *world*. *God* and *world* are different words that refer to that which eternally exists. "This whole universe that encompasses us," Seneca writes, "is one and it is God" (*Ep.* 92.30). "All that you behold," he later tells Lucilius, "both god and humanity, is one—we are the parts of one great body" (*Ep.* 95.52).

Yet, and here Seneca's language again becomes more complex, *God* is not simply the word for everything that is—as if *God* and *everything that is* could be substituted for each other without a loss of meaning. *God,* rather, is the word for what is ultimately rational in what is—the order of the world, or the laws by which we are to live. "Creative reason," Seneca tells Lucilius, is the first cause of all things—"in other words, it is God" (*Ep.* 65.12; see also *Ep.* 90.29).[24] "Divine reason," he says, "is set in supreme command over all things, and is itself subject to none" (*Ep.* 92.1). And when speaking about human rationality, Seneca is quick to say that *ratio* is "nothing else than a portion of the divine spirit set in a human body" (*Ep.* 66.12). Human reason is "the same" as divine reason, precisely "because it is derived from divine reason" (*Ep.* 92.1). *God,* therefore, refers not only to the rational ordering principle of the world but also to its presence within the human being. In a very strict sense, then, when referring to certain constitutive parts of their reality, both the world and human beings can be called divine (see, for example, *Ep.* 85.19–20).

Elsewhere, of course, Seneca's word for the ultimate ordering principle of the cosmos is *Natura.* "Nature," says Seneca, continuing on in his effort to establish the oneness of humanity, "produced us related to one another, since she created us from the same source and to the same end" (*Ep.* 95.52). This natural end is to exercise our reason in a life of virtue; that is what distinguishes humans from mere animals (see *Ep.* 76.9; 121.3; 124.8). In a kind of self-consistent circularity, Seneca teaches Lucilius that human reason is linked with Nature. "What is reason?" Lucilius asks Seneca. "It is," Seneca straightforwardly says in reply, "the imitation of Natura" (*Ep.* 66.39). We are to take Nature as our teacher, "conforming to her laws and living as she commands" (*Ep.* 45.9). In Seneca's letters, Nature is thus virtually synonymous with the set of words we moderns tend to think of as more explicitly theological: *God/god/gods/divinity/divine.* For Seneca, to follow Nature by using our reason is to pursue the alignment of the divine with the divine, the aspect of God that is in every human being with the reasonable aspect of the world, that is, with God. Nature after Nature, God after God.

As an aspiring philosopher, Lucilius would have no trouble swallowing Seneca's invectives against superstition. In his more rigorous moments, however, Lucilius might wonder how the other two ways Seneca speaks of God can fit together. "Why," for example, "should we pray to the world?" he might ask. "What sense does it make to call upon God if God means only a certain aspect of the world?" "What can the reasonable part of the world actually *do* in response to our invocations?" Such questions, we imagine, would not worry Seneca.

"O Lucilius!" he could easily respond. "Come now, let's not invite superstition in through the back door!" *Pray, invoke,* and so on, is all mythical language, a way to speak piously about the need to train the rational soul—the divine within us—to be in accord with Nature.

In Seneca's letters, then, there is at bottom a kind of dualism inherent in what is.[25] *God/Nature* and *Fortuna,* that is, are simply different ways to name the character of what is. Neither God nor Fortuna is personal in any kind of significant sense. They are, rather, textures of the cosmos, reasonable and wild, respectively.[26] To survive the wild, Seneca counsels his pupil, our lives must become aligned with the reasonable; we thereby live in accordance with nature and ourselves become God, thus achieving divine happiness in the midst of the world's wild, excessive power (see *Ep.* 48.11; 59.14; 82.1).

Assuming he follows Seneca thus far, Lucilius's most natural question would seem rather obvious: if this is so, O master, how then do we align ourselves with Nature? Ah, Seneca would say, let's consider the passions.

PASSIONS

The Stoics are so well known throughout history for their austerity that even today people who know nothing of what a Stoic was can use the term with accuracy to describe someone whose emotional reactions are exceptionally reserved. "You needn't be such a Stoic," we often say to those who don't display their emotions. And with good reason. Over against the Aristotelian tradition's emphasis on moderation, in its orthodox, Chrysippean form, Stoicism taught the extirpation of the passions.[27] Seneca himself, however, is more complex. His organizing theoretical language in his letters to Lucilius is obviously more Stoic than Aristotelian, but in practice he is somewhat less concerned with extirpating the passions than were his Stoic predecessors.[28] Still, he resolutely believes that it is from "the passions that one passes over to vice" (*Ep.* 85.10), and his clear desire is to guide Lucilius toward a life free from the damaging influence of human affect. He begins with the body.

In contrast to those who worry too much about bodily appetites as a ground for passion run amok, Seneca rejects the view that the body's most basic biological needs are in themselves affectively problematic. It is true, of course, that the body's appetites can enslave us (*Ep.* 14), that the body must be well managed to achieve freedom (*Ep.* 65), and that the soul alone is worthy of wonder (*Ep.* 8). Still, for Seneca, as long as we refrain from overindulgence, it is only natural that hunger should be relieved, thirst quenched, cold kept away with clothes, and bad weather fought with good shelter (*Ep.* 8.5; 21.11 et passim).

Seneca's acceptance of the body's appetites, however, is not predicated on a strict division between body and soul (or mind) that would allow him to locate the passions in one place rather than another. Indeed, for Seneca, both the body and the soul are, well, bodily, and both are subject to the influence of affect.[29] Indeed, Seneca not infrequently presses Lucilius to see the corporal nature of affect or the passions: "You will have no doubt that emotions are bodily things . . . like wrath, love, sternness; unless you doubt whether they change our features, knot our foreheads, relax the countenance, spread blushes, or drive away the blood? . . . Do you think that such evident marks of the body are stamped upon us by anything else than the body? And if emotions are corporeal, so are the diseases of the spirit—such as greed, cruelty, and all the faults that harden our souls." Moreover, he continues, virtues are corporally manifested in discrete "symptoms" that indicate their presence: "Do you not see how a spirit of bravery makes the eye flash? How prudence tends toward concentration? How reverence produces modesty and tranquility? How joy produces calm? How sternness begets stiffness? How gentleness produces relaxation? These qualities are therefore bodily; for they change the tones and the shapes of substances, exercising their own power in their own kingdoms" (*Ep.* 106.5–7). For Seneca, therefore, freeing oneself from the power of the passions will involve training the soul toward wisdom through the exercise of reason or the practice of virtue, as well as developing practices focused on the body for the sake of the soul's reasoning capacities.

In order to see how Seneca hopes to shape Lucilius to deal with affect, we may focus on three letters in particular. In two of the letters, Seneca explicitly differentiates his view from the Aristotelian model; we are thereby enabled to see the sharp edges, as it were, of his thought about the passions vis-à-vis a particularly powerful alternative. In the third letter, written originally to his friend Marullus but included for Lucilius's benefit, Seneca deals with the most potent affect, love, and its power in the midst of the deepest loss: that of a beloved child. Reading these three letters together discloses *in nuce* Seneca's attempt to work against the destructive pressure of the passions.

In *Ep.* 85 and 116 Seneca explicitly contrasts his view of the passions with that of the Peripatetics. "The question has often been raised," Seneca tells Lucilius, "whether it is better to have moderate emotions or none at all." We Stoics, he says, "reject the emotions; the Peripatetics keep them in check" (*Ep.* 116.1). Take grief, for example. The Aristotelians argue that "it is not the way of human nature that a man's soul should be exempt from sadness"; human nature requires the acknowledgment that we are in some way meant to grieve. Indeed, even the sage grieves, though of course in proper proportion to his stature of wisdom: "The wise man is not overcome by grief but merely touched by it." By admitting grief into the category of nature, the Aristotelians forgo the ability to "abolish the passions; instead, they can only moderate them" (*Ep.* 85.3).

Seneca's view of the usefulness of moderation is clear: "Would you call a man well who has a light fever?" he asks. "I do not understand how any halfway disease can be either salutary or useful" (*Ep.* 85.4; 116.1). "Well," Lucilius might respond, "you're less sick. Cancer under control is better than cancer on the rampage, is it not?" True enough, Seneca could say, if the disease were of that kind. But in fact the disease of affect is inescapably and aggressively progressive: it grows, dear Lucilius, faster than you can treat it. Even when the start is small, once the emotion is set on its way, it gains strength every step of the way (*Ep.* 85.3; 116.5). "Small evils . . . grow, and as they grow will hamper" us. It is no different with pleasure, which grows until it overtakes and enslaves us. As he says in an earlier letter, pleasure tends to run headlong into the abyss of sorrow (*Ep.* 23.6). "It is easier to stop [the passions] in the beginning than to control them when they gather force" (*Ep.* 85.9). But why can we not simply reason our way through the passions? Why must we fear their growth? Quite simple, Seneca says: "Reason is no match for them" (85.6). Don't forget, Lucilius, we're talking about the full range of human affect, not one simple passion.

> If by [the Peripatetic] definition the wise man has any passions whatever, his reason will be no match for them and will be carried swiftly along, as it were, in a rushing stream—especially if you assign to him not one passion with which he must wrestle, but all the passions. And a throng of such, even though they be moderate, can affect him more than the violence of one powerful passion. He has a craving for money, although in a moderate degree. He has ambition, but it is not yet fully aroused. He has a hot temper, but it can be appeased. He has inconstancy, but not the kind that is very capricious. . . . He has lust, but not the kind that is violent. We could deal better with a person who possessed one full-fledged vice than with one who possessed all the vices but none of them in extreme form. Again, it makes no difference how great the passion is; no matter what its size may be, it knows no obedience, and does not welcome advice. (*Ep.* 85.6–8)

The passions, in short, cannot be held in check. According to Seneca, our disease requires a drastic intervention—something much closer to a surgical amputation than a treatment medication.

The prescribed intervention, of course, is a life of wisdom by way of the exercise of reason/virtue. The only way to deal with the passions, Seneca says again and again, is to subject them to reason: "The passions, which are heavy taskmasters, sometimes ruling by turns, sometimes together, can be banished from you by wisdom, which is the only real freedom. There is but one path leading there, and it is a straight path; you will not go astray. Proceed with a steady step, and if you would have all things under your control, put yourself under the control of reason; if reason becomes your ruler, you will become ruler over many" (*Ep.* 37.4). To observe reason's healing efforts at work, we turn to Seneca's counsel to a sorrowing friend.

Iunius Marullus, consul designate in 62, was stricken with inconsolable grief upon the death of his "little son."[30] Marullus was apparently unable to gain control of his weeping over time, and word reached Seneca's ear that his friend was exhibiting "womanish grief." Seneca thus wrote him a lengthy letter of rebuke in which he makes four central points that should, he thinks, help to reorient Marullus toward reason.[31]

Seneca's first point runs throughout the letter: to grieve like this, he instructs Marullus, is entirely out of keeping with what is natural, with Nature. But Seneca, his friend might ask, am I not supposed to grieve at all, to cry or to weep? And would this not support those who "accuse [you Stoics] of too great a strictness, slandering your precepts because of supposed harshness—because (they say) we declare that grief should either not be given place in the soul at all, or else should be driven out immediately"? (*Ep.* 99.26). Surely you cannot think that Nature asks so much. True enough, Seneca would say. Do you think "that I am advising you to be hard-hearted . . . not allowing your soul even to feel the pinch of pain? By no means! That would display inhumanity, not virtue." "But," he continues, "suppose I forbade you to show emotion?" It would not matter. "There are certain feelings which claim their own rights. Tears fall, no matter how we try to check them, and by being shed they ease the soul." Should we, then, weep and cry after all? Yes, says Seneca the Stoic, here apparently giving some ground to the Aristotelians: "Let us allow [the tears] to fall. . . . Let us weep according to the emotion that floods our eyes" (*Ep.* 99.16). But not as much as we want; indeed, only as such tears are "wrung from us by the necessity of Nature" (*Ep.* 99.18). There is a crucial difference, Seneca chides, between tears that fall by "their own force" or "against our will" and tears that we "allow to escape" (*Ep.* 99.18–19). The former come unbidden "when the first news of some bitter depravation has shocked us, and when we embrace the body that will soon pass from our arms to the funeral flames." The latter occur not while we are alone but only in the presence of others as a kind of display, and, further, upon our overindulgence of "sweetly sad" memories of those who have died (*Ep.* 99.19). It's simple, Seneca tells his friend, "You should either check or pour forth your tears" (*Ep.* 99.20).[32]

For Seneca, the crucial matter is that there is a proper natural grief: to grieve according to Nature is to avoid the display of grief that comes only in the presence of others and to stop the soul from grieving before its grief becomes mingled with pleasure. "We may, I assure you, obey Nature"—weep in the initial stage of bereavement—"and maintain our dignity"—control our tendency toward grief thereafter (*Ep.* 99.21; see esp. 99.27).

Seneca's second point pertains to the unity of human affect, or the final inseparability of different emotions. Against the Epicurean Metrodorus, who thought that pleasure was good salve for sorrow, Seneca counsels Marullus to beware the pleasure that often accompanies grief (*Ep.* 99.25). Pleasure's presence, indeed, is a sign that grief has deviated from the course of Nature, an indication that one has begun to extend grief beyond the immediate and normal impact of unexpected loss. Seneca's argument here presumes a complex account of the unity of human affect that sees how temporarily distinguishable emotions can intertwine and shade into each other. Grief, anger, joy, and so forth do not exist in discrete impermeable compartments within the human being called "grief," "anger," and "joy," but are tied together in a larger more complicated unity.[33] The problem for Marullus, therefore, is not only that "chasing after pleasure in the very midst of mourning is base"; the problem is also that the intertwining of pleasure with grief makes it doubly hard to excise excess grief. If one begins to pursue pleasure "by means of" (*per*) grief, then one must now work not only against the grief, but also against the pleasure (*Ep.* 99.26, 29–30). And who wants to be rid of pleasure?

But how do we actually use reason to get rid of excessive grief, or prevent it from coming our way? What should Marullus have done?

Seneca's third major point in his "critical" letter is that Marullus's extreme grief derives from a faulty basic judgment. Though there are various aspects to it, the faulty judgment amounts to one central matter: death, even early death, is not an evil. More facetiously put, Seneca's point is that in actual fact it's hardly as bad as Marullus has made it out to be. Much of Stoic doctrine was of course predicated on the notion that things that do not depend upon us, that are not within our control, are neither good nor evil in themselves. Our great mistake is to treat them as if they are. On this point, Seneca is no different from his forebears: "Life is neither a good nor an evil; it is only the locus of good and evil" (*Ep.* 99.12, 22, 32, etc.). Death is not something we can prevent or control, and is therefore no evil—nothing that could actually cause a wise man pain.[34] The wise man, says Seneca, knows that the inner fortress that defends our souls against Fortuna is built brick by brick on judgments that separate things that we control from things we cannot. Where we err, Fortuna's breach is certain. Marullus has erred. He has misjudged this death as an evil, and allowed it to cause him unnatural grief. In short, his wall has been breached on account of faulty cognition: "I am not exhorting you to make an effort and rise to great heights," Seneca scolds, "for my opinion of you is not so low as to make me think that it is necessary for you to summon every bit of your virtue to face this trouble. Yours is not pain; it is a mere sting—and it is you yourself who are turning it into pain" (*Ep.* 99.14).[35]

Seneca buttresses his argument about Marullus's flawed judgment with two main observations. The first is that a consideration of time and eternity ought to help knock Marullus's reason into shape: "Let us say this also to him who mourns and misses the untimely dead: that all of us, whether young or old, live—in comparison with eternity—on the same level as regards our shortness of life. For out of all time there comes to us less than what anyone could call 'least,' since 'least' is at any rate some part; but this life of ours is next to nothing, and yet (fools that we are!), we marshal it in broad array!" (*Ep.* 99.31; cf. esp. 99.10–11). Come Marullus, Seneca argues, seen in proper perspective, your son's life was hardly shorter than yours. Moreover, you will go his way soon. "It is foolish to lament one's loss when there is such a slight interval between the lost and the loser. . . . We follow closely those whom we have lost" (*Ep.* 99.6).

The second observation turns on the unknowability of the course a human life will take. It is true, Marullus, that you might have taught him well so that "he would have turned out temperate and prudent." But then again—and this "fear is the more reasonable"—he might "have become just like the many." Indeed, Seneca continues, consider "the youths of the noblest lineage whose extravagance has flung them into the arena; note those men who cater to their passions . . . whose days never pass without drunkenness or some signal act of shame." Think on lives such as these, Marullus, and you will see "that there was more to fear than to hope for" (*Ep.* 99.13; cf. 99.3, the child was of "uncertain hope"). Probably you were spared.[36]

Taken together, Seneca's two observations reinforce the sense that both life and death are things beyond our control and therefore should not be allowed to break through the wall of the rightly reasoning soul. Conversely, coming to correct cognitive judgments can treat diseased affect. Yet, Marullus—or Lucilius in his stead—might respond: have you not required me to forget my son?! To merge his life into eternity as if his existence didn't matter?! Ultimately to dishonor him by saying he mattered not?! Not at all, says Seneca.

So, fourth, Seneca argues that when grief is appropriately in accord with Nature, memory is the proper way to honor the time we have had with a friend or a son.[37] Indeed, "to forget the beloved dead, to bury their memory along with their bodies, to bewail them bounteously and afterward think of them but scantily—this is the mark of an inhuman soul. For that is the way in which birds and beasts love their young; their affection is quickly roused and almost reaches madness, but it cools away entirely when its object dies. This does not befit a prudent man. He should continue to remember, but"—and here is the key—"cease to mourn" (*Ep.* 99.24). The past can "serve for our delight" precisely because memory is able to make present "a great part of those we have loved—though chance has removed their persons. . . . The past is ours," Marullus, "and there is nothing more secure for us than that which has been" (*Ep.* 99.4–5).

To a modern reader it would seem that by the end of his letter Seneca has accused Marullus of false grief. By definition, true grief is what fits with Seneca's construal of grief. If Marullus grieves too much, he is causing his own tears to fall. Conversely, if his tears are still falling, he is grieving too much. For Marullus's grief to appear real to Seneca, it has to be reasonable on the latter's terms. Of course, Seneca himself would not put it this way; nor would he agree with the overall point. He would instead say that the kind of grief toward which he directs Marullus (and Lucilius) is not his individual construal but that which is embedded in Nature and which the strength of the passions demands.

Putting it this way helps to show that Seneca's argument about the passions depends upon judgments about two different but related matters: first, a judgment about what Nature is and what is therefore required of human beings; and, second, a judgment about the power of the passions and the corresponding ability of the virtuous soul to keep them under control. As we have seen, Seneca counsels Lucilius not to moderate his passions but to eliminate them. Yet, when it comes to speaking directly to a grieving father, Seneca softens his account of Nature to include shock, tears, and sorrow at initial bereavement, and he risks reigniting the passions by recommending the practice of remembering the dead. Seneca is clear that "desires and pleasures can torment us" (*Ep.* 24), and that our passions, once activated, are far too powerful to be moderated by reason. Yet by allowing Lucilius to overhear his advice to Marullus, Seneca teaches his pupil about the importance of love for the humanity of the soul. He does not recommend moderation in good Aristotelian fashion, but he does see that denying the love for a son by refusing to remember him leads not to a life that is freed from the tyranny of the passions but to a gnarled, inhuman soul.

PHILOSOPHY

In a sense, most of what has been said thus far could be said with almost exclusive reference to the realm of ideas. Lucilius's training, that is, could appear as a training of the mind alone—you ought to think in this way rather than in that way, Seneca would be saying. Of course it is both obvious and true that Seneca is attempting to (re)train Lucilius's habits of thought, but to believe that the primary target of his teaching is the mind is to overlook the most basic thing of all: what Seneca takes philosophy to be. For Seneca, philosophy is practice. His teaching on death, Fortuna, God/Nature, and the passions can be understood only when it is lived inside a way of life that makes its intellectual content take human shape in the world. Conversely, living philosophically actively discloses the intellectual content of Seneca's teaching. In short, there can be no division between *morales* and *intellectus*.

This unity of the moral and intellectual life, however, results in something of a paradox—a paradox, in fact, of which Seneca himself is acutely aware. As he tells Lucilius, "Philosophy cannot exist without virtue, nor virtue without philosophy. Philosophy is the study of virtue by means of virtue itself; but neither can virtue exist without the study of itself, nor can the study of virtue exist without virtue itself. For it is not like trying to hit a target at long range, where the shooter and the object to be shot at are in different places. Nor, as roads which lead into a city, are the approaches to virtue situated outside virtue herself; the path by which one reaches virtue leads by way of virtue herself. Philosophy and virtue coinhere" (*Ep.* 89.8).[38]

If we take him seriously, there is no way to resolve or dissolve the paradox Seneca articulates. Yet precisely through this paradox we can see clearly the central thrust of his philosophical teaching: he is engaged in chiseling a virtuous soul for the full breadth of a human life.

It is oddly difficult, however, to analyze this purpose simply because it is all-pervasive. Indeed, scrutinizing Seneca's many remarks on philosophy is a bit like talking about the wetness of water—philosophy, for Seneca, really is that obviously about life. Still, we can understand *philosophia* according to Seneca by concisely organizing his language into three central themes: his larger point about what philosophy is and is therefore intended to do, his view on how it actually does this work, and the results of philosophy's work.

First, then, is Seneca's repeated claim that philosophy is nothing short of the *lex vitae*, the "law of life," that according to which we must live if we are to live well in this world (see *Ep.* 94.39), and the *ars vitae*, the "art of life," the actual manner by which we live the law of life (see *Ep.* 117.12). Philosophy "moulds and constructs the soul," he tells Lucilius early on; "it orders our life, guides our conduct, shows us what we should do and what we should leave undone; it sits at the helm and directs our course as we waver amid uncertainties" (*Ep.* 16.3).

Where university students today frequently experience philosophy courses as exercises in logic chopping, Seneca mocks this conception of philosophy.

Constructing a silly syllogism, Seneca says, "'Mouse' is a syllable. Now a mouse eats cheese; therefore, a syllable eats cheese. Suppose now that I cannot solve this problem; see what peril hangs over my head as a result of such ignorance! What a scrape I shall be in! Without doubt I must beware, or someday I shall be catching syllables in a mousetrap, or if I grow careless, a book may devour my cheese! Unless, perhaps, the following syllogism is shrewder still: 'Mouse' is a syllable. Now a syllable does not eat cheese. Therefore a mouse does not eat cheese."

His verdict on the usefulness of such exercises is clear: "What childish nonsense!" Seneca continues, "Would you really know what philosophy offers to humanity?" He answers immediately and with only one word: "Counsel" (*Ep.* 48.6–7).[39]

Such counsel, however, is not merely advice; the Counselor's attempt is fully to transfigure its human object: "I feel," says Seneca, "that I am being not only reformed but also transfigured" (*Ep.* 6.1). Such transfiguring does not, of course, happen all at once, and—except in the case of the Sage—it always remains incomplete. Still, Seneca has no doubt about where to look for help: "Tell me what to avoid," he says to philosophy, "what to seek, by what studies to strengthen my tottering mind, how I may rebuff the waves that strike me abeam and drive me from my course, by what means I may be able to cope with all my evils, and by what means I can be rid of the calamities that have plunged in upon me and those into which I myself have plunged. Teach me how to bear the burden of sorrow without a groan on my part, and how to bear prosperity without making others groan; also, how to avoid waiting for the ultimate and inevitable end, and to beat a retreat of my free will, when it seems proper to me to do so" (*Ep.* 117.21). As his dramatized plea shows, philosophy according to Seneca is nothing more than a matter of both life and death. It is the way we are wisely in the world such that we may be ready to leave it.

Second, if philosophy is the practice of a wise life, its truth cannot be learned apart from its embodiment. Precisely, that is, because philosophy is "practicing the truth" (*Ep.* 98.17), apprenticeship is the requisite form of study and learning. "Cleanthes could not have been the express image of Zeno, if he had merely heard his lectures," Seneca tells his pupil. That is why "he shared in Zeno's life, saw into his hidden purposes, and watched him to see whether he lived according to his own rules" (*Ep.* 7.6). "What ought to be done," my dear Lucilius, "must be learned from one who does it" (*Ep.* 98.17). Practice, Seneca repeatedly insists, is correlated with apprenticeship because knowledge comes by observing a master at work and being trained by his example. For this reason, says Seneca, "I hold that no man has treated humanity worse than he who has studied philosophy as if it were some marketable trade, who lives in a different manner from that which he advises" (*Ep.* 108.36). Such a person, Seneca's logic runs, actively prevents the possibility of learning how to live, for he severs the necessary relation between knowledge and life. "A teacher like that can help me no more than a seasick pilot can be efficient in a storm. He must hold the tiller when the waves are tossing him; he must wrestle, as it were, with the sea; he must furl his sails when the storm rages; what good is a frightened and vomiting steersman to me?! And how much greater is the storm of life than that which tosses any ship!" (*Ep.* 108.36).[40]

Lucilius may well understand Seneca's point already; after all, their very correspondence is a form of apprenticeship. But he may nevertheless legitimately wonder, What if there isn't a Sage or a philosopher nearby? How then do I learn to live, O master?

My dear Lucilius, Seneca could reply, of course there will not always be master philosophers around us, but that is precisely why we Stoics require you to have ready at hand so many exempla from which to learn. Why else would I spend so much time on Cato's life? Or on Socrates? Or any of the others? Or tell stories about Stilbo's response to Demetrius the City Sacker, or Calvisius Sabinus's ridiculous attempt to appear learned by educating his slaves and having them whisper poetry in his ear to quote to his guests, or Scipio's voluntary exile, or the Spartan lad who committed suicide rather than become a slave, and countless other matters? Go ahead, Lucilius, "and choose a Cato; or, if Cato seems too severe a model, choose some Laelius, a gentler spirit." The main thing is "to choose a master whose life, conversation, and soul-expressing face have satisfied you; picture him always to yourself as your protector or your pattern (*exemplum*)" (*Ep.* 11.10; cf. 25.6).[41]

Moreover, Seneca both recommends and presupposes the practice of "spiritual exercises."[42] Such exercises are both contemplative and mundanely physical. The philosophical life, Seneca tells Lucilius, is not a thing to be done here and there but is a "daily, ordinary practice" (*Ep.* 53.9, *ordinaria est*).[43] It therefore requires "daily meditation" and "continuous study" (*Ep.* 16.1–2). From his reading, for example, Lucilius should each day acquire a thought that does some particular work—fortifying him against death, or poverty, or misfortune (*Ep.* 2.4). Indeed, for this purpose Seneca graciously promises to send Lucilius some books with the profitable passages already marked; the pupil can thus save time and begin his memorization immediately (*Ep.* 6.5). Such lines, when often repeated to oneself, train thought in their direction, order the world's appearance in certain ways rather than others, and thus influence one's decisions about how to act. This is the logic that also informs Seneca's injunctions to memorize certain Stoic precepts. "The mind," he tells Lucilius, "needs many precepts in order to see what it should do in life" (*Ep.* 94.19; cf. 13.1). Of course precepts themselves are but small pieces of larger Stoic doctrinal convictions—*decreta*—that "simultaneously include the whole of life and the universe in its completeness" (*Ep.* 95.12). Contemplation of Stoic doctrine inducts us, therefore, into a more holistic way of seeing the world in which the Stoic way of life comes to make a kind of natural sense. Thus is Lucilius also to develop a keen awareness of his own way of being in the world. Self-observation, Seneca advises, comes by way of imagining oneself from the perspective of another: "Act in whatever you do as you would act if anyone at all were looking on" (*Ep.* 25.5). In this way we learn to hold ourselves accountable to the philosophical exemplum we seek to imitate and to see ourselves "Stoically" in the world.

Seneca also recognizes the necessity of physical training for philosophical development. "A great step toward freedom," he says, "is a stomach that is willing to endure maltreatment" (*Ep.* 123.4). Indeed, Lucilius should spend a predetermined number of days "content with the scantiest and cheapest fare, [and] with coarse and rough dress" (*Ep.* 18.5). And in *Ep.* 108, Seneca speaks of the practices he learned as a young man from his teacher Attalus and how they have continued to shape his pursuit of the philosophical life. Whenever Attalus "extolled personal purity, moderation in diet, and a mind free from unnecessary . . . pleasures, the desire came upon me to limit my food and drink. And that is why some of these habits have become permanent, Lucilius." "I have forsaken," Seneca continues, "oysters and mushrooms forever since they are not really food but are relishes to bully the sated stomach into further eating. . . . I have also throughout my life avoided perfumes. . . . My stomach is unacquainted with wine . . . and I have shunned the bath." Now, truth be told, Lucilius, "other resolutions have been broken. But all in such a way that in cases where I ceased to practice abstinence, I have observed a limit which is indeed next door to abstinence" (*Ep.* 108.14–16). By focusing on his dietary and other practices, Seneca reminds Lucilius not only of the physical counterpart to successful contemplation but also of the concrete seriousness of his central point: philosophy truly is about an embodied way of being. OK, a trainee like Lucilius might respond, but what does such apprenticeship and practice actually bring about in the life of the apprentice-practitioner? I see that philosophy is a way of life, but what does that way of life lead to, result in? What's its point after all?

Third, then, Seneca argues that "one thing is basically settled: there is a difference between philosophy and wisdom. . . . Philosophy does the going, wisdom is the goal" (*Ep.* 89.7). And wisdom? "Wisdom's course is toward the state of happiness; there she guides, there she opens the way for us" (*Ep.* 90.27).

"Do you ask," says Seneca to Lucilius, "what the Sage has found out and what he has brought to light?" His answer is striking: "First of all, it is truth and nature. . . . Second, it is the law of life" (*Ep.* 90.34).[44] Truth, Nature, and How We Must Live—these are the coordinates of Seneca's practical philosophy.

When the truth about nature is known through a way of life called wisdom, the philosopher becomes God-like. "That is exactly what philosophy promises me," Lucilius, "that I shall be made equal to God. For this I have been summoned, for this purpose I have come" (*Ep.* 48.11). The Sage himself, Seneca later says, actually "lives on a plane with the gods" (*Ep.* 59.14).[45] Does this mean, then, that the philosopher withdraws from worldly affairs, hides from social and civil life behind his philosophical pursuit?

By no means, Seneca would answer. "The Sage is content with himself," Seneca tells Lucilius, is a phrase "incorrectly explained by many; for they withdraw the Sage from the world, and force him to dwell within his own skin" (*Ep.* 9.13).[46] Indeed, the Stoics as a whole commended an active political life. It is true that a philosopher may need to retire, as Seneca himself tried to do. But even here, retirement should be construed not as abandonment of public life altogether but as an attempt to focus on important matters for the sake of others. "My object in shutting myself up and locking the door is to be able to help a greater number. . . . I have withdrawn not only from men but also from my affairs, especially my personal affairs. I am working for later generations, writing down some ideas that may be of use to them. There are certain wholesome counsels, which may be compared to prescriptions of useful drugs; these I am putting into writing; for I have found them helpful in ministering to my own sores, which, if not wholly cured, have at least ceased to spread" (*Ep.* 8.1–2; cf. *Ep.* 68.1–7).

As Seneca presents it to Lucilius, Stoic philosophical life is fundamentally for the good of oneself—that cannot be denied—but such self-focus turns out to be relevant to the good of others, too. When Stoics have "withdrawn into privacy," it has been "for the purpose of improving human existence and framing laws for the human race" (*Ep.* 14.14).[47] Though this *telos* stands in some tension with such statements as "the highest good calls for no extrinsic instruments; it is developed at home, and arises entirely within itself" (*Ep.* 9.15), Seneca seems unbothered. The philosopher ought to strive to be "in want for nothing" (*Ep.* 9.15), and yet he can help with the wider human predicament. "On all sides people are stretching out imploring hands to the philosopher; lives ruined and in danger of ruin are begging for some assistance; people's hopes and resources depend upon you. They ask that you deliver them from all their restlessness, that you reveal to them, scattered and wandering as they are, the clear light of truth. Tell them what nature has made necessary, and what superfluous; tell them how simple are the laws that she has laid down, how pleasant and unimpeded life is for those who follow these laws, but how bitter and perplexed it is for those who have put their trust in opinion rather than in nature" (*Ep.* 48.9–10).

Philosophy, Lucilius is told, is in principle for everyone (*Ep.* 44), though admittedly he also learns that only a few will become wise—most, Seneca observes, would rather just mindlessly watch sports (*Ep.* 76.1–4). Still, they all need the invitation: even the mob can be helped by the witness of the philosophers.

Taking things as a whole, Seneca insists that philosophy is not a discrete subject, something to be learned in a university alongside other matters of human knowledge and concern, but is instead a redemptive mode of being. It rescues us from the inevitable perils that accompany human life on all sides and press us from without. It treats the diseased soul and the cancers that plague us from within. It shapes us mentally and physically by practices that develop the existential pattern that heals. Philosophy, in short, is the wise way of life that enables us to die daily, to build and fortify the inward fortress against Fortuna, to become aligned with God and Nature, and to control the passions—and therefore to walk the only path that grants happiness in the world in which we find ourselves.

2

Epictetus

> Tell me: can all the things that seem to certain people to be good and fitting simultaneously be right? Now, is it possible that all the opinions that Jews and Syrians and Egyptians and Romans hold about food can be right? How is that possible? I think it totally necessary that if the Egyptians are right, the others cannot be, or if the Jews are right, the others cannot be.
>
> —*Epictetus,* Discourses

"Epictetus is a thinker we cannot forget, once we have encountered him, because he gets under our skin. He provokes and he irritates, but he deals so trenchantly with life's everyday challenges that no one who knows his work can simply dismiss it as theoretically invalid or practically useless. In times of stress, as modern Epictetans have attested, his recommendations make their presence felt."[1] So begins A. A. Long's laudable study of Epictetus. Like Seneca, Epictetus lives on.

DISCOURSES AND *MANUAL* OF EPICTETUS

While Seneca was born in the purple, Epictetus was probably born a slave, and was certainly one by adulthood. As far as slaves go, however, Epictetus was hardly on the bottom rung of life. Indeed, his last owner was the prominent Epaphroditis, himself a freedman and secretary for two emperors, Nero and Domitian. In fact, Epictetus was familiar with the imperial court, and Epaphroditis allowed him while still a slave to hear the famous Stoic teacher Musonius Rufus.[2] After Domitian expelled the philosophers from Italy, moreover, Epictetus formed a Stoic school in the metropolitan Roman colony Nicopolis, where his chief clientele consisted of young Roman noblemen on their way to lucrative and envied careers. It was there that he achieved considerable renown. Still, his life as a slave indelibly marked him, as we can easily see through the abundance of material in which Epictetus employs the slave-master image as a way to make his point.

As far as we know, Epictetus never wrote a word. His onetime student Arrian, an accomplished author in his own right, compiled from notes a series of *Discourses* that show Epictetus at work in his school. Four of Arrian's original eight books remain. Were we to take these four *Discourses* as Epictetus's *ipsissima verba*, we would go too far; yet as a comparison with Arrian's own compositions show, neither are the *Discourses* Arrian's in any sort of vigorously constructive sense. They are best read as "the gist" of how and what Epictetus taught.[3] Arrian also produced a *Manual* of some of Epictetus's central convictions—many of which find their philosophic grounding in the content and pedagogical style displayed in the *Discourses*. For this chapter, therefore, we will take the *Discourses* and the *Manual* together and draw upon both works in our presentation of Epictetus.[4]

In contrast to Seneca's letters to Lucilius, Epictetus's *Discourses* are not addressed to a single person; they are, instead, "records" of his Socratic-style engagement with his students (and occasional visitors and passersby). Like Seneca's letters, however, the *Discourses* of Epictetus depict a Stoic master in the attempt to shape Stoically the lives of those who would learn from him.[5] Epictetus deals, therefore, with a vast range of subjects. Still, like any good teacher, he knows how to repeat himself. We shall thus focus on five animating themes that regularly occur in both the *Discourses* and the *Manual*: God, right judgments, philosophy, anthropology, and society. The obvious aim of this focus is not only to select matters that allow constructive comparison and juxtaposition with our other ancient authors but also to present the normative coordinates of Epictetus's works.[6] We begin with God, for it is Epictetus, above all other Stoics, who could earn the title of theologian, so central is his talk about God to his broader philosophical discourse and practice.

GOD

Any reader who turns from Seneca to Epictetus will no doubt be surprised at the dramatic increase in God-talk. Not only does Epictetus talk about God much more frequently than Seneca, he also speaks with a more pious accent. For Epictetus, God is the possibility and direction of the philosophical life.

As would any serious philosopher, Epictetus assumes that superstition is inherently problematic. He therefore spends little time ranting against its deforming influence, though he does occasionally take aim at the confusion cultic practice can cause between what is truly God and what is not (see *Disc.* 1.22.14–16; cf. *Ench.* 18.1; *Disc.* 2.8.13; 2.16.16).

Where we moderns, however, might think such views on superstition would preclude going to the diviner, seeking an oracle, listening to the interpretation of bird entrails, and so on—all such things look rather like Tarot cards and psychic hotlines to us—Epictetus offers a surprise. He does not say "don't go to the soothsayer" but rather "go in the right way," that is, as a philosopher who already knows that whatever the predicted outcome, "it will be possible for you to turn it to the good" (*Ench.* 32.2). Indeed, "go in confidence," as Socrates himself counseled, and with a willingness to play the part of the philosopher regardless of predicted peril (*Ench.* 32.2). Epictetus does not, therefore, teach contempt for traditional religious practices but rather focuses on the only sure way to avoid falling into superstition: the right posture of the philosopher.

This posture depends essentially upon the philosopher's knowledge of God. Thus Epictetus instructs the young man Naso that the "first thing" aspiring philosophers "must learn is that there is a God . . . and that in everything [the philosopher] says and does, he must act as an imitator of God" (*Disc.* 2.14.11–13; cf. 4.1.98–99). Yes, Naso might reply, but you also say that I ought to begin by "understanding the meaning of terms" (*Disc.* 2.14.14). What, O Teacher, does the word *God* mean?

Epictetus's reverence for God extends well beyond his respect for the natural order or awe at the world's beauty. He does of course, like any Stoic, believe deeply in the divine character of the world's good order (see *Disc.* 1.6.1), but God for Epictetus is not simply identical with a certain shape of the world. Again and again, Epictetus instructs his pupils about the meaning of the word *God* through a way of speaking that displays what could only be called a kind of personal warmth or trust.[7] To those who struggle with the rigors of philosophical life, Epictetus says, "Be bold to lift up your neck to God like a man freed from bondage and say, 'from now on, use me for whatever you wish; I am of one mind with you; I am yours. I don't want to be excused from anything that seems good to you; lead me where you will, clothe me with what you want. Do you want me to hold public office or stay in private life? Remain here, or be exiled? Be poor or be rich?'" It matters not, Epictetus implies. "'In all such states or places, I will defend you to humanity'" (*Disc.* 2.16.42).

Considering the way Providence has marvelously provided for all our true needs ought to bring forth hymns of praise to God. "Shouldn't we," says Epictetus, "as we dig and plow and eat, sing a hymn of praise to God?" God has given us what we need, "hands, and power to swallow, and a belly, and power to grow without thinking about it and to breathe while asleep." Above all, "God has given us the faculty to comprehend these things and to follow the path of reason." Indeed, Epictetus continues, it is nothing less than our very nature to sing in praise of God. "If I were a nightingale, I should sing as a nightingale; if a swan, as a swan. But, look, I'm a reasoning being (*logikos eimi*). I must therefore sing hymns of praise to God. This is my work. I do it, and I will not desert this post as long as it has been given to me to fill. I exhort you to join me in this same song" (*Disc.* 1.16.16–21).

As this prayer shows, Epictetus's pious expressions are not simply mythological language intended to express intellectual truths.[8] For Epictetus *God* means something that calls forth song, praise, prayer, and devotion. God is not simply identified with a correct set of reasoned judgments about the world. There is an irreducible *flavor* to Epictetus's speech that cannot be eliminated by achieving conceptual clarity. Indeed, conceptual clarity about his addresses to God requires us to assume that Epictetus was serious. To study in Nicopolis was to learn that the word *God* means someone you can talk to.

Such warmth does not, however, prevent Epictetus from making more formal statements about God, as if his pedagogical program could only verge on theological sentimentality. Far from it. "What is the *ousia* (essence, being) of God?" he asks in a classically Greek turn of phrase. "Might it be flesh? No! Land? No! Fame? Never!" The *ousia* of God is "mind, knowledge, right reason" (2.8.2, *nous, epistēmē, logos orthos*).[9] Elsewhere, while emphasizing the importance of becoming self-sufficient, he continues a Greek metaphysical tradition about God: we ought to strive to be like Zeus, says Epictetus, who "communes with himself, and is at peace with himself, and contemplates the character of his governance, and occupies himself with ideas that are appropriate to himself" (*Disc.* 3.13.7).

Indeed, his students would not be wrong to think that Epictetus's warm piety presupposes a particular judgment about God over and against other options. For in fact it does: there are four wrong views, Epictetus teaches, that would-be philosophers must reject in order to submit themselves to the truth. First, the notion that the Deity (*to theion*) does not exist; second, that it exists but is idle, indifferent, and exercises no forethought; third, that it exists, and does exercise forethought, but only for great and heavenly things and not at all for earthly matters; and, fourth, that it exercises forethought for earthly and human things but only in a general way, not according to each individual (*Disc.* 1.12.1–3). In contrast to these four ways of thinking about God, Epictetus says, we ought to side with Odysseus and Socrates, those wise men who knew that not even when we move are we concealed from God (*Disc.* 1.12.3, citing the *Iliad*, 10.279). The fifth, and correct, view about God thus makes several different but equally important judgments about God: that God exists, that God has forethought, that this forethought includes both important heavenly matters and earthly and human concerns, and that such forethought is related to human beings on an individual basis. God, Epictetus might say, relates not just to *us* but to *you* and to *me*. After all, we are God's children.

God has made us, fashioned us as a master craftsman, begotten us as a father would his children. "Zeus has made you"; "you are the workmanship of the Craftsman" (*Disc.* 2.8.19, 21, *dēmiourgos*). Even Caesar can only adopt a divine son, says Epictetus, taking aim at standard imperial practice for securing an heir. "But you," he tells a student, simply "are the son of God" (*Disc.* 1.3.2; cf. 1.9.6).[10]

How so? a new student might wonder. I have already heard you say many times over that God is "the Father of all humans" (*Disc.* 1.3.1; 3.22.82; 3.24.15–16 et passim). But in what way? Simply by my existence as such am I a son of God?

Epictetus's answer to this question is "not exactly." It is not so much the human being as such but our capacity to reason (*hē dynamis hē logikē*) that secures our kinship with God (*Disc.* 1.1.4). When I say, dear boy, "You are a fragment of God," I mean that "you have a part of him in yourself" (*Disc.* 2.8.11), and that part, of course, is your reason (*logos*).[11] The fact that Zeus has given each of us our own *daimōn*, Epictetus could continue, does not mean that we have returned to a superstitious view of little gods that control us for this or that. *Daimōn* refers, rather, to our reason as a way to describe its essentially divine character (*Disc.* 1.14.14).[12] In fact, argues Epictetus, by virtue of our rationality, we are not "inferior to the gods"; indeed, we are their equals (*isos tois theois*, *Disc.* 1.12.26–7; cf. *Disc.* 1.14.11).[13] That is why even as individuals, Epictetus famously declares, we are never apart from God: "When you close your doors and make darkness within, remember never to say that you are alone. For you are not. God is within you, and your divine reason is, too" (*Disc.* 1.14.13–14, *daimōn*). We are, then, fundamentally "intertwined with God through reason" (*Disc.* 1.9.5).

Yet for Epictetus it is not only through human rationality that God is intertwined with the world. So, too, says Epictetus, God's "seeds have descended not only to my father and grandfather but to all things that are begotten and grow upon the earth" (*Disc.* 1.9.4). God is everywhere already "present in his works" (*Disc.* 1.6.23–24) and made manifest in them: "Every work reveals its Artificer."[14] God in his Providence (*pronoia*) has made not only colors but the faculty for seeing them; and not only that, but light to see them by. God made not only men but also women, and complementary organs by which to unite them. Dark and light. Rain and sun. And so on, almost *ad infinitum*. "Who is it,"

Epictetus asks, "that has fitted this to that and that to this? Who is it that has fitted sword to scabbard and scabbard to sword?" (*Disc.* 1.14.1–10). The very fit of "this to that" shows the intertwining of God and world.

Epictetus in fact does not finally differentiate between God and the cosmos; "all things are united as one" (*Disc.* 1.14.1–10). The Artificer is not someone who is "outside" his work. He is, in a very strict sense, part of the work itself. They are united, one, intertwined—ultimately the same reality.[15] Yet in Epictetan grammar *God* is not simply another word for the world in its entirety. It names instead a certain character of the cosmos, a direction or grain within its overarching unity.

Epictetus's theological language is thus clearly complex. God is not a "person," or even quite a "universal mind," as if God or God's "thoughts" were distinct from the world in which his *pronoia* comes to pass.[16] Nor could Epictetus be called a panentheist, as if all things were somehow in God, because all things are not "in" some other thing called God, or even intertwined with some other thing called God—and this for the simple reason that there is no distinction that would allow God to mean "another thing."

Epictetus himself saw no disjuncture between his theology and his piety: "Piety toward the gods," he once taught, "is chiefly having right opinions about them" (*Ench.* 31.1). Of course, as it turns out, right opinions about divine things should bring forth hymns as a result of true understanding; piety and knowledge are interconnected. Epictetus knew neither Goethe nor Wordsworth, but he would have sensed in them a remarkable similarity in sensibility. The world—at least in part—is sublime, godlike, indeed, God itself. That this is so should call forth, from the philosopher who is trained to see it, a contentedness of soul that extends even unto the moment of death. If, Epictetus tells his students who are still anxious over the prospect of death, I am occupied with philosophy when "death finds me . . . it is enough for me if I can lift up my hands unto God and say, 'The faculties that I received from you to enable me to understand your governance and to follow it—these I have not neglected. As far as the power lay in me, I have not shamed you. See how I have dealt with my sense; see how I have dealt with my preconceptions. Have I ever blamed you? Have I been discontented with any things that happen, or wished it to be otherwise? Have I at all violated my duty toward others? I am grateful that you have begotten me. And I am grateful for that which you have given me. However long I have had the use of your gifts is enough for me. Take them back again and assign them whatever part you wish, for they were all yours, and you had given them to me. Is there any more fitting end than this?'" He continues, "Is it not enough for you to take your departure from the world in this way?" (*Disc.* 4.10.14–17). To see how Epictetus would educate his students to arrive at the ability to utter the dying prayer, we turn to his attempt to form their judgments.

RIGHT JUDGMENTS

It is hardly accidental that Arrian chose to open the *Manual* as follows: "Some things are under our control, and some things are not" (*Ench.* 1.1). For it is this distinction that forms the foundation of Epictetus's philosophy. All Stoics would, in a sense, share it, but no other makes so much of it, returns to it so frequently, or expounds its meaning as much as Epictetus. By beginning the *Manual* with this distinction, Arrian conveys structurally what must be the case philosophically, as the *Discourses* repeatedly confirm: even to get off the ground in learning how to live the way Epictetus commends, a student will have to ingest this most basic difference between things that are under human control and things that are not.

Of course, stated so generally, such a distinction could hardly raise an eyebrow. Even Nietzsche did not think everything was subject to his will. The philosophical contour of Epictetus's statement, therefore, comes through specification. "Under our control," he immediately continues in the *Manual,* "are conception, choice, desire, aversion, and, in a word, everything that is our own doing." Things that are not under our control, he says, are "our body, our property, reputation, office, and, in a word, everything that is not our own doing" (*Ench.* 1.1).

Yet in real life things such as these do not automatically sort themselves for our sake. Nor do we automatically sort them correctly; indeed, Epictetus might say, the very need for philosophy itself testifies to our ineptitude in distinguishing between things that are and are not under our control. How then do we learn to distinguish?

Epictetus's answer depends upon several interrelated decisions, all of which relate to the way we know the world. As he says over and over again, we experience the world in terms of "impressions" (*phantasiai*). Some external impressions are of course insignificant: that grass is green in the spring, that water is wet, that some apples are sweet, and so on. Some impressions are simply trustworthy accommodations of our common sense to nature: when we try to eat a piece of bread, do we not always put it in our mouth rather than somewhere else?[17] But other impressions are powerful or "disturbing"—a favorite Epictetan word—and bring with them the possibility of unhappiness and eventual existential ruin. This possibility is realized, however, only when we fail to sort our impressions into the right categories and respond on the basis of our error.[18] "Study immediately every disturbing impression (*phantasia*)," Epictetus once said, "so that you can say to it, 'You are an impression and not at all what you seem to be.'" He continues: "After that examine it and test it by these rules that you have, the first and most important of which is this: Whether the impression has to do with things that are under our control or with things that are not under our control. And if it has to do with things that are not under our control, be ready to answer 'It is nothing to me'" (*Ench.* 1.5).

Epictetus holds that "it is not the things themselves that disturb us human beings." The problems, rather, stem from "our judgments (*dogmata*)" about external impressions of things (*Ench.* 5). Where we judge wrongly and misidentify the category to which an impression belongs, we allow ourselves to be disturbed and put ourselves at risk. Since the use of external impression falls within our control (*Ench.* 6)—we don't just instantly react to impressions but can hold them at bay to analyze—the crucial matter is learning how to make right judgments.

In order to judge rightly, we must first realize, says Epictetus, that impressions come to us in four different ways. Things either "are and seem so to be; or are not, and do not seem to be; or are, and do not seem to be; or are not and yet seem to be" (*Disc.* 1.27.1). For Epictetus learning how to sort impressions is learning a full orientation to the world. Making a correct judgment includes a range of other commitments that must be in place if we are to make correct use of external impressions.

The first such commitment is to nature (*physis*). For Epictetus, making the correct judgment about an impression always means that one has read its nature accurately. "Whenever you have made use of impressions according to nature (*kata physin*), you should be elated; for then your elation will be at your own good" (*Ench.* 6).

Epictetus is no epistemological simpleton and is well aware that impressions are conditioned by traditions of thought and life, the broad course of history, human relationships—even certain biological constraints—and so on. Impressions must thus be uncoupled from their normal vehicles before their nature can be seen.

Despite the fact that countless daily matters would teach us otherwise, we should not, for example, see a wife as a wife *kata physin*. Or a child. What is more natural is to see them as human beings. "If you kiss your own child or wife," Epictetus teaches, "say to yourself that you are kissing a human being; for when it dies you will not be disturbed" (*Ench.* 3.1). The death of *my wife*, to understate the matter, is a quite different thing from the death of *the human being who is mortal in the first place*. To respond to the first, Epictetus argues, is to mistake contingency for nature and thereby risk existential demolition.

To win through to the second is to read the human being according to its nature.[19]

Sorting impressions requires a certain level of abstraction, an ability to see through the way something first appears to its more fundamental nature. Once seen, an object's nature tells us in which category to put the impression: over the death of my wife or child I have no control—the impression thus sorts easily into the category "things over which I have no control."

According to Epictetus, discerning a thing's nature is nothing more than learning how to apply our "preconceptions (*prolēpseis*) to particular cases" (*Disc.* 1.22.9). These preconceptions are shared by all humans (*Disc.* 1.22.1), though we do not emerge from the womb with "an innate concept of a right-angled triangle, or a half-tone musical interval." Preconceptions, for Epictetus, are not pure concepts, mathematical-like truths available to the mind quite apart from the course of our lives or the history of a word's use. Preconceptions are more directly related to the distinctions one needs to make for a philosophical life: "Who has come into being without an innate concept (*emphyton ennoian*) of what is good and evil, beautiful and shameful, appropriate and inappropriate, and happiness (*eudaimonia*)"—the philosopher's perennial pursuit—"and proper and obligatory, and of what we must do and what we must not do?" (*Disc.* 2.11.3).

As we travel through life, however, we lose the ability to apply our innate preconceptions correctly to particular cases. Take the preconception "healthy," for example. Why is the word *healthy* used so very differently and in contradictory ways, Epictetus asks. To be healthy, "one person says, 'Keep abstaining from food,' and another, 'Give nourishment'" (*Disc.* 2.17.9). The reason, he argues, is that we "are unable properly to apply the preconception 'healthy' to specific instances" (*Disc.* 2.17.9). We have lost the right meaning of terms and no longer know how to use them well (*Disc.* 2.14.14). The first step to apply them rightly is simply to admit our ignorance. In good Socratic fashion, Epictetus would have his students rid themselves of the idea that their common notions count as knowledge (*Disc.* 2.17.1, *apobalein oiēsin*; cf. 2.17.39–40). What they must then learn, he says, is the Stoic "general principles" (*theōrēmata*), the system of classification that tells us what things are grouped under which preconception, and thus how to use terms such as *healthy* both accurately and well. Only so, Epictetus says, can we hope to apply our preconceptions correctly to specific instances, or particular impressions (*Disc.* 2.17.3–13).[20]

For Epictetus, therefore, preconceptions cannot be recovered and rightly applied by anyone in any way of life whatsoever. They are in their mature form specifically Stoic configurations, knowable in relation to particular cases only through the Stoic pattern of sorting.[21] This is why Epictetus confidently asserts that there can be no contradictions in our preconceptions (*Disc.* 1.22.1–21; 2.11.13–18; 2.26.1–7): different sorting, and hence different application, would lead to a different life, and we cannot live incompatible lives simultaneously. "Is it possible that all the opinions that Jews and Syrians and Egyptians and Romans hold about food can be right? How is that possible? I think it totally necessary that if the Egyptians are right, the others cannot be, or if the Jews are right, the others cannot be" (*Disc.* 1.11.11–14). In terms of a habitual practice of consumption, Epictetus knows, one can either eat pork or not, but one cannot both eat pork and not eat pork at the same time. Or, to put it in terms of the philosophical schools, no one can be both a Stoic and, say, an Epicurean concurrently. The different ways impressions are interpreted and the resultant differences in the lives of the school's adherents are incompatible in one human life. In Epictetan grammar, the meaning of *preconception* thus turns out to be synonymous with his specific sort of Stoic teaching and pattern of life. Hence when he says that we should "have our preconceptions clear, polished like weapons, and ready at hand," he means that we should train as Stoics (and no doubt preferably in Nicopolis).

It is of course true that Epictetus says that it is our capacity to reason—the "most excellent faculty of all"—that allows us to discriminate among impressions (*Disc.* 1.1.4–7). But by capacity to reason (*hē dynamis hē logikē*), he means not so much a general power shorn of its specific incarnations as he does the Stoic version of the *logos*—which is itself, of course, nothing other than aligning ourselves, in both thought and practice, with nature.[22] "And what does 'rationally' mean?" he asks. "In perfect accordance with nature," comes the predictable answer (*Disc.* 3.1.25, *logikōs*).[23] The power of reason is thus learning from the Stoic master how to apply our preconceptions rightly in order to know whether an impression should be grouped as under our control or not. In short, for Epictetus, to judge impressions well and rightly, one must become a Stoic philosopher. We thus turn to his language about philosophy itself.

PHILOSOPHY

Speaking of philosophy as the way we learn how to make right judgments about impressions could lead to the notion that philosophy according to Epictetus was primarily intellectual exercise. Nothing could be farther from the truth. It is true that the "first and greatest task of a philosopher is the ability to test and discriminate between impressions, and to apply none that has not been tested" (*Disc.* 1.20.7). But such discrimination already occurs within the context of a philosophical life. Like Seneca, Epictetus sees philosophy as a habit of being or a comprehensive style of existence, an emancipatory mode of living that includes not only thought but also the full range of human action.

Of the learned Chrysippus, Epictetus says, "When a person gives himself airs because he can understand and interpret the books of Chrysippus, say to yourself, 'If Chrysippus had not written obscurely, this man would have nothing about which to give himself airs.'" Suppose I then learn how to interpret Chrysippus, Epictetus continues, if "I admire the mere act of exegesis, have I not become a grammarian instead of a *philosopher*? . . . Far from being proud, therefore, whenever someone says to me, 'explain Chrysippus to me,' I blush when I can't display deeds that match and harmonize with his words" (*Ench.* 49; cf. *Disc.* 1.26.8–9).

Philosophical meaning cannot be read off a page. It must be woven from a life. If Epictetus's students cannot see Chrysippus exegeted in daily habits and patterns, then Epictetus's teaching is implicated. But come now, a student could reasonably say, "I wish to know what Chrysippus means in his treatise on *The Liar*"; can you not expound it to me? If you want to take short cuts in understanding, expect me to lay out truths for your examination as a vendor might spread the goods he has to sell, "if that is your design," Epictetus replies, "go hang, you wretch! What good will that do you? With sorrow you'll read the whole treatise, and with trembling you will then talk to others." Wisdom cannot be acquired simply by explanation nor understanding solely through dialogue. In an unformed life the truth will have no effect. Despite the fervor, nothing will be accomplished. You will doubtless end up like my current students who fawn over each other's hermeneutical abilities all to no good: "You will go back to the same things again; you [will] have exactly the same desires as before, the same aversions, in the same way you [will] make your choices, your designs, and your purposes; you [will] pray for the same things and be interested in the same things" (*Disc.* 2.17.34–36). Philosophy unlocked from life is only show. Interpreting Chrysippus is never an end in itself, something toward which we should strive for its own sake. Philosophy is working on yourself! It is more like rough training for the Olympics than reading a book (*Ench.* 29), more like the contest of the event itself than lifting weights and flexing your bronzed muscles (*Disc.* 1.4.13)! Do not say, "See how I have mastered the treatise *On Choice*" (*Disc.* 1.4.14). It is "not *that* I'm looking for, you slave, but how you act in your choices and refusals, your desires and aversions, how you go at things, and apply yourself to them, and prepare yourself, and whether you are acting in harmony with nature therein, or not. For if you are acting in harmony with nature, show me that, and I will tell you that you are making progress; but if out of harmony, be gone with you!" (*Disc.* 1.4.14–15).

Reading, study, exegesis—all these, Epictetus says, are useless without the lives that make the interpretations worth taking seriously in the first place. Understanding Chrysippus, in short, is a full-time job. Even the great Chrysippus himself "has no place for pride if he merely interprets the will of nature but does not himself follow it" (*Disc.* 1.17.17). Indeed, I will go farther than that, Epictetus would say. "We have no need of Chrysippus on his own account, but only insofar as he helps us to follow nature" (*Disc.* 1.17.18). Could we see what he saw without him, we could dispense with his writings. But alas, we cannot see without help.

How, then, do we learn philosophy, learn to see according to nature and therefore how to make right judgments about impressions in the daily living of life? In a sense, of course, it is the entirety of his remaining corpus that shows how Epictetus would answer this question.[24] Still, there are two recurrent features of his language about learning philosophy that focus his answer more specifically: his teaching on the passions, and his insistence on the various exercises required of would-be philosophers.

If philosophy for Epictetus is a full-time job, this is in no small measure because human passions are full-time realities. It is no accident that the first and "most crucial" division of philosophy concerns the passions (*ta pathē*). It is pointless to move on to the second (ethics) and third (logic) divisions before conquering the passions. Progress in philosophy depends fundamentally upon the practical use of reason, but the passions, argues Epictetus, "make it impossible for us even to listen to reason" (*Disc.* 3.2.1–4; cf. *Disc.* 1.4.11; 3.12–14; 4.10.13).[25]

Take love, for example. "Only the Sage can truly love," says Epictetus, in a phrase that links inextricably the treatment of the passions to the right judgments of reason. But how can this be? For I am foolish and yet love my child (*Disc.* 2.22.3–4). Ah, Epictetus replies, but let me tell you what that love—and love, more generally—amounts to in real life. "Did you never see dogs caressing one another and playing with one another, and say, 'Nothing could be more friendly.' But to see what love (*philia*) is, throw a piece of meat between them, and you will know." It is no different with people. Despite the fact that you provide for your son, show him affection, believe that he loves you, and so on, see what happens to "love" as it meets money and women: "Throw between yourself and your son a small piece of land, and you will find out how much your son wants to bury you, the sooner the better—and how earnestly you pray for your son's death. Then you will change your mind again and say, 'What a child I have raised! For a long time he has been carrying me to the grave!'" Or, "Throw a pretty woman between you, and the old man as well as the young will love her" (*Disc.* 2.22.9–11).[26] Love as you see it, Epictetus argues, is not a state of right *dogma* (*Disc.* 2.22.37) but a destructive force subject to error and whim, a passion whose inevitable effect is to wreak havoc not only upon ourselves but also upon those whom we claim to love most.

I see your point about love, O Teacher, but what about the desire to help those who sorrow or hurt? If we are to rid ourselves of the passions (*Ench.* 2.2), are we to become emotionally immovable, cold and hard and unable to render help to those who suffer? Epictetus's answer is complex.

Precisely because the disturbing influence of the passions comes on the heels of desire unattained (*Disc.* 3.3.3), and precisely because the suffering undergone by others is something that is out of our control—it results from their own wrong judgments about what *they* can control—we must eradicate our desire to alleviate their suffering. We cannot make their judgments for them and therefore cannot help them and must not try. The only one we can help is the one over whom we have control. "The grief of another is another's, but my own grief is mine" (*Disc.* 3.24.23).

But this does not mean that you cannot be present with and to those who suffer; indeed, if things are dire enough, you can even *fake* sympathy. Of course, Epictetus would not really put it quite that way, but he comes close enough in a passage that is as famous as it is revealing. "When you see someone weeping in sorrow, either because a child has gone on a journey, or because he has lost his property, beware that you are not carried away by the impression that the man is in the midst of external ills, but immediately keep before you this thought: 'It is not what has happened that distresses this man . . . but his judgment (*dogma*) about it.' Do not, however, hesitate to accommodate yourself to him as far as words go, and if the occasion offers, even to groan with him. Nevertheless, be careful not to groan inwardly!" (*Ench.* 16).[27] Epictetus's answer eliminates true empathy as a possibility within the philosophical life. The Sage's inner security must not falter in the face of that which might disturb him (*tarassein*).

This does not mean, however, that the Sage cannot appreciate the gifts Providence brings his way, or exhibit affection toward wife or children; indeed, Socrates himself quite clearly "loved his own children." Yet he loved them as a "free man who remember[ed] that it is first necessary to be a friend to the gods"—which is to say that Socrates' "love" was free of pathos; it was an affection shaped by reasonable judgments about the mortality of his offspring (*Disc.* 3.24.59–60). To the question "How shall I be affectionate?" Epictetus answers: "as a man of noble mind, as a man of good fortune; for it is against reason (*logos*) to be dejected, or broken in spirit, or to depend on someone else [for your well-being], or to blame either God or man" (*Disc.* 3.24.58). Affection, in short, is allowed because it is not passion. Far from being a force that disturbs the philosopher's *autarkeia*—self-sufficient independence—affection is simply reason enjoying its concert with nature. It is therefore quite appropriate for those whose lives are shaped by the judgments of reason.

A young student who has followed Epictetus thus far may be forgiven if he were to think that Epictetus's view of the relationship between philosophy and the passions presents something of a problem. On the one hand, he says that right judgments about what is under our control and what is not are rendered difficult, or even near to impossible, by the passions. We must therefore treat the passions in order to discriminate correctly between our impressions. On the other hand, however, he says that in order to eradicate desire, we must make right judgments about impressions. We must therefore discriminate correctly among impressions in order to treat the passions. Where desire is aflame, our judgments are compromised. And where our judgments are incorrect, desire becomes inflamed. How can we learn to sort our impressions if our passions interfere with reason and *at the same time* eliminate the passions by means of our rightly formed judgments of reason?

Well, Epictetus might say, I never claimed it would be easy. "The lecture hall of the philosopher is," after all, "a hospital. You ought not to leave in pleasure but in pain" (*Disc.* 3.23.30). Philosophy is the arena of the hard, painful work that is healing.[28] Understanding the tensions in philosophy may well amount to discerning the best shape of human life we can hope for. All this is to say that the problem you detect is in fact a real and inescapable paradox. It cannot be resolved intellectually in abstraction from the course of your life; nor can it be dismantled and rebuilt into a stepwise method by which you can see through its tension. Yet, remarkably, it can be lived.

To live the paradox that Stoic philosophy is, the pupil must not only "learn but also add exercise and then training" (*Disc.* 2.9.13, *meletē* and *askēsis*). As the rest of his corpus shows, Epictetus's "then" (*eita*) should not be read here in the sense of a progression (and then . . . and then . . .). His point, rather, is that learning itself is inseparably intertwined with particular practices and disciplines that treat the passions.[29] True, you may be a quick learner, Epictetus could admit, but the fact is that "it's not a fair match between a pretty girl and a beginner in philosophy" (*Disc.* 3.12.12). Learn by exercise and discipline, and the needed discrimination between impressions will appear all the more clearly to you through the course of your action. Conversely, the clearer the distinction between what is in your control and what is not, the easier it will be to act accordingly.

Of course, Epictetus might continue, by exercise and training I do not mean such silly things as "practicing walking on a tightrope" or, as the Cynic Diogenes was wont to do, "throwing our arms around a statue" to toughen ourselves. True, these require discipline because they are both hard and, in the case of the tightrope at least, rather dangerous. "But not every difficult and dangerous thing is suitable for training, but only that which facilitates success in achieving the object of our effort" (*Disc.* 3.12.1–4). What sort of exercises, then, discipline us to make right judgments?

To this question, Arrian's records of his master's teaching display a range of practices that includes both physical markers of the philosophical life, such as the traditional beard and cloak (see *Disc.* 1.29.22; 3.1.24; 4.8.5–6), and exercises geared more strictly toward conceptual development, such as reading, copying, and memorizing (see *Disc.* 1.1.25; 1.10.8). Epictetus obviously never had the chance to read Foucault on discipline or punishment (though Foucault did read Epictetus), but he did know how to guide his students toward a type of self-criticism that Foucault himself brilliantly thematized two millennia later: by conducting his relations with others "as if Another is looking on from above" (*Disc.* 1.30.1–2), the student constructs a Monitor who keeps watch over his life. But precisely because the Monitor is nothing other than the student's own projection, the Monitor turns out to reflect what the student has learned philosophically about how to act. That is, Epictetus's pupil has learned to monitor himself—and, more specifically, to see his behavior in light of the Stoic philosophy that forms the basis and shape of the projection.[30]

There are many other techniques that Epictetus would consider exercise and training. For example, he admits that the sheer vividness of an initial impression can "sweep you off your feet," but he counsels a kind of active patience bolstered by internal speech: "say to the impression, 'Wait for me a little, O impression; allow me to see who you are, and what you are an impression of; allow me to put you to the test.'" He also encourages his pupils to imagine vigorously the future train of events unleashed by acquiescing to desire (2.18.24–26). Or, to mention only one other example, he exhorts them to "tell yourself first of all what kind of man you want to be, and then go ahead with what you are doing," that is, live into the paradigm you hold before you (*Disc.* 3.23.1). But perhaps no passage shows as clearly as his remarks in *Disc.* 2.18.1–18 how Epictetus conceives of the interdependence of thought and practice as necessary to his philosophical program. It is worth citing at some length.

> Every habit and faculty is confirmed and strengthened by the corresponding actions, that of walking by walking, of running by running. . . . If you lie in

bed for ten days, get up and try to take a rather long walk, and you will see how wobbly your legs are. In general, therefore, if you want to do something, make a habit of it; if you want not to do something, refrain from doing it, and accustom yourself to something else instead. The same is true for the things of the soul. When you are angry you may be sure not merely that this evil has befallen you [a misjudgment], but also that you have strengthened the habit [of misjudging and being angry], and have, as it were, added fuel to the flame. . . . In this way, without doubt, our illnesses arise, as the philosophers say. For when once you conceive a desire for money, if reason is used to reveal this desire as an evil, the passion is stilled and the governing principle (*hēgemonikon*) is restored to its original authority. But if you do not apply the remedy of reason, your governing principle does not revert to its previous condition, but being aroused the next time by the same impression, it bursts into the flame of desire more quickly than it did before. And if this happens over and over again, the next stage is that a callousness results and the illness strengthens the avarice.

He continues:

For the man who has had a fever, and then recovered, is not the same as he was before the fever, unless he has experienced a complete cure. Something like this happens also with the passions of the soul. Certain imprints and welts are left behind on the soul, and unless a man erases them perfectly, the next time he is scourged upon the old scars, he has welts no longer but wounds. If, therefore, you wish not to be hot-tempered, for example, do not feed your habit, and set before it nothing on which it can grow. As the first step, keep quiet and count the days on which you have not been angry. "I used to be angry every day, after that every other day, then every third, then every fourth." If you go so much as thirty days without a fit of anger, sacrifice to God. For the habit is first weakened and then utterly destroyed. (*Disc.* 2.18.1–14)

On the one hand, Epictetus's remarks offer a commonplace that all but the least reflective students would already know: both for good and for ill, habits are hard to break. On the other hand, however, Epictetus binds the right use of reason together with the health of the soul.[31] Reason, that is, does not work alone. For Epictetus, there is no such thing as thought itself, or judgments about impressions which can be made in abstraction from the philosopher's own habit. Reason cannot "apply its remedy" apart from the ability of reason's carrier to remain healthy. Precisely because reason all too easily follows the crooked lines laid down in the soul by repeated submission to the passions, it can be said to have a trajectory, and this trajectory is in large part identical with the effectiveness of the discipline of the philosopher. To read the etching upon the soul, Epictetus argues, will be to discover the shape of a person's (un)trained reason. And to discover in the etching one who is free from the power of the passions is to see the shape of reason's remedy habitually well applied.

In short, for Epictetus, to come to school in Nicopolis is to expect to be cured. Philosophy has nothing to do with learning principles (*theōrēmata*) that do not treat our illness, as if it were only offering us "eye salve" when we have nothing wrong with our eyes (*Disc.* 2.21.15–22). It is instead the only way we can be healed, or—to switch to Epictetus's favorite metaphor—to be set free from bondage. "For what purpose did you go to the philosophers?" he asks (*Disc.* 4.1.83). "To be set free" is inevitably his answer. Indeed, "every day when you are training yourself as you do in the gymnasium, do not say that you are 'philosophizing'—what an arrogant phrase!—but rather that you are a slave presenting your Emancipator in court. For that," he says, "is true freedom" (*Disc.* 4.1.113).

That the freedom offered by philosophy is fundamentally sustained by erecting an impenetrable inner citadel (*akropolis*) is as obvious in Epictetus as anything he teaches (see *Disc.* 4.1.86). Yet a savvy student might wonder how the intertwining between reason and exercise or training could allow Epictetus such confidence in the ability of a person to build the wall needed for the citadel. If reason and the passions are that intertwined, the student might ask, how can we ever get free of passion-shaped, and thus deformed, reason? Must there not be some "space," some "place" where reason can operate free of the passions' influence—at least to get things started in the right direction? Do you not presuppose a picture of the human being in which our freedom ultimately rests on the exercise of an already and always free faculty? How else could we even begin our emancipation? Indeed, yes, would come the reply, I do so presuppose. My picture of the human being is exactly coordinated with my understanding of the work philosophy can do.

For the next section of this chapter, we thus turn to a particular Epictetan presupposition about the human being. What we shall discover is that Epictetus is remarkably confident in our capacity to transform ourselves and to live the philosophical life.

HUMAN BEING

A. A. Long argues that when it comes to the human being Epictetus is an "optimist." Taken by itself, Long's evaluation is hard to swallow. Where, for example, the Aristotelians thought we could moderate the passions—control their excesses while enjoying their gifts—the Stoics thought not. In their view, the Aristotelians were simply naïve. Human beings are too weak to wrestle with the power of the passions, the Stoics thought, or even to make basically wise decisions about how to live. Indeed, as Epictetus puts it, the first thing an aspiring philosopher must admit is his profound weakness in the face of life's most crucial matters: "The beginning of philosophy with those who take it up as they should and enter in by the gate, as it were, is an awareness of humanity's weakness and impotence concerning what really counts" (*Disc.* 2.11.1). Yet readers of Epictetus can get Long's "optimism" down—and this for the simple reason that he is ultimately correct.

The fundamental presuppositions required by Epictetus's language about humanity can be seen most clearly through his use of a single term, *prohairesis*. How best to translate this word has long been a point of debate—particularly since Epictetus is the first philosopher to employ it systematically—but no ancient student of Epictetus would ever have been in doubt about its importance or its basic meaning.[32]

"You have a *prohairesis* that is by nature unhindered and incapable of being compelled" (*Disc.* 1.17.21, *prohairesin echeis akōluton physei kai ananankaston*). Most fundamentally, *prohairesis* refers to the faculty that by nature lies beyond the reach of any external influence, the "capacities and dispositions" (Long) that are entirely up to us.[33] It is an essential inborn feature of the human being rather than something achieved through time and discipline. Indeed, Epictetus continues, a person's *prohairesis* is nothing other than a part of God's own being, given to us by God as an irrevocable gift. Defending the inability of one's *prohairesis* to be hindered or compelled from without, Epictetus says, "For if God had so constructed that part of his own being that he has taken from himself and given to us so that it could be hindered or compelled either by himself or from another, he would no longer be God, nor would he be caring for us as he ought to" (*Disc.* 1.17.27). So basically independent, so sovereign in its operation, so internally secure is our *prohairesis* that even God who gave it cannot now interfere with it or compel it in any way.

If it's the case that our "*prohairesis* and all prohairetic works" are under our control (*Disc.* 1.22.10), then isn't it so that all we have to do is rely on our internal, untouchable freedom? Why is it so difficult? What is the problem?

Through a life deformed by bad judgments about impressions, Epictetus would answer, and a consequent inability to live the distinction between what is up to us and what is not, our prohairetic capacities are in an important sense diminished—hidden from us, one might say, behind the unreasonable pattern of passionate life. It becomes all the more difficult, therefore, to live naturally (by the guidance given through exercising our *prohairesis*) in conformity with nature (the purpose of prohairetic living). So, too, to speak of "progress" (*prokopē*) in philosophy is to speak of an active cultivation of the natural capacity of our *prohairesis*. "Where is progress?" Epictetus asks. It is there where a man has "withdrawn from external things and turned his attention to his *prohairesis*, cultivating and completing it so as to make it harmonious with nature—elevated, free, unhindered, untrammeled, faithful, and honorable" (*Disc.* 1.4.18).[34] Thus, for Epictetus, the degree to which the natural freedom of our *prohairesis* is exercised is itself closely linked with the degree to which we exercise our natural freedom.

A tautology! A tautology! some pupil might well accuse. Doesn't such an expression reveal a deep contradiction in your notion of our natural capacities? Wouldn't that mean, despite your assertions, that the *prohairesis* can in fact be hindered (or helped)?

Well, Epictetus could respond, no and yes. No: the freedom of the *prohairesis* is ultimate or absolute in the sense that the *prohairesis* cannot be fundamentally corrupted, rendered utterly depraved; no matter how foolish his life, a man's *prohairesis* always remains a "place" from which to gain a foothold against the passions. Our *prohairesis* is in this way untouchable—not even by God.

Yes: in a sense our freedom is relative for the simple reason that a foolish life increases our sickness, deepens the human problem by making it more difficult to exercise the freedom that is ours to begin with. But worry not, such damage is never beyond repair.

Indeed, prohairetic living for Epictetus is nothing short of the human good. "If you ask me, 'What is the human good?' I can give you no other answer than that it is a kind of *prohairesis*" (*Disc.* 1.8.16; cf. 1.29.1; 2.23.27). Of course, Epictetus does not mean "good" in a nonspecific sense but rather in a specifically Stoic philosophical sense. That is to say, the human good is developing the natural freedom of our *prohairesis* by building our citadel and cultivating our ability to deal from behind its wall with the world as it comes to us. Living prohairetically makes "us ready to meet the things that come upon us" (*Disc.* 3.10.6) and brings "our will[s] into harmony with what happens" (*Disc.* 2.14.7). This is the purpose of the *prohairesis* and the raison d'être of human freedom.

Because of his belief in an inalienably free space within the human being, Epictetus's anthropology is indeed remarkably optimistic. He may rant and rave against his students' foibles and foolishness, offer grim accounts of their success in discriminating among impressions, and chide them again and again for their inability and refusal to deal well with their passions. But in the deepest sense, Epictetus is absolutely confident that they can do better. He acknowledges that they can't do better all at once, and advises them that the path to self-sufficiency starts with small things—by adopting the right posture toward a spilled jar of oil before moving on to the death of one's wife or child (*Ench.* 12.1; *Disc.* 2.18.1; 4.1.11). But grow they can. Given his picture of the human being, his confidence is perfectly placed and satisfyingly coherent: the philosophical life is achievable because of the kind of free thing the human being is; conversely, the human being is just the kind of thing that needs the philosophical life for its freedom.

SOCIETY

But what about the fact that we have to cultivate our freedom within a range of relationships? Are we to retreat, to hide socially as well as existentially behind the wall of our inner acropolis? What about family and our obligations to civic life?

Ah, Epictetus could say, you've done well: coming to understand the importance of the *prohairesis* is an education in how to articulate the necessary condition for a call to self-sufficiency. But if you mean by your questions that we *need* such relationships for our freedom or happiness, then of course you are quite mistaken. They and all their twists and turns are entirely out of our control (they go into *that* column, not the other).

Yet Epictetus argues that self-sufficiency does not require us to move out of our relational embeddedness. Indeed, as it turns out, the case is quite the reverse. Prohairetic living—exercising our natural freedom, making right judgments about what is under our control and what isn't, eradicating the passions, and so on—is the indispensable condition of discharging well one's relational responsibilities, of playing excellently the roles that specify our particular natural duties. Consider the family: "Our duties are in general measured by our social relationships. He is a father. One is called upon to take care of him, to give way to him in all things, to submit when he reviles or strikes you." If someone says, "But he is a bad father," Epictetus would reply, "Did nature bring you into relationship with a good father? No, but simply with a father." Or what about a scoundrel for a brother? "My brother does me wrong," someone says. Epictetus replies, "Very well, then, maintain the relation that you have toward him; and do not consider what he is doing, but what you will have to do, if your *prohairesis* is to be in harmony with nature. For no one will harm you without your consent: you will have been harmed only when you think you have been harmed. In this way, therefore, you will discover what duty to expect toward your neighbor, your citizen, your commanding officer, if you acquire the habit of looking at your relations with them" (*Ench.* 30; cf. *Disc.* 3.3.5–10).

The possibility of behaving well toward both father and brother depends upon the judgment that their character is not up to us. By observing this basic distinction, Epictetus teaches, we can be in accord with nature quite apart from how we are treated by father or brother; we can thus fulfill our natural duties irrespective of the behavior of others. The effectiveness of our accordance with natural duties, moreover, is not limited to the philosopher's family dynamics. As the last sentence of this passage says, because of his harmony with nature, the philosopher's relation to political life is not fundamentally different from that to his family.

It is true, Epictetus acknowledges, that some have thought "philosophers were not active in civic affairs" (*Disc.* 1.10.8, *praktikoi*). Moreover, Epictetus's teaching about the independence of philosophically shaped reason was sufficiently bold to elicit the question, "Do you philosophers teach us to despise our kings?" But Epictetus's answer was as clear as it was direct: "Far from it. Who among us teaches you to dispute their claim to the things over which they have authority?" (*Disc.* 1.29.9).[35] Stoics, argues Epictetus, make excellent citizens precisely because they can acknowledge natural duties and act on them in harmony with nature.

Contrasting the politics of Stoic philosophy with that of the Epicureans, Epictetus mocks the latter as utterly impractical, neglectful of duty, and foolish. "By God, I ask you, can you imagine an Epicurean *polis*? One man says, 'I don't marry.' 'Neither do I,' says another, 'for people should not marry.' 'No, nor have children, nor perform the duties of a citizen.' And what do you suppose will happen then? Where are the citizens to come from? Who will educate them? Who will take charge of the political formation of the young men? Who will be in charge of the gymnasium? . . . Your judgments are bad, subversive of the polis, destructive of the household, not even suitable for women. Throw these ideas away, man! You live in an imperial city. It is necessary for you to rule, to judge justly, to refrain from what is someone else's" (*Disc.* 3.7.19–21).[36]

Through the contrast with a rival school, Epictetus pointedly makes it clear that, unlike those Epicurean fools, the Stoics know that the freedom won by philosophy is exercised in wider circles of relationships and not apart from them. We have roles to play: father, son, city councilor, and more; indeed, we must never forget that such roles are not social constructions but are instead given by God, required by nature (*Disc.* 2.10.7–12; *Ench.* 17). When offered a provincial governorship, for example, those trained in Nicopolis will simply say, "I accept." But then they will continue, "and having accepted it, I will show how an educated man behaves" (*Disc.* 1.29.44). "Govern us," says Epictetus to a Roman official, "as rational beings by pointing out to us what is profitable, and we will follow you; point out what is unprofitable, and we will turn away from it. Bring us to admire and emulate you, as Socrates brought people to admire and emulate him" (*Disc.* 3.7.33–34).

No matter that Socrates persuaded "only one in a thousand" to give serious attention to his own life (*Disc.* 3.1.19); the normative point is the same. For Epictetus, the human being most fully becomes itself in freedom when it neither needs others nor neglects them but, instead, shows them a better way. Epictetan Stoic philosophy, therefore, is for society exactly to the extent that its practitioners both refuse to participate in the confusions that make its members sick and exhibit the natural way we ought to live through playing the roles in which they are cast.

Epictetus, like Seneca, believes that Stoic philosophy is the cure for what ails human beings. For both men, philosophy is the art of living (*Disc.* 1.15.2).

Of course, they have their differences. Epictetus, for example, is much less concerned than Seneca about the ravages of Fortuna (*Tychē*). And, though Epictetus does once say that the "epitome of all the ills to come upon us is the fear of death" (*Disc.* 3.26.38), he is much less existentially troubled by the problem of human mortality than is Seneca. Epictetus believes, as Seneca principally does, that death returns us to dust (*Disc.* 4.7.15), but he evidently sees no reason to dwell upon our end. And though both figures think deeply about Providence, Epictetus's confidence in God is the greater. Where Seneca tirelessly warns Lucilius against even the good things in life, Epictetus counsels his students to sing hymns. Where Seneca sees Fortune's snares, Epictetus discerns God's gifts. Where Seneca says, "Beware!" Epictetus says, "Trust God." To risk a reduction of their complexity and refinement: the world we inhabit is not quite as scary for Epictetus as it is for Seneca.[37]

Epictetus, moreover, is much more concerned with epistemology than is Seneca, and in particular with the question of how we know what "nature" is. Both philosophers exhort their pupil(s) to align their lives with nature, but Epictetus emphasizes the need for detailed conceptual resources to describe how we know exactly what that is (preconceptions, principles, judgments, impressions). Of course, Epictetus is not a "pure" but a "practical epistemologist," at least in the sense that his question about the foundation of natural knowledge is not finally distinct from his determination to know how best to live. There can be no contradictions in our preconceptions not because of intellectual aesthetics but precisely because we cannot live more than one life at the same time. Nevertheless, much more so than Seneca, Epictetus tends to present "how to live" through the lens of "how we know how to live." So, too, Epictetus develops the necessary anthropological correlate to preserve human freedom in face of the inextricable unity between our passions and our judgments, but *prohairesis*—or its Latin approximation *voluntas*—is hardly the center of Seneca's philosophical counsel.

Still, theirs is obviously a common conversation, a practical philosophical tradition in full swing whose basic, normative moves can easily be adapted in different directions by its seasoned practitioners. Human beings are sick, they both think, because we have lost our harmony with nature. We become healthy by returning to nature and living according to its pattern. But this pattern, they hold, is not discernible simply by looking. We have to be taught how to look and what to see. Nature, as it turns out, is for both men quite specific, graspable in its particularities only through the practice of a certain shape of thought. Stoic philosophy, with its doctrines and disciplines, is thus the particular educational program that inducts its participants into the existential style that heals—a wise and happy life.

3

Marcus Aurelius

Do not behave as though you had ten thousand years to live.
Your doom hangs over you. While you live,
while it is permitted, become good.
—*Marcus Aurelius*, Meditations

"Soon," says Marcus Aurelius in his *Meditations*, "you will have forgotten everything. Soon, everybody will have forgotten you!" (7.21). As Pierre Hadot observes, however, "Marcus Aurelius was wrong. Eighteen centuries—almost two millennia—have passed, and the *Meditations* are still alive. Nor have their pages been reserved to a few aristocrats of the intellect, like Shaftesbury, Frederick II, or Goethe: on the contrary, for centuries they have brought reasons to live to innumerable unknown people, who have been able to read them in the multiple translations of the *Meditations* which have been made in every corner of the earth; and they still do so today."[1]

MEDITATIONS

Like several Roman emperors before him, Marcus Aurelius was not born in line for the imperial throne. He was instead adopted by his predecessor Antoninus Pius and became emperor in AD 161 upon Antoninus's death. Marcus immediately invited his adopted brother Lucius Verus to reign as his co-regent, which Verus did until his death in 169. From then until his own death on the Danubian front in 180, Marcus ruled as sole imperator.

It is no surprise that Marcus received a first-class education—studying rhetoric with the famed Fronto, for example—and paced rapidly through the *cursus honorum.* His exposure to philosophy came through a variety of tutors and professors, but it was his teacher Rusticus who made the greatest impression upon him and with whom Marcus maintained a long relationship. In fact, it was Rusticus who first lent Marcus a copy of Epictetus's sayings, texts that were in time to form the philosophical foundation of Marcus's life and thought. It is not clear, however, at exactly what point Marcus became a serious Stoic. The Emperor Hadrian, for example, took to calling him *verissimus*, "the most truthful one," in his late teens. This nickname stuck well enough to be known to the Christian Justin Martyr, who links it with Marcus's reputation as a young philosopher. Justin's *First Apology* addresses not only Emperor Antoninus but also Antoninus's son "Verissimus, the Philosopher" (1.1).[2] And Marcus himself credits one of his earliest teachers, Diognetus, for showing him at a young age the worth of the short cloak and hard bed—traditional outward markers of the philosophical life (*Meditations*, 1.6). Regardless of when the transition occurred, by the time Marcus ruled the empire, he had long been devoted to Stoicism and understood himself in light of the Epictetan stream of Stoic tradition.

Marcus's *Meditations* are the only real written work he left behind, and are in many respects notoriously difficult to interpret. Like the present form of Pascal's *Pensées* and much of Wittgenstein's work, Marcus's *Meditations* are loosely arranged jottings, prompts for memory, directions from Marcus to himself about a wide variety of both important and more mundane matters. In this way the *Meditations* are truly an insider's conversation—much that we would need to know to achieve specificity of understanding is forever hidden behind the wall that separates us from Marcus and the immediate context of his life. We do know that book I is a different kind of thing from books II through XII and that the *Meditations* come more or less from the last decade of Marcus's life. But specific chronological or geographical markers are few and far between. Indeed, by far the two most important markers—the mention of the River Gran in the land of the Quadi and the military base Carnuntum—are situated between books I and II and between II and III, respectively, thus making it impossible to know whether the notes are pre- or postscripta to the books, or even whether Marcus himself or an editor wrote them.[3] Marcus rarely writes more than a few sentences and hence supplies almost no larger hermeneutical help.[4]

It is tempting to assume that we are thus reduced to reading random sayings within our best guess at a helpful interpretive context. Such an assumption, however, only betrays our failure to see how the chapters on Seneca and (especially) Epictetus prepare the way for the present chapter on Marcus. For in fact the *Meditations* are not simply random reflections but are part of a particular tradition. As Pierre Hadot observes, "Marcus Aurelius' *Meditations* . . . are not the spontaneous outpourings of a soul that wants to express its thoughts immediately, but rather an exercise, accomplished in accordance with definite rules. . . . [The *Meditations*] presuppose a pre-existing canvas, upon which the philosopher-emperor could only embroider."[5] This does not mean, of course, that the *Meditations* exhibit a tight order that comes to light once one has read Epictetus. Indeed, book I bears no direct relationship to the rest of the work, and books II through XII do not systematically unfold complex themes or suggest an underlying narrative or existential trajectory such as we find in St. Augustine's *Confessions*, for example.[6] Yet as Hadot has persuasively argued, the *Meditations* as a whole have a kind of practical center of gravity that corresponds to Marcus's recurrent attention to three core Stoic disciplines: the disciplines of judgment, of desire, and of action.[7] By no means does this gravitational center pull every statement into its orbit.[8] But once posited, it does provide a plausible organizing structure by which to interpret Marcus's words.

Still, reading the *Meditations* in this way is hampered by the significant fact that their arrangement is not according to the three Stoic disciplines. Moreover, there are recurrent emphases that lend themselves more to thematic analysis than to structural display. In the end, however, we do not have to choose between persistent themes or the three Stoic disciplines: the themes disclose the primary arenas in which Marcus hopes to work on himself by means of the disciplines, and the vast amount of repetition is itself the actual manner by which the disciplines are practiced in these arenas.[9] Because I am most interested in displaying the shape of the Roman Stoic tradition vis-à-vis Seneca and Epictetus, we will focus upon six of the *Meditations*' repeated themes and note their relation to the disciplines Hadot identifies when helpfully illuminating them.[10] This procedure also allows us to treat Marcus more briefly than Seneca and Epictetus. Marcus is not so much an innovator as he is a disciple, a faithful repeater of what he learned from Rusticus and other teachers, from Epictetus, and from the Stoic tradition more generally. The *Meditations* themselves, therefore, are not a work of philosophical construction in a strict sense. They chart no fundamentally new territory, nor do they develop human thought in previously unknown directions.[11] They are instead the record of a faithful disciple in action.

DEATH

Like Seneca, Marcus regularly ponders death, both his own and the phenomenon more generally. Given his life, this focus is hardly surprising. Not only did Marcus accompany his army on campaign, he also doubtless knew that many emperors did not die peacefully in bed of old age. But Marcus's work upon himself was not merely to recognize open-eyed the dangers that surrounded him. More deeply, it was also an attempt to position himself existentially vis-à-vis his own particular mortality and to come to grips with what this end entails for the human being's best-lived life. Marcus's grammar of death reveals four regularly recurring patterns of speech.

First, Marcus often reflects on the universal reach of death's power. Being emperor elevates him not one step higher than a slave on death's ladder (9.1). Indeed, he reminds himself, death laid low not only "Alexander the Great but also his muleteer" (6.24). Time, says Marcus, reflecting on the deathward movement of life, is a rushing river that bears away everything that comes into being (4.43): "How many a Chrysippus, how many a Socrates, how many an Epictetus" has already been swept away (7.19). Nor does death miss those whose divinity is assured and proclaimed far and wide: the Divine Augustus and all his court are gone; Vespasian, Trajan, and their families, all dead (8.31, 4.32). "Think it over," Marcus tells himself; "someone, after all, must be the last of the line" (8.31). Even those who fight to master death eventually succumb: the physicians who care for their patients, the astrologers who predict the demise of others, the philosophers who discourse upon our end, the warriors who kill countless numbers, the tyrants who abuse their power over human life—all these, Marcus meditates, come to the same final spot, the grave (4.48, 9.33).

Second, death in Marcus's grammar is part of the way things most truly and deeply are, that is, *kata physin* (according to nature). Like Epictetus, Marcus repeats *kata physin* again and again, reminding himself of the reason he need not fear his end. "Not even death can bring terror on him who regards as good that which comes in its own good time" (12.35). Death, like winter or summer, is a regular part of the way the world goes: it would be as unreasonable to fear snow in a steamy Roman July as it would be to fear our mortality. "Dissolution is but one of the processes of nature, such as to be young and to grow old . . . to grow teeth and beard and gray hairs"; a reasonable man, therefore, "should await death as one of the works of nature" (9.3). It is true that Marcus admits that death itself is an inscrutable mystery of nature—he says this also of birth—but such an admission does nothing to lessen death's naturalness. No matter how mysterious, death appears clearly to well-trained reason as a work of nature; "and if one is afraid of a work of nature, why that's childish!" (2.12). Even now, "look for the hour when the soul shall emerge from its sheath just as you await the moment when the child your wife carries shall come forth from the womb" (9.3). Of course, looking forward to death as the birth of the soul depends upon at least some notion of what death is. One could hardly look forward to death were the prospects thereafter to include, for example, going to a low level of purgatory or to hell (to think of the Christian Middle Ages). For Marcus, disciplining his fear of death by focusing on its naturalness is inseparably bound with his view of what death entails.

Third, then, Marcus often reflects on the outcomes of death. He does not offer a systematic account to himself—canvassing all the various options and weighing the strengths and weaknesses of each—but instead focuses primarily upon three central possibilities. In 7.32 Marcus straightforwardly names the three: "Concerning death: if we're atoms, then we're scattered; and if we're a whole, then it's either extinction or translation." Elsewhere he says much the same thing; in 11.3, for example, he talks of a soul that, when released from the body, is released "to be extinguished, to be scattered, or *symmeinai*"—a word that is best rendered "to be left intact" (cf. 8.25). Yet, as with "translation" (*metastasis*), by "left intact" Marcus does not envision the soul's personal postmortem existence in the sense that he Marcus-Aurelius-with-all-the-particularities-that-make-the-thing-that-Marcus-Aurelius-is will continue on in this exact arrangement. Even in his most confident moments about the possibility of some sort of continuing life (*bios*), it is clear that he does not view this "translation" as something that involves the ongoing existence of personal identity: "The one who fears death is afraid of either nonsensation or another sensation. But you will either have no sensation—and therefore no ability to sense evil—or you will acquire a different kind of sensation because you will be another living thing and life will not cease" (8.58; see 3.3, 5.33).

But what, we might wonder, could the Stoic emperor mean by "another living thing"? Is this some version of reincarnation? Since Marcus will not continue on as Marcus, will he come back as another person, or an inanimate object, or—surely not—some chicken or goat?

No, Marcus would reply, continuity in life as I would consider it depends upon our Stoic cosmology, in which that which exists is recycled through periods of dissolution and reconstitution—all of which are directed, of course, by the Reason that directs the cosmos. To continue on or to be translated, therefore, means that if the soul outlives the body in some way, the soul, too, will nevertheless be dissolved and reabsorbed into the "seminal reason of the whole" (4.21; cf. 6.24).[12] "We will," in short, "vanish into that from which we came" (4.14). If, Marcus could continue, we were thus to speak of a pre- and post-mortem continuity, we could do so only through the participation of the stuff that made "our" reason in the broader redistribution of reason throughout the eternal cosmic cycle. Of course, this strains the meaning of *continuity* to the breaking point if not past it. But as I say, it may be much more reasonable simply to assume that death brings scattering or extinction.

Marcus's refusal to decide between the options reflects his honest agnosticism about the specifics of postmortem human reality. More deeply, however, as he senses again and again, they ultimately amount to much the same thing: there will be no more "Marcus" after Marcus dies, for everything that dies is finally "dissolved into the elemental constituents of the cosmos" (8.18). As a result, Marcus's recurrent meditations on one or the other of the three postmortem outcomes produce in him the same basic existential-philosophical consequence: the need to focus on the present.

Finally, then, as he reflects upon death, Marcus consistently admonishes himself to concentrate upon living in the moment. "Isolate the present," Marcus says, for "this is the mark of a perfected habit of life (*ēthos*): to pass through each day as if it were the last" (7.29 and 7.69, respectively; cf. 2.5, 7.56). We know not whether we will be here tomorrow or the next day and must therefore let "every deed and thought be as a man who can depart from life at any moment" (2.11; cf. 3.1). Marcus's meditation on living each day in view of death serves to direct himself toward a constant pursuit of the philosophical life: "A moment and you will be dead, and not yet are you honest, undisturbed, free from the fear of harm from externals, gracious to all, or convinced that just action is the only wisdom" (4.37; cf. 4.26).

Such constancy is geared toward an explicit posture of readiness vis-à-vis death itself. One cannot say of a man whose mind is philosophically disciplined, Marcus muses, that "his life is cut short, when the day of destiny overtakes him, as we might say of a tragedian's part, who leaves the stage before finishing his speech and playing out his piece" (3.8). Were someone to complain that he had been given the chance to play only three of the full five acts, Marcus would respond: "Really, in life three acts can be the whole drama" (12.36).

Death, for Marcus Aurelius, is thus to be judged as natural and something for which he can prepare—even desire—by articulating to himself the way in which this natural good leads to right action in the present. It is true, of course, that Marcus's basic judgment about the naturalness of death derives partly from the observable fact of its universal reach. But more significant, his judgment about death is also inseparably intertwined with his understanding of nature itself. We turn, therefore, to Marcus's language about nature, which is to say about God.

GOD AND NATURE

Though Epictetus was his philosophic master, Marcus's *Meditations* lack the deeply pious tone of Epictetus's *Discourses* and *Enchiridion*. It is true that Marcus was initiated into the Eleusinian mysteries with his son Commodus, and it is equally true that Marcus can at times speak of the gods with reverence, as he does in 12.28: "To those who ask the question, 'Where have you seen the gods, or how have you apprehended that they exist, that you worship them so?' [I would reply]: First, they are visible to the eyes; second, I have not seen my own soul, and yet I honor it; so it is with the gods: from my experiences each moment of their power . . . I know that they exist, and I reverence them" (cf. 6.23, 7.70, 9.40). Yet such speech is hardly a part of the dominating pattern of Marcus's God-talk.

Marcus returns much more frequently to the basic Stoic dogma that "there is one cosmos made up of all things, and one God through all things, and one substance, and one law, and one reason common to all intelligent living beings" (7.9).[13] But pantheism, for Marcus, is not self-evident. It is, rather, something that he has to discipline himself to see: "Meditate often upon the interconnection of all things in the world and upon their relation to one another. For all things are in a way intertwined with one another and, because of this, all things have a certain friendship with one another" (6.38; cf. 2.9, 9.1). Profound, observable difference among the vast variety of the world, Marcus tells himself, does not erase the basic unity of the whole (7.23).

Yet such a unity is not static. "All substance," says Marcus, echoing Heraclitus from long before, "is a river of ceaseless flow" (5.23). The interconnection of the whole, for Marcus, is thus tied to the world's constant motion. Nature enjoys nothing more than to renew itself through dissolution and reconstitution: "Contemplate continually all things that happen because of change, and train your mind to think that Nature loves nothing so much as to change the things that are and to create new things in their likeness. For in a certain way everything that exists is the seed of that which will come out of it" (4.36; cf. 5.13, 9.35, 10.7). Around and around and around it goes, says Marcus, for all time, never ceasing, world without end.[14]

While it is true that Marcus does not have any kind of robust teleological sense, such flux and cyclicality should not be construed as a kind of mindless jumble. The directedness of the eternal flux is quite real for him. It is not, however, something that is easy for him to hold, as his constant posing of a central alternative attests: "Remember . . . either Providence or atoms!" (4.3.2; 8.17; 9.28 et passim). Or again: "It's either a medley—a mutual intertwining of atoms and their scattering—or oneness, and order, and Providence. If the former, why would I desire to waste my time and remain in such a random aggregation and confused mass of chaos? . . . Whatever I do, the scattering of atoms will come upon me. But if the latter, I bow in reverence, I become calm, and I take courage in the ordering principle" (6.10; cf. 4.27; 9.39; 10.6

et passim).[15] Epicureanism, at least of the type we know from Lucretius, is thus a serious alternative for Marcus, but it is finally rejected.

Here, as elsewhere, Marcus denies Fortune an independent base of operation and instead disciplines himself to see its working within the context of a broader affirmation about the reasonableness of Providence. These, then, are the Stoic doctrines I should think on, says Marcus: "The works of the gods are full of Providence: the works of Fortune are not divorced from Nature or from the interweaving and binding of the threads by the guiding hand of Providence. From such guidance come all things" (2.3; cf. 2.11; 6.5; 7.23, 75).[16] The world is shot through, if not with the grandeur of God, at least with the divine reason (*logos*) that moves the cosmos and all its workings (9.1; cf. 6.1; 9.29). Admittedly, says Marcus, this is not always immediately apparent. "The lion's wrinkled brow, the foam from the boar's mouth," and countless other matters are hardly beautiful "when taken in isolation." But for those who train themselves to see more deeply into "the workings of the whole," even the more grotesque items take their place nicely within the wider cosmos (3.2). "Everything that happens," Marcus says in the face of Fortune, "happens justly" (4.10)—that is, according to the direction of reason.

Marcus's language about the divine *logos* extends also to his speech about human beings, thus making them divine in at least one crucial respect. To speak of God in Marcus's grammar is also to speak of human reason. "'Live with the gods,' they say. But he is living with the gods who continuously show his soul to them as satisfied with its lot and doing whatever the *daimōn*—the portion of himself that Zeus has given to each man to guard and guide him—wills. And this *daimōn* is each person's mind and reason" (*nous* and *logos*, 5.27). Primarily because of its range of meaning, *daimōn* is always a difficult word in Greek. Yet here Marcus's thought is clear: it is God in the human being. So, too, in 3.5–7, where Marcus warns himself against the dangers of rhetorical frills and superfluous deeds and admonishes himself to attend to the god within. "Let the god within you be the guardian of a real man, a man ripe in years, a statesman, a Roman, a ruler, who has taken his post like one waiting for the retreat to sound, ready to depart. . . . Nothing better is known than the *daimōn* that is within you. . . . A man who puts first his own mind and *daimōn*—and the practices that cultivate its excellence—avoids melodrama, utters no groans, and needs neither the refuge of absolute solitude nor the crowded streets" (3.5–7; cf. 5.27, 34; 7.53; 9.39; 10.6; 12.2, 26).[17]

For Marcus, then, the word *God* refers both to nature/the cosmos and to the reason that directs it. This reason is also present within human beings and constitutes their divinity—the mind of each is, as Marcus says, "God" (12.26).

What is most deeply natural for the human being, therefore, is to know its own divinity and live in accordance therewith—that is, *kata physin*. In the musing of the *Meditations*, anthropology thus turns out simply to be the other side of the coin of divinity. Or, as Marcus puts it to himself, "The man who does not know what the cosmos is does not know what he is. And the one who does not know the purpose of the cosmos does not know who he is or what the cosmos is" (8.52). We thus turn to two features of Marcus's anthropology—right judgments and the commitments that make right judgments a possibility in the first place.

HUMAN BEINGS AND RIGHT JUDGMENTS

Like Epictetus before him, Marcus regularly emphasizes the dependence of the philosophical life upon right judgment. We travel through life beset by a wildly diverse panoply of impressions (*phantasiai*), the emperor learned from the former slave, and must rightly sort them in order to achieve happiness. Wrong sorting of impressions paves the road to existential instability and, ultimately, to misery. Sorting impressions, therefore, is a work of great importance; it is the work of judgment.

For Marcus, as for Epictetus, the most basic distinction needed for the right sorting of impressions is between things that lie within our control and things that do not (externals). Marcus learned well from his reading of the *Discourses* that externals "cannot touch the soul" and that "disturbance" arises only from within, as a result of our mistaken opinions (*hypolēpseis*) about impressions (4.4). Proper therapy for his troubling disturbance entails the correction of wrong opinions about impressions, and the ability to make this correction lies entirely within his control: "It is in your power to rid yourself of many unnecessary troubles, for they exist entirely in your opinions" (9.32; cf. 9.15 or 12.26, "everything is opinion").

But surely not, Marcus might catch himself thinking, after leaving his tent to look at one of his wounded soldiers. This man's thigh has a nasty gash in it, and the resultant pain is not because of his misjudgment but because—quite simply—things like that hurt. Yet as he would quickly recognize, this is a false objection. Marcus does not mean that the body is immune from pain; to the contrary, his affirmation is only that such pain need not disturb us inwardly. The reason? It does not of necessity reach the soul or mind: "Harm can come to you," he reminds himself, "only from your own power, your own judgment over what is bad" (4.39). It is true, he says, that we should give attention to the body because the mind (*dianoia*) can show itself in the face (7.60). But nowhere does he press for a basic unity of body/mind/soul; indeed, Marcus's advice to himself is coherent only on the supposition of a division between them. "Even if your body be cut, burned, ooze pus, or rot from gangrene, let the part that makes judgments about these things rest at peace" (4.39). "Rid yourself of the opinion 'I am harmed' and the harm itself disappears" (4.7; cf. 8.40). Even with physical pain, Marcus reassures himself, we have the power to restrict its reach to the body and to remain at peace.

Yet as he knows well, there are other types of suffering that seem to emerge from within. There may well be an initial external stimulus, of course—news from a herald, something one sees—but the pain itself seems to arise in the soul/mind rather than the body. In an example taken from his own potentially devastating loss, if also directly from the pages of Epictetus, Marcus reminds himself that even though a "little child" is diseased and may die, it is not in danger. Death, Marcus has taught himself again and again, is both natural and entirely out of our control. The *phantasia* "diseased child" can thus be judged "out of my control" and sorted in such a way as to render the opinion "not in danger" (8.49; cf. 9.40).[18]

But how, we might well wonder as we encounter impression after impression, do we actually do the work of sorting? We have learned *that* we must sort, but we want to know *how*. What enables us to get from "diseased child" to "not in danger"? Marcus's answer is, once again, materially the same as Epictetus's: *dogmata*. By *dogmata* Marcus means judgments-formed-by-Stoic-principles, or, in brief, the way in which the Stoic tradition sorts the world. "Nothing so enables greatness of mind as the ability to examine systematically and truthfully everything that meets us in life" and to situate things vis-à-vis their place in the cosmos and their relation to humanity (3.11). In each case ask, "What is this now that is giving me this impression, what is its composition, and what is its duration?" (3.11). Hold an impression at bay, Marcus thinks, and scrutinize it according to principle-formed judgment. Where it suggests the possibility of false opinion—for example, that licentious behavior is desirable or even according to nature (5.36)—principle-formed judgment intervenes. Reminding himself that "happiness is a good *daimōn* or goodness itself," Marcus addresses a potentially countervailing impression, "What, then, are you doing here, O *Phantasia*?! By the gods, depart as you came. I have no need of you" (7.17; cf. 7.29).[19]

Yet the daily life of a Roman emperor was hardly unhurried and relaxed; even on his less than very busiest days Marcus might easily doubt that we have time to subject every impression to the kind of scrutiny he would like. What about those things that come upon us quickly, out of the blue, too fast for leisurely examination, in the middle of work or war? "Just as the doctors have their instruments and scalpels always at hand for cases that require emergency therapy," Marcus writes, "so you have your prepared *dogmata*" (3.13).[20] Totally surprising and unbidden *phantasiai* can be treated—that is, rightly sorted—and undesirable opinions avoided. As his analogy with the tools needed for trauma surgery suggests, however, it is too late to begin looking for the correct Stoically formed judgments once the impression strikes. We need the *dogmata*, in a favorite phrase of his, "right at hand."

Marcus disciplines himself vis-à-vis his impressions through a process of shaping his judgments by repeated meditation upon Stoically derived ways of seeing the world. In so doing, he creates a kind of Stoic filter, or grinds a Stoic lens, so that as he moves through the world *phantasiai* are rightly sorted and his life thus well and happily lived. The repetition is, of course, integral to the effectiveness of the discipline: the more he meditates, the more the *dogmata* lie close at hand; the closer the *dogmata*, the more automatic the sorting; the more automatic the sorting, the happier the man.

HUMAN BEINGS AND THE POSSIBILITY OF RIGHT JUDGMENTS

If we were to ask Marcus how exactly "Nature has given us authority over impressions," he would respond with one word: the *hēgemonikon* (governing-faculty within us).[21] The *hēgemonikon*, for Marcus, is both reason's sovereign potential and the locus of its active direction. Of the three constitutive parts of humanness—the flesh, the spirit, and the *hēgemonikon*—it is the latter that provides the possibility of living according to reason; flesh and blood are to be disdained, spirit is only "wind" or "air," but the unfettered *hēgemonikon* brings a reason-directed life (2.2).[22] "Externals must stand outside the door by themselves," Marcus notes, "until the *hēgemonikon* tells us about them" (9.15). Neither "fire nor steel nor despot nor abuse" can threaten the innermost part of us (8.41), for "the *hēgemonikon* becomes invincible when it withdraws into itself and is content with itself, doing nothing that it does not will" (8.48). It is then the "inner citadel" from which the life of reason is pursued; "a more impregnable fortress a man does not have" (8.48; cf., e.g., 4.3.1; 7.28 et passim). By returning again and again to the utter impenetrability of the anthropological space, as it were, named the *hēgemonikon*, Marcus thus reminds himself that wrong opinions about impressions do not have to be: they are avoidable, and thus also is the consequent damaged existence. We need not admit any "opinion that is discordant with Nature and the constructive reasoning of the rational being" (3.9).[23] "Reason," says Marcus, "and the reasoning faculty are sufficient in themselves and for their own works" (5.14).[24]

It does occur to Marcus, however, to wonder about the fact that we seem to be in conflict with ourselves. If the *hēgemonikon* is an unassailable acropolis, why do we have so much difficulty sorting impressions? Why can't we simply exercise our reason securely from within our fortress and live *kata physin*?[25] Reflecting on the fact that the primal cosmological elements that help constitute his bodily existence—spirit and fire—"obey" earthly restraints despite their "natural tendency to ascend," Marcus asks, "Is it not dreadful that only the thinking part of you should be disobedient and irritated about its proper place?" It is true, he continues, "that nothing is forcefully imposed upon it—only that which is in accordance with its own nature. Yet this it does not accept, but instead is led in a contrary direction. For the movement toward injustice and licentiousness, wrath, sorrow, and fear is nothing other than a severance from Nature." And further, says Marcus, when the *hēgemonikon* becomes "discontent, this, too, is a desertion of its proper place" (11.20).

To questions about the cause of such a "dreadful" reality, Marcus offers no direct answers. But throughout the *Meditations* he assumes that the problem is due to our ignorance rather than to a fundamentally broken *hēgemonikon*. "Wrongdoing," says Marcus to himself, "is involuntary" (4.3.2). Lest we think that Marcus is simply excusing himself, he would be quick to point out that his view of the problem of ignorance applies as much to others as it does to himself: "Whenever someone does something wrong to you, think immediately what opinion of good or evil he had that has caused him to do wrong. For once you see what this opinion is, you will have mercy on him and be neither astonished nor furious" (7.26). The offender, that is, commits his wrong because he is confused and knows not the right way to sort his impressions: he is ignorant of what is up to us and what is not, forms a wrong opinion, and therefore acts in a damaging way. "How is it bad or strange that the untutored act in untutored ways?" (9.42.3).

But thanks be to the gods, the wrongdoer can be taught! The correlative of Marcus's view of ignorance as the root of the self's conflict with its own best interests is that error is in principle corrigible by teaching. By locating the problem outside of the *hēgemonikon* rather than within it, Marcus names a lack that teaching can fill. Where there is ignorance, let there be teaching. Of course there will always be the slothful, the rogues, and others who simply will not listen, but their refusal to be taught speaks not against my view, Marcus would say, but for it: they remain ignorant and thus act accordingly. "As a whole," he reminds himself, "it is possible to teach the errant a better way" (9.42.2, *metadidaskalein*).

Of course, as Marcus's use of the word *metadidaskalein* shows, "teaching" is much broader than "do or don't do this specific thing." More comprehensively, *metadidaskalein* points to the need to adopt a new frame of reference, or mode of understanding the world, or—most basically—a new pattern of life. At its deeper levels, therefore, corrigibility for Marcus is conceived in a very particular way: the Stoic philosophical tradition. "Teach them a better way of life" means "show them how to be a Stoic."[26] That such a possibility even exists—that a man is not in principle stuck in his ignorance—is itself thus dependent upon Stoic philosophy. It is a hardly a surprise to see that Marcus's anthropology both emerges from and returns to Stoic philosophy. He is, after all, striving to live the Stoic life, which is to say, to discipline himself in the way of philosophy.

PHILOSOPHY

In contrast to both Seneca and Epictetus, Marcus does not often speak directly of philosophy. Given the genre of the *Meditations*, however, this is unsurprising. The pope probably rarely if ever reminds himself to think and live like a Roman Catholic. Yet his intense engagement in the actual thinking and living as a Roman Catholic would be constant. Thus it is also with Marcus, the Stoic. The entirety of the *Meditations*, as Hadot has shown, is the work of philosophy itself.

Where Marcus does speak of philosophy, his language is clear and predictable. Philosophy is therapy, salve, ointment for the struggles of human life. "There comes a time in a man's life when his existence is in flux, his insight clouded, his body's entire composition decaying, his soul a cyclone, his fortune unpredictable, his fame uncertain. In short: all the things of the body are a river, and all the things of the soul are as a dream and a mist, and life is a war and a journey in a strange land, with a posthumous fame only of oblivion. What, then, can be his escort through life? One thing and one thing only: Philosophy" (2.17).[27]

Marcus continues with a brief digest of what he takes this one and only thing to be. Philosophy, for Marcus as for the other Stoics, is not intellection alone but is instead "to keep the Reason within you unwronged and unharmed, master of pain and pleasure, doing nothing without purpose, nothing through falsehood or with hypocrisy . . . and, above all, to await death with the merciful knowledge that it is nothing other than a release of the elements of which every living thing has been composed . . . for this is *kata physin*, and nothing bad can be *kata physin*."[28]

Philosophy is therefore for Marcus a style of life, a disciplined way of living according to nature by the light of reason—toward *eudaimonia* and away from chaos (cf. 7.17). How many times, Marcus reminds himself, "have I strayed from philosophy and nowhere found the good life—not in logical arguments, not in wealth, not in glory, not in self-indulgence, nowhere! Where, then, is the good life to be found? In doing what Nature demands of human beings" (8.1; cf. 9.29; 10.2 et passim).

But how, most basically, do we achieve the kind of happy life that comes from the practice of philosophy? Marcus's answer is simple: turn inward. "Go into yourself" (7.28). "Look within" (6.3). When the world's chaos rages, Marcus says over and over again, "go immediately into yourself" (6.11). People seek "retreats for themselves—the country, the seashore, the mountains—and you, too," Marcus says to himself, "are rather prone to experience this yearning." "But all this," he continues, "is most unphilosophic given the fact that you can retreat into yourself at any hour you wish. For nowhere can a person retreat into more tranquility or solitude than in his own soul, especially the one who has the sort of inner habits of thought that immediately bring comfort. And by 'comfort,' I mean a well-ordered life. Continually, therefore, grant yourself this retreat and renew yourself" (4.3).[29]

Marcus's convictions about the impregnability of the inner citadel are thus correlated not only with the possibility of making right judgments but also with a particular method of philosophizing. Look not, Marcus says, to the things that lie beyond the bodily border but instead go deep within.[30]

Yet, and once again like his inscripted mentor Epictetus, Marcus Aurelius does not follow Platonic accounts of anamnesis or foreshadow the Cartesians. Turning inward, for Marcus, does not mean that we recall or discover innate truths waiting for us inside. The turn inward is a specifically Stoic kind of turn, one that corresponds to the Stoic ordering of practical reason. Reason, for Marcus, is not some pure "thing" waiting to be found within himself as much as it is the active operation of the inward strength of the *hēgemonikon* in an existential pattern of repair and renewal—the *technē*, or craft, of the self in the Stoic life.[31] "What is the 'self'?" Marcus asks himself. "Reason," he answers, and then objects, "But I am not Reason." Quickly, however, he comes to the point: *estō*—"Let it become so" (8.40).[32] Marcus's *estō* gestures to the profound sense in which the dichotomy between intellection and practice is overcome in the discipline of Stoic existence: for Marcus as for Epictetus and Seneca, Reason itself is a becoming, an ongoing practice of Stoically disciplined thought in the shape of a Stoic philosophical life. Inwardness, therefore, turns out to be Marcus's specific way of speaking about philosophy in the ancient sense: a way of being in the world.[33]

Still, someone might object, in a very mundane or practical sense doesn't this whole inward move detach us from our compatriots and therefore lead to social chaos? What kind of a life is that for a Roman emperor? Marcus's clear answer to these questions is that turning inward in the Stoic sense neither severs my connection with other human beings nor relieves me from my deep and extensive civic responsibilities. Indeed, precisely because the inward turn is a Stoic turn, it will always entail corresponding Stoic convictions about *physis* (nature). "My nature," after all, is simultaneously "rational and political" (6.44, *logikē kai politikē*).

SOCIETY

The *Meditations*' numerous statements about civic responsibility are no surprise. In contrast to the Epicureans, for example, the Stoic tradition emphasized the compatibility of philosophy with civic life; indeed, many went a good deal farther than this and stressed the necessity of civic engagement as part and parcel of what it meant to be a Stoic. Marcus himself, moreover, was a man of serious intelligence. As emperor, he could hardly help but reflect on the connections between his philosophical pursuit and his rule. It is true that the *Meditations* do not evidence how Marcus used his philosophical understanding to make particular "policy decisions," but they do display his repeated effort to discipline his thinking vis-à-vis other human beings. For Marcus, the Stoic devotee of the Logos, there could be no higher summons to society than to know that "the rational is at once the political" (10.2).

This integration of "rational" and "political" shapes Marcus's language about society in two primary ways. First, he consistently trains himself to think of our rational nature as the basis for a common humanity. "If our intellectual capacity is common to us all," he says, "then so, too, is the Reason by virtue of which we are all rational creatures. If this is so, then the reason that tells us what to do or not do is also common. If this is so, then there is a common law. If this is so, we are all citizens. If this is so, we are all members in a commonwealth. If this is so, the world is like a city" (4.4). By virtue of our common reason, Marcus's logic implies, all humans are bound together in a network of interwoven commitments and obligations—the "world-city" (10.15; cf. 10.33.4 et passim).

Second, therefore, Marcus continually reminds himself that our rationality is exercised in community, that our common humanity is no less than a common rational project. "The good of a rational creature," says Marcus, "is community" (5.16, *koinōnia*).[34] Our purpose or end (*telos*), he thinks, is to live rationally according to the polity of the cosmos (2.16). For this reason, we are, quite simply, "made for one another" (8.59). Rational polity entails other people.

Surely, a trusted counselor might say, this is rather naïve, Marcus. You mean to tell me that I'm made for that poor wretch over there? Marcus's initial reply, of course, would be utterly unsentimental. While it is true that we rational creatures are made for one another, in practice this often means that those of us who live *kata physin* must either "teach or bear with" our fellow humans (8.59, *ē didaske ē phere*). But Marcus's *Meditations* also cut much deeper: the common rationality that constitutes our common humanity entails a particular kind of moral claim. "Treat unreasoning creatures and lifeless things and objects generally with magnanimity and freedom," Marcus admonishes himself, "for they do not have reason as you do. But precisely because human beings do have reason, treat them as neighbors" (6.23, *koinōnikōs*). That is, reason itself prohibits the confusion between the human and nonhuman world and, Marcus implies, requires us not to treat each other like beasts.

Of course Marcus never works this out in connection to the Christians, for example, or to the objects of conquest along the battle fronts where some of his *Meditations* were probably composed,[35] but he does insist that our common reason necessitates the practice of justice. Indeed, injustice toward our fellows is an impious offense against Nature herself: "Injustice is impiety. For inasmuch as the Nature of the whole cosmos has fashioned rational creatures for the sake of one another, to benefit one another on account of their worth—but not to injure each other—the one who transgresses her will acts with obvious impiety toward the most esteemed of the gods" (9.1; cf. 4.33).[36] For Marcus, in short, to harm others is to contradict Nature and thus to contravene the truest meaning of *human being* in its Stoic sense: it is "human nature to care for all humans" (3.4).[37]

As any reader of the *Meditations* would admit, however, Marcus's language about the moral claims of common reason should not be loaded with more than it can bear. Still, as is true of both Seneca and Epictetus, Marcus's commitment to philosophical life does not remove him from politics. His politics will rather naturally, of course, be a Stoic politics—which is to say that he will ultimately be indifferent to all that happens outside of the control of his inward fortress (9.1.4)—but the discipline of his *Meditations* nevertheless trains him to see reason as inescapably political: "Will only one thing," says Marcus, "to act or not to act, as political reason requires" (9.12, *ho politikos logos*).

Like the raison d'être for the philosophical labor of both Seneca and Epictetus, Marcus's *Meditations* are an attempt to slake a certain kind of existential thirst—the thirst to be in the world in a pattern of happiness and healing, to deal with the damage brought to our door by our own action and by the far less scrutable workings of the wider world. And like both Seneca and Epictetus, Marcus knows that to slake this thirst is to be disciplined by a particular pattern of a thinking life. Twenty years from the turn of the second century, the Stoic tradition is alive and well.

Marcus shows no real interest in general prescriptions for our predicament, nor does he even display much individuality.[38] Instead, the *Meditations* evidence Marcus's repeated effort to conform his thinking life to the pattern that he is attempting to learn. Have these Stoic principles "at hand," the reader of the *Meditations* hears Marcus say to himself again and again. Remember them, learn them, live them. Indeed, the whole of the *Meditations* shows Marcus's commitment to the particulars of Stoic disciplinary training.

Marcus is no simpleton, however, and knows that all will not easily be well, at least not all of the time. He knows that the human tendency toward failure is but the presupposition of the need for serious and prolonged training—the kind that finds him meditating in the midst of war—in how to discern the truth *kata physin*. The Stoic philosophical life is the pattern by which we learn how to continue on in the face of moral breakdown and simple, ordinary recalcitrance. In a testimony to his sense of philosophy's power to heal the wounds inflicted by human failure, he admonishes himself, "Don't be disgusted, don't give up, don't be impatient if you don't always succeed in acting from right judgments-formed-by-Stoic-principles (*dogmata*). But after you fail, return again, and rejoice if most of your conduct is worthy of humanity. Love that to which you return. And don't return to philosophy as if to a schoolmaster but as a man with sore eyes to the sponge and salve, or another to his poultice and lotion. In this way you will show that obedience to reason is not a burden but instead brings rest and relief. . . . What could be sweeter than wisdom itself?" (*Med.* 5.9).

Throughout the *Meditations* Marcus never gives the slightest indication that there is any other way to be successfully in the world. Sorting impressions, memorizing the principles that allow us to form right opinions, moving inward to the inner fortress, accepting the naturalness of death, grasping the nature and interconnections of the cosmos and one's place within it, exercising reason's politics—for Marcus Aurelius, this is the only chance to taste the sweetness of wisdom. "A man has but one life," he tells himself, "and yours is nearly over" (2.6).

Part Two

4

St. Paul

For me, to live is Christ and to die is gain.
—*St. Paul,* Letter to the Philippians

As influential as the Stoics treated in this book have been, even their cumulative weight is virtually insignificant compared with St. Paul's. Already within the New Testament itself, Paul is acknowledged as a foundation upon which the Christian tradition has begun to rest, and he has been both hero and foe in turns to almost everyone concerned with the rise of Christianity and its enduring impact. This is not to say he was always well and clearly understood. Indeed, the author of the little New Testament letter 2 Peter admits as much. In Paul's letters, he says, there are some things "that are hard to understand, which the unlearned and unstable distort" (2 Pet 3:16). But it is to say that Paul's legacy has been enormous. Down through the centuries from his time to ours no less than theology, philosophy, politics, law, literature, architecture, and visual and material art—in short, the whole field of human life we call a culture—experienced the gravitas of Paul.

LETTERS

As the records have it, Saul of Tarsus never intended to become a devotee of Jesus of Nazareth or to join the community that eventually took his name. Indeed, by Saul's own admission he persecuted the fledging Christians with considerable zeal. Yet sometime in the mid-30s on the way to the city of Damascus something dramatic happened that changed the course of Saul's life. As he and his sometime travel companion Luke both tell it, the once-dead Jesus of Nazareth appeared to Saul. The encounter was of such magnitude—it left

Saul blind for a time—that Saul ceased persecuting Jesus' followers and instead joined their mission. Over time Saul became "the Apostle to the Gentiles" and traveled to and fro around much of the Mediterranean basin preaching and establishing churches. Saul's ministry was not without controversy, and he suffered for it regularly. He was eventually martyred in Rome toward the end of Nero's reign—beheaded, as tradition has it. History has remembered him by his Roman name, Paul; the Christian church by the claims made for the texture of his life: *Saint* Paul.

Paul not only founded Christian communities, he also counseled them both in person and from a distance. To do the latter he sent letters, which in antiquity were read aloud and counted more as personal presence than as a written word. Of the letters Paul wrote, many have survived. Not all that bear his name are his own—his letters spawned a whole tradition of writing in his name—and of the thirteen that are currently found in the New Testament, only seven are considered by modern scholars to be Paul's beyond doubt.[1] The strength of the modern arguments for and against Pauline authorship varies widely, but no reasonable soul would object to a reading of Paul that depended primarily upon his letters to the Romans, Corinthians, Galatians, and Philippians, as well as upon the first letter to the Thessalonians and the short note to the early Christian man named Philemon.

Though Paul has been called the first Christian theologian, and though his letters have often served as a rich source for much Christian systematic reflection, the letters themselves are not systematic treatises. They do display tight arguments, thematic development, and theological profundity. Yet they make no attempt to grasp things in their entirety and to relate points on the dogmatic compass one to another for the sake of internal self-consistency. Instead, as readers of Paul from John Locke until today have tirelessly emphasized, the Pauline letters are ancient mail. They were written to particular communities with particular problems in mind—or a message that needed to be heard—and were delivered by a carrier as a "word on target."[2]

Despite the fact that they deal with a broad range of local issues, the church quickly realized that Paul's letters could be read with considerable profit well beyond their initially intended destination.[3] Such a realization reflects not only Paul's growing authority but also the (implicit) judgment that Pauline particularity opens out upon a more universal Christian experience. His words to the struggling Corinthians, the early Christians learned, spoke wisdom to all the faithful. Modern scholars have noticed this, too, though they have put it in different terms. Paul's letters, they say, reveal a "coherent gospel" or a consistent "narrative substructure."[4] The assumption of both the ancients and the moderns is that Paul's letters can be read together on a variety of topics and can be seen—when read in this way—to disclose substantively similar judgments about God, Christ, humanity, world, and so forth.

In what follows we will attend both to the particularities of the initial recipients of Paul's letters—where such matters can be known—and to the common themes that emerge from a reading of his epistolary corpus. As befits the larger project of this book, the importance of the Pauline particularities will emerge inside of the focus on specific themes. We begin with God.[5]

GOD

In what Philipp Melanchthon once called Paul's "compendium of doctrine," the Letter to the Romans, the most common noun is *theos*, God. This is no surprise. Romans is not only Paul's most theologically elaborate missive, it is also where he says what Christianity is most basically about.[6] And that, for Paul, is God.

God, however, is not a general term in Paul's grammar, a word that points to whomever or whatever anyone thinks is the Highest Power.[7] Nor is God simply a bucket into which to pour general metaphysical claims, though of course Paul knows how to make them (for example, Rom 1:20). The term *God* is quite specific and bound to a particular history. God is the God who elected Israel to be his people (Rom 11:2), and "the one who raised Jesus from the dead" (Rom 8:11), or as Paul also says, "the God of the Jews" and of "Gentiles, too" (Rom 3:29). Both in and beyond Romans, Paul's language about God is multifaceted and complex, but there are several features that recur again and again across his letters and bring this larger picture into focus.

Were someone to ask Paul, "Who exactly is this God you speak of?" Paul would begin to tell a story. Paul was a pastorally nimble soul, and where he would begin the story would probably depend upon who asked.[8] No matter where Paul actually began, however, he would soon get around to speaking about Israel, or the Jews. For Paul, God is he who has done what Israel's history recounts. Abraham, Isaac, Jacob, and all of their progeny—collectively known simply as "the people of Israel"—are the names and history that specify what "God" means.[9] Most central among the relatively early events of the history of Abraham's seed were the Exodus from Egypt, the giving of the Torah (Jewish Law), and the self-revelation of God's proper name, YHWH.

The Tetragrammaton, as the name later came to be called, was the Bible's way of articulating the significance of God for the categorical difference between "the religion of the Hebrew people" and "revelation." The former, a modern Paul might have said, is the stuff of Feuerbach, Marx, and Freud, the human attempt to make "God" in our own image (Rom 1:21–23). The latter is God's apocalypse, or the self-disclosure of God that comes from God's side of the Creator and creature distinction—a knowledge that human beings cannot achieve or fashion on their own precisely because it is in principle beyond their reach. "O the depths of the riches and wisdom and knowledge of God! How unsearchable are his judgments, how inscrutable his ways! For who has known the mind of the Lord or been his counselor?" asks Paul in his dramatic voiceover of Isaiah 40:13 (Rom 11:33–34).

By Paul's time, the original Hebrew version of God's name was considered so sacred that it was no longer said aloud (except on Yom Kippur, and then only by the high priest himself). It could, however, be said in Greek. When Paul read the Greek version of the Old Testament that was his Bible, he therefore saw and heard the Tetragrammaton regularly rendered as *Kyrios* or Lord.[10] It was "the Lord" upon whose name Israel would call to be saved (Joel 2:32; Rom 10:13). For it was the Lord who brought the Israelites out of the land of Egypt and gave them the Law, who rescued them from the Babylonian Exile—communally, the most traumatic event in Israel's history—who subsequently allowed the temple to be rebuilt in Jerusalem, and who raised Jesus from the dead (Gal 1:1). For Paul, this last action is the culmination of God's purpose in electing Israel and the place where God's act in the world is most fully concentrated. In the Messiah Jesus, writes Paul to the Corinthians, "all of God's promises are yes!" (2 Cor 1:20).

But surely not, a skeptical reader might say. I can agree that God ought to mean the one from whom all things come (1 Cor 8:6). But, Paul, certainly you don't mean that the God who creates all things and is over all things acts most fully in the life of a singular human being, just one man? The meaning of "God" is that particular, that restricted in scope? The high point of the story that names who God is comes through a fleshly Jew? *That* can't be the claim.

Au contraire, Paul might reply, God's eternal majesty and glory as Creator leads precisely to this: "In the fullness of time, God sent forth his Son, born of a woman" (Gal 4:4). Indeed, Paul would continue, the glory of the God who made "the light shine in the darkness" is seen most fully "in the face of Jesus Christ" (2 Cor 4:6). To see God's glory, says Paul, one must believe in the life, death, and resurrection of his Son—that is, after all, what it is to look on the face of Jesus.

Why can't we all see it? Why isn't it obvious, self-evident, or at least humanly discernible? To look at Jesus of Nazareth and then to say "here is the glory of the God of the cosmos" seems rather foolish, does it not? Paul's considered reply would doubtless develop the distinction between God's wisdom and human wisdom (for example, 1 Cor 1–2), as well as articulate the damaging effects of sin on human perception (for example, Rom 5:12–21), but he may well simply begin his answer with the identity of God himself. To know God in Jesus Christ, says Paul, we need the Spirit.[11] "No one can say 'Jesus is Lord,'" Paul says, "unless it's by the Holy Spirit" (1 Cor 12:3).

The Spirit in Pauline grammar is the Holy Spirit (Rom 5:5; 9:1 et passim), the Spirit of God (Rom 8:9, 11, 14, et passim), the one who "knows the things of God" (1 Cor 2:11) and who, in a striking phrase, "searches even the depths of God" (1 Cor 2:10). "What no eye has seen, nor ear heard, nor the heart of man conceived . . . God has revealed through the Spirit," says Paul (1 Cor 2:10). It is this Spirit that "God has given in our hearts as an *arrabōn*," a down payment or deposit—an assurance that God's act in Christ leads to salvation (1 Cor 2:22).

Though the Holy Spirit is the subject of action verbs in Paul's language and can be the object of God's action, the Spirit is not other than God. The Spirit is not a distinct entity external to God's own life. Neither is the Spirit simply reducible to modern categories such as immanence, as if *Spirit* were the best word Paul could use to express God's relation to human beings or to the world. For Paul, the Spirit is God and distinct within God. "The Kingdom of God," he tells the church in Rome, "is righteousness, peace, and joy in the Holy Spirit" (Rom 14:17).

Yet, for Paul, the Spirit is not only God's but also Christ's. The link between God and Jesus Christ, that is, is not general, amorphous, or only historical, but specific, formed, and currently present. It is the Spirit of God's Son, Paul informs the Christians in Galatia, that enables them to cry out to God as "Abba! Father!" (Gal 4:6). Reminding the Roman Christians about their exit from "life in the flesh"—the preferred way to speak of wayward and wasteful existence—Paul juxtaposes the two ways of identifying the Spirit: "And you are not in the flesh, you are in the Spirit since the Spirit of God (*pneuma theou*) dwells in you. But anyone who does not have the Spirit of Christ (*pneuma Christou*) is not his" (Rom 8:9). And in his discussion of the need for the Spirit to open the eyes to the truth of Scripture's testimony to Christ, Paul even speaks of the Lord Jesus as "the Spirit of the living God" (2 Cor 3:3, 16–18).[12] In the Pauline patterns of speech, therefore, the same Spirit is inextricably bound both to God and to Jesus Christ; moreover, the language of Spirit articulates the complete presence of God in Christ and the way by which human beings come to know this presence in the here and now.

But this all sounds rather muddled, one of Paul's plenteous opponents might say. God, Jesus, Spirit, and so on appear all mashed up together. Isn't God just supposed to be "one"? Monotheism with all that it entails for worship and thought seems here to be thrown to the wind, the typical and predictable casualty of thought enflamed by zeal.

"Hear O Israel, the Lord your God, the Lord is one," has always formed the foundation of my life, Paul would respond (Deut 6:4). Morning and night I have recited the Shema, morning and night I have upheld the oneness and utter uniqueness of God. You can read of "the one God" in one of my letters to the Corinthians, for example, and to the Galatians (1 Cor 8:6; Gal 3:20). And that God is the only God—and therefore the God of all—you can read in what I wrote to the Romans (3:29).

Yes, but let's press the point: what about Jesus? In fact, when I read "God is one" in 1 Corinthians 8:6, I immediately read thereafter: "and there is one Lord, Jesus Christ." Unless I'm mistaken, this "one Lord" is a direct commentary on the Shema itself.

> For us there is one God, the Father,
> from whom are all things and in whom we exist,
> and there is one Lord, Jesus Christ,
> through whom are all things and through whom we exist. (1 Cor 8:6)

It appears, does it not, that you have inserted Jesus into the middle of the fundamental confession of God's oneness. Aren't there now *two* powers in heaven?[13]

No indeed, Paul would respond. There are not two powers in heaven. The Lord of heaven is the only Lord; "the same Lord is the Lord of all," as I put it for the Roman church (Rom 10:12). But, and here's the trick, to speak of this Lord we need to speak both of God the Father and of Jesus Christ. As I also said to the Christians in Rome, "If you confess with your lips that the Lord is Jesus and believe in your heart that God raised him from the dead you will be saved" (10:9). And I concluded, citing the prophet Joel, "All who call on the Name of the Lord shall be saved" (Rom 10:13).

Now notice what the Roman Christians have learned: the Lord whom we are to confess is Jesus, and yet the Lord spoken of in the book of the prophet is obviously the one Lord of the Shema. The proximate juxtaposition of these two statements enlarges the referent of the word *Lord*—again, God's own name in Israel's Scripture—to include Jesus without placing him in competitive relation to God. In God's case, oneness can include distinction without ceasing to be oneness. This is the underlying logic of 1 Corinthians 8:6, too, and the reason that I can say in my letter to the Philippians that "at the name of Jesus every knee shall bow and every tongue confess that Jesus Christ is Lord to the glory of God the Father" (Phil 2:10–11).[14] The one Lord is both God the Father and Jesus Christ.

In short, Paul's reply would affirm that neither Jesus nor the Spirit contradicts the oneness of God. Indeed, they express it, or articulate it historically, concretely, humanly. Conversely, God's oneness articulates the final significance of Jesus the Messiah (1 Thess 3:2 and 2:8, 9). There is no competition between God and Jesus. The one God is for us and with us as the Lord Jesus. Had Paul lived after Kant, therefore, and learned about "monotheism" as a philosophical principle, he might have said his opponents thought of oneness or monotheism as abstractions, properties or attributes that match the highest form of speculative reason or even religious thought. Not so the biblical God. That God is one in exactly the way the Bible depicts his oneness: a dynamic, living oneness that culminates historically in the life of Jesus of Nazareth, who is made currently present by the power of the Holy Spirit.

Paul's way of telling the story that names who God is thus includes three points of reference: God the Father, Jesus, and the Holy Spirit. "The grace of the Lord Jesus Christ and the love of God and the fellowship of the Holy Spirit be with you all," says Paul in his last recorded communication with the Corinthians (2 Cor 13:14; cf. 1:21–22; Rom 15:30).[15] Having already heard much about "the same Spirit, the same Lord, and the same God" (1 Cor 12:4–6), they would hardly be surprised by such language.[16] Obviously, Paul was not a Trinitarian in any later sense of the term. But his theological grammar is nevertheless irreducibly triadic in shape. "God" in its fullest sense means the one whose identity is known by speaking together of the Father, the Son, and the Holy Spirit.

In the end, putting the question "who is God?" to the Pauline letters elicits an answer that entirely resists simplicity. It requires, instead, a nimble movement between three distinct but inseparably related terms, with a willingness to hold onto the oneness of Israel's God all the while. To tell the story that names who God is according to Paul, therefore, we have to speak distinctly and concurrently of God the Father, Jesus of Nazareth, and the Spirit that is their Holy Spirit. To leave out one of these would reduce Paul's theological language to the point of destroying it; or, to say it another way, refusing the Pauline complexity results in the telling of another story and thus in the naming of someone other than the God about whom Paul writes. The fillip for the complexity, of course, is Paul's reflection on Jesus.

JESUS CHRIST

A first reader of Paul's letters may be surprised at the absence of talk about Jesus' earthly life or an argument for his identity as Israel's Messiah (lest we forget, the meaning of the term *Christ* in the first place). In contrast to the four canonical Gospels, for example, Paul rarely speaks of Jesus' miracles, message, or ministry. There is, of course, one striking exception to this rule: Jesus' crucifixion and death. But as a whole Paul focuses more upon the impact and meaning of the totality of Jesus' life, death, and resurrection—what theologians have often called the "Christ-event."[17]

For Paul, Jesus was a real—blood, flesh, and bones—human being. In the twenty-first century, and well after the rise of the "historical Jesus" industry, the truth of such a belief goes almost without saying. In Paul's day, however, for both Jews and pagans there were other options on offer: mediating angels, say, or exalted patriarchs, or divine or semidivine heroes. But Jesus was none of these things. He was, as Paul put it at the beginning of Romans, "descended from David according to the flesh" (Rom 1:3), or, as he says in Galatians, "born of a woman, born under the law," that is, as a Jew with a Jewish mother.

But doesn't Paul also argue that Jesus is the "image of God" (2 Cor 4:4)? How can a human being be an image of God? Moreover, don't his letters imply that to speak of God is to speak of Jesus? Isn't this simply idolatry, the confusing of the creature with the Creator, as he says of the "images" in the opening paragraphs in Romans (1:23)?

Well, Paul might say, it is true that the human creation of images of God is idolatry. No serious reader of the infamous Golden Calf episode could disagree.[18] Images abrogate the second commandment. On the other hand, however, as Genesis 1:26 teaches us, God can image himself in human form: "In the image of God, he created him"—the first human creature, the *anthrōpos*.[19] With images, you see, it's all a question of the right direction. We cannot fashion God "in the image of a mortal human being" (Rom 1:23). But when God sends forth his Son in the fullness of time, he can come as a human being, as God's image. From his side of things, as it were, God is free to do this.

Christ Jesus "was in the form of God" and "equal to God," as Paul says to the Philippians, but took "the form of a slave" and "was born in the likeness of human beings"; indeed, he continues, "being found in the scheme of human life, [Jesus] humbled himself and was obedient unto death, even death on a cross" (Phil 2:6–8).[20] Yes, says Paul, Jesus was a human being—like Adam himself. Proof positive? He could die.

Jesus' death was not, however, the ordinary natural death of every individual. It was, rather, a singular event in time. He died a real human death, but one whose significance was utterly unique. Later readers of Paul spoke about this significance with the Latin catchwords *pro nobis*, "for us." Again and again, to the Corinthians, the Galatians, the Romans, and others, Paul speaks of this for-us-ness of Jesus' death. Citing an early piece of Christian tradition, for example,

Paul tells the Corinthians that he taught them what he himself had learned: "that Christ died for our sins according to the Scriptures" (1 Cor 15:3). They later hear that "Christ died for all" (2 Cor 5:5). The Romans are told that Jesus was put to death "for our trespasses" (Rom 4:25), and the Galatians are warned to repent of their error, lest they render Christ's *pro nobis* death gratuitous (Gal 2:21). Indeed, in an arresting phrase, Paul even says that Christ became "a curse for us" (Gal 3:13).

Paul's language has partly to do with the way in which Jews could read Scripture in the first century—he cites the book of Deuteronomy's "cursed is he who hangs upon a tree" as evidence, for example (Gal 3:13)—but also with his overall understanding of the world as a place of profound brokenness. As modern readers of Paul now tirelessly emphasize, Paul did not first discover this brokenness and then discern Jesus' death as the healing event. Paul's reading of things, in fact, moved from Jesus to the world; the former became the lens through which the latter was seen. And what he saw in light of Christ was a place in which human beings themselves stood condemned (see Rom 3:9–31). They were, in a word, the "ungodly" (Rom 5:6). Yet the problem was also deeper: the ungodly existed in an age in which the curse of sin held sway, the "present evil age," as Paul tells the Christians in Galatia (Gal 1:4).[21]

Paradoxically, perhaps, for Paul even the Jewish Law itself testified to this brokenness.[22] Contrary to Martin Luther's understanding of the Law, obedience to Torah was actually possible, thought Paul, as he says in his letter to the Philippians (3:6). But in fact, as Paul argues in his effort to keep the Galatians focused on the significance of Christ's death as an act of love-for-the-sake-of-deliverance (Gal 2:20), Israel has historically failed in its attempts at obedience, and the Law that promises life now cannot deliver it. Indeed, says Paul in light of his reading of Deuteronomy, we live in an age in which the Law itself now pronounces the curse.[23]

Christ's death, however, delivered us from the curse precisely by freeing us from the age in which its power was paramount. "The Lord Jesus Christ," Paul declares, "gave himself for our sins to deliver us from the present evil age" (Rom 1:4). "At just the right time," he says to the church in Rome, "while we were still weak . . . Christ died for the ungodly"; or again, "God demonstrates his *pro nobis* love in that while we were still sinners Christ died *pro nobis*"; and "while we were enemies [of God], we were reconciled to God by the death of his Son" (Rom 5:6, 8, 10). In short, and to put it rather simply, Christ assumed the enmity and the curse himself, and his death set things on a new footing.

The significance of both Jesus' life and his death hangs on his resurrection from the dead. In attempting to wake the Corinthians up to the consequences of rejecting the resurrection (1 Cor 15:12), Paul emphatically denies any significance to Jesus' life or death apart from the resurrection. "If Christ has not been raised," he tells the church in Corinth, "then our preaching is in vain and your faith is in vain." "If Christ has not been raised," he repeats, "your faith is in vain"; moreover, "you are still in your sins." So much, in fact, does the entirety of the Pauline gospel depend upon the resurrection of Jesus that "if for this life only we have hoped in Christ, we are of all men most to be pitied" (1 Cor 15:14, 17, 19). For Paul, speaking of Christ's death by itself was as pointless as setting sail on a boat with thousands of holes in the bottom. Not for Paul the Liberal Protestant attempts to wring meaning from the dead Jesus. Death without resurrection sinks the Christian faith, pure and simple.

Why not, however, just talk platonically about the freeing of Jesus' soul from his body? Why speak of the significance of Jesus' death only with the language of "resurrection from the dead"? The primary reason, Paul would say, is that Jesus was raised bodily. After all, the whole point in using the language of "resurrection" is simultaneously to say "body."[24]

But someone—a lapsed Corinthian, say—might press, What kind of body? Are you speaking, Paul, of a Lazarus-like miracle, a waking up with the same exact body, warts and all, or perhaps flying corpses, or simply visions? And Paul would say, as he did to the Corinthians who were vexed by the question of the body:

> O fool! What you sow cannot be made to live unless it dies. And what you sow is not the body that is to be, but a bare kernel, perhaps of wheat or some other grain. But God gives to it a body he has chosen. . . . So it is with the resurrection of the dead. What is sown is perishable; what is raised is imperishable. It is sown in dishonor; it is raised in glory. It is sown in weakness; it is raised in power. It is sown a natural body; it is raised a spiritual body. If there is a natural body, there is also a spiritual body. Thus it is written [in the book of Genesis], "The first man, Adam, was a living natural body"; the last Adam, a life-giving spiritual body. But it is not the spiritual body that is first but the natural body, and then the spiritual body. . . . This I tell you, brothers and sisters, flesh and blood cannot inherit the kingdom of God; nor does the perishable inherit the imperishable." (1 Cor 15:36–50)[25]

Or, having tired of such long-winded teaching, Paul might simply say what he wrote to the Philippians when he assured them that their resurrection would be like Christ's: "The Lord Jesus Christ will transform our lowly body to be like his glorious body" (Phil 3:21).

Throughout his letters, then, Paul's logic is clear enough: when Jesus died, he was dead—not partly dead, as if he possessed a soul that escaped death, but really, truly, and fully dead. Paul consistently speaks, in fact, of Jesus' resurrection in the passive voice, as something that can only be attributed to the act of God (see Rom 4:25 et passim). Because he was dead, Jesus could not raise himself; it was God who raised Jesus from the dead. And when he was then alive again, he was alive with the body by which he lived his earthly life. This body, however, was not flesh and blood *simpliciter*, a resuscitation like Lazarus's in John's Gospel or a revivified corpse; it was, rather, transformed flesh, transformed blood, a body that required the word *spirit* to describe it.

As a Jew, Paul knew that God created the world and had declared it good. The resurrection of Jesus testified, for Paul, to God's commitment to redeem the stuff of the world rather than to reject it, to validate its goodness by going to its material foundations and remaking them. Jesus' body, that is, is the first sign of the new creation that God wrought through Christ's faithful obedience unto death. Jesus Christ was the new Adam, redeeming and restoring by his faithfulness the creation broken by the disobedience of the old one (1 Cor 15; Rom 5:12–21). The curse has been borne and taken away. "If anyone is in Christ," Paul tells the Corinthians, "he is a new creation" (2 Cor 5:17). Or again, "neither circumcision nor uncircumcision is anything—only new creation" (Gal 6:15). Of course, Jesus is a great many other things for Paul, but "new creation" is the sum and substance of the life, death, and resurrection of the Christ. The entirety of the Christ-event, in which death was the culmination of a life of faithful obedience, was *in nuce* a redoing of the human project. Jesus Christ is the new Adam according to Paul, and as a result there is nothing less than new life in a new world.

HUMANITY: CREATION AND SIN

By speaking of Jesus Christ as the new or second Adam, Paul invokes a history that displays what it is to be human. Paul never reflects on humanity in abstraction from this history, as if he believed it were possible, for example, to get down to an essence or a capacity that distinguishes us from the rest of the animals. Instead, for Paul, anthropology is what the human being has been through its history from the first Adam until the second—and, then, what it can become in light of the Christ-event.

Modern Old Testament scholars frequently read the creation stories in Genesis 1 and 2 as reflecting separate and differing traditions—or "sources"—about God's creation of the world. Such scholars often assume that Genesis 1 and 2 are difficult to read together. Paul did not. When Paul read the opening chapters of Genesis, he saw that God created the human being—the *anthrōpos* as such (Gen 1:26)—which was differentiated into male and female (Gen 1:27). The name of the male was Adam (*adam*, Gen 2), and the unfolding of his history was simultaneously the history of humanity (Gen 3). *Adam*, for Paul, signified *anthrōpos*, marked its character and being, and said what it was to be human in two foundational ways: the first was created by God in his image (Gen 1–2), and the second was fallen, broken, in need of redemption (Gen 3).[26]

As Paul read further in Scripture he would have encountered a second differentiation, that of Jew and Gentile.[27] The election of Abraham divided humanity into two fundamentally separate ways of being in the world, the Jewish way and the other way (whatever its internal variety). The Jewish way was the way of Torah and covenant—or, to use another figure, the way of Moses—and the other way was the way of estrangement from God and the practice of false worship. By Paul's time, of course, these two different ways of being were both existential and historical facts, practically dense forms of chronologically elongated life that predetermined, as it were, much of the material that Paul had to work with in his thinking about human promise and predicament.

In Romans 5, for example, Paul turns from a lengthy discussion of Abraham in chapter 4 to construct an Adam/Christ typology that abbreviates dramatically the entire history from Adam through Moses to Christ. Through one man sin—and thus death—entered the entire world and spread to all human creatures. As a result of Adam, "all have sinned." Death, therefore, "reigns" through the one man, and the verdict upon the history of Adam, confirmed by the Torah itself, is "condemnation." Precisely in his universal reach, Adam is a "type" of another man, "the one to come." Through the just act of this other man, says Paul, life is given to all human beings. The obedience of the one man Jesus Christ results not in condemnation but in its exact opposite, acquittal, and in the free gift of righteousness to all. Thus, according to Paul, what it is to be human is determined by the first and the second Adam.

But what about our freedom? we moderns might like to ask. Doesn't your schema overdetermine our sense of embeddedness within the world, our historicity? Moreover, what about the individual, Paul? You seem to speak as if humanity can be grouped all together, seen as a chunk whose individual contours are smothered. What about the "I," Paul? What about the cultivation of the self, the ability to move through the world determining my own "I" as I go?

Had he lived to taste the modern flavor of such questions, Paul's answer would prove profoundly unsatisfying to the champions of innate individual freedom and the exaltation of the "I" in the projects of self-determination. Anthropology is participatory at its core. Our humanity is determined on the one hand by our participation in Adam's sin and, on the other, by our participation in the new life in Jesus Christ. To go even farther, freedom as moderns conceive it is an abstract property of the human being in isolation from heaven or hell, something that supposedly exists entirely within the "immanent frame." But in point of fact freedom is not entirely immanent and is not abstract: it exists only in participation in Christ. "Do you not know that if you yield yourselves to any one as obedient slaves, you are slaves of the one whom you obey, either of sin, which leads to death, or of obedience, which leads to righteousness?" (Rom 6:16). We are slaves either to the one Adam or to the other. Freedom is, quite simply, becoming a slave of Christ. As Paul went on to tell the Roman Christians, "Thanks be to God that you who were once slaves of sin have become obedient from the heart to the pattern of teaching to which you were delivered, and, having been freed from sin, have become slaves of righteousness" (Rom 6:17–18). Left to ourselves, we are not "ourselves" but rather agents of sin.

Contrary to the reductive way sin is often spoken of in regular discourse, the Pauline epistles evidence not one but three complexly intertwined ways of speaking about what sin is. It is, first, a cosmic condition, an inescapable fact about the (broken) structure of the world in which humans emerge and out of which they cannot extract themselves (see Rom 8:18–26). It is, second, a description of certain behaviors, dispositions, or acts that contravene the moral order of God's law—"sins" (see Rom 7:5), "trespasses" (see Rom 5:14; Gal 3:19), or "transgressions" (see Rom 5:16–18; 11:11–12). And it is, third, a power (see Rom 7:7–25), something that can, it seems, act within the world, seizing even the best that life can offer to its own destructive purposes.

Precisely because of its multifaceted reality, sin's reach is broad and its damage deep. What normally appears as wisdom, for example—the quintessence of the philosophical quest—turns out to be nothing of the kind. Foolishness, says Paul, is the real name for human Sophia in the sight of God. Standing the truth on its head, he tells the struggling church in Corinth that genuine wisdom is what looks like foolishness. "Where is the wise man? Where is the scribe? Where is the debater of this age? Has not God made foolish the wisdom of the world? For since in the wisdom of God the world did not know God through wisdom, it pleased God through the folly of what we preach to save those who believe . . . [and] we preach Christ crucified" (1 Cor 1:20–21). In short, Paul argues, sin blinds us, and our quest for the wise life leads us to reject as foolishness that which is really wise, the crucifixion of Christ (1 Cor 1–3).

"But what about the Torah?" a thoughtful reader might ask Paul. Did not God give his holy law for our guidance in a world conditioned by sin and populated by those who commit transgressions? Indeed, he did, Paul would say. The Law is "holy," and the commandments are "holy, just, and good" (Rom 7:12).

God gave the Law to the Jews so that by the witness of their life they might be a light to the nations. In fact, Paul argues, the Law was intended to be our tutor, our educator toward Christ (Gal 3:24).[28]

But sin dramatically intervened, and seized the Law to work through it toward our debilitation. "I should not have known," says Paul, offering a particular instance of what he took to be generally true, "what it is to covet if the law had not said, 'You shall not covet.' But sin, finding an opportunity in the commandment, wrought in me all kinds of covetousness." Paradoxically, and tragically, "the very commandment that promised life proved to be death to me. For sin, finding an opportunity in the commandment, deceived me and by it killed me" (Rom 7:7–11; cf. 1 Cor 15:56). Was it, then, the Law—"that which is good"—that became death to me? Paul reasonably asks. "By no means!" he answers. "It was sin, working death in me through what is good" (Rom 7:13).

Sin, here, is a power. It is a reality that can toxically twist the relation between human beings and the God-given gift for directing us toward patterns of repair and, ultimately, toward the Christ. Paul may leave the finer-grained aspects of sin's activity shrouded in mystery, but for him its active power is real all the same. True enough, the Law enables us to know what we should not do, but sin can use the Law to intensify our bondage to that which we should not do, taking us over and acting on our behalf to malform our lives. "I do not know what I'm doing," says Paul in one of his most famous passages,

> because I don't do what I want to do but, instead, do exactly the thing I hate. But if I do the thing I don't want to do, I agree that the Law is good—that is, the Law shows me what I ought not to want to do. Now then, it is no longer I myself that do it but sin dwelling within me. For I know that good does not dwell in me, that is, in my flesh. To will the good is present within me, but to do it is not. For I do not do the good that I want, but the evil that I do not want—that's what I do. But if I do that which I don't want to do, it is no longer I myself who am doing it but sin dwelling within me. I find it to be the case even with the Torah that whenever I'm wanting to do the good, evil lies ever so close to me. For I delight in the Law of God in my inner person, but I see another law in my members at war with the law of my mind and making me captive to the law of sin that dwells in my members. I am so wretched! Who will deliver me from this body of death?—Thanks be to God through Jesus Christ our Lord!—So then, I myself serve the Law of God with my mind, but with my flesh I serve the law of sin. (Rom 7:15–25)

Even where the Law discloses the good, even where we perceive the good, even where we will to do the good, sin dominates. It takes over, divides the self, and prohibits the possibility of self-direction for repair. Left to ourselves, sin works in and upon and even despite us to bear fruit for death, sin's *telos* and its most profound consequence (see Rom 7:5; cf. 6:23 et passim). We are, irreducibly and inescapably, creatures headed for ruin and death.

In Pauline theology, being human thus turns on the question that arises from the history that describes who we are: how shall we be delivered from our history of sin and death? It would not be too much to say that, for Paul, death destroys our humanity, inasmuch as it destroys us. The question about the deliverance from death is thus simultaneously a question about recovering our humanity.

HUMANITY: DEATH AND RESURRECTION

Had Paul lived in our time, he would have understood Ernest Becker's claim that death "haunts the human animal like nothing else."[29] Paul would also have understood one of Becker's primary predecessors, Kierkegaard, when he argued that postlapsarian human self-consciousness was exactly concomitant with our dread of death. For Paul, death itself—the condition of our humanity and the power that reduces us to being dead—is awful, terrible, a curse, the enemy.

Scattered throughout his letters are remarks about the power of death to shake and even undo us. In his earliest surviving letter, for example, Paul assumes that grief is what results when the intimacy of our connection to others is severed by death. Do not grieve, Paul tells the Christians in Thessalonica, "as others do who have no hope" (1 Thess 4:13; cf. 2 Cor 7:9–10). Paul's point is not that the Thessalonians have no cause for grief but rather that their grief need not be hopeless. Grief exists, but it can be intertwined with hope. When writing to the Corinthians about his afflictions in the province of Asia, Paul uses death language to express the nadir of his suffering: "We were so utterly, unbearably crushed that we despaired of life itself. We even felt as if we had received the death sentence" (2 Cor 1:8–9; cf. 4:11–12; 11:23). Still more arresting is Paul's placement of death in the consummation of all things: "Then comes the end, when [Christ] delivers the kingdom to God the Father after abolishing every ruler and every authority and every power. For he must reign until he has put all his enemies under his feet. The last enemy to be destroyed is *death*" (1 Cor 15:24–26). Death is an enemy greater than rulers, greater even than demons. One may imagine a power, the ultimate enemy, unyielding though all his allies have crumbled. So significant is death's demise that it marks the completion of Christ's work.

Remember, Paul would say, death is not simply the natural close to things; it is inseparably connected to sin. Indeed, "the sting of death is sin" (1 Cor 15:56).

Death is ours due not simply to the way the world runs but to the curse. Death conquers and swallows up all perishable life. Rulers may harm, demons may torment, but to have to die is to perish and to be cursed. "When the perishable puts on the imperishable, and the dying puts on the undying, then the word that is written will come to pass: 'Death is swallowed up in victory'" (1 Cor 15:54). For Paul death is a deep enough threat to the human creature that its defeat cannot come simply by existential posturing. Even the well-adjusted, authentically alive creatures are in the end defeated by death. Defeating death requires a great deal more than a well-adjusted soul; it requires, in fact, nothing less than the transformation of death to life.

Thanks be to God, then, that "he who raised the Lord Jesus will raise us also with Jesus" (2 Cor 4:14). "Christ, having been raised from the dead," Paul proclaims to the Roman church, "will never die again. Death is no longer able to lord it over him. The death he died," Paul continues, "he died to sin, once for all, but the life he lives he lives to God. So you, too, must consider yourselves dead to sin and alive to God in Christ Jesus" (Rom 6:9–11). When it comes to victory over death, Paul's basic point throughout his letters is the same: the history of Jesus Christ discloses what to expect and, therefore, provides the hope that suffuses even the darkest grief. As Christ is, so shall we be, says Paul. Mysteriously, but not for that reason any less factually, we are united with Christ by faith and participate in him. His reality becomes ours. "Do you not know," Paul asks the Christians in Rome, "that all of us who have been baptized into Christ Jesus were baptized into his death? We were buried with him by baptism into death, so that as Christ was raised from the dead by the glory of the Father, we, too, might walk in newness of life. For if we have been united with him in a death like his, we shall certainly be united with him in a resurrection like his" (Rom 6:3–5).

According to Paul, therefore, hope in the face of death is rooted not in a particular philosophical anthropology—predicating immortality as a necessary property of the soul, say—but in God's action in Christ. It is true that Paul can speak about different aspects of the human being—the "spirit, soul, and body" in 1 Thessalonians 5:23, for example, or the "inner" and "outer man" in 2 Corinthians 4:16, or the "mind" in Romans 7:23, and so forth.[30] But the ability to withstand death is not constitutive of any of these various aspects. To put it slightly differently, the complexity of the human being does no strictly philosophical work against death. For Paul, it is the new life of the second Adam that discloses the future of the human being. "The first human was from the earth, made of dust; the second human is from heaven. . . . Just as we have borne the image of the man of dust, so, too, we will bear the image of the man of heaven" (1 Cor 15:47, 49). Our resurrection will follow that of Jesus: like him, we will finally be raised with a body transformed from death to life, a spiritual body (1 Cor 15:35–43; cf. Rom 8:23 et passim).

Of course, as a Pharisee, Paul would have already believed in the Living God's power to raise the dead before he encountered the risen Jesus himself.[31] Jesus, thought Paul, was the "firstborn" of those who would be raised (Rom 8:29), the sign that foretold of the character of the final consummation of all things.

But, Paul, any of his congregants might wonder, haven't you now introduced an interval, a time between our death and the bodily resurrection on the last day? Our future beyond death is given to us in Christ Jesus—so far, so good—but we are not yet at the last day, and there are plenty who have died and whose bodies are yet in the tomb. Doesn't this give death a provisional victory?[32]

No—and, well, yes, Paul could reply. Death has no victory: the resurrection of the body is our assured future. But in a sense it's true that death defeats the physical body in the meantime. It is simply a fact: the bodies of those who have died rot and decay and, eventually, entirely disappear—ashes to ashes and dust to dust.

Death's momentary defeat of the body is not, however, the final word; moreover, Paul could continue, there is life in the meantime for those who die before the last day. Your loved ones, and the other saints, too, are "with Christ." And this "with-ness" is not a disappointing waiting, or a holding pattern. It is a true being-with, and a joyful anticipation of death's ultimate demise. Indeed, when pondering my Roman trial and the potential for death, I found it easy to tell the Philippians that it's better to "depart and be with Christ" than it is to remain alive on earth (Phil 1:23).

The Pauline language for human reality in the interval between our death and the consummation of all things derives from his sense of our participation in and union with Christ. Prepositions are theologically strong words for Paul. The human being cannot be divided from Christ because we are in him; when we die we are therefore with him. Nowhere in his letters does Paul explain how this can be so, that is, what part of the human being it is that can exist with Christ without its transformed body, how God relates to this part without a body, how this requires us to think differently about time, and so on. What Paul does express quite clearly, however, is the belief that God's act of love in raising Christ from the dead defies the power of death to separate us from him in any way: "Who shall separate us from the love of Christ? Shall tribulation, or distress, or persecution, or famine, or nakedness, or peril, or sword? . . . No! In all these things we are more than conquerors through him who loved us. For I am sure that neither death, nor life, nor angels, nor principalities, nor things present, nor things to come, nor powers, nor height, nor depth, nor anything else in all creation, will be able to separate us from the love of God in Christ Jesus our Lord" (Rom 8:35–39). Or, still more simply, "whether we live or die, we are the Lord's" (Rom 14:8).

Christians thus do not finally need to fear death. "To live is Christ, and to die is gain," says Paul to the Philippians (Phil 1:21). Suffering for Christ's sake, the Corinthians hear, is simultaneously a visible proclamation of his death and the proleptic announcement of his victory over death. Affliction may well lead to death for Paul and other Christian missionaries, but this death is to be welcomed for its potential to testify to Jesus. We are "always carrying the death of Jesus in our bodies so that the life of Jesus may also be manifested in our bodies. For while we live we're always being given up to death for Jesus' sake, so that the life of Jesus may be manifested in our mortal flesh. So death is at work in us, but life in you" (2 Cor 4:10–12).

It is thus precisely the hope of resurrection that allows death to appear as the enemy that it is and permits Paul to challenge its claim upon the human race. Death is the power of annihilation about which human beings can do nothing whatsoever. The head must bow, the body give way. Only the God who is life itself can defeat death. But this, Paul believes, God has done in Christ and will do at the end when he will be all in all (1 Cor 15:28). Isaiah's words will yet come true: "Death is swallowed up in victory" (1 Cor 15:54, citing Isa 25:8).

Human life is a historical thing in relation to God, one that takes time and unfolds its reality through time as sin, death, redemption, and hope. If there is an essence to being human, we would not learn what it is from Paul. For him, to be human is, on the one hand, to emerge as participants in the patterns of brokenness named sin and, therefore, in the unavoidable trajectory toward death. On the other hand, it is to participate in the reality that declares the end of sin and death—new creation. The startling thing, in the ancient world no less than now, is that new creation according to Paul is itself human at its heart. Indeed, it even has a name, Jesus Christ. In Pauline logic, therefore, to participate in Jesus Christ is to renew and repair our humanity.

THE WAY OF REPAIR: FAITH AND COMMUNITY

If in Pauline thinking the human creature is not simply and only a being unto death but a being that can live toward what it was created to be, how does this happen? If the resurrection of Jesus discloses the future of humanity as that in which we can hope, what are we supposed to do or be in the meantime? On page after page Paul's letters reveal a great care with human life in the meantime.

Worship of God, pagan cults, proper eating, court cases, marriage, children, and virtually countless other matters both great and small receive comment. Nothing, it seems, is exempt from Christian life in the meantime. Still, there are two characteristic patterns of speech that tend to dominate Paul's language about the meantime. The first has to do with faith and the second with community.

No reader of Paul's letters would disagree with the statement that faith forms a crucial part of Paul's theological vocabulary. As he says in the opening words of his letter to the Roman Christians, "I give thanks . . . because your faith is proclaimed throughout the whole world" (Rom 1:8; cf. 1 Thess 1:8, etc.). *Faith* is the primary word Paul uses to describe the human response to Jesus' own faith, or, better, faithfulness.[33] For Paul, as many recent studies have emphasized, the latter evokes the former. Paul frequently speaks of Jesus' faith—by which he means his trustingly obedient life rather than a pious feeling—as the source for human faith. God's power to set things right was disclosed "through the faithfulness of Jesus Christ," says Paul, "to all who believe" (Rom 3:22). Earlier in the letter, he abbreviated the same interconnection rather simply: "by faith for faith," wrote Paul in Rom 1:17.[34] And in his letter to the Galatians he tirelessly argues not only that God's justifying power is effected through the faithfulness of Christ but also that this marvelous truth evokes faith: "For we know," says Paul, "that a human being is not justified by works of the law but through the faithfulness of Jesus Christ—and we have believed in Christ Jesus in order to be justified by the faithfulness of Christ" (Gal 3:16). The Christ-event establishes the possibility of faith. We are summoned, says Paul, to believe in God through Christ.

It is true, as Ed Sanders and others have long noted, that a significant portion of Paul's "faith/not works" antithesis occurs in polemically shaped passages. It isn't works or righteous deeds, Paul argues, that can bring about new creation or life from the dead. Only God can free us from bondage to sin and death and re-create the world in which we can freely serve him.[35] Paul also, however, speaks paradigmatically of the faith of Abraham as the prefiguration of the trust that is the Christian response to God's act in Christ.

In the fourth chapter of Romans, for example, Paul discusses Abraham's faith at length. Paul's discourse is lengthy not only because he needs to argue from Scripture that God's present work in Christ is continuous with his past dealings with Israel—"faith" is the fundamental way God always works, Paul thinks—but also to suggest that the kind of trust in God that Abraham exhibited speaks now of Christian trust. Paul's point is that Abraham trusted God to bring him children in the face of obvious evidence to the contrary—he was quite old, Paul knows from Genesis—and was right to do so. God himself is "the faithful one," says Paul again and again in calling Christians to trust in his power to give life (see 1 Cor 1:9; 10:13 et passim). Both the circumcised and uncircumcised—which means, of course, everyone—can heed the summons to follow "the example of the faith of our father Abraham" (Rom 4:12; cf. Gal 3:7, 9).

Well, Paul, thinking about Abraham, I can see faith as a kind of deep trust in the God who keeps faith, a Pauline congregant might wonder, but does this trust entail particular content? Is it simply a general feeling about divine benevolence, or do we actually have to believe specific things?

"If you confess with your lips that Jesus is Lord and believe in your heart that God raised him from the dead, you will be saved," Paul would respond (Rom 10:10). Indeed, he could continue, it has even been said of me that I preach "the faith I once tried to destroy" (Gal 1:23), thus implying something with rather specific and identifiable content that I tried to decimate but now preach (cf. 1 Cor 1:23). In fact, there is content to the faith. But such content is more like the total story of God's dealings with the world as reflected in Scripture and in Christ than it is, say, a properly numbered set of statements (if you believe three out of five essential truths, you have "faith" whereas two out of five is not enough to count as faith). Our trust, therefore, does have content to it—it is not the general Romantic sense about the goodness of the divine—but the content does not replace the act of trusting with the whole being of one's life through thick and thin (see 2 Cor 11:23–33).

To put it into later terms, had Paul known of the distinction between the *fides qua creditur* (the faith by which it is believed, that is, trust) and the *fides quae creditur* (the faith which is believed, that is, content), he could well have understood it. But he would not have taken these distinctions to name fundamental differences in "faith." Rather, for Paul, trust simply was trust in the life-giving power of the God who raised Jesus of Nazareth from the dead even when things appeared to the clear-eyed to indicate the foolishness of that trust. In the meantime between the now of new creation and the not yet of its final consummation, Paul would say, "We walk by faith, not by sight" (2 Cor 5:7).

Faith, however, was not for Paul the remarkably individualized experience it has become in the late-modern West. Faith did include personal response, of course—the "I" of Romans 7 does receive transformation—but the primary thrust of faith in the Pauline epistles is toward community. So, second, the Pauline grammar of the meantime is irreducibly communal. All of the letters indisputably by Paul, to name an obvious but striking fact, are written to churches. Even the letter that bears a man's particular name is written not just to Philemon but to the church that gathered in his house (Phlm 1:1–2). And Richard Hays has argued persuasively that the *telos* (aim, goal, purpose) of

Paul's scriptural interpretation as a whole—not only in this or that instance—is ecclesial. Through his readings of Scripture, Paul aims to form the church that God is creating.[36]

If there is a primary emphasis to Paul's churchly grammar, it doubtless falls upon his continual attempt to bring Jew and Gentile peacefully together in one body. Modern Christians may have forgotten how loudly this issue reverberates throughout the pages of the entire New Testament, but the division between Jew and Gentile was the most delicate and theologically charged social problem of the first century. In the variety of opinions that swirled about, Paul's position was clear: "There is no distinction" between Jew and Gentile, as he bluntly tells the Roman church two times over (Rom 3:22; 10:12; cf. Gal 3:26–28). When some of Paul's opponents attempted to reintroduce a division in Galatia along the lines of Torah observance, Paul erupted. "I am astonished that you are so quickly deserting him who called you in the grace of Christ and turning to a different Gospel—not that there is another Gospel, but there are some who trouble you and want to pervert the Gospel of Christ. . . . If anyone is preaching to you a Gospel contrary to that which you received, let him be accursed!" (Gal 1:6–7). Nothing should threaten the unity of Jew and Gentile in Christ.

The unity of Jew and Gentile in one community does not mean, as Paul is at pains to demonstrate to the Roman church, that the Jews who have yet to see Jesus as the Messiah are "cut off" (see Rom 11:17–24). Despite modern misunderstandings, Paul is no supersessionist. Israel according to the flesh will yet come to faith, says Paul (Rom 11:25–36). Still, in the meantime, those who share Abraham's faith, who respond to Christ's faithfulness, and who trust the faithful God to resurrect them on the last day are to gather together in one body—on the same footing, without distinction.

Much is at stake here for Paul. The oneness of the Christian community, in fact, mirrors to the world God's own identity as the one and only God (Rom 3:29–30; 10:12–13). Paul's drive to establish and preserve the unity of Jew and Gentile, that is, isn't a social program alone, as if social life for Paul had its own raison d'être and normative direction. It is rather that the social shape of humanity in Christ derives from the call to witness to the identity of the one God. To divide the people of God is to threaten the unity of God's identity as the one and only God. Long before St. Augustine in the ancient world or John Milbank today, Paul knew that Christian theology entails claims about a particular kind of sociology. As he puts it to the Corinthians, "For just as the body is one and has many members, and all the members of the body, though many, are one body, so it is with Christ. For by one Spirit we were all baptized into one body—whether Jews or Greeks, slaves or free—and we all drank of one Spirit" (1 Cor 12:12).

Precisely because Paul understands Christian community as a witness to the identity of God as Israel's God, the one and only God, Paul also exerts considerable energy toward helping his congregations to distance themselves from the normal pagan habits of their pre-Christian lives (see 1 Thess 1:9). Though he mentions the necessary break from paganism in almost every situation, this aspect of Paul's community building is on display nowhere more prominently than in his first surviving letter to the Corinthians. There Paul chides them for their immoral sexual practice, their love of Greco-Roman wisdom, their unruliness in worship, their view of the body, and—most elaborately—their confusion over what to do about eating the food that has been sacrificed to the pagan gods, that is, "idols" in Paul's language. Over a span of about three complex chapters, Paul argues essentially two points, both of which illustrate the interconnection between God and the Corinthian church.

First, says Paul, bend to the weak. There are some who do not know that food in itself is nothing and who "fall" on account of eating food associated with pagan religious practices; accommodate their ignorance. Knowledge is for the sake of serving those "for whom Christ died" not for "puffing up" (1 Cor 8:1–13). In Paul's view, theological knowledge leads to the kind of practical wisdom that characterizes and reflects God's self-disclosure in Christ as the one who is strong precisely when he is weak. That weakness conditions the unity of the Christian community's witness in Corinth should come as no surprise to readers of Paul's wider corpus. The man who could write that the one in the form of God took the form of a slave (Phil 2:5–11) is a man who works at the deepest level of his theological grammar with the link between God in Christ, the unity of the church, and the necessity to be weak with those who are weak (cf. 2 Cor 11:29–30).

Second, Paul argues that the Corinthians must not go to the festivals in pagan temples to eat. The reason? Participation in Christ and in idolatrous practice are mutually exclusive (1 Cor 10:14–11:1). "You cannot," Paul instructs them, "drink the cup of the Lord and the cup of demons. You cannot partake of the table of the Lord and the table of demons" (1 Cor 10:21). In continuity with the vocation of historic Israel, to witness to the God who brooks no rivals (1 Cor 10:22), the Christians need to be distinct from the "nations."[37] As would later become crystal clear, their refusal to go to the temples or to sacrifice to the pagan gods marks the Christians socially as a group whose form of life visibly testifies to the exclusive authority of—or, even, freedom to serve (*exousia*, see 1 Cor 8:9)—Israel's God in Christ Jesus.

The meantime community of Jews and Gentiles is thus for Paul a profound sort of social difference, one that is predicated on the response of faith and visibly apparent. Inasmuch as this social difference is also a political difference, Paul positions his congregations critically vis-à-vis certain constitutive features of the Roman Empire. He does not explicitly contest Caesar's rule—indeed, he can even see the authorities as allowed by God (Rom 13:1–7). Nor does he overtly criticize the imperial cult or judicial miscarriages or any other obviously problematical political practices. But he does, simply by placing all things under the dominion of Christ, help to create the political conditions under which Christian communities can live out the demotion of Caesar from "a god" to a servant of God. Implicitly, that is, Paul's way of conceiving of Caesar's authority is finally an uncompromising challenge to Rome's construal of the emperor. For Rome, precisely because the emperor founds the political order and is the fulcrum on which it all turns, he requires ultimate and unchallenged allegiance. Caesar not only is "the Lord of the whole world," as an inscription in Greece once said of Nero, he can also be nothing less than what his politics require: a god, the extrinsic founder of the political reality called the Roman Empire. For Paul, however, such claims would smack of idolatry: for him, as for other Jews, only the true God can found a political order. All other political players are but actors on this more fundamental, God-given stage. As Paul tells the Corinthians, the Gentiles may well think there are "many lords and many gods" in the world—with Caesar among them—but "for us there is only one God . . . and one Lord" (1 Cor 8:6). At bottom, therefore, while Paul may remind the Romans to "pay taxes to whom taxes are due and give honor to whom honor is due," he does so only because he can judge such realities momentarily to cohere with the divine economy.[38] When push later came to shove, congregants schooled in Pauline logic would have no difficulty discerning the Christian difference from *Dea Roma*, her emperor, and the wider religiopolitical practices that held them necessarily together. Final allegiance belongs only to Christ.

The Christian difference is not, however, only a negative difference, that is, a difference constituted only by its distance from the pagan world's regular runnings. It is also a place where Christian life itself is developed, enhanced, furthered, and, in short, grown. Husbands, wives, single women and men, parents, children, and so forth are all taught to see their lives first through their identity as Christians. Moderns may have good reasons for disliking some of Paul's instructions, but his basic attempt was to train his communities to subordinate their "natural" roles and affections to the witness of the community.

It is no real surprise, therefore, that some interpreters of Paul have thought him implicitly to endorse the status quo when it comes to ancient slavery, for example. While he does at times counsel his readers to remain as they were when called, more fundamentally he sees slavery as something that is transcended by the unity of the one community in the new creation—which is to say that "neither slave nor free" gains specific application in the case of the Christian slave Onesimus.

It is true that though Paul acknowledges his authority to command Onesimus's owner to do what is required (Phlm 8), his letter to Philemon does not explicitly say "set Onesimus free." But like any effective pastor, Paul knows how to apply intense spiritual and personal pressure to assure this same result.

Not only is the letter read aloud in the presence of the other Christians who meet in Philemon's house—thereby creating a pressurized structure of accountability for Philemon—it also suggests that Onesimus is equal to Paul as a human being ("in the flesh"), in Christ ("in the Lord"), and in his work for the Gospel ("receive him as you would me"). Paul sends the runaway Onesimus back to Philemon "no longer as a slave but more than a slave, as a beloved brother . . . both in the flesh and in the Lord. If, then, you consider me your partner, receive him as you would me" (Phlm 16–17). Don't let money stand in the way, Paul coaxes further; I'll pay what is owed on his account (Phlm 18–19). Of course, Paul immediately thereafter says, "Even though you owe me your own self, I'll pay," thus implicitly directing Philemon to overlook financial matters. Paul then tightens the screw. Further challenging the normal understanding of indebtedness and repayment, he shifts the sense of "benefit" to a more spiritually charged plane: in fact, "*I* want some benefit from *you*," he declares to Philemon, turning the tables. "Refresh my heart in Christ" (Phlm 20).

In closing, Paul essentially says, I won't compel you to free your slave because I know you'll do the right thing: "Confident of your obedience I write to you, knowing that you will do even more than I say" (Phlm 21). And, lest Philemon doubt Paul's sincerity, Paul mentions his plans for a personal visit and adds that he hopes Philemon will pray that the visit transpires: "Prepare a guest room for me, for I am hoping through your prayers to be granted to you" (22). As a pastoral strategy, "I know you'll do the right thing, and to make sure I'll come check up on you," would always receive low marks from those who want individual autonomy. But Paul had no such worries. By the end of the short but intense letter, Philemon would have seen that to refuse Onesimus his freedom would have been to oppose Paul's counsel and challenge outright his authority—and that this would have to be done in front of the other Christians who met in his house and then again to Paul's face when he later came to visit. Thus, while the Christians had to wait for a sermon from Gregory of Nyssa in AD 379 to see a robust condemnation of slavery as an institution, Paul's letter to Philemon began the kind of work that could eventually be done under the vision of a common humanity in Christ. Once again, one Lord, one people.[39]

Elsewhere, however, Paul's letters do not display as much concern with the issues that have become important in modern civil debates as they do with broader constructive practices that make for growth in holiness. "To the saints in Christ Jesus in Philippi," Paul begins his letter to the Philippians (1:1). To all those who are called as saints, he says to the Corinthians and to the Romans (1 Cor 1:2; Rom 1:7). "All the saints" of here or there greet you, Paul writes time and again (see 2 Cor 13:12). Saints—those who are holy or set apart—is as much a part of Paul's way of speaking about community as is his family vocabulary (for example, "brothers and sisters"). *Saints* in Paul's grammar is less an individual term than it is a characterization of the community's identity and trajectory. Quite simply, "saints" means Christian communities who live as they are called to live in witness to the one and only God. Later ecclesial understanding would of course reduce the number of people to whom "saint" could legitimately be applied, but for Paul "saints" are not necessarily those whose lives have already displayed remarkable holiness. Most of the Corinthians, for example, are—at the very best—just beginning to learn the disciplines that make holiness possible.

Such disciplines, as Paul's letters repeatedly attest, were manifold. Restraining the pull of the passions (see 1 Cor 7; Gal 5:16–25), cultivating the communal priority of the weak (see Rom 14–15:7), redistributing finances to aid the poor (see Rom 12:13), table fellowship (see 1 Cor 11), baptism (see Rom 6:3), refusal of retributive violence (see Rom 12:17–19), enemy love (see Rom 12:14), contemplation of the truth (see Phil 4:8), prayer (see Rom 1:9), and many, many other things are all part of Paul's vision for the community that repairs the old creation by the life it lives in the new.

All this might seem rather laborious. Quite a lot to do and much at which we can fail. Yes, Paul would reply, the pattern of Christian community is that comprehensive—even more so!—and we must constantly examine ourselves to see whether we are "holding to the faith" (2 Cor 13:5–7). And, though God's grace is not worn out by our misdeeds, we are nevertheless responsible for the things we do "in the body" as we come before the throne of Christ (2 Cor 5:10). Failing is a serious problem. Conducting the Lord's Supper, for example, in such a way as to reinforce the division between those who have enough to eat and those who don't "profanes the body and blood of the Lord." Those who do this "drink judgment" upon themselves (1 Cor 11:27–29).[40]

But, drawing on one of the more mysterious paradoxes in the epistles, Paul could continue: Fear not, however, for the disciplines that we practice are finally dependent upon God's own work in us. We are not left to our own effort but can instead rejoice in the fact that Christian practices are at their deepest the work of

God. "Work out your salvation with fear and trembling," Paul tells the Philippians, "for God is at work in you, both to will and to work for his good pleasure" (Phil 2:12–13). "I am sure," he had said earlier in the letter, "that he who began a good work in you will perfect it until the day of Christ Jesus" (Phil 1:6).

With the phrase "until the day of Christ Jesus" Paul explicitly acknowledges the dialectic that marks all his speech about Christian life. Modern New Testament scholars have often referred to this dialectic with the cumbersome but accurate phrase "now/not yet." You have "now," says Paul to the Roman Christians, "received reconciliation through Christ" (Rom 5:11). "There is therefore now no condemnation for those who are in Christ Jesus" (Rom 8:1). Holiness is really possible. Now, the community can really be, in one of Paul's most loved images, the "body of Christ."

Still, the pattern of this world is passing away; it has not yet passed away (1 Cor 7:31). Christ will return (Phil 4:5), but he has not yet done so. The night may be far gone, but the day, though at hand, is not yet here (Rom 13:12). The Corinthians, Paul says, should still pray "our Lord, come!" (1 Cor 16:22), for he has not yet returned to release the full creation from its groaning (Rom 8:18–25). God will "have mercy upon all," but this final redemption has not yet occurred (Rom 11:32).

For Paul the Christian community thus embodies the tension at the "ends of the ages" (1 Cor 10:11). Its existence is fully marked by the time between the promising beginning of new creation and the wait for its consummation.

Trying to help the readers of Paul's letters understand what sort of literature they had on their hands, John Locke once wrote that Paul "was, as 'tis visible, a Man of quick Thought, warm Temper, mighty well vers'd in the Writings of the Old Testament, and full of the Doctrine of the New: All this put together, suggested Matter to him in abundance on those Subjects which came his way: So that one may consider him when he was writing, as beset with a Crowd of Thoughts, all striving for Utterance. In this Posture of Mind it was almost impossible for him to keep that slow Pace, and observe minutely that Order and Method of ranging all he said, from which results an easie and obvious Perspicuity."[41] Postmodern anxieties about divining an author's state of mind notwithstanding, it would be hard to improve on such a statement.

The whirring, buzzing, palpable passion of Paul's letters that Locke speaks of evidences a man possessed by a great and joyful truth and at considerable pains to communicate its impact on virtually every dimension of human life that comes to his mind. Of course Paul himself would give the truth that has possessed him a particular human name: Jesus. And that, most simply, is what his letters are: witnesses to the way in which God's revelation in the Messiah

Jesus should and do shape human life—both now and for the future in which God shall complete the work begun "in the fullness of time."

Paul is, however, hardly an optimist. Indeed, in his view our natural capacities to seek God and do the good—or to quench our thirst for truth and beauty—inevitably lead us away from that which we seek. Sin overpowers us, enslaves us, and makes us sick unto death. And no amount of spiritual exercise or striving against our illness can make us well. Recovery and repair come to us from the outside, from God's side of the human predicament. Paul's letters, therefore, are not lessons in self-cultivation or community organizing or social criticism or any such things in themselves. They are rather more like passionate summonses to receive and undergo the disciplines of the free life that only God can grant. Faith, not available knowledge of the immanent world, is the gift—and, subsequently, the virtue—that imparts true vision (Gal 3:15). And church is the name for faith's "meantime," reparative pattern of life in the world.

5

St. Luke

Inasmuch as many have undertaken to write a narrative
about the things that have been fulfilled among us, it also
seemed good to me to write an orderly account.
—*Luke 1:1–4*

As a living personality within the pages of the New Testament, Luke pales in comparison with Paul. In terms of influence, however, he compares to Paul as sun does to sun. To have written one of the four canonical Gospels is to have penned one of the most influential texts in the past two millennia of human existence. To have written the first and only canonical story of the church's birth and earliest growth—the Acts of the Apostles—is to have furnished the most basic linear shape of our knowledge of crucial first years of the church.[1] It is, further, to have offered the anecdotes and images that fund much of our subsequent imagination about the earliest period. Raphael's work of Paul on Mars Hill in Athens or in prison, Rembrandt's alarming rendering of the stoning of Stephen, Caravaggio's splendid depiction of the blinded Paul—and virtually countless other works of art, sculpture, literature, and so on—draw their inspiration from Acts. To a startling degree, all such inspiration depends upon Luke.

WORKS

In contrast to Paul's letters, for not one of the four canonical Gospels is authorship claimed by the person to whom they are attributed. Such self-effacing biography was of course part of the point: the Gospels are about the life of another man, Jesus of Nazareth.[2] Yet, from the earliest surviving manuscript on, the Gospel of Luke has never been attributed to anyone other than "Luke."[3]

If, as ancient tradition holds, this is the same Luke who was St. Paul's onetime companion, then what can be known of his biography is relatively slim. He was born a Gentile and, at some point, became intimately familiar with the Greek translation of Jewish Scripture. When his induction into the Christian way of life took place is not known, but in the little letter to the Christian man Philemon, St. Paul calls Luke his "co-worker," and in the second letter to Timothy, Luke is Paul's "sole companion" (Phlm 24; 2 Tim 4:11). And indeed, there are portions of the later story in Acts in which the author seems to include himself with Paul in the travels around the Mediterranean.[4] But beyond the events described in these passages, there is little that can be said about Luke's life.

It is true that the letter to the Colossians speaks of Luke as a "beloved physician" (Col 4:14). Two other sources from about the end of the second century also refer to him as a physician.[5] Yet there is no distinctively medical vocabulary in either Luke or Acts, and the technical gap between the physician and nonphysician in the ancient world was not the enormous gulf it is today.[6] There is thus relatively little that can be made from Luke's role as a practitioner of medicine. He was, however, a writer.

His two surviving works are both addressed to the same man, Theophilus, "lover of God."[7] In these addresses, Luke makes clear his literary aim: by means of a carefully arranged narrative, Luke will establish the solidity or foundation—or, as some English translations have it, the truth—of the things into which Theophilus has been catechized (Luke 1:1–4; cf. Acts 1:1). Luke's works are thus stories about Jesus and about the early church that seek to instruct Christians in the truth that they claim to live.

While it is true that some type of narrative underlies all meaningful statements—or at least our ability to perceive them as meaningful—it is nevertheless the case that a discursive presentation of a story requires some extraction and resetting of its main themes.[8] Comparison and/or juxtaposition of the kind I intend, that is, coincides exactly with the way in which one must talk intelligently about narratives in the first place. This chapter will thus cover five themes that emerge from the Gospel of Luke and Acts and best befit our larger task. We begin where Luke himself does, with the story of Israel.

ISRAEL

All of the Gospels begin their stories in different places vis-à-vis the life of Jesus of Nazareth: Matthew with Jesus' lineage, Mark with Jesus already an adult, John before even creation. Luke begins a few months before Jesus is conceived, and the focus of the story is upon his relatives—Elizabeth and Zechariah, the parents of John the Baptist.

What is perhaps most striking about the opening of the story is the vast amount of detail that is best described simply as "Jewish." Readers unfamiliar with Israel's history are drawn immediately—indeed, without narrative warning—deep into the specifics of Jewish religious life. Luke chronologically marks the ensuing events by Herod the Great, the king of Judea, and then formally begins his story with the Jewish priest Zechariah and his wife, Elizabeth. Zechariah, the reader is told, is from the division of Abijah—a name unrecognizable to all but the most scripturally conscious Jewish readers—and Elizabeth from the line of Aaron. Zechariah is serving at the temple in Jerusalem and is providentially (or, in a more modern way of thinking, randomly) chosen by lot to enter the temple and offer incense.

From there the story moves inside the temple itself, to the right side of the altar of incense, and to a named messenger from God, Gabriel. It is Gabriel who speaks for Luke: the history of Israel will move forward anew and afresh in the womb of Elizabeth. "Your son," the troubled and fearful Zechariah hears, "will be filled with the Holy Spirit, even from his mother's womb. And he will turn many of the sons of Israel to the Lord their God, and he will go before him in the spirit and power of Elijah, to turn the hearts of the fathers to the children, and the disobedient to the wisdom of the just, to make ready for the Lord a people prepared" (Luke 1:15–17). And conceive Elizabeth does.

Gabriel's next appearance is what Christians later called the Annunciation, a scene artistically rendered time and again world over. "Gabriel was sent from God to a city of Galilee named Nazareth, to a virgin espoused to a man whose name was Joseph, of the house of David; and the virgin's name was Mary" (Luke 1:26–27).

The announcement that the virgin is to bear a remarkable son is accompanied not so much by acclamations of general greatness as by a series of promises that are specifically tied to the royal history of Israel: Jesus, says Gabriel, will be called "the Son of the Most High, and the Lord God will give to him the throne of his father David, and he will reign over the house of Jacob forever, and of his kingdom there will be no end" (Luke 1:32–33). As Mary then says in the Magnificat, God "has helped his servant Israel, in remembrance of his mercy, as he spoke to our fathers, to Abraham and his posterity forever" (1:54–55). Upon regaining his speech at the birth of his son John, Zechariah the priest is even more explicit. "Blessed be the Lord God of Israel, for he has visited and redeemed his people, and raised up a horn of salvation for us in the house of his servant David, as he spoke by the mouth of his holy prophets from of old, that we should be saved from our enemies, and from the hand of all who hate us; to perform the mercy promised to our fathers, and to remember his holy covenant, the oath which he swore to our father Abraham, to grant us that we, being delivered from the hand of our enemies, might serve him fearlessly and in holiness and righteousness before him all the days of our life" (Luke 1:68–75).

And when the infant Jesus is presented in the Jerusalem temple, the old prophet Simeon exclaims to God, "my eyes have seen your salvation which you have prepared in the presence of all the people, a light for a revelation to the Gentiles and glory for your people Israel!" (Luke 2:30–32).

In addition to these explicit statements, the entirety of the birth/infancy story is written in a diction almost identical to that of the (Greek) Old Testament, and there are echoes of the Old Testament in virtually every line. As Nils Dahl once put it, Luke composes the "continuation of biblical history."[9] Moreover, when the curtain on Jesus' youth comes to a close, he is in the Jerusalem temple itself, instructing the doctors in the things of God (Luke 2:41–52). Not only does this show the theological locus from which Jesus' authority comes, it also brackets the infancy narrative itself with scenes in the temple: for Luke, the movement of God in the coming of Jesus is the "fulfillment" of what God began in the election of Israel (cf. 1:1). Luke's narrative echoes the theological foretelling of the prophet Malachi about the "day of the Lord." On that day, says Malachi, "the Lord will come suddenly into his temple" (Mal 3:1). And, indeed, that is exactly where the Lord is found.[10]

But, an astute reader of Luke might say, doesn't the continuation of biblical history in the fulfillment of God's promises to David end in rather mixed results? Throughout the story, Jews of various types seem not to understand Jesus as the continuation of God's gracious dealings with Israel and instead say rather more accusing things: "He casts out demons by Beelzebul, the prince of demons," for example (Luke 11:15). To be sure, Jesus has a ready reply, as he always does, but such parrying does little to convince those who cannot see what Luke claims is there. He is rejected by his home crowd (and nearly killed), "tested" again and again, plotted against, and ultimately crucified. In short, the people of Israel itself seem to be divided over the truth of Jesus' identity.

Yes, but this, too, Luke would reply, is part of the way in which Israel's story is carried on. As Simeon prophesies, Jesus is set for the "fall and rising of many in Israel, and for a sign that is spoken against" (Luke 1:34; cf. 11:16–17). Even Jesus himself knows this: "The Son of Man," he says of himself, "must be rejected by the elders and chief priests and scribes, and be killed" (Luke 9:22, etc.).

And as before the resurrection, so after it: all the way through my second volume, Luke could say, you will see a division among the Jews who encounter the messengers of Jesus. Some accept—indeed, there are large-scale conversions, even of priests (Acts 6:7)—and some do not. In particular, Paul's success among both Gentiles and Jews is mixed.

Paul? Does not Paul, Luke's reader could object, explicitly say that God is finished with the Jews, that he has moved on to the Gentiles—that those who were once "chosen" are no longer so? Paul, such a reader might argue, is hardly an example of the continuation of Israel's story in the mission of the early church. Listen to him with Barnabas in Pisidian Antioch, for example: "It was necessary that the word of God should be spoken first to you. Since you thrust it from you, and judge yourselves unworthy of eternal life, behold, we turn to the Gentiles" (Acts 13:46). Or when in Corinth, he says this: "Your blood be upon your heads! I am innocent. From now on I go to the Gentiles!" (Acts 18:6). And could the end of the story be any clearer? Paul says to the Jews who do not yet believe, "Let it be known to you then that this salvation of God has been sent to the Gentiles; they will listen" (Acts 28:28).

But surely, Luke might reply, any good reading of the story in Acts would attend to the wider context of these comments and the overall narrative pattern into which they fit. For in fact in each case Paul's comments are nestled within scenes that tilt their meaning in a completely different direction from what your extractions imply. And the three scenes as a whole, moreover, display a narrative pattern that is basic to the way that God has always dealt with his people—that of prophetic rebuke for the sake of repentance and life.

Looking closely both at the whole sweep of the Acts story and at the individual scenes in which Paul's seemingly harsh sayings occur does not reveal a theology of rejection. Instead, Paul acts fundamentally as an Old Testament prophet. Paul's stinging rebukes are no more against the Jews than the words of the prophet Isaiah that he uses to rebuke them in Antioch. Indeed, Paul's purpose there is to say to his brother Jews that precisely by his going to the Gentiles will Israel be a light to them (Acts 13:47). And what does he do next? He goes immediately to Iconium and enters the synagogue to preach (Acts 14:1). So, too, after his words in 18:6—harsh, yes, but not up to those from the flaming heart of Jeremiah or the thundering voice of Amos—where does he go? He moves into the house *next door* to the synagogue (Acts 18:7) and goes to work on the ruler of the synagogue, Crispus, who as it turns out comes to believe "in the Lord [Jesus], together with all his household" (Acts 18:8; cf. 18:13; 1 Cor. 1:14). Then Paul, says Luke, remained in Corinth for eighteen straight months (Acts 18:11).[11] Hardly a rapid departure.

By the time readers reach the end of the story, Luke could argue, they should be able to construct the basic outline of the scene vis-à-vis Paul's interaction with other Jews: Paul preaches, some accept and some do not, he issues an Old Testament–like prophetic rebuke in the hope of bringing to repentance those who reject his teaching, and he then continues to engage with other Jews (and Gentiles, too, of course). And, lo and behold, that is what we find at the end of the story. Arriving as a prisoner in Rome, Paul declares that his imprisonment is "for the hope of Israel" (Acts 28:20) and attempts to show the consonance between Scripture and his claims about Jesus. Some "were convinced by what he said, while others did not believe him" (Acts 28:25). Paul then issues a prophetic rebuke by citing the words of Isaiah. For two more years after this initial encounter, says Luke, Paul lived in Rome at his own expense and welcomed "all who came to him" (Acts 28:30). The narrative logic of these three passages excludes the possibility that Luke conceives God's relation to "unbelieving Israel," to borrow a phrase from Paul, as one of abandonment or rejection. The relation, instead, is a kind of double call to embrace the fulfillment of the old promises in the life of Jesus: the initial proclamation of God's act in Jesus, and the subsequent prophetic rebuke of those who do not hear the first call—both with the hope of acceptance.

For Luke, the continuation of God's dealings with the Jewish people thus results in a division within Israel itself between those who see Jesus as "fulfillment" and those who do not.[12] Nothing in the story suggests that God has passed Israel by or left behind those Jews who do not see fulfillment. The narrative pattern of Acts shows rather that they continue to receive the prophetic call of their own Scriptures. Paul may well shake the dust off his feet—and then move in next door.

Of course the central point of division is Jesus. And it is to him that we thus turn.

JESUS

Luke knows what Paul and all the other earliest Christians knew: like every other human being that has ever been, Jesus was born of a woman, umbilical cord and all (Luke 1:31; 2:6–7). Indeed, of all the Gospels it is arguably Luke that places the most emphasis on Jesus' humanity. He is human in the other three Gospels, of course, but only in Luke do we read that the little child Jesus "grew and became strong, filled with wisdom" (2:40) and, later, that the older child was "obedient to [his parents]" and "increased in wisdom and years and in favor both with God and man" (2:52). In short, as all humans do to one degree or another, Jesus matured.

It was once thought that Luke's emphasis on the humanness of Jesus was due to a "Gnostic" view that threatened to erase Jesus' humanity because of an antimatter philosophy that required Jesus to have been human only in appearance.[13] The Gnostics, however, came later than Luke, and his emphasis on Jesus' humanity is more readily understood as a simple correlative of the fact that Jesus was a human being. He was born into the world as humans are and left it as humans do—upon death.

No less human, in fact, was Jesus' death than his birth. It is true that, unlike in Mark's Gospel, Jesus does not cry out in the language of forsakenness upon the cross, but this truth does nothing to lessen the reality of his suffering and crucifixion in Luke.[14] Upon facing the likely outcome of his ministry in Jerusalem, Jesus is struck by its difficulty, and falls to his knees alone and prays to God his Father, "Father, if you are willing, take this cup away from me!" While the conclusion to his prayer—"yet, not my will but your will be done"—does express profound trust in God, it also explicitly voices Jesus' rather human desire to avoid the suffering that is on the way (Luke 22:41–42). And well he might wish this. Not long after his prayer, Jesus is taken captive, and "the men who were holding him mocked him and beat him." They also blindfolded him and taunted him, "Prophesy! Who is it that struck you?" And with many other words, Luke writes, they reviled him still further (22:63–64). It was no less the case with Herod Antipas, who "disdained Jesus and, with his soldiers, ridiculed him," including dressing Jesus up as a mock "king of the Jews" before sending him back to the Roman governor Pontius Pilate for a verdict. Pilate himself may well have found Jesus innocent of any crime worthy of the death penalty (23:4, 14–25), but justice was not to prevail. Unjustly sentenced to death, Jesus was ignominiously crucified between two bona fide criminals.

We do not know the "tone" with which Jesus uttered his last words according to Luke, but their meaning is clear: "Into your hands I commend my spirit" is not the tranquil acceptance of death, but a "cry with a great voice" for vindication from God (Luke 23:46). The words are those of Psalm 31:5, and the larger context of that psalm supplies the right resonance to Jesus' words. "Be gracious to me, O Lord," Jesus says through the echoes of the psalm,

> for I am in distress; my eye wastes away from grief, my soul and body also . . . my strength fails because of my misery, and my bones waste away. I am the scorn of all my adversaries. . . . I have passed out of mind like one who is dead; I have become like a broken vessel. For I hear the whispering of many . . . as they scheme together against me, as they plot to take my life. But I trust in you, O Lord; I say, "You are my God." My times are in your hand; deliver me from the hand of my enemies and persecutors. Let your face shine upon your servant; save me in your steadfast love. Do not let me be put to shame, O Lord, for I call on you. . . . Let the lying lips be stilled that speak

insolently against the righteous with pride and contempt. . . . Blessed be the Lord for he has wondrously shown his steadfast love to me when I was beset as a city under siege. I said in my alarm, "I am cut off from your sight." But you heard my supplications when I cried out to you for help. (Ps 31)

Heard in concert with the Old Testament prayer it evokes, "Into your hands" turns out to be Luke's way of expressing Jesus' final cry to God for ultimate vindication.[15] As the centurion recognizes, the one being crucified is innocent and therefore has a just claim for vindication (Luke 23:47). Yet die he does. Joseph from Arimathea "went to Pilate and asked for the body of Jesus. Then Joseph took the body down and wrapped it in a linen shroud, and laid him in a rock-hewn tomb, where no one had ever yet been laid" (Luke 23:52–53).

Whatever else Luke says about Jesus, he says clearly that the man from Galilee was a human being. The parentheses of all human life are inerasably his, too: Jesus of Nazareth, born of a woman and dead in the grave.

And yet. No reader of Luke's two volumes could suffer the illusion that Jesus is a human being in exactly the same way that all others are. Where other ancient biographers wrote the lives of illustrious men, Luke was clearly out to say more than that. But how? someone might ask. How can a human being be entirely human and yet something that others are not?

Luke's answer would begin at the exact place where Jesus shares his humanity with other humans: his existence in his mother's womb. For it is just there that the difference becomes apparent.

You shall bear a son, says Gabriel to the unwed Virgin. Her response to this news is the only reasonable one: "How can this be, since I have not known a man?" Unlike ancient Pompeii's murals or more contemporary cultural productions, the Bible as a whole does not dwell on the basics of reproduction. It simply assumes them. No one needs to be told, Luke might say, that the shock of Gabriel's announcement occurs against the background of the physiological necessities for human life.

The answer to Mary's question is simple, if also startling. "The Holy Spirit will overshadow you." With "Holy Spirit" Luke speaks of God in the dynamic way of the Jews. For Jewish tradition, as for Luke, God was alive—"the living God," as Scripture said again and again—and such life meant for them that God could never be understood as a monad or an analogy to any of the philosophical accounts of "God" as the top Being in a variously tiered universe. God was, rather, a self-relational God, one whose internal life required the Jews to speak with a more subtle theological grammar: to talk of the Living God was to talk not just of his being God but of his Word and Spirit and Wisdom and Presence.[16]

Does not such dynamic language threaten the oneness of God, risk compromising God's uniqueness through the suggestion of other modes of being? Not at all, Luke would reply. As Jesus himself says in my narrative of his life, "God is one" (Luke 18:19) and this one God is the only God there is (cf. 5:21).[17] The point is simply that to understand the oneness and uniqueness of the Jewish God is to understand that (a) there is distinction within God, and (b) such distinction requires the very specific language of the Holy Spirit. In fact, in my follow-up story about the rise of the church, the Holy Spirit is the principal character by which God himself moves in the church.[18] To speak of God's Holy Spirit is to speak of God himself. It is God, therefore, who overshadows the Virgin and whose act results in the human Jesus. This overshadowing, Luke could continue, is finally why I can refer to Jesus himself as "the Lord."

And, indeed, the first time the human Jesus enters the narrative, it is in the womb of his mother—and it is there that Luke first employs what will become his most noteworthy way of referring to Jesus: the Lord.[19] "How can this be," says an inspired but also astonished Elizabeth to Mary, "that the mother of my Lord comes to me?" (Luke 1:43). Where modern New Testament scholars have routinely believed that Jesus was acclaimed Lord only after his death and resurrection, Luke makes clear that he was Lord from the moment of his existence. Jesus' identity is inseparably bound to his emergence in the world as the Lord. To be Jesus, Luke's story line says, is to be the Lord.

Yet what is it to be the Lord? Were there not countless "lords"? Rulers, gods, heroes, local dignitaries, and the like could all be styled "Lord," could they not? Moreover, even Israel's God himself was called "the Lord"? How are we to understand Jesus as the Lord?

Consider the flow of my narrative, Luke could begin. The term *Lord* (*kyrios*) occurs more than twenty times before its use for Jesus in the womb. In each case it refers to the God of Israel. "The commandments and ordinances of the Lord" (Luke 1:6), the "temple of the Lord" (1:9), the "angel of the Lord" (1:11), and so on. Readers' expectations are thus shaped to understand "the Lord" as God. But the sudden introduction of Jesus into the story as *kyrios* complicates these expectations by creating a dual referent for the one word. After "the mother of my Lord" (1:43), the reader hears not one but two possibilities: Jesus and God. Moreover, the sense of a dual possibility is immediately heightened as the story progresses. In only the second sentence after Elizabeth's acclamation of Jesus as Lord, she speaks of God as the Lord: "And blessed is she," says Elizabeth of Mary, "who believed that there would be a fulfillment of what had been spoken to her by the Lord" (1:45). Mary, too, in the very next phrase says her soul rejoices in "the Lord" and her spirit in God her Savior (1:46).

In fact, each occurrence of *Lord* after Luke 1:43 refers again to God—until 2:11, where the angels announce to the shepherds that the baby born in Bethlehem is not only Christ and Savior but also Lord. "For you there was born today in the city of David a Savior, who is Christ, the Lord" (2:11). This is the second and last time Jesus is called *kyrios* in the story of his birth and youth, and it activates the memory of 1:43, simultaneously highlighting both verses. From 2:11, the story moves to God yet again, and until the close of the period of Jesus' youth, it is God who is directly named Lord.

The overall pattern of the story about Jesus' conception and birth is thus one in which the reader is tutored to hear in *kyrios* a resonance that encompasses both God and Jesus in the one word. Luke situates Jesus' identity as Lord, that is, within an overall narrative line that says he bears the same acclamation as the God of Israel.

But surely, a modern critic might say to Luke, readers can discriminate between the two *kyrioi* in the opening of your story? Did you really write this ambiguity into the story, cleverly suggesting an association of Jesus and God through the resonance of this word?

The very first scene after the shift in time from Jesus' youth to his adulthood begins to answer the critic's question. John the Baptist erupts into Jewish history at the river Jordan, proclaiming the words from the Old Testament book of Isaiah. "The voice of the one crying in the wilderness: Prepare the way of the Lord! Make his paths straight! Every valley shall be filled, and every mountain and hill shall be brought low. And the crooked shall be made straight, and the rough ways shall be made smooth. And all flesh shall see the salvation of God!" (Luke 3:4–6; Isa 40:3–5). Now, Luke might say, who is the Lord in John's announcement?

On the one hand, the *kyrios* John speaks of is the one of whom the prophet Isaiah speaks—the God of Israel. In Isaiah, as elsewhere in the Old Testament, the Lord is God. On the other hand, however, the order of Luke's narrative makes clear that the Lord of whom John speaks is Jesus. As New Testament scholars have long seen, the opening chapters of the Gospel of Luke work with a John-then-Jesus pattern: John's birth announcement, then Jesus'; John's birth, circumcision, and appearance, then Jesus'.[20] Literarily, this pattern's point is that John prepares for Jesus. In Luke 3:4–6 the text of Isaiah is thus used to articulate John's preparatory role for the coming of Jesus. John is the voice of the one preparing the way of the Lord Jesus. The Lord in Luke 3:4 is, in short, both God and Jesus at the same time.[21] The one who comes in the name of the Lord is God in the life of Jesus the Lord. What it is for Jesus to be the Lord according to Luke, therefore, is for him to share an identity with the God of Israel. Read all the way through Acts, Luke might say, and the accumulation of nearly two hundred uses of the word *kyrios* would point ineluctably to this same conclusion. Precisely because Jesus shares in God's identity as Lord can he be said to be, as Peter puts it to the centurion Cornelius, the Lord of all (Acts 10:36). For Luke, to express Jesus' identity literarily is to narrate it as a complex both/and: Jesus is both the human being he obviously was and simultaneously the human exposition of Israel's God.

But what about Jesus as Israel's Messiah? Isn't that the most important claim of your story? It is doubtless true, Luke would say, that Jesus was Israel's Christ. From the moment of Gabriel's announcement, Jesus is said to be David's heir. Other angels, too, speak of Jesus as the Christ (Luke 2:11). Even those who mock Jesus on the cross get it right, though of course the truth they speak is ironic and unintended (23:35–43). Yet when it comes to the titles that Jesus bears, it is important to think well about how he wears them.

Modern scholars have made much of this same point. It is philosophically somewhat backward, they have realized, to reconstruct the meaning of a title such as Messiah and then apply that meaning to Jesus. The meaning of the titles in Luke and Acts, rather, will be determined by the figure of Jesus in the story.[22] It is he that gives them their most significant shape.

This is particularly important to remember for the title Christ, for in fact nowhere before Jesus is there any indication that the Messiah was expected to be denounced by the leaders of the Jewish people and subsequently killed by pagan decree. Luke himself articulates the novelty of this notion through the mouth of Cleopas and his companion on the road to Emmaus. The two are returning home after Jesus' death at Passover and meet a stranger along the road.[23] In response to his question about the cause of their obvious dejection, they say, "We had hoped that he was the one to redeem Israel" (Luke 24:21; cf. Acts 1:6). The implication could hardly be more apparent: their messianic hope went unfulfilled. The rest of the Gospel, together with Acts, then develops the transformation in the meaning of Messiah to include suffering and death. In the final scenes of the Gospel, for example, an exegetical lesson is given by no less than Jesus himself. And what did he teach? "O foolish men, and slow of heart to believe all that the prophets have spoken. Was it not necessary that the Messiah should suffer these things and enter into his glory? And beginning with Moses and all the prophets, he interpreted to them in all the Scriptures the things concerning himself" (Luke 24:25–27). The idea of a suffering and dying Messiah is unexpected enough to require a lesson by the Messiah himself.

Modern scholars who have worried over the fact that there are no passages in the Old Testament that directly say that the coming Messiah will suffer and die have missed Luke's theological style from the outset.[24] Luke's reading of the Old Testament is anything but wooden, and the way in which messianic prefiguration works for him hinges not on simplistic one-for-one textual proofs but on something much more dramatically outside the frame of human possibility: Jesus' resurrection.[25]

For Luke, as for all other early Christians—as well as the mockers at the crucifixion—Jesus' death did in fact complicate, even threaten, the truth of his messianic identity. Had Jesus lain in the grave until he rotted away, there would be no need to discern the correspondence between his life and the Old Testament. The cross would have been the end of any messianic identity and, simultaneously, the hopes of his disciples. Yet precisely because God raised him from the dead, it was no less than God himself who confirmed Jesus as the Messiah. The suffering Jesus was vindicated by an act that overturned the observable end of the messianic claims about him. And, therefore, Luke's hermeneutical reasoning ran, because God confirmed Jesus as the Messiah, the Scriptures that were fulfilled in him spoke about him. "God has confirmed the crucified Jesus," Peter preaches, "as both Lord and Christ" (Acts 2:36; cf. Luke 2:11).[26] As Paul tells King Agrippa II, "I say nothing but what the prophets and Moses said would happen: that the Christ is one who suffers and that as the firstborn of the dead he proclaims light to Israel and to the Gentiles" (Acts 26:22–23).

Jesus is thus unquestionably the Jewish Messiah in Luke's writings, the "Coming One" who was to deliver his people (Luke 7:18–30; 19:38; cf. 13:35; 3:16). But in the light of the course of his life, such deliverance was shifted from its typically more mundane sense of temporal political hope to the effect of the resurrection (see also "community" below). Yes, Jesus is the Christ, Luke would say, but precisely in this identity transforms the meaning of the word *Messiah* to fit the particularity of his life, death, and resurrection.[27]

Contemporary students of Luke's Christology have often been much concerned not only with titles but also with categorizing Luke's view of Jesus as either "high" (more toward God) or "low" (more toward a human being). Luke, however, did not work with opposing categories of this kind, and the fact that the human Jesus shares an identity with God as Lord already suggests their interpretative insufficiency. Where New Testament scholars in the nineteenth and twentieth centuries would see opposing poles—humanity and divinity—Luke instead sees only one thing: the Lord himself in the human life of the Messiah, Jesus of Nazareth.

But Luke also calls him Son, does he not? any observant reader might ask. How, then, should we understand the term *Father*? Who, that is to say, is really God in Luke and Acts?

GOD

The word *God* (*theos*) occurs nearly three hundred times in Luke and Acts. With good reason, therefore, Luke's two volumes have been called "theocentric."[28] Such a description, however, does not by itself do the work of clarification. After all, one might as easily say that the Gospel obviously "centers" upon Jesus and Acts upon the community that takes his name. Still, it is true that Luke's two narratives display the conviction that God is ultimately the one who is at work in the life of Jesus and the nascent church. It is God, so Luke would say, whose plan guides the hope of the world (see Luke 7:30; Acts 4:28). All that comes to pass in the history of Jesus and its subsequent effects unfolds according to the will of God (see Acts 2:23; 20:27).

It is thus hardly a surprise that careful scholars of Luke's works have repeatedly conceived of his works in terms of "salvation history." History, on this view, is the medium of God's Providence. And there is something obviously correct about this reading of the Gospel and Acts: the Lukan literature itself is the most historically oriented of the New Testament writings and reveals on page after page a historically shaped literary imagination. Nowhere else, for example, do we learn the details of Roman political and legal history as a way to mark the times and places of God's salvific work in Christ and his community (see esp. Luke 2:1–2). Nowhere else are the events of both past and current Jewish history so consistently drawn as a way to show their fulfillment in the life of Jesus in a specific time and place (see esp. Luke 1:1–4). In this way Luke's choice of what sort of literature to prepare for Theophilus both constitutes and reflects his claim about the identity of God, that is, that what it means to be "God" is historically displayed both in its fulfillment of the promises made to the Jews and in relation to the wider Roman world.

Yet for Luke, to see history as theologically shaped is not at all to read it in Hegelian or Troeltschian fashion where "the Spirit" or "God" becomes what is discovered through the philosophical or religiously sensitive contemplation of history's unfolding—the meaning of the world's running divined. Nor is *God* impersonal, a Deist-like word that would ultimately function only to describe the power that set and/or keeps the world in motion. In the Lukan corpus God is instead named as Father. "Be merciful," Jesus concludes a lengthy sermon, "just as your Father is merciful" (Luke 6:36; cf. 9:26; 11:13; 12:30–32; Acts 1:7).

But Father, one might say, tells us only so much. There are all sorts of fathers. What does Father mean? First of all, a modern Luke would reply, I did not look around at human fathers and decide that they provided the best way to think about God—as if by observing human life we could see a part of it that corresponded to

"God." This, as all thinkers about religious matters ought to know, is the problem of projection. Nor does the Father-language arise from a Harnack-like conception of the universal "Fatherhood of God"—"Our Father who art in heaven" refracted amorphously off the lens of liberal Protestantism. In my two narratives, rather, God is called Father because he has a Son. It is Jesus, after all, who most clearly speaks of God as his Father.

Early in the story, for example, after discovering that Jesus was not among their group of pilgrims home from Passover, Mary and Joseph return to Jerusalem to find him. When they finally locate Jesus in the temple, he responds to Mary's worry by invoking his relationship with the Jewish God: "Didn't you know," he says, "that it's necessary for me to be about my Father's business?"[29] Given that Mary explicitly names Joseph as his father in her expression of worry—"Your father and I were anxiously looking for you"—Jesus' reply raises the question of who his father really is. The hometown crowd in Nazareth also wonders about exactly this issue: after Jesus speaks well, they ask, "Is this not Joseph's son?" (Luke 4:22).[30] His bearing, as it were, seems far to exceed his birth. Isn't Joseph his father?

Keep reading, Luke would probably say again, for in fact the story clarifies the way in which Joseph is Jesus' father—by adoption and special dispensation. Mary conceives Jesus without Joseph's help, yet it is through Joseph that Jesus is the heir of David's throne, the royal Messiah (Luke 1:27, 32; 3:23–38).

When it comes to Jesus' own language about his Father, however, he speaks not about Joseph but continues what he began in Luke 2:49. "I praise you, O Father, Lord of heaven and earth," says Jesus to God, "that you hid these things from the wise and intelligent and revealed them to babes. Yes, Father, for this was well pleasing to you. All things have been handed over to me by my Father, and no one knows who the Son is except the Father, or who the Father is except the Son and anyone to whom the Son chooses to reveal him" (Luke 10:21–22). "My Father," he later tells his disciples, "has given me a kingdom, and I give it to you" (22:29). And after his resurrection, Jesus speaks to them about what is now to come: "the Promise of my Father" (Luke 24:49; cf. Acts 1:4; 2:33).[31]

Narratively speaking, Jesus' Father-language is substantiated by no less than God himself. In what are the two most explicit statements about Jesus from the perspective of heaven, he is unambiguously declared to be "God's Son." When Jesus "had been baptized and was praying, heaven was opened, and the Holy Spirit descended upon him in bodily form like a dove, and a voice came from heaven, 'You are my Son, my Beloved One; with you I am well pleased'" (Luke 3:22; cf. 20:13). And in the Transfiguration scene, when Peter, John, and James witness Jesus' "glory" as he converses with Moses and Elijah, a cloud overshadows them—as in Exodus and elsewhere, a sign of God's presence—and "a voice came out of the cloud, saying 'This is my Son, the Chosen One; listen to him'" (Luke 9:35).[32] The Acts of the Apostles is no different. With reference to the restoration of Israel, Jesus tells the disciples that it is "not for you to know the times or seasons that the Father has fixed by his own authority" (Acts 1:7; cf. 1:4). Peter tells the listeners at Pentecost that Jesus has received and poured out the Holy Spirit, the "Promise of the Father" (Acts 2:33). And after Paul's dramatic change from persecutor to preacher, he spent "several days in Damascus with the disciples and immediately began to proclaim Jesus in the synagogues, saying, 'This one is the Son of God'" (Acts 9:19–20)—implying, of course, that God is the Father. In the Lukan corpus, then, God is the Father of the Son, who is Jesus. God's fatherhood is not separable from his relation to the Son; indeed, as the language obviously implies, the relation is mutually constitutive. Father, for Luke, means Father in a very particular way: the Father of the Son Jesus. To speak of God as Father in Luke and Acts is simultaneously to speak of Jesus as his Son.

OK, a persistent reader might ask, but this still leaves open the question of the Father's character. We can well understand that "projection" is not your way of thinking. But how, then, should we know what to think when we say "Father"?

At this point Luke's answer would probably seem needlessly redundant—"Read the story" can become as tiresome to sympathetic inquirers as the answer "Read my book" does to friendly academics who ask each other serious questions. But it would doubtless be the hermeneutically appropriate reply. Luke has not, however, left his readers without some more simple guidance.

In one of the most famous stories in any of the Gospels, Luke explicitly portrays the Father in accordance with one of Jesus' most striking phrases about God: the Most High, says Jesus early on in the Gospel, is "kind to the ungrateful and wicked" (Luke 6:35). The parable of the prodigal son shows what this means in practice.[33]

The narrative arc of the parable is as easily discerned as it is well known: a son leaves home for a foreign land, falls on hard times, and returns. Along his journey numerous details combine to paint this son's leave-taking and subsequent squandering of life in the starkest terms: his request for an early inheritance not only reveals a desire to be finished with his family but may also declare to his father that he is as good as dead to his son; his "besotted living" implies immoral fraternizing among pagans; and his willingness to tend pigs—unclean animals according to Jewish law—and even eat their food paints him as a Jew suffering the abhorrent consequences of a man gone entirely wrong; he is, as the parable later goes on to say, "dead and lost" (Luke 15:24, 32). His realization that he can return home depends most fundamentally upon an understanding of his father.[34] "When he came to himself, [the son] said, How many of my father's day laborers have more than enough bread while I perish here in famine! I will arise and go to my father, and I will say to him, 'Father, I have sinned against heaven and before you. I am no longer worthy to be called your son; treat me as one of your workers.' And he arose and came to his father. But while [the son] was yet at a distance, his father saw him and had compassion upon him, and ran and embraced him and kissed him. And the son said to him, 'Father, I have sinned against heaven and before you. I am no longer worthy to be called your son'" (Luke 15:17–21).

At this point, the father interrupts his son's speech, and the son never finishes what he planned to say. "Treat me as one of your workers" is replaced by the father's action: "But the father said to his servants, 'Bring quickly the best robe, and put it on him; and put a ring on his hand, and shoes on his feet; and bring the fatted calf and kill it, and let us eat and rejoice because this one—my son—was dead and is alive again; he was lost and is found.' And they began to make merry" (Luke 15:22–24).

Throughout the history of interpretation, New Testament exegetes have wondered whether the parable is most directly about the lost son, or the younger and older sons in contrast, or the father. But there is of course no reason to choose. Contra Adolf Jülicher, parables are by nature multivalent, and readers can inhabit different perspectives in different readings.[35] Still, in this short segment of the story, the word *father* occurs seven times, highlighting his role in the return of the son and filling out for the reader what "father" means in Luke's Gospel. The prodigal bets on the fact that his father will not turn him away. But in a surprising, almost *über*-display, the father himself dramatically exceeds the son's calculations of his goodness and enacts what in first-century terms could be seen only as extravagant kindness or love. For complete rejection, he returns kindness, even love, to the wicked.

The description of the father's kindness or love is then deepened in his response to the prodigal's older brother. Understandably irked, the older brother challenges the justice in his father's response. To his father's plea to join the celebration, the elder boy spits out his accusation: "Look here, *Dad*, I have slaved for you these many years, and I never disobeyed your command. And yet, you never gave me even so much as a kid that I might have a party with my friends! But when this son of yours—the one who squandered your life's work with whores—came home, you killed the fatted calf for him!" (Luke 15:29–30). Rather than chastising his older son for his speech or laying on the guilt that derives from ideals about sibling love, the father instead displays kindness in the face of ingratitude. "Child, you are my constant companion, and all that is mine is yours" reminds the older brother of his place with his father and his de facto wealth while simultaneously gesturing to the father's own coming death.[36] The father's estate will be for the older son without remainder. An invitation to see his brother anew and to join the rejoicing then follows the reminder: "We had to be merry and rejoice, for *this brother of yours* was dead and now lives, and he was lost and was found" (15:32). In good Lukan fashion, we are not told what the older brother actually does. But in the face of painful accusation, it is clear that the father returns kindness, even love, to the ungrateful. The parable of the prodigal son thus shows in story form what Luke takes to be the truth of God's character. The Father is this kind of Father: kind to the ungrateful and the wicked (6:35).[37]

Whether this parable is meant more to map sinners and Pharisees, or Gentiles and Jews, or waywardness and self-righteousness in more general terms is impossible to decide.[38] For in fact it is all of them in turns or at once. At each level and in every case, the Father is the one whose mercy is worked out as kindness to the wicked and ungrateful. In Luke's Gospel, this is the God whom Jesus calls Father.

As the previous section on Jesus illustrates, Luke's theological grammar becomes considerably more complex as one moves beyond his naming of God as Father. To read Luke's two volumes closely is, in fact, to see that, like Paul's, Luke's linguistic patterns include Jesus in what it means to be the God of Israel on earth in human form and the "Holy Spirit" as a mode of God's being. Acts in particular not only reads Old Testament texts that spoke of God as now speaking of Jesus,[39] it also consistently displays an overlap of God, Jesus, and the Spirit in some of the more basic features of early Christian life.

In retrospect it is no surprise that Acts portrays the Christians as engaged in a considerable amount of preaching. From Jesus himself onward, the Nazarenes preached. If, however, one asks what they preached, the answer is more subtle when it comes to God. To be sure, the early Christians proclaimed the "kingdom of God" (see Acts 8:12) and the "word of God" (see Acts 4:31). But they also preached "the name of Jesus" (see Acts 5:40) and "the word of the Lord"—where "Lord" is frequently ambiguous (Acts 8:25; 13:48–49; 15:36). When it came to faith, moreover, the Christians in Acts held that faith was in Jesus' name (3:16), the Lord (9:42), the Lord Jesus and God (16:31, 34), and Christ Jesus (24:24). Confession of creation's one Lord was made both of God, the Lord of heaven and earth (17:24), and of Jesus, the Lord of all (10:36). And salvation was predicated both of God the Savior (28:28; cf. Luke 1:47) and Jesus, for "there is no other name under heaven that has been given among humanity by which we must be saved" (Acts 4:12; cf. Luke 2:11).

Upon examining Luke's language about the Spirit, the question "whose Spirit" yields an irreducibly complex answer. As more recent scholarship has shown, in narratological terms the Holy Spirit is a "character" in Acts; the Spirit is the subject of numerous verbs, for example, and directs or leads the church, and even speaks in the first person. Says the Spirit to Peter in Joppa, "Behold three men are looking for you. Rise and go down, and accompany them without hesitation; for *I* have sent them" (Acts 10:19–20). So, too, in Syrian Antioch the Spirit begins a further step in the early Christian mission by saying, "Set apart for *me* Barnabas and Saul for the work to which *I* have called them" (13:2). And yet, the Spirit of the Lord is the Spirit both of God and of Jesus (Acts 8:39 and Acts 5:3–9; 16:7).

The complexity of the answer mirrors both volumes' depiction of the Spirit. The Spirit is both the "Power of the Most High" and the one whom the Father gives (see Luke 1:35; 11:13). The Spirit is also the one in whom Jesus rejoices when he prays to his Father, the one by whom Jesus baptizes and instructs the apostles, and the one who fills and anoints Jesus.[40]

In both Luke and Acts, God the Father, Jesus, and the Spirit are intertwined within the narrative to the degree that to separate them would be to tell a different story. Lukan narrative grammar requires, therefore, that a description of the word *God* use language about the Father, Jesus of Nazareth, and the Holy Spirit as the way the one God of Israel works his kindness and mercy in human history. "God" in Luke's sense is the one whose (hi)story the Gospel and Acts tell by speaking of the Father, Jesus, and the Holy Spirit.

But, Luke, if the meaning of "God" is tied to that specific history and those specific names, how can you expect non-Jews to know of God? Well that, Luke could say, is a question about the relation of God to human beings more generally, and to understand this we must consider the human condition.

HUMAN BEINGS

If Luke thinks humanity has an essence, he never hints at what it might be. If he thinks human beings are best understood within a wider physiological account of living things, he never says so. If he thinks humans basically develop the same way in every culture or different ways in different cultures, he does not tell us. Instead, he presents the human being as something entangled in (hi)story.[41] To understand humanity in the Lukan writings is thus to see its "caught-up-ness" in the history of God's dealing with the world through Jesus of Nazareth.

Despite the considerable variety in the portrayal of individual characters in the stories, there are fundamentally two ways in which all individual lives are determined by their participation in the larger human drama. The first is the need for a turn or return to God—that is, the history of sin—and the second is the manner by which such a (re)turn happens and its subsequent effects.

In Luke's Gospel Jesus straightforwardly says, "Those who are well have no need of a physician, but those who are sick. I came not to call the righteous but sinners to repentance" (Luke 5:32; cf. Matt. 9:13; Mark 2:17). Jesus' statement, of course, is his response to a recurrent accusation: "This man," say the Pharisees and scribes again and again throughout Jesus' ministry, "eats and drinks with tax collectors and sinners" (Luke 5:30; 7:34; 15:2 et passim). Such language shows the obvious fact that sin is a problem at which Jesus aims. "Your sins are forgiven," he declares to the paralytic whose friends lowered him through the roof to be near Jesus (5:20).[42] "Your sins are forgiven," he says again, this time to the woman who was publicly known as a "sinner" in her town (7:37, 48). "Which one of you," Jesus begins a parable, "having one hundred sheep, if he has lost one of them, does not leave the ninety-nine in the wilderness, and go after that one that is lost until he finds it? And when he has found it, he lays it on his shoulders, rejoicing. And when he comes home, he calls together his friends and his neighbors, saying to them 'Rejoice with me, for I have found my sheep that was lost.' Just so, I tell you, there will be more joy in heaven over one sinner who repents than over ninety-nine righteous persons who need no repentance" (Luke 15:3–7; cf. 15:10).

And in Acts it is no less clear, as Peter and the apostles say, that Jesus' life, death, and resurrection were "to give repentance to Israel and the forgiveness of sins" (Acts 5:31). Paul, too, declares in Pisidian Antioch that "through this man forgiveness of sins is proclaimed to you" (13:38). And Jesus himself—in Paul's retelling, of course—instructs Paul to go to the Gentiles so that "they may receive forgiveness of sins" (26:18).

Yes, but what is sin in the first place? What, a reader might wonder, are these people forgiven *for*? Furthermore, you speak of those who are "righteous" and "have no need for repentance." Elizabeth and Zechariah, you write, are not only "righteous" but "blameless" (Luke 1:6). Does this mean that Jesus is the "Savior" only for some, that there are those who have no need of the forgiveness he effects?

Luke's language about sin is less easily systematized than Paul's, but Luke's works nevertheless display a similar understanding of the human problem of sin. As one should by now expect, however, his answer to these questions would be couched much more in terms of the unfolding of redemptive history than in Pauline-like dialectical argument.

Sin, Luke might thus begin, is difficult to define in any abstract way.[43] It is, rather, something that is exhibited in concrete acts and over the course of history.[44] It is a sin, for example, to stone Stephen to death. "Lord," cries the dying Stephen, "do not hold this sin against them" (Acts 7:60). And Paul, according to his recounting of Ananias's words, sinned in persecuting the fledgling church (Acts 22:16, with possible wider reference as well). But sin is also—to use a central biblical metaphor—the accumulation of debt that only God can forgive.[45] "A certain creditor had two debtors," Jesus says to Simon the Pharisee, "and one owed five hundred denarii and the other fifty. When they could not pay, he remitted the debts of both. Now which one of them will love him more?" (Luke 7:41–42).[46] Indeed, to speak of the forgiveness of sins is often to speak of the cancelation of debts (see Luke 13:1–5). So, too, sin shows itself as ignorance not only in pagan idolatry (Acts 17:23, 30) but also in the particularity of Jesus' death: "Brothers," says Peter to his Jewish audience under Solomon's portico, "I know you acted in ignorance, as did also your rulers. . . . Repent and return [to God] that your sins may be blotted out" (Acts 3:17–19).

Yet sin is also historical for Luke in a much more comprehensive sense: it characterizes the age into which Jesus comes—"this wicked generation" (Luke 11:29)—and is manifested in relation to him especially and in particular. When Luke writes that "both Herod and Pontius Pilate, with the Gentiles and the peoples of Israel," gathered against Jesus, he indicates that the reach of the human problem is made explicit in the death of Jesus; humanity's predicament includes everyone, Jew and Gentile alike.[47] Indeed, the best way to understand the apparent tension between Luke's statements that all human beings need to repent and his language about the "righteous" or Elizabeth and Zechariah is to see it in terms of the difference Jesus himself makes in and for the history of sin. In Luke's view, the righteousness and blamelessness before the Torah of any particular person neither negates nor repairs the basic human predicament. Blamelessness before the Torah is simply living in light of the ways in which the Law itself makes it possible to atone for sin.[48] It is undeniably good, Luke might say, that Jews such as Elizabeth can live in faithful obedience to the covenant God made with them. It would be a mistake, however, to assume that covenant maintenance is the same thing as the repair of the human condition. The burden of Luke's stories is that only in relation to Jesus do we see this latter thing become possible on the stage of human history. Jesus himself effects a change in the history of human sin.

In sharp contrast to Matthew's use of an Abrahamic genealogy to begin his Gospel—he starts with Abraham and works forward in time to Jesus—Luke begins with Jesus himself and works back in time to Abraham and then beyond him to Adam. "Jesus was about thirty years old when he began his work, being the son (as was supposed) of Joseph, the son of Heli, the son of Matthat, the son of Levi . . . the son of David . . . the son of Jacob, the son of Isaac, the son of

Abraham . . . the son of Enos . . . the son of Seth, the son of Adam, the son of God" (Luke 3:23–38). In naming the other pole of the genealogy "Adam, the son of God," rather than Abraham, Luke implies that Jesus is the one who carries forward the history of Adam. Immediately before the genealogy, Jesus, too, is named "the Son of God" at his baptism, and thus it is that one Son of God mirrors the other.[49] Jesus is Adam redux.

Lest a reader wonder whether such a theologically charged connection is to be made, Luke eliminates all room for doubt by moving directly from Adam to the scene of Jesus' temptation. "If you are the Son of God," the Devil tempts (Luke 4:3, 9), if you are the son of Adam, then go the way of Adam—and sin.[50] Three times the Devil tempts, and three times Jesus parries the temptations. The son of Adam repeats his father's history of temptation, but this time God's son does not sin. Humanity, it is implied, is given a new beginning in the second son of God.

Whether or not Luke had read any of Paul's letter to the Romans—most modern New Testament scholars think he had not—the substantive similarity between Paul's argument in Romans 5:12–21 and Luke's narrative portrayal of Jesus as the son of Adam is striking. For Luke, no less than for Paul, the figure of Adam is used to reflect on the history of sin in light of the advent of Jesus Christ. For Luke, no less than for Paul, Adam was a type of the one to come in the sense that both Adam and Jesus determined the human condition vis-à-vis sin. And for Luke, no less than for Paul, Jesus altered the conditions by which God deals with human sin. To be sure, there are differences between Paul and Luke, but they are primarily in form rather than content: where Paul spoke directly of the new creation begun by the son of God, Luke told its story.[51]

But Jesus gets killed, does he not? What does his death have to say about humanity? Would sin not here have the final word?

It would indeed, Luke would have to acknowledge, were death to be the end. The new beginning that the second son of God inaugurated by his resistance to the Tempter would have met its end. But precisely because Jesus' death was not his end, Luke would continue, there is more yet to say about the human being.

In contrast to Seneca's or Paul's letters, for example, the Lukan works do not contain a prolonged discussion of death as the terminus of the human—both its being and its projects. Luke takes it for granted, however, when he portrays the two dejected disciples on the road to Emmaus (Luke 24:12–35). Of course the irony in the scene could hardly be thicker—that the disciples tell Jesus about Jesus is only the tip of the iceberg—but its entire effectiveness depends upon the "natural knowledge" that death spells the end of human striving and hopes.

Given their assumption about Jesus' death, Cleopas and his companion are rightly downcast (24:17).

In fact, such a view of death is the presupposition of the central Lukan kerygma, namely, that God has raised Jesus from the dead (see Acts 3:15; 4:2, 10; 10:41; 13:30, 34; 17:3). The "pangs of death could not hold him" (Acts 2:24), says Peter, nor did "his flesh see corruption" (Acts 2:31).

Though Luke knows a central consequence of Jesus' bodily resurrection for the human being is the hope of the same kind of resurrection (see Acts 17:31; 23:6; 24:15, 21; 26:23; cf. "eternal life" in Luke 10:25; 18:18, 30; Acts 13:46, 48), his emphasis lies elsewhere.[52] For Luke, the impact of Jesus' resurrection is primarily focused on the present. By virtue of his resurrection, says Paul, "light" was proclaimed to both Israel and the Gentiles (Acts 26:23). By "light" Luke does not mean to point only to a change in perception or intellectual vision, as if apprehension alone were the telos of Jesus' resurrection. Rather, as the sweep of the Acts narrative shows, he principally means that human beings have a shot at repair, that their lives can incarnate forgiveness or the release from sins. The promise, Peter preaches to his fellow Jews, is "for you, for your children, and for all that are far off—everyone whom the Lord God calls to him" (Acts 2:39). Therefore, "turn from your wickedness" (Acts 3:26) and "receive forgiveness in his name" (Acts 10:43; cf. 17:30).

In the Lukan view of things, *metanoia* (repentance) is not simply a sequence of sorrow, confession, and pardon. The *metanoia* kind of turning is instead a more fundamental change in the lived structure of human existence that moves us from the patterns of waywardness and ignorance into patterns of release and repair. It is, in short, a "repentance unto life," as the apostles realize from Peter's testimony (Acts 11:18). Through the obedience and resurrection of God's Son, humanity—both Jews and Greeks, Paul tells the Ephesian elders (20:21)—is given the possibility of life. When it comes to the human being Luke's theology of new creation is simultaneously a theology of repentance.

But what does such a change look like? I can well understand, a reader might want to say, that you think of the human being in relation to its situation within history and its possibility for a turn to life. But what is the human being once it has made this turn?

Luke's reply could doubtless point to particular instructions for individual relationships. Jesus teaches, after all, that repentance in any given case can be a recurrent thing and that, as such, it provides the chance for repeated forgiveness (Luke 17:3–4). But, more basically, Luke would once again challenge the modern notion that anthropology is best conceived vis-à-vis the individual and argue instead that repentance unto life is best understood when we think of church.

CHURCH AND SOCIETY

Critics of various types have often expressed disappointment about the transition from Jesus to early Christianity. Jesus of Nazareth came proclaiming the Kingdom of God, they say, and we got the church instead.[53] Luke, on the other hand, would put it rather differently: Jesus came proclaiming release to the captives, and the church is the place where the captives are released. For Luke, Christian community is the necessary consequence of the total event that was Jesus' life, death, and resurrection. The book of Acts follows the Gospel of Luke not only as a matter of literary order but also as a material theological necessity. Of all the New Testament writers, Luke is the one who most explicitly conceived ecclesiology as internal to the way we should understand the life of Jesus.[54]

Precisely for this reason, however, discerning the Lukan view of the church is deceptively difficult. Ecclesiology cannot be disentangled from Christology or anthropology, for example. Church, for Luke, is what it is to be publicly caught up with one's being in the life of Jesus of Nazareth. Ecclesiology as it is displayed in Acts thus turns out to be less about this or that defining aspect of Christian community than it is about the whole thing: the visible human witness to the Lord Jesus Christ in a world that did not know him.

Displaying "the whole thing" that is Christian community according to Acts is obviously impossible. Still, something of its distinctive profile can be seen by situating Acts' political vision within the wider Roman world. This will allow us to focus on the features of the profile that most directly exhibit Luke's animating ecclesiological judgments. There are three such features.

First, Luke depicts the formation of Christian community around the Mediterranean basin as a culturally destabilizing force. No sooner have the apostles regrouped in Jerusalem and begun to tell about the resurrected Jesus than they are arrested in the temple (Acts 4:1–3). Not much later, the apostles are again imprisoned by the Jerusalem leadership and, after a miraculous jailbreak, subsequently forced to appear before the Sanhedrin and give account (Acts 5:17–42). The high priest himself levels the accusation: "We strictly charged you not to teach in this name, yet here you have filled Jerusalem with your teaching and you intend to bring this man's blood upon us" (Acts 5:28).

Modern readers have found this charge puzzling, but in fact it is rather clear. As Gamaliel's subsequent comparison with the brief movements started by Theudas and Judas the Galilean shows, the high priest's worry about blood is politically sensible (Acts 5:33–39).[55] Both Theudas and Judas were prophetic, messianic pretenders who aroused the worry of the Roman leaders over the possibility of revolt. Roman governors in antiquity had little patience with such a worry and often acted with utmost quickness to dispel it. In the cases Gamaliel mentions, both men were killed, and their followers were either killed or imprisoned—or scattered of their own accord. The high priest knows what modern exegetes have sometimes forgotten: a Jerusalem that follows a messianic claimant will attract the attention of the Roman governor and inevitably become bloody. The Sanhedrin's desire to kill the apostles for refusing to be quiet about the Messiah Jesus is thus rooted not in some supposed jealousy but in the understanding that the apostles' proclamation runs a politically grave risk for all (Acts 5:29–33, 40–42).[56] For the moment, the apostles are spared from death as Gamaliel's counsel prevails: they are beaten, charged once again "not to speak in the name of Jesus," and let go. But the political potential of emerging Christianity has been seen.

As the narrative progresses, the early Christians again and again appear as problematical figures. It is true, of course, that some people join the new movement—even a "great many of the priests in Jerusalem itself!" (Acts 6:7)—but as a whole the potential for sociocultural unraveling is discerned and resisted with force. After Stephen's stoning and the beginning of a more widespread persecution of the fledgling community, the Christians range beyond Judea into the towns and cities of the Gentile world. It is there that their potential for cultural dismantling is most immediately evident.

In the town of Lystra, for example, Paul and Barnabas are acclaimed as gods for their healing of a cripple. But their response to the Homeric liturgy—"the gods have come down to us in the likeness of men!"—is one of dramatic rejection. When the priest of Zeus brings oxen to sacrifice to them, Barnabas and Paul rend their clothes, declare pagan worship to be profoundly misguided, and speak of the break between God and the world that requires such worship to be discarded: "Men, why are you doing these things? We ourselves are humans just like you. . . . You should turn from these worthless things to the living God who made heaven and earth and sea and all that is in them" (Acts 14:15). Paul is subsequently stoned and dragged out of the city.[57]

In the Roman colony of Philippi the immediate catalyst for confrontation is different, but the substance is not. Paul rescues a "prophetic" slave girl by exorcising the spirit that made her fortune telling possible. In so doing he simultaneously destroys the economically exploitative work of her owners. Seeing the destruction of their business, the girl's savvy masters carefully rephrase their worries in dangerous political terms. Going before the Philippian magistrates, they accuse Paul and Silas: "These men are Jews and are disrupting the city, and they advocate practices that are unlawful for us Romans to accept or to do" (Acts 16:21). Given the gravity of the accusations against the Christian missionaries, it is no great wonder that the magistrates "tore their clothes off, gave orders to beat them with rods," and "after they had inflicted many blows upon them," threw them into prison (16:22–23). Of course the two men are freed from prison, but the businessmen and magistrates have rightly intuited the potential for cultural wreckage in Philippi.

And in the Asian metropolis of Ephesus, where the massive Artemisian temple functioned as a societal center, the Christian missionaries once again portend the dismantling of constitutive pillars of pagan culture. Vast quantities of the virtually ubiquitous magical books are burned upon conversion (Acts 19:18–20), and the local craftsmen are persuaded by one of their more discerning members that their business and that of the larger city is in serious danger. "Men," says the shrewd shrine maker Demetrius, "you know that our prosperity comes from this business. And you see and hear that not only in Ephesus but almost throughout all Asia this Paul has persuaded and turned away a considerable company of people, saying that gods made with hands are not gods. And there is danger not only that this trade of ours may come into disrepute but also that the temple of the great goddess Artemis may count for nothing—and she may even be deposed from her magnificence, she whom all Asia and the world worship" (Acts 19:25–27).

With such a threat, it comes as no surprise that the craftsmen are able to whip up the crowd to a riotous pitch and blunder their way to the theater. Indeed, there was enough disorder that the most powerful local official worried about the charge of *stasis*. His rhetorical suavity and political clout are sufficient enough to dissuade the crowd from further rioting, thereby averting the charge of *stasis*. But the troubling fact of Demetrius's point remains. Where the Christians come in, Artemis goes out—and with her, all of the business that depended upon her vast reach.

But what about the scene in Athens? Isn't it the case that Paul has a more debatelike philosophical approach there? Doesn't he show that the Christian gospel is intelligible in pagan philosophical terms? What of cultural unraveling?

Though modern interpreters have long considered the scene in Athens to be a placid philosopher's dialogue, the ancients would have read it differently. In antiquity it was known not only that Athens grew its own philosophers but also that it could try and kill them. Socrates was the best remembered, but he was not the only thinker who met his doom in Greece's most famous city. In fact, Paul's appearance before the court of the Areopagus is a trial. Luke's Paul is enough of a rhetor to combine a skillful avoidance of the capital charge—bringing in strange deities, as did Socrates—with a comprehensive critique of pagan "piety" as "superstitious" idolatry.[58] Turning to the God who is now newly known in Athens would in fact expose the city as a place "full of idols" rather than of wisdom (Acts 17:16–34).

Well now, there's the rub. If you continuously show that the Christians are disruptive, aren't the Athenian prosecutors basically right to try Paul? Wouldn't the Philippians or the Ephesian Demetrius have correctly discerned that the economic unfolding of Christian practice is a threat to religiously based economic or political order? Wouldn't the Romans be right to judge Christians seditious, guilty of the crime of riot-causing revolt—the dreaded *stasis*, the punishment for which is death? Wherever they go, the Christians upset normal cultural patterns, which in turn leads to disorder. What more in the way of evidence is needed?

You are very close to the truth, Luke might reply, but, alas, sit on the wrong side of it. The Christians do in fact bring the possibility of disorder, but such disorder is not the same thing as *stasis*. In fact, Paul was accused of this very crime—and declared innocent.

The second feature of Luke's view of church is thus his negation of a particular way of interpreting the cultural disorder brought by Christianity's arrival. Over the course of a long stretch of the end of Acts (24:1–26:32), Luke tells of Paul's trial for *stasis*. This trial is the narrative culmination of a long series of occasions when the Christians have been brought before local authorities and accused of disruption. In this particular case, Paul's opponents have a good argument, at least prima facie. Paul has incited a riotous crowd in the capital of Judea—in Roman eyes, one of the more incendiary provinces of the ancient world—and drawn the attention of the local tribune Claudius Lysias (Acts 21:27–23:35). Upon learning that Paul is a Roman citizen and dealing with a plot to take his life, Lysias does the most politically careful thing he can and sends Paul under protective escort to Judea's governor in Caesarea for trial.

In Caesarea Paul's opponents let the hired lawyer they've brought present their case to governor Felix. The lawyer Tertullus's charge is what one would expect given Luke's depiction of the trouble that follows Christian missionizing. Says Tertullus to Felix, "We have found this man to be a pestilential inciter of seditious riot among all the Jews in the entire world and a ringleader of the school called the Nazarenes. He even tried to profane the [Jerusalem] Temple, but we seized him" (Acts 24:5–6).

"I am innocent of this crime," Paul argues before Felix. And then again, says Paul before the new governor Festus, "I have done nothing against the law of the Jews, against the Temple, or against Caesar" (Acts 25:8). If I'm a criminal, Paul continues, "and have committed a crime worthy of death [that is, *stasis*], then I do not seek to escape death" (25:11). And the verdict? "This man," the

Romans agree, "has done nothing that deserves death" (26:31; cf. 23:29; Luke 23:4).

But how can Paul say these things? And how can he be found innocent given what we see of the early Christians in Lystra, Philippi, Athens, Corinth, Ephesus, and Jerusalem, to mention only a few of many possible places? Doesn't the narrative fudge on the political realities here?

There is a small story, Luke could reply, that addresses the tension we're encountering. The story takes place in the free city of Thessalonica, and the charge there against the Christians is that they are "acting against the decrees of Caesar and proclaiming another king, Jesus" (Acts 17:1–9). Now, are these charges true or false? The proper answer is both.

According to the Acts narrative, it is true that the early Christians proclaim an ultimate sovereign other than the Roman emperor. It is Jesus, rather than Caesar, who is the "Lord of all" (Acts 10:36). It is also true that the implication of such a proclamation is that where a loyalty oath to Caesar must be taken—such as in the city of Thessalonica—the Christians could refuse such an oath on the basis of competing loyalties. At this point, the Kingdom to which they belong could conceivably compete with the imperial kingdom. Moreover, the competition would be socially explicated, or visible: there is a new community, those whom outsiders will eventually name "Christians" (Acts 11:26; 26:28; cf. 1 Pet 4:16). But it is false to say that such competition is intended as sedition with the purpose of some sort of revolt (*stasis*), or that the disruption that occurs when such an oath is refused should be read as direct political subversion. As the innocent Jesus went peacefully to his death proclaiming the Kingdom, so I will go to mine doing the same, Paul argues. No violent resistance, only proclamation.

There is thus no ontological necessity to a violent disruption of a culture's order, a modern Luke might reason, because in fact the proclamation of another king is made in peace and could be received in peace (Acts 10:36; cf. especially Luke 2:10–14). True, receiving a proclamation that would relativize Caesar's sovereignty in light of Jesus of Nazareth could be expected to reorder the world in significant ways. But such disordering and reordering would be in the spirit and with the telos of peace. In the vision of the Acts of the Apostles, cultural destabilization and dismantling is at one and the same time the call to a community of peace.

For Luke, therefore, the negation of the charge of *stasis* is necessary precisely because the Christian denial of the Roman gods—Caesar and his requirements for ultimate loyalty among them—is premised on a communal life grounded in the peaceful witness of self-sacrifice rather than the violence of revolt. Before

Christianity Roman political vision had no categories through which to understand a "yes-disorder, no-*stasis*" form of life. So Luke wrote a story that attempted to create them.

The intractable difficulty, of course, is that Luke's way of looking at things will inevitably appear either insane, as Festus thinks (Acts 26:24), or irrationally, superstitiously obstinate in the face of Caesar's demands, as Pliny the Younger and others after him found it—unless and until one is inside the society that obeys Jesus as its final Lord. The dialectic that can claim "the devastation of constitutive patterns of your culture is actually the salvation of God in human time—and therefore not to be resisted but embraced with rejoicing" is internal to the Christian thing itself. It is not a claim that is verifiable apart from its acceptance. On their own terms alone, the Romans have cause to suspect the Christian society of engendering disorder. On Luke's terms, turning from the darkness to the light will enable the needed political vision.

So what if we do turn, what then? a Roman might ask. What is put in the place of such cultural dismantling?

Well, first of all you join a new family, Luke might say, articulating the third essential feature of an ecclesial profile. You become a brother or a sister (Acts 6:3; 9:30; 10:23; 11:1, 29; et passim), and you are bound by your new ties to your siblings around and across the great sea. Wherever there are those who follow Jesus, you will find your brothers and sisters. Indeed, you are closely enough knit that when one part of this great family suffers, the others are expected to share their burdens (see Acts 6:1–7; 11:29–30; 12:25).

Familial language, however, does not preclude hierarchical order, as if calling each other "brother" automatically distributed theological insight and practical wisdom in an equal measure to all. Luke's sort of hierarchy is not the kind that so worries postmoderns of various stripes but the kind that is inevitably a necessary part of any communal organization. Even the Quakers have leaders. The more difficult issue is that systematizing Luke's structure of authority has proved notoriously difficult for modern scholars of his work. To be sure, there are the twelve (with Matthias for Judas), Peter, James, Paul, Stephen, elders, deacons, and so on. But beyond the most obvious observations, arranging these various people and offices into clear tiers has simply not been possible. Still, what is obvious from Acts is Luke's conviction that the new society cannot flourish without orders of authority that guarantee both the movement's continuity with the earthly Jesus and the pattern of life that is its ethic.

The one who fills Judas's place, says Peter, must have "accompanied us during all the time that the Lord Jesus went in and out among us, beginning from the baptism of John until the day when he was taken up from us—one of these men must become with us a witness to his resurrection" (Acts 1:21–22). "Constructing" Jesus may have gained great ground in (post-)modernity, but the Acts of the Apostles displays a more serious concern with history: the resurrected Jesus is not he-who-we-construct-him-to-be but the particular person who lived on earth and was crucified under governor Pilate. The humanity of the real and only Jesus, that is, is transmitted via the authority of those who can name the resurrected one as Jesus of Nazareth crucified and dead.

And where the potential for the first real rift in the church arises, the twelve respond by establishing the office of deacon. As the number of family members grew, the Greek-speakers began to murmur against the Aramaic-speakers because their widows were neglected in the daily distribution of goods. So "the twelve summoned the body of disciples" and, among other things, said, "Pick out from among you seven men of good repute, full of the Spirit and wisdom, whom we may appoint" to ensure the sharing of provisions (Acts 6:1–7; cf. Acts 2:41–47; 4:32–37). As this passage shows—admittedly, more between the lines than through them—the new family will have crises, as all sociologically close groups do over time in one way or another. Luke's understanding here and elsewhere in Acts is that the maintenance of communal life is inconceivable without the structure that makes the wise use of authority possible.[59]

Communal order, however, is not only for internal maintenance. It is also for outward witness. Indeed, insofar as a reader could attempt a one-word summary of Luke's thinking about church, the most likely candidates would doubtless be variations on *witness*. "You shall be my witnesses," says Jesus in the programmatic commissioning before his final departure, "in Jerusalem, and in all Judea, Samaria, and to the end of the earth" (Acts 1:8). And it is this mission that the story of Acts tells. To the best of all historical knowledge, never before had the Mediterranean world encountered a missionizing form of communal life that simultaneously required the extinction of polytheism. Various pagan cults spread with differing degrees of success, but there was no mission in any kind of stricter sense of the word, and none of the cults threatened to tear the basic polytheistic fabric. And it is true, of course, that for the most part pre-Christian Jews thought pagan gods to be worthless idols and had no theological truck with them. But mission in the Jewish sense was more by way of example than by strategic evangelizing and communal formation in the attempt to convert any and all pagans to their way of life. But as Acts relates it, the Christians did exactly this latter sort of thing.

To be baptized, to be devoted to the apostles' doctrine, to share all things in common, to suffer for "the name" of Jesus, and—for pagans—to reject all gods but the God of Israel was not only to be resocialized in the profound sense of strong new community identity. It was also to undergo socialization in a particular orientation toward the "other," namely, that the other was always an insider-in-waiting, a potential member of the new community and recipient of the blessings that came with heeding the call to join.

In short, the Lukan understanding of Christian community implies a nuanced "church/world" distinction. Luke does not have a "macrotheory" of societal correction or construction. Some version of an ancient socialism, for example, was not his. The church has its own way of knowing and being: peaceful devotion to Jesus Christ in a new sociological pattern is not *stasis* but salvation in the here and now. And this ecclesial self-understanding is not, strictly speaking, compatible with the self-understanding of the larger Roman world.[60]

Yet the distinction between the church and the world is more complex than modern sociological theories might at first allow. Where moderns would likely see a "sect" anytime the wider world is described as existing in "darkness," Luke would counter that the darkness can give way to light. A careful reader of Acts, in fact, could well imagine that the church/world distinction was the ecclesial counterpart not to a sociological dualism but to a grand theology of invitation. For Luke, the world is always invited to church. Were the world to accept such an invitation, the distinction would dissolve. And in this, perhaps latent, sense, Luke does turn out to have a practical theory for the world.

Jesus will be a light of revelation to the Gentiles and glory to the people of Israel, says the old prophet Simeon (Luke 2:32). Insofar as characters in a story can speak for their authors, Simeon says with economy what Luke exhibits narratively over nearly a third of the entire New Testament. Jesus brings the redemption that God promised to the people of Israel and opens the way out of darkness for the Gentiles.

In Luke's view, however, he is not just telling stories. He is instead writing about the foundation of Christian truth in the life of Jesus of Nazareth and in the community to which he gave rise. Reading Luke's narratives, as he tells Theophilus, deepens the catechesis Christians have already undergone. It is through the story that Christian readers develop their understanding of the one whom they already worship as Lord and learn the historically normative shape of the new family to which they now belong.

Perhaps better than any other writer within the New Testament, Luke intuits what is on the immediate horizon for the Christians. He reflects on the way they earned their name, and he understands the dialectical nature of the emerging church. Like Jesus, Christians are the innocent who may well face trial and death. They cannot prove their innocence because their truth requires repentance to be understood. And they cannot resist their death because it would betray the practical shape of their truth. They therefore must be prepared to go to their deaths proclaiming the truth in which they have been instructed and trusting, as did Jesus himself, in the resurrection of the dead.

6

St. Justin Martyr

"I have tried to become acquainted with all teachings. But I have committed myself to the true teachings of the Christians, even though they may not please those who hold false opinions."
The prefect Rusticus said, "You do admit, then, that you are a Christian?"
"Yes, I am," said Justin.
—*The Acts of the Christian Martyrs*

In the first century after the writing of the New Testament documents, perhaps no Christian is quite as engaging a figure as Justin Martyr.[1] There are others who were more learned and others who were martyred, but Justin's claim to be a philosopher who practiced the only true philosophy, his development of the "apology" as a Christian political genre, and his extended engagement with Judaism prove to be a remarkably intriguing combination.

WORKS

As we learn from his *First Apology*, Justin was born in Palestine about the year AD 100. He was not raised as a Christian. By his own account, like the author of the *Pseudo-Clementine Recognitions* in the third century and St. Augustine in the fourth, Justin traversed various pagan philosophies before converting to Christianity (at which time he was still a relatively young man). As a Christian he lived in Ephesus and became known as a debater for the faith, most notably through a disputation with the Jew Trypho. But at some point, probably around the year 150, Justin moved to Rome. The changing of cities also brought a change in what he intended to accomplish. In the emperor's city Justin not only continued debating, he also composed some of his works and opened a school for training Christians. Due perhaps to a particularly virulent debate with the Cynic philosopher Crescens, Justin was eventually arrested and brought to trial, along with some of his students. The judge was the city's prefect, Q. Iunius Rusticus, one of the influential teachers of Marcus Aurelius. After hearing Justin's admission that he was a Christian and—in two of the three recensions of the case's transcript—learning that he would not sacrifice to the gods or obey the edict of the emperor, Rusticus ordered him scourged and executed. Rusticus did not know, of course, that his decision would create the conditions under which the Christian teacher would be forever remembered: martyrdom. Justin and those tried with him were not, of course, the first Christians to lose their lives because of their faith. But as posterity would have it, Justin's witness—the original meaning of *martyr*—became part of his name. The man whose writings we still read is known to all as Justin Martyr.

Of Justin's several writings, only three authentic works have survived: the *First Apology* (*1 Apol.*), the *Second Apology* (*2 Apol.*), and the *Dialogue with Trypho* (*Dial.*).[2] All three contain textual difficulties or evidence lacunae, but the *Second Apology* clearly presents the thorniest questions. Most scholars, to put it simply, do not think the *Second Apology* is a second apology at all. The proposals about exactly what it is instead vary according to particular readings of the text—some believe it's an appendix to the *First Apology*, some think a follow-up reminder about the original petition, some see a set of notes for a rough draft, and so on—but they all have a point to make. The *Second Apology* is quite difficult to take as a single, stand-alone document. For my purposes, however, this matters relatively little. As readers will by now have learned, the intellectual effort required for this book is to see things whole. Taking account of the *Second Apology*'s compositional oddity, therefore, occurs both before and through the overall coordination of Justin's thought. In keeping with the constructive aims of this book, we will focus upon the animating themes of Justin's three works that best befit creative conversation with our other five authors. As with Paul, so with Justin: we begin with God.

GOD

In a sense, it is hardly surprising that Justin speaks frequently about God. It is finally his view on God, after all, that makes Justin a Christian. Like Paul's letters, his language about God in the *Dialogue* and *Apologies* is rife with biblical terms, echoes, images, and the like. Yet because his surviving works are not directed primarily to Christian audiences, Justin's theological grammar is also markedly different from Paul's and evidences substantial reflection on newly arising questions and problems in Christianity's encounter with the wider world. Precisely because Justin is trying to cover so many bases, his way of speaking about God is culturally complex. He reaches both for Moses and for Plato; he champions continuity with the Jewish God while distinguishing the Christian view from the Stoic; he affirms the existence of other so-called gods but reduces them to God's creatures gone wrong, and so forth. Still, there are some basic linguistic continuities that appear across his works and impart a kind of organizing force to his talk of God. We shall focus upon three types of speech as a way to see the larger contours of what Justin says with the word *God*.

First, claiming continuity with Jewish tradition, Justin repeatedly states that there is only one true God and that this uniqueness is the ground of proper worship. Only the true God can be worshiped. Trypho, however, observes that Justin does not keep all the commandments of the Torah, and expresses his astonishment—quite logical from his perspective—at Justin's claims about God: how can "you try to convince us that you know God," Trypho questions, "when you fail to do those things that every God-fearing person would do?" (*Dial.* 10.3). Justin replies that the connection Trypho draws between God and complete Torah observance is now not necessarily as tight as Trypho insists. Though Justin does not observe the commandments in the way the Jews do, he clearly affirms that "there never will be, nor has there ever been from eternity, any other God except him who created and formed this universe" (*Dial.* 11.1; 56.3, 4; et passim). Moreover, Justin continues, citing the book of Deuteronomy, "We do not claim that our God is different from yours, for he is the God who, 'with a strong hand and outstretched arm, led your forefathers out of the land of Egypt.'" And since there is no other God in whom to trust, "we have placed our trust in . . . the God of Abraham and of Isaac and of Jacob" (*Dial.* 11.1, Deut 5:15). Justin differs with Trypho, of course, on how Gentiles in particular should relate to the God of Abraham, Isaac, and Jacob—indeed, the difference is exactly that between emerging Christianity and traditional Judaism—but about the uniqueness of this God and his relation to the world Justin and Trypho are agreed. For both sides of the debate, *God* means the one true God and "the Father and Creator of all things" (*Dial.* 7.3; 68.3, 4, et passim).

Speaking of God as the one and only Creator of the world also entails in Justin's logic the crucial distinction between God and everything that is not God. God, for Justin, is not part of everything that is—the efficient cause of order within the more comprehensive category of being, say—but is the one who made everything that is. It is true, of course, that in the beginning of the *Dialogue* Justin offers a definition of God that uses the word *cause* (*aitia*). "God is the one who is always the same and in the same way and who is the cause of being for all other things" (*Dial.* 3.5). But not only is this definition spoken by the pre-Christian Justin, it is also given a Jewish explication as the *Dialogue* unfolds and in the *Apologies*. "Cause" means not "power internal to" but "maker of, outside of, external to" whatever is (cf. *2 Apol.* 6.9). When Justin says, as he frequently does, that God is "unbegotten," he is invoking this absolute distinction between what is created and what is not (*1 Apol.* 14.1; cf. *Dial.* 127.1).[3] God is uncreated or unbegotten, and all things that exist that are not God have been created by this one and only God.

Such a distinction does not, however, lead to a denial of the existence of other powerful and sentient beings, as it does for many modern "monotheists." On the contrary, Justin simply takes it for granted that there are more powerful things in the world than humans. There are good angels, for example, as well as angels gone wrong, or demons. What Justin denies is that these beings have any claim to be the true God. When Trypho cites biblical texts—"your God is a God of gods and Lord of lords" (Deut 10:17)—to make his point, Justin simply agrees. Says Trypho, "Such words are used, not as if they were really gods, but because the word is instructing us that the true God, the Creator of all, is the sole Lord of all those who are falsely regarded as gods and lords" (*Dial.* 55.1). Or, more simply, in the words of both the biblical Chronicler and the Psalmist, "The gods of the nations"—although reckoned as gods—"are idols of demons and not gods" (*Dial.* 55.2, citing 1 Chron 16:26 and Ps 95:5). "From your quotations," Justin says to Trypho, "I know that they who worship these and similar objects are justly condemned" (*Dial.* 55.3). The images that stand at the center of the pagan cults, he tells the Roman emperors in his petition, are "called gods" but are in fact "dead and lifeless and do not possess the form of God. . . . Rather, we suppose that these things have the names and shapes of those wicked demons who were seen in apparitions" (*1 Apol.* 9.1). Justin's view of God, that is, requires a rejection of the theological legitimacy of the polytheism in which he was born and reared and which formed the fabric of Greco-Roman life. He does not deny the existence of the beings with which such polytheism was intertwined, but he most emphatically denies that they are God and, hence, denies the legitimacy of their worship.

How then, Trypho cleverly objects, can you speak in the way you do about Jesus of Nazareth? Don't you speak of him, too, as God? If the correlate of God's uniqueness as Creator is that we worship him alone, don't you commit the same basic error as the polytheists when you speak of Jesus as God? Isn't this exactly the confusion between Creator and creature? Prove to us, he says, that we can admit the existence of "another God" (*Dial.* 55.1; 48.1; et passim).

Justin replies, as he does throughout the argument with Trypho, by turning to specific scriptural passages that speak to the point in question. If he can make his argument from the texts that both he and Trypho take as Scripture, Justin reasons, Trypho will be won over. Justin therefore explicates several intriguing passages in the Old Testament and argues that, when seen in the right light, they do speak of another as God (*Dial.* 56–62).[4] Of course, moderns know this as "christological exegesis" and see that it works only in hindsight. Absent the first advent of Christ, no one would have thought these passages to mean what Justin says they do. As it turns out, however, Justin himself is quite aware of this difficulty and uses the language of prophecy and fulfillment to speak of the necessary conditions for a right understanding of Scripture's speech about God.[5] Given Justin's premises—these texts have been fulfilled in Christ—the prophecies do speak of another, "second" God. This other "God" is the begotten God.

Second, then, Justin also uses the word *God* to speak of the one whom God has begotten. "So, my friends," he says to Trypho and the others, "I will now show from the Scriptures that God has begotten of himself a certain rational power at the very beginning, *before* all created things."[6] Throughout Scripture various titles are used to describe this power—Wisdom, Son, Lord, for example—but they all point to the same reasonable reality, the *Logos,* the one who "performs the Father's will and . . . was begotten by an act of the Father's will" (*Dial.* 61.1; cf. *2 Apol.* 5.3). Though Justin missed Origen by many years, and therefore could not have known the latter's view on the "eternal generation" of the Logos/Son from the Father, Justin's language about God's begetting is not far from the main point of the later wording. "Begetting," Justin implies, is a kind of grammar that excludes "making," which is the way of speaking that applies to all creatures. God did not *make* the Logos, says Justin, he *begat* him (*Dial.* 62.2 et passim); the Logos stands on God's side of the Creator/creature divide. And in begetting the Logos, God did not become less, lose anything of himself, or reduce his "God-ness," as it were. It is like speech, Justin explains, reaching for an everyday analogy: "When we utter a word, it can be said that we beget the word, but not by cutting it off, in the sense that our power of uttering words would thereby be diminished" (*Dial.* 61.2).[7] Or it is like fire: one fire kindles another without losing anything of itself, yet "the enkindled fire seems to exist of itself and to shine without lessening the brilliancy of the first fire" (*Dial.* 61.2). The Logos proceeds from God as fire from fire, and is himself God as fire remains fire. For Justin, therefore, though the word *Logos* can mean "word" or "deed," the Logos is not simply God's way of speaking (his word) or acting (his mighty deeds) but is instead a distinct, uncreated mode of being God a second time in a second way (cf. *1 Apol.* 13.3). God from God is God.[8] Readers of the opening chapters of the book of Genesis can see this divine multiplicity easily enough, he tells Trypho. The words "Let us make," argues Justin, should be read along with "Adam has become one of us" (Gen 1 and 3). What else does the plural pronoun show except that "there were a number of persons together, numbering at least two" (*Dial.* 62.3)?

Of course, Justin does not speak of the Logos as an undetermined or amorphous second mode of God's being. For Justin, in the course of time the Logos is none other than Jesus Christ. In him the Logos has become human and received exact specification. He is Jesus of Nazareth, the Messiah of the Jews, and the one who was crucified and raised from the dead for our sake. Trypho is thus right, in Justin's view, in what his question about Jesus presupposes, namely, that only God can be God and that Jesus, if not God, is an idol. Justin's full reply, that is, takes for granted the truth of the biblical God's uniqueness. Precisely because Jesus is the Logos in the flesh and is therefore on God's side of the Creator/creature distinction, Justin answers, he can legitimately be called "God."

The begotten God is thus God exactly in the same sense as the unbegotten God; they are together "God." Yet for Justin, there is a kind of order to God's life that prevents simply identifying Jesus with the Father, as if the terms were interchangeable because they share the same description as God (cf. *1 Apol.* 13.3; *1 Apol.* 32.3).[9] Moreover, there exists yet another figure whom Justin positions inside the meaning of God—the Holy Spirit.

The Holy Spirit is the third primary way in which Justin speaks of God. Though Justin rarely reflects directly on the work of the Spirit, no reader of the *Dialogue* or *Apologies* can doubt his central role: the Holy Spirit is the one who speaks prophetically through Scripture of the future work in God's economy (*Dial.* 25.1). Scarcely can Trypho get an exegetical question out before Justin has responded with "the prophetic Spirit said" this or that through the book of Isaiah (or the Psalms or elsewhere) to testify to what was on the way in the first advent of Christ (see *Dial.* 32.3; 38.2; 43.3, 4, et passim). Indeed, the vast amount of scriptural quotation in the *Dialogue* in particular makes it almost possible to say that the Spirit is the key ingredient of Justin's argument with Trypho. Of course, this is not quite right. Trypho could (and does) agree with Justin that "God's prophetic Spirit" speaks through Isaiah and the rest without agreeing that these texts apply in the particular way Justin claims they do (see *Dial.* 49.6; 56.3). But the overstatement prevents the suspicion that Justin has not given much thought to the role of the Spirit vis-à-vis God's identity and draws attention to the fact of the Spirit's importance for Justin's overall language about God. It is finally God who speaks when the Spirit speaks. "In yet another way," Justin tells Trypho and his friends, "*God* indicated the power of the mystery of the cross when he said through Moses" (*Dial.* 91.1, citing Deut 33; emphasis added). For Justin, "God" and "the Spirit" are interchangeably appropriate words to describe the voice of the one who speaks in Scripture. The Spirit may well speak often in "parables and similitudes," but speak as God he does (*Dial.* 77.4).[10]

When, therefore, the Roman officials read of the baptism of the new Christians "in the name of the Father of all and Lord God and of our savior Jesus Christ and of the Holy Spirit," they would be justified if they supposed that these three referred to one divinity (*1 Apol.* 61.3). Of course, earlier in the petition they would have heard that "the prophetic Spirit" was third in the divine order, after the true God and his Son; and later they would learn that Christians are those who "bless the Creator of all through his Son Jesus Christ and through the Holy Spirit" (*1 Apol.* 13.3; 67.2).[11]

Like Paul's, Justin's language about God exhibits irreducibly complex patterns. God is the Father of all, the Logos who is Jesus Christ, and the prophetic Spirit all at once, and yet these three are not simply different words for saying the same thing, interchangeable without loss or remainder. The Unbegotten is not the Begotten; the Spirit is different still. But to speak of the God who creates and sustains the world (*Dial.* 29.3), watches over it in justice (*2 Apol.* 12.6), establishes a covenant with the Jewish people (*Dial.* 11.1), guides them through prophetic prediction (*Dial.* 7.1), acts dramatically in the first advent of Christ Jesus (*Dial.* 14.8), and will again in the second, is to speak of one and only one God. Again like St. Paul, the primary impetus for the complexity in Justin's theological grammar is Jesus Christ himself.

JESUS CHRIST

Unlike Paul, Justin had access to the four Gospels. He could therefore read about the life of Jesus. Though he does cite them, he does not make as much explicit use of the Gospels—or, as he also calls them, the "memoirs of the apostles"[12]—as modern authors who write about Jesus might expect. Implicitly, however, the ways in which he describes Jesus of Nazareth, attempts to prove Jesus' identity from the Old Testament as Messiah and God, and develops his own christological reflection in new directions are fully intelligible only upon the supposition that Justin knows the things careful Gospel readers can learn. Foremost among such things is the fact that Jesus himself really is the sticking point between Christians and all others.

Justin and Trypho, in fact, agree on many more things than modern scholars give them credit for. Of course, Justin himself writes Trypho's part and, as in many of Plato's dialogues, agreement through argument and repartee is literarily necessary to move the dialectic forward as a whole. Still, agree they do, and on a vast number of things that the knowledgeable reader can see as potential areas of convergence. But not on the one thing that makes all the difference: Jesus Christ. The Romans, too, could understand much of Justin's petition—that he and they are committed, theoretically at least, to justice and piety, to wisdom and reasonableness, that he and they are invested in citizenship, uphold the importance of the law, recognize the distinction between crime and innocence, and so forth. But they could not agree on the one thing that mattered: that devotion to Jesus Christ was true freedom rather than a sociopolitical problem. Who, then, is this Jesus Christ in Justin's view? Why stake so much on him?

Justin would answer these questions in multiple ways, but again and again his answers would reveal four central convictions that said for him who Jesus Christ is. First, throughout his works, Justin both assumes and repeatedly affirms that Jesus was a human being. Again, this affirmation may strike us moderns as bland or superfluous, but given the bloom of overspiritualizing tendencies in the second century ("Gnosticism"; cf. *Dial.* 35.6), speaking of Jesus' humanity was actually a way for Justin to put a stake in the ground. Jesus, he tells Trypho, was a human being who had flesh and could suffer as we do (*Dial.* 48.3; cf. 57.3; 98.1; 99.2; et passim).[13] Had Justin the chance to hear of Piaget, he might have said that Jesus grew up in a developmentally appropriate way—"like any other man," that is to say, who "exercised the appropriate powers at each stage of growth" (*Dial.* 88.2). Can there be any doubt to his humanity?

Jesus was born of a woman—as any human must be—but this woman was a virgin. As Isaiah said, "The Lord himself shall give you a sign. Behold, a virgin shall conceive and bear a Son, and his name shall be called Emmanuel" (*Dial.* 66.2). But Justin, Trypho argues, that text does not say a *virgin* shall conceive; it says a *young woman* shall conceive. Moreover, the text speaks of the birth of Hezekiah, not of Jesus (*Dial.* 67.1). Trypho's exegetical objection here depends upon a difference between the Hebrew and Greek of Isaiah 7:14. In Hebrew, the word *almah* does not require the meaning "virgin" but can be read instead simply as "young woman" (of marriageable age). The Septuagint, however, nudges the word toward its more restricted meaning and translates *almah* as *parthenos*, virgin.[14] Justin acknowledges that some Jews do not rank the Greek translation as high as the Hebrew text (see *Dial.* 71.1), but he insists that the Septuagint is no less inspired by the prophetic Spirit.[15] And once the legitimacy of the Greek text is granted, it is but a small step for Justin to the obviousness of Jesus as the only fit for "born of a virgin." Since Jesus, not Hezekiah, was born of a virgin, the text must apply to him.[16] Who else, in fact, has been born of a virgin?

Why Perseus of course, Trypho replies (*Dial.* 67.2; cf. *1 Apol.* 22.5; 54.8). Don't you remember the myth, Justin, how Zeus in the form of a golden shower descends upon the virgin daughter of King Argos, Danaë, from whom Perseus then subsequently issues forth? Justin's reply, which is understandably surprising to many moderns, is to grant the similarities of the case and then argue that they result from the work of the Devil and his demons. No archetypal images of purity, no broader metaphysical positions on flesh, no oedipal relation to fathers—nothing of this kind can serve to explain the similarities. The Devil and his minions, Justin tells Trypho, know the scriptural prophecies and have used them to fabricate and circulate the myth among the Greeks (*Dial.* 69.1 et passim). The Perseus story, that is, is not a stand-alone "parallel" from another frame of thought or life, but is instead a story that depends upon the Old Testament for its origin. True, the Old Testament prophecy is mediated by demonic exegesis and pagan amplification, but the ground of the Greek stories remains.[17] There is only one truth—that of the fulfilled prophecy in Jesus—and all other comparable stories are only derivative and counterfeit imitations of this truth. Jesus was a human being born of a virgin.

That seems a rather difficult claim. Indeed, it's a bit like saying Jesus is human and not human at the same time. Or, as Trypho himself puts it, he is a "human but not of human origin" (*Dial.* 48.1).[18] Justin might well point out that Adam was human and not of human origin—indeed, neither Adam nor Eve was born of a woman (cf. *Dial.* 84.1–4)—but Justin's central claim to paradox is something else: that the human Jesus was also God in the flesh.

So, second, to say who Jesus is Justin speaks simultaneously of God (as we also saw above). Precisely because this claim is also bound together with the question of whether or not the Jewish Messiah was expected to be God, Justin spends considerable time trying to convince Trypho that Scripture speaks of the coming Messiah as God and/or Lord. If, Justin reasons, he can convince Trypho of this truth, and subsequently show that Jesus was the Messiah, he will have shown that Jesus is also God. Q.E.D. Trypho, however, responds, "It seems to me that they who assert that [Jesus] was of [purely] human origin, and was chosen to be anointed and became the Christ, propose a doctrine much more credible than yours. We all expect that the Messiah will be a man of [purely] human origin. . . . If this man appears to be the Messiah, he must be considered a man of [purely] human origin" (*Dial.* 49.1).[19]

But consider these texts, says Justin, who throughout the work cites multiple passages from Genesis, Exodus, Deuteronomy, Psalms, Proverbs, Isaiah, Jeremiah, Malachi, Daniel, and more besides. Indeed, just before reassuring the tiring reader of the *Dialogue* that the long-winded exegesis and frequent repetition are done with an eye to persuasion, Justin says that he has proven "at length that the Holy Spirit calls the Messiah *God*" (*Dial.* 124.4; cf. *Dial.* 36.2; 137.4).[20] What else could it mean when David says, "God is ascended with jubilee, and the Lord with the sound of a trumpet. Sing praises to our God, sing praises. Sing praises to our King, sing praises" (*Dial.* 37.1, citing Ps 46)? Does this apply to the immutable and unbegotten God? He neither ascends, nor descends, nor goes anywhere else at all (*Dial.* 127.1). It must therefore apply to God's Messiah. Who, dear Trypho, ascends to heaven? The one who has been raised from the dead and ascended, Jesus of Nazareth (*Dial.* 36.2–6).

The messianic God, however, is not God *simpliciter* or in general. He is rather the begotten Son of God the Father, and "everybody will admit that the Son is numerically distinct from the Father" (*Dial.* 129.3; cf. 128.1 et passim). For Justin, the God who is the Son of God is also the Logos—the Word, Speech, Reason, or even Pattern, of God the Father. As he puts it in his petition, the Logos "acquired the form of a human and was born as a human being and was called Jesus Christ" (*1 Apol.* 5.4; cf. *1 Apol.* 23.2 et passim).[21] The Logos lived a human life, says Justin, and this human life was exactly the life of Jesus—which is to say that to know what God's Logos is, O Romans and Jews, you need to look at the life of Jesus. The power of this thought should not be missed. In Justin's texts, Christ is not the Christian name for what is rational, but something much more difficult to swallow: what is rational is who Jesus Christ is (see esp. *2 Apol.* 10.8; cf. *1 Apol.* 13.3).

And Trypho sniffs the difficulty immediately. Your claims about Jesus as the Logos entail, do they not, that the Logos himself was crucified, that he was made a curse? Preposterous! Not only does this offend against common sense, nowhere in Scripture does it even say that the Messiah is to be crucified. We can agree, Justin, that "your quotations from Scripture prove that we must look forward to that glorious and great Messiah who, as the Son of Man, receives the everlasting kingdom from the Ancient of Days" (*Dial.* 32.1, see Dn 7:13). And we can even see from your reading of Isaiah 53 that in some sense "the Messiah was to suffer" (*Dial.* 90.1; cf. *Dial.* 89.1–2). But what we cannot stomach is crucifixion, the fact that the one who was to save "was to be crucified and subjected to so disgraceful and shameful a death (which even in the Torah is cursed). We find it impossible to think that this could be so" (*Dial.* 90.1; cf. *Dial.* 10.3).[22]

Justin replies, as is his wont, with figural readings of Scripture that purport to counter Trypho's objections and show that the cross was all along part of God's providential plan. Moses' prayer with outstretched hands in Exodus 17, for example, was in the shape of a cross; his posture was a foreshadowing "sign" of Jesus' own outstretched hands on the cross (Moses held his arms out for a long time; so, too, were Jesus' arms held out for a long time; Moses sat on a stone; Jesus was prefigured as a "stone," and so on; *Dial.* 90.4–5). Justin's larger point, however, is that a reading of the total grain of Scripture, as well as a clear-eyed look at the manifest problems of the real world, shows the just judgment of Deuteronomy 27:26. Precisely because we have not kept the law of God, "the entire human race will be found to be under a curse" (*Dial.* 95.1; see also *Dial.* 93–95).[23] "If then," Justin continues, "the Father of all willed that his Christ should shoulder all the curses of the whole human race, fully realizing that he would raise him up again after his crucifixion and death, why do you accuse him, who endured such suffering in accordance with the Father's will, of being a cursed man, instead of bewailing your own iniquity?" (*Dial.* 95.2; cf. *Dial.* 94.5).[24]

It is significant, however, that Justin ultimately invokes the vocabulary of hiddenness and mystery to speak about the crucifixion.[25] Echoing the opening of 1 Corinthians, Justin tells Trypho that "the hidden power of God was in the crucified Christ" (*Dial.* 49.8) and later speaks of "the power of the mystery of the cross" (*Dial.* 91.1). And early in his petition, he locates the incomprehension of the Christians at the point of the crucifixion, and insists that this "mystery" has been misunderstood: "For it is there [at the point of the crucified man] that they declare our madness to be manifest, saying that we give second place after the unchangeable and eternal God . . . to a crucified man, being ignorant of this mystery, to which we urge you to give your attention, as we expound it" (*1 Apol.* 13.4). Justin's language displays his awareness of Paul's argument about the cross in 1 Corinthians, namely, that it is finally foolishness to the Greeks and a stumbling block to Jews. Justin does not think that recognizing the truth of the "paradox" over which he and Trypho argue, or which the Romans mock, is as simple as learning about it. He had not read John Henry Newman, but he knew well enough that assent could be vastly more complicated than a simple formula of presentation-then-reaction (assent).[26] In fact, for Justin, to see God in the crucifixion is already to have understood something of the effect of Jesus' crucifixion upon human life.[27]

Third, then, the aim of the Logos's human existence was to save human beings from the condition from which they could not deliver themselves. Jesus Christ taught, as Justin tells the Roman officials, "with a view to the alteration and restoration of the human race" (*1 Apol.* 23.2; cf. *1 Apol.* 14.3). The Logos, he says again later, became "a human being by the will of God for the sake of the human race" (*1 Apol.* 63.10; cf. *1 Apol.* 50.1), so that "as a sharer in our sufferings, he might also bring healing" (*2 Apol.* 13.4). Modern readers may all too easily assume that healing relates primarily to individuals. And of course Justin would hardly deny that the human race could be healed without the healing of its component parts.

Yet this *pro nobis* human existence of the Logos was not a treatment that left the more fundamental condition of disease and illness unchanged. In Christ, says Justin, God established "a new covenant for the whole world" (*Dial.* 43.1; 122.6; cf. *1 Apol.* 10.6). Jesus Christ does not, that is, simply help humans on an individual basis; instead, Justin argues, the whole God/world relation has been renewed and reconfigured in Christ. This reconfiguration and renewal are consistent with the way in which God has always worked (*Dial.* 30.1; cf. *Dial.* 122.5),[28] but it is nevertheless both historically and ontologically—in time and in possibilities of being—a genuinely new start for humanity.

Fourth, the enfleshed Logos Jesus, however, is not only our "helper and redeemer" (*Dial.* 30.3), he is also our King and Lord and Judge, says Justin. Citing Isaiah 43:15, he asks Trypho, "Now, when Scripture says, 'I am the Lord God, the Holy One of Israel, who showed Israel your King,' will you not admit that Christ the eternal King is meant?" (*Dial.* 135.1). Of course Justin's is a rhetorical question—he neither expects Trypho to answer it nor gives him the chance—but the point is one he repeatedly makes. As he puts it in his petition, "We know none who is a more kingly or just ruler" than the Logos (*1 Apol.* 12.7). Jesus' kingly, just rule is "eternal" as the Logos is eternal, but it also takes shape in time. In particular, argues Justin, his rule claims the final political allegiance of the Christians in the present, and it orients them toward his return in the future to render just judgment.

Throughout his argument with Trypho over the messianic prefigurations in Scripture, Justin distinguishes between two advents of the Christ, the first, which has happened and involves suffering, and the second, which has yet to occur and will involve the final judging and redemption of the world (see *Dial.* 14.8; 31.1; 120.4). The messianic return is the vision of the book of Daniel, says Justin, and Jesus will be the Son of Man coming on the clouds. All people will then recognize his Lordship, know him as the one who enacts justice, and receive from him their just judgment. For Justin, therefore, Jesus Christ's kingship determines human existence in the present by his two comings, the first, which calls us to new life under his rule, and the second, which will simultaneously measure the quality of our lives and end all things.[29]

Such claims as these obviously permit little in the way of compromise over the significance of Jesus Christ. Where Trypho says that turning to Jesus Christ is turning away from God toward man (*Dial.* 8.3), Justin replies not by arguing that Jesus, too, is a legitimate way but by claiming that he is the only way to God (*Dial.* 43.2; 44.4). To be ignorant of Christ, says Justin, is to be ignorant of God and, hence, to miss the chance to be healed (*Dial.* 136.3). For Justin, nothing less than the knowledge of God himself and the healing that such knowledge brings is at stake in knowing Jesus Christ. To put it this way, of course, is to assume that "knowledge" is much more than simple understanding of a logical truth. Knowledge of Jesus Christ is more like a way of life, according to Justin, which is to say that it's more like philosophy than anything else.

PHILOSOPHY

The *Dialogue with Trypho* opens with the hailing of Justin as a philosopher. "Good morning, Philosopher," says Trypho (*Dial.* 1.1). Trypho recognizes Justin as a philosopher because of his dress, the standard cloak (*tribōn*) worn by those who publicly profess to be philosophers. Justin's garb makes an interesting claim to all who care to inquire, namely, that as a Christian he is a philosopher. In fact, not only is the *Dialogue* written in standard philosophical style—dialogues came in with Plato and never really went out—the entire work is cast as Justin's answer to Trypho's question, "What is your philosophy?" (*Dial.* 1.6). For Justin, the answer is rather straightforward: Christianity.

By philosophy, however, Justin does not mean what most moderns mean—an analytical discipline that applies solely to the intellect, a kind of rigorous exercising of pure reason. Justin doubtless places heavy emphasis upon philosophical reasoning, but for him reasoning philosophically means living in a certain way of life. Philosophy for Justin, as it was for Seneca, Epictetus, and Marcus, is practice, an intellectually dense form of living whose justification is its ability to lead people to new life.

The most obvious way in which Justin's works display his sense of philosophy is the autobiographical account of his conversion to Christianity (*Dial.* 2–8). It is true that Justin exercises some literary license here, but so would most everyone else who wanted not to bore his audience. Moreover, precisely because Justin's narrative is somewhat stereotyped, his main concerns emerge all the more clearly. As he tells Trypho, Justin tried several different philosophies before finally embracing the truth of Christianity.

He first attached himself to a Stoic teacher, and then to a Peripatetic (Aristotelian), but both philosophies proved inadequate, the former because it taught him nothing new and the latter because the teacher's fees were too high. Justin next approached a famous Pythagorean but found the reputed man unwilling to take him on as a pupil without the requisite knowledge in "music, astronomy, and geometry"; at last, having almost despaired, Justin found the Platonists, and one of their sages began to train him in the Platonist way of being. Justin progressed day by day and began to think that his progress would soon enable him to behold God, "for this is the purpose/goal/aim of Plato's philosophy" (*Dial.* 2.6). Believing solitude, and perhaps the beauty of the landscape, to be most conducive to the practice of meditation, Justin went to a place near the sea. It was there that he met "an old man," who through a mixture of argument and preaching led Justin through the door to the Christian faith.[30]

Justin first tells the old man why he had come beachside: "I take great delight in such walks, where I can converse with myself without hindrance because there is nothing to distract my attention. Places like this are most suitable for philology" (*Dial.* 3.2). Where Justin echoes Plato's definition of dialectic—the soul's conversation with itself—as the means by which philosophy is practiced, the old man asks him bluntly, "Are you, then, a lover of words, rather than a lover of deeds and of truth? Do you not strive to be a practitioner rather than a sophist?"[31]

It is true that this objection turns Plato himself against Justin, but it also begins the argument that will tie practice inseparably with true knowledge of God. Justin cleverly replies that thinking itself is a kind of deed, and philosophical thinking is precisely the sort of deed one needs in order to develop virtue and happiness. "What greater deed could one perform than to prove that reason (*logos*) rules all and that the one who rules reason and is sustained by it can look down upon the errors and undertaking of others, and see that they do nothing reasonable or pleasing to God? . . . Human beings cannot have prudence apart from philosophy and straight thinking" (*Dial.* 3.3).[32] "But," the old man interrupts, cutting to the chase, "does philosophy lead to happiness?" Knowing this question to be as old as philosophy itself, Justin answers, "Assuredly, and it alone" (*Dial.* 3.4).[33]

"Philosophy," he says, responding to yet another question, "is the knowledge of that which exists, and a clear understanding of the truth. Happiness is the prize of this knowledge and understanding" (*Dial.* 3.8). Having heard Justin join the knowledge of truth to human happiness, the old man then directs the conversation to the main point: God. "How do you define God?" he asks.

Within the context of the second century, Justin's answer is predictably bland—"God is the being who always has the same nature in the same manner and is the cause of everything else"—but the old man takes it for what it's worth and moves on. After a lengthy discussion of various matters, the conversation culminates in the old man's straightforward assertion: "What I say is the truth and here is how you may learn it" (*Dial.* 6.1). Over against the Platonist position, the old man argues that life is not a property of the soul itself but is instead something given by God. The soul cannot generate itself from itself, says he. That would make it God (*Dial.* 6.2). The soul is, of course, a living thing, but only derivatively so; it "partakes of life because God wishes it to live" (*Dial.* 6.2).

The old man then speaks of the soul's continued existence and destiny after death, and Justin is convinced that the Christian is right: our fate as human beings really does depend on something the philosophers had not seen, the sustaining power and just judgment of the unbegotten God.

If the philosophers, Justin then asks, "do not know the truth, what teacher or method shall one follow?" (*Dial.* 7.1).[34] Justin's question is revealing. He does not ask, "How shall I know the truth?" as if all it took to develop the right epistemology was the correct list of logical propositions. Instead, Justin takes it for granted that learning the truth involves an adherence to a preexisting pattern of knowing that requires a teacher and a tradition. Knowing the truth philosophically, for him, is synonymous with becoming a disciple.

The old man's answer appropriately describes the teachers and tradition into which Justin should be inducted to learn the truth. The Old Testament prophets, the Christian says, are the real philosophers. They, and they alone, told the truth; moreover, they told it long before the "so-called philosophers." Their knowledge of the truth did not come about because they achieved special insight of their own accord. They were virtuous, yes, but more important, they were "loved by God" and "spoke through the inspiration of the Holy Spirit." Indeed, they "reiterated only what they heard and saw when inspired by the Holy Spirit" (*Dial.* 7.1). To know the truth they knew is thus to know things that in principle reside on God's side of our knowledge of him.

Were Justin to have worried that he missed the chance to hear the prophets, the old man would have assuaged his worry immediately: "Their writings are still extant," he tells Justin. And "whoever reads them will profit greatly in his knowledge of the beginning and end, *provided that he has believed in them*" (*Dial.* 7.2, emphasis added). With this last phrase, the old man complicates the kind of reading Justin must do if he is to know the truth of which the prophets speak. While the prophets did provide a particular kind of testimony to the truth of their words—the events of which they foretold are happening even now, says the old man, and they performed miracles—more fundamentally their reliability is "beyond proof" (*Dial.* 7.2). The reader must not look to the prophets to provide knockdown arguments to win his trust, the old man implies, but must instead trust them ahead of time, as it were, have a basic faith in their reception and communication of the truth. Only in this way will Justin understand the writings. "Above all," says the Christian to Justin, teaching him how to read, "beseech God to open to you the gates of light, for no one can perceive or understand these truths unless he has been enlightened by God and his Christ" (*Dial.* 7.3).

Evidently the old man had much more to say, but Justin thinks it unnecessary to pass along (*Dial.* 8.1). The main point has been made, and Justin's "spirit was immediately set on fire." He developed "love for the prophets and for those men who are friends of Christ," and, meditating on what he had heard, he found that Christianity was "the only solid and profitable philosophy" (*Dial.* 8.1). "Thus it is," Justin tells Trypho and his companions, "that I am now a philosopher" (*Dial.* 8.2).

On the one hand, Justin clearly seeks to create a sense of deep continuity with the pagan tradition and to use this continuity for his own rhetorical advantage in communicating what Christianity actually is. He uses the familiar tropes of the philosopher such as the cloak and the movement through various philosophies to draw his readers in by means of something they already understand. This communicative strategy culminates in Justin's audacious claim that in becoming a Christian, he has become a true philosopher.

"You could use other words," someone might say to Justin. Yes, perhaps I could, Justin would reply, but *philosophia* is what best gestures toward something we Christians need to say about our way of life, namely, that it is a pattern of being that is staked on our knowledge of the truth about God. Moreover, dear friend, *philosophy* is a word that we can use to our benefit.

When composing my petition, for example, I repeatedly appealed to a common understanding of a philosopher as one who loves the truth and exhibits piety in its pursuit. I used this understanding, and the fact that it was projected onto the emperor and his sons, to call the Roman treatment of Christians into question. "Reason prescribes that those who are truly pious and philosophers should honor and hold in affection truth alone," said I (*1 Apol.* 2.1). And then, "Turning to you [emperor and sons] then, you hear on all sides people calling you pious and philosophers and guardians of justice and lovers of learning" (*1 Apol.* 2.2; cf. *1 Apol.* 1.1; *2 Apol.* 2.16). "But whether in fact you are," I continued, "remains to be seen" (*1 Apol.* 2.2).

Here, and indeed throughout his work, Justin returns to the "type" of philosopher as a way to exhibit a standard to which he wants the emperors to be accountable. If you are called philosophers—and even, in the case of Marcus Aurelius, "Verissimus, the Philosopher"—then behave like philosophers. Seek the truth of the case, rule with justice. Of course there are always those who contradict their name, who "assume the name and appearance of philosophers," but who act "in no way worthily of their profession" (*1 Apol.* 4.8; cf. *1 Apol.* 26.6). Be not like them. Follow not "the path of violence and tyranny," admonishes Justin, "but of piety and philosophy" (*1 Apol.* 3.2; 12.5; 70.4).

Philosophy, for Justin, thus names something of very deep worth in the pagan world not only because it describes a way of life founded on the truth, but also because it can potentially draw attention to the necessity of particular virtues for proper Roman rule. Implied in Justin's language about truth and political virtue, therefore, is the judgment that even outside of Christianity there are better and worse options for structuring human life; philosophy is clearly better than run-of-the-mill paganism.[35]

On other hand, however, Justin fundamentally criticizes pagan philosophical tradition(s). For all their insight into this or that, as he puts it through the mouth of the old man in the *Dialogue*, they "know nothing about such matters" as God, life after death, or even the soul itself, "since they cannot even explain the nature of the soul" (*Dial.* 5.1). Pagan philosophers may well exhibit a similarity to Christian teaching on a particular point. Plato, for example, taught that our souls will carry on past death (*1 Apol.* 18.2–6; cf. *1 Apol.* 8.4–5; *2 Apol.* 10.2). Christians, too, acknowledge that death is not the final word for the human being. But such similarities are not the result of mutual, independent insight, or even coincidence. Instead, where Plato or any other philosopher agrees with the teaching of Scripture, it is the result of his dependence upon the Old Testament. "Moses is older than even all the writers in Greek," says Justin. Plato took his wisdom from Moses. "And everything that both the philosophers and poets said concerning the immortality of the soul or punishments after death or contemplation of heavenly things or similar teachings, they were enabled to understand and explain because they took their starting points from the prophets" (*1 Apol.* 44.8–9; cf. *1 Apol.* 59.1–5). "For this reason," Justin continues, "there appear to be seeds of truth among all" (*1 Apol.* 44.10). Thus where we moderns would tend to see parallel tracks of human reason, Justin argues for a genetic, historically determinative relationship as the cause for the similarities between Christians and pagan philosophers. The "seeds of truth" that appear among the philosophers are not God's gifts of insight strewn about through the whole of human history but specific understandings made known through the prophets. Justin's genetic relationship cuts off the possibility of true theological insight independently of God's relation to historic Israel and now to the Christians. "It is not we, then, who have the same opinions as others, but everyone speaks in imitation of what we say" (*1 Apol.* 60.10).[36] More still, Justin never retreats from his basic claim that Christianity is the only philosophy; if one wants to learn philosophical truth, Justin says in a myriad of ways, learn the manner of life that is trust in the prophets and love of the friends of Christ.

In short, Justin's narration of his conversation with the old Christian and his conversion to Christianity establishes a yes/no dialectical relation to pagan philosophy that runs throughout the rest of the *Dialogue* and the two apologies. Justin does not want to deny certain insights he sees in Greek philosophy ("yes"), but he describes these insights in such a way as to eliminate their originality, tie their truth directly into the history of Israel, and show their utter inadequacy for the transformation of human life apart from Christianity ("no"). The Greek philosophical tradition, Justin might say, has a lot to offer in the way of confirming the truth of the prophets, but on its own it can do little for us.[37]

But what about human reason itself? Don't you speak of the logos as a faculty that can reason its way to certain things about God? Isn't this the whole point of your celebrated teaching on the "*logos spermatikos*"?[38] Answering your question, Justin could reply, requires me to say more about the human being who exercises its logos; it's impossible for me to answer the question about reason without saying what it is that reasons. Reason can't be divided from the thing that reasons.

For Justin, therefore, the scheme for human life (philosophy) and the human being itself (anthropology) are intimately and inseparably intertwined. Indeed, the dialectical yes/no relation to pagan philosophy is exactly what a reader of Justin should expect if the human being is what he thinks it is.

HUMAN BEING

Justin speaks of the problems and promise for the human being throughout his writings. Over against any notion that God created the mess we now find ourselves in, and over against any notion that our fate is predetermined in such a way as to demolish our freedom or the meaningfulness of our choices, Justin repeatedly affirms that humanity was created free and able to obey God (*Dial.* 88.5; 141.1–2; 2 *Apol.* 7.1). "At the beginning," Justin tells the Romans, "God made the human race with intelligence and able to choose what is true and to behave well." Human beings are therefore "without excuse with regard to God, for they have come into existence as rational and sentient beings" (*1 Apol.* 28.3, *logikoi kai theōrētikoi*; cf. 1 *Apol.* 10.3–4; 2 *Apol.* 7.1). Without excuse?

Well, yes, Justin would say. We misused our freedom, chose evil rather than good (*Dial.* 88.5), and were deceived by those angels who had already gone bad, the demons (2 *Apol.* 4.1–6). Our subsequent history has been one long repetition of this original choice, with the result that ignorance, a tendency to sin, and a vulnerability to deception by demons marks humanity through and through (*1 Apol.* 10.6; 14.1; *Dial.* 141.1–2; cf. 2 *Apol.* 9.3–4, where the demons work even on a systemic, sociocultural level by making laws).

It is true that we maintain some moral knowledge and some sense of guilt—intuitions founded on what remains of our originally good creation—but even these are easily smothered by our habits of being or hidden from us by the acts of unclean spirits (*Dial.* 93.1). The demons, moreover, ally themselves with the "evil desire in each person, which by nature (*physis*) is universal and various," and seek to enslave us (*1 Apol.* 10.6; 14.1). Our problem is more severe, therefore, than a crack in the otherwise sturdy edifice of reason. Ignorance of God and all that comes with it can take root in the soul itself (*1 Apol.* 12.11), making our need for help run that much deeper. The trick is that precisely because we are active participants in the problem that plagues us—we both produce and reinforce it—there is relatively little, or rather virtually nothing, that we can do either to exonerate or heal ourselves.

The good news, says Justin again and again, is that the human being is not stuck in the cycle of ignorance, sin, and guilt. Of course, Justin is no simpleton. He knows that "it is not easy to bring about a sudden change in a soul taken hold of by ignorance." But he holds that it is nevertheless completely possible "to escape ignorance when truth has been presented" (*1 Apol.* 12.11). Presenting the truth, however, is not as easy as simply making a statement about the human condition and the possibility for change; for Justin, rather, it is exactly the same thing as proclaiming the truth of the Christian way of life for all people. Overcoming ignorance in Justin's teaching, therefore, has relatively little to do with the intellect per se, as if the human being was the kind of thing that could simply think its way out of ignorance to a new life. Justin thinks rather of a more comprehensive deliverance and healing, one that touches our "evil desires," our acts of injustice, our choice to pursue anything other than the good; in short, Justin thinks of repentance (*metanoia*), the turning around of a whole life. Indeed, in some ways the worst of us are better off: Christ, says Justin, echoing the words of Luke 5:32, summoned to repentance not the just, but the "impious, the undisciplined, and the unjust" (*1 Apol.* 15.7; cf. *Dial.* 116.1). Yet not only the obviously problematic specimens of goodness but "everyone who repents" will find God's mercy (*Dial.* 141.2; cf. *1 Apol.* 15.7). And repentance, for Justin, is the beginning of repair.

Throughout Justin's works, the human being appears as the sort of thing that can be repaired, and Jesus' teaching is the instruction that enables this repair by altering us toward the good (*1 Apol.* 23.2). In practice this means that the Gospels provide the pattern that educates us into the one true philosophy, the way of God's healing made known through Jesus Christ. Wish to be healed? Read the words of Jesus in the Gospels and live thereby. Learning our way out of ignorance and the tendency to sin is for Justin the process of being conformed to the teaching of Jesus (*1 Apol.* 23.2).

But we eventually die, do we not? For all the healing and repair you speak of, the human being is still indisputably a deathward creature.

Yes, "all are obliged to die," Justin would reply (*1 Apol.* 11.2; 57.2; cf. *2 Apol.* 11.1). But death is not, in a strict sense, the end of human life.[39] The soul continues on. We are conscious after death; "consciousness endures for all who have been," says Justin (*1 Apol.* 18.2). Of course, Plato said as much, as Justin himself readily acknowledges. What Plato and Co. did not say and would never have affirmed, however, is what Justin says about the body. "We believe in God even more" than the Greek philosophers, Justin tells the Roman officials, because we "expect even to receive our own bodies again, after they have died and been put in the earth" (*1 Apol.* 18.6). Justin goes on forthrightly to acknowledge the seeming implausibility of such a belief—over time buried bodies become something much less recognizable than a human form, not to mention the fact that bodies are hacked, hewn, and otherwise destroyed beyond recognition well ahead of their eventual decay—but he never wavers from his basic scriptural belief that "nothing is impossible for God" (*1 Apol.* 18.6; see Gen 18:14; Luke 1:37; Matt 19:26).

As his confession hints, Justin's affirmation of the postmortem reception of the body does not strictly follow from his body/soul anthropology.[40] Justin does believe in the unity of the human person, namely, that the human being is not fully a human being without a body (cf. *Dial.* 6.2), but his faith in the importance of the body for life after death derives from his commitment to think about death in light of the bodily resurrection of Jesus of Nazareth. Jesus was raised bodily; ergo humans will be raised bodily (*1 Apol.* 19.3–8). Indeed, says Justin to Trypho, those Christians who "assert that there is no resurrection of the dead and say instead that their souls are taken up to heaven at the very moment of their death" are not real Christians. By denying the importance of bodies to life after death, these Christians "blaspheme the God of Abraham, Isaac, and Jacob" and forfeit the name "Christian" (*Dial.* 80.4).

But Justin, one might say, there are corpses all over. I can well understand those Christians who say no more than that the soul is released upon death. If bodies are raised to life after death, why do corpses remain for all to see? The resurrection of the body, Justin would respond, is something that occurs with Christ's second advent. Not until then will those who have died receive their bodies. But upon his coming, Christ will "raise the bodies of all human beings who have existed" (*1 Apol.* 52.3; cf. esp. *1 Apol.* 19.4).

And that is not all, Justin would continue. The raising of the body is simultaneously the final verdict on our eternal habitation. Some will be forever with God in everlasting bliss, others in Gehenna, where they will endure everlasting punishment (see *1 Apol.* 19.8; 28.1; 52.7–9; *Dial.* 35.8 et passim). Not for Justin is today's liberal Protestant discomfort with fates unpleasant to contemplate. For him, death and resurrection was really that serious a thing; everything was at stake. Receiving our bodies after death meant that we were ultimately accountable to God for the life that we lived in the flesh (see *Dial.* 39.6). Justin does not go so far as to say that we ourselves are primarily responsible for the location of our eternal habitation, or even that God's goodness to humanity is conditioned by our virtuous response, but he does place great weight on our responsibility to live our lives of repentance toward their proper eternal end. According to Justin, the manner by which our humanity is displayed is something of eternal consequence.

As a whole, then, like Paul, Justin does not conceive of the human being in abstraction from the history of God's dealings with his creatures. He shows no interest in finding a human essence, or in articulating a universally acceptable definition of what it means to be human. It is true that he makes much more of the soul than the writers of the New Testament, say, but even here his understanding is conditioned by the economy of God. Souls are created things, in need of redemption, incomplete without a fleshly body, and with a proper eternal end. To think "soul" vis-à-vis the human is to think of a history of embodied relations with God from the beginning, in the election of Israel, and finally in Jesus Christ—a history that is marked not only by sin and waywardness and death, but also by the possibility of forgiveness and return and eternal life.

POLITICS AND DEATH: ROME AND THE CHRISTIANS

The reality of death as a marker of the injustice of the world was obvious to Justin even before his own demise. What surprised Justin, however, was the way in which Christians would courageously endure suffering and death at the hands of the Roman government. "When I myself took delight in the teachings of Plato, I heard the Christians slandered and saw that they were fearless in the face of death and everything thought fearful" (2 *Apol.* 12.1). When he wrote this, he did not know that he, too, would eventually join the Christian witness to a politics of death.

Historians know that official persecution of Christians did not happen until the reign of Decius in AD 251. But focusing on official, legally sanctioned violence can obscure what on any reading is an obvious fact: on a local level and/or ad hoc basis persecution was a part of Christian life from at least the middle of the first century. And from the beginning of the second century—thirty years or so before Justin's death—the name "Christian" had already become an important political marker.[41] With the clarity of hindsight, the attention given to the name is unsurprising: persecution of Christians qua Christians depends upon the ability to see them as a community, or at least as a particular kind of thing, a way of naming a category or group such that it made sense to try them as *Christianoi*, Christians.

Justin, obviously, tells Trypho repeatedly that Christians are a particular kind of thing.[42] Yet their particularity comes not from ethnicity or geographical locale—there isn't a single race where there aren't Christians, says Justin (*Dial.* 117.5; cf. *1 Apol.* 1.1)—but from their devotion to Jesus Christ. That is, after all, what the name *Christianos* means, follower of Christ. Justin does not immediately mention the name "Christian" in the opening of his petition, but it isn't too long before he begins to discuss its significance for Roman practice.

Surely, Justin begins, "something is not judged to be either good or bad by the name it is called without consideration of the actions that are associated with that name" (*1 Apol.* 4.1). A name by itself tells you nothing. "Neither commendation nor punishment could reasonably be based on a name unless actions can show something to be virtuous or wicked" (*1 Apol.* 4.3). But "with us you take the name as proof" of some crime (*1 Apol.* 4.4). We are "accused of being *Christianoi*" (*1 Apol.* 4.5; *2 Apol.* 2.1; *Dial.* 96.2). This makes no sense: why not accuse us of specific crimes? We are quite willing for any and all charges to be investigated (*1 Apol.* 3.1).[43]

Indeed, Justin continues, "if one of those accused [as a *Christianos*] becomes a denier and merely says that he is not a Christian, you release him, as though you were in no way able to convict him of doing anything wrong" (*1 Apol.* 4.6). Justin's point here, like Tertullian's three decades later, is that the Romans' jurisprudential practice is bizarre and illogical. If, he argues, being a Christian is worthy of punishment, there ought to be some crimes associated with the name. But if someone is declared innocent on the basis of verbal denial, then there cannot be any crime associated with the name (no one accused of murder or gross theft, for example, is let off simply because he denies his crime). Legally speaking, then, what exactly are we accused of?

If, Justin could have said, you answer that the name itself is sufficiently problematic, we Christians would reply that our beliefs may be strange in your eyes, but they hurt no one. If any of you think our faith is "incredible or impossible, the delusion hurts us, and no one else, so long as it is not found that any of our actions are wrong" (*1 Apol.* 8.5). Of course if upon hearing the things that we believe "they seem to you to be not far from reason and truth, honor them. But if they seem to you to be portentous nonsense, despise them as nonsensical matters and do not decree death against those who do nothing wrong, as though they were enemies" (*1 Apol.* 68.1).

I will go farther still, Justin says. "We more than all people are your allies and fellow soldiers for peace, since we think it impossible for one who does evil . . . to escape God's notice" (*1 Apol.* 12.1). You want to collect taxes? "Everywhere we attempt to be the first to bring taxes and levies to those appointed by you, as we were taught by him [Jesus Christ]" (*1 Apol.* 17.1). In fact, except in this sense of having an arena where we can show our loyalty to God's commands, we are not interested in a human kingdom. "When you heard that we were awaiting a kingdom, you rashly supposed that we were talking about one that was human, though we were talking about the one that is with God. . . . If we were awaiting a human kingdom," you see, "we would have denied [the accusation that we were Christians] in order to avoid being killed, and we would have tried to escape detection in order to obtain what we were waiting for" (*1 Apol.* 11.1–2; cf. *1 Apol.* 17.3). I admit, of course, that "some of those who have already been caught were shown to be criminals" (*1 Apol.* 7.1).[44] But simply as a sociological fact, surely you could see that this would be true of any group, as it demonstrably is with, say, any of the philosophical schools (*1 Apol.* 7.2–5). In-group deviance is unsurprising if for no other reason than that it is simply a part of human life, and we make no complaints about the just punishment of criminals for their crimes (*1 Apol.* 7.2–5).[45]

Naturally, Justin could continue, we will not sacrifice to the gods, but we are not "atheists" (*1 Apol.* 6.1; 13.1).[46] That charge will not stick. We do reject the *daimones.* And yes, in our view, worship belongs to the one true God alone, to whom all, including emperors, are subordinate (*1 Apol.* 3.5; 17.10–11; 40.11; cf. *Dial.* 49.8).[47] But worship God we most certainly do. Do not forget, O lovers of law and justice, that we Christians could easily appeal to your father Caesar Hadrian's rescript concerning our treatment. "On the basis of [his] letter, we are able to insist that you command that judgments be given in accordance with our petition." We see no reason to do that, however, since our case is just on its own terms (*1 Apol.* 68.3).

Of course Justin does then actually append Hadrian's rescript as a reminder—one must cover the bases after all (*1 Apol.* 68.4). But his main point remains clear. The Christian case is on the side of justice.

If the justice of the Christian case is so obvious, a critic might ask, why can't the Romans see it? Justin's answer is simple, though, once again, surprising to moderns. It is not solely because of their upbringing or their education or their innate inabilities that they cannot reason their way to accept the Christians. It is rather, says Justin, because they are deceived by demons (*1 Apol.* 57.1).[48] "When it comes to us, though we bind ourselves to do no wrong and not to hold atheist opinions, you do not conduct the inquiry with sober judgment but with irrational passion, and driven under the whip of wicked demons you punish us without discernment and imprudently" (*1 Apol.* 5.1).[49] Yet hate such people we do not, says Justin. "As is apparent, out of pity we wish to persuade them to change" (*1 Apol.* 57.1).

In short, says Justin, Christians are the best citizens Rome has. They are not interested in the kind of power that sustains Roman political practices—they do not play the game Rome plays—but they are profoundly interested in living lives of peace and justice. If you want peace and justice, says Justin, let the Christians flourish. He does not shrink from declaring that Jesus is the true King and Lord (*1 Apol.* 12.7; cf. *Dial.* 135.1), and on many occasions he threatens the Roman rulers with the judgment of God (*1 Apol.* 17.4 et passim). He seems rather content, moreover, to describe the socially dense effects of Christian transformation in a way that could only irritate the Roman sense of social order (*2 Apol.* 2.1). But for all that, Justin's argument about justice and peace is completely sincere. If they care about justice and peace, truth and piety, Justin believes, the Romans should recognize these things in the Christians.

Whether or not Justin's petition was ever seriously considered is unknown. What Roman officials would make of his argument in this period of history, however, is not. It was foolishness. The Christians were not interested in justice but were stubbornly resistant to reasonable demands to give up their practice and return to regular Roman life—so stubborn in fact that torture and death would not dissuade them. Justin himself was one of them, and he was killed. Yet by his own account, he was not damaged. "You have the power to kill us," he says early in his petition, "but not to harm us" (*1 Apol.* 2.4; cf. *Dial.* 46.7).[50]

JUDAISM

No study of Justin would be complete without serious consideration of his relation to Judaism. The very existence of the *Dialogue with Trypho* says as much. Yet both because the entirety of the *Dialogue* is directly relevant to this issue and because the broader historical questions surrounding the "parting of the ways" between Judaism and Christianity are so complex and heavily debated, condensation is remarkably difficult.[51] Still, it is hard to miss what is the most distinctive feature of Justin's relation to Judaism, that of a complexly interwoven and profound dis-agreement. Characterizing Justin's relationship to Judaism as dis-agreement may well be orthographically awkward, but it is conceptually necessary for the simple reason that the hyphen gets to the truth of the matter: the simultaneity of agreement and disagreement occurs at the deeper level of things and cannot be dissolved (or, for that matter, resolved in ordinary time).[52] Justin and Trypho say "yes" together and "no" together on the question of God and Scripture, and it is this peculiar yes/no on these matters of fundamental, structuring importance that leads to the tension that characterizes the *Dialogue* as a whole. For the purposes of presentation, of course, we have to take Justin's yes and no successively, but it should be borne in mind that they actually occur simultaneously—as one complex relation.

The yes: By Justin's account, he and Trypho worship the same God, and they read the same Scriptures. The importance of this agreement is hard to overestimate. Over against all forms of pagan life about which we know anything much at all, Justin and Trypho agree that the only God is the one spoken of in the Scripture preserved and carried forward by the Jewish people. The Christians, like the Jews, worship only one God, the one who called Abraham and promised to send the Messiah. And the Christians, like the Jews, are a people of the book.[53] That this book is the same book, that it tells the same history of the same God with his people, distinguishes Justin and Trypho from their pagan neighbors and draws them into the shared theological framework that makes their argument both possible and intelligible.[54] Apart from this agreement, as Trypho says, their discussion could not have even gotten off the ground. "We would not have listened to you thus far had you not constantly cited the Scriptures in your attempts to prove your point, and had you not stated that there is no God superior to the Creator of the world" (*Dial.* 56.16). But with it, they inhabit a profoundly and materially similar world, one which is all the more distinctive given its areas of demarcation from constitutive aspects of wider pagan society.

The no: The trouble is, of course, that Trypho and Justin cannot agree on how the Scriptures position their readers in relation to God. Justin says that Trypho's teachers are ignorant of the meaning of the Scriptures (*Dial.* 9.1), but Trypho's reading of the Christian writings has hardly convinced him that they provide the key to scriptural knowledge and wisdom (*Dial.* 10.2; 18.1). Though they both affirm that the creator God will send the Messiah, they diverge on when and whom. For Justin, of course, the Messiah has already come for the first time, and he is none other than Jesus of Nazareth, the crucified one. It would be an overstatement, but not by much, to say that the *Dialogue* is one long work that attempts to illustrate the truth of this claim from the Old Testament. The prophecies in Scripture, says Justin numerous times and in various ways, have been fulfilled in the life, death, and resurrection of Jesus. For Trypho, the Messiah has not yet come, but when he does, he most certainly will not be crucified. The Old Testament prophecies about the Messiah, ipso facto therefore, do not refer to Jesus.

Jesus, then, is the hermeneutical sticking point. If he is the Messiah, as Justin holds, the Old Testament prophecies will be read in a fundamentally different way than if he is not, as Trypho believes. It is thus hardly surprising that their evaluation of the continuing force of the particularities of Old Testament Law depends upon their judgment about the significance of Jesus in God's ongoing work in the world. Nothing, Trypho would say, has changed in God's economy. The entirety of the Old Testament Law remains in force. True, the destruction of the Jerusalem temple has required certain legal adjustments—the laws stipulating what is and is not to be done in temple sacrifice, for example, cannot directly apply at the moment—but their enduring force has not been lessened (cf. *Dial.* 46.2). Justin, on the other hand, claims that much indeed has changed, that Jesus was a turning point in the ages—the definitive marker of the different way in which God will now deal with his people. Not all of the Old Testament stipulations are to be literally observed. Many must now be spiritually interpreted. The festival of unleavened bread, for example, should be coordinated with Christian baptism of repentance. The "symbolic meaning" of the festival is a life that avoids the "old deeds of the bad leaven" (*Dial.* 14.2). And true circumcision, Justin argues, echoing a motif that runs from Jeremiah to Paul, is of the heart rather than the flesh (*Dial.* 15.7; cf. *Dial.* 43.1–2). "What you really need," Justin tells Trypho, "is another circumcision, though you prize that of the flesh." Further, "the New Law demands that you observe a perpetual Sabbath, whereas you consider yourselves pious when you refrain from work one day a week. In so doing you [show that] you don't understand the real meaning of that precept" (*Dial.* 12.3).

But, says Trypho, there are Christians who continue to observe the Torah, are there not? There are, Justin replies, and though there are differences among genuine Christians over how to think about such observance, I believe it is just fine. It neither adds to nor takes anything away from salvation in Christ—all people, Jews and Gentiles alike, must repent to inherit the gifts of God (*Dial.* 25.6–26.1)—and if they wish to observe the Law, so be it (*Dial.* 47.1–3).

Well, this is just the problem, Trypho might say. Aside from these few who continue in their obedience to the Torah, the rest of you "do not observe a manner of life different from that of the Gentiles, for you do not keep the feasts or Sabbaths; nor do you practice the rite of circumcision. You place your hope in a crucified man, and still expect to receive good things from God when you disregard his commandments" (*Dial.* 10.3). But, Trypho, Justin would reply, we Christians are quite distinct from our neighbors precisely because of what you say at the end: we hope in a crucified man. And this itself is enough, as you well know, to enable us to be identified by our neighbors, tried by our officials as if we were criminals, and ultimately killed for continuing to confess this very hope.

As their comments about Torah observance illustrate, both Justin and Trypho recognize that their argument is not simply about hermeneutical theory—one should read Scripture in this way and not in that, and so on. Rather, Justin and

Trypho are ultimately arguing over the truth of different ways of being in the world. Scriptural interpretation is inseparably intertwined with these ways of living—both Jews and Christians claim to be scripturally shaped—but the sheer density of the lived difference can hardly be overstressed. Put simply, neither communities nor individuals can live at one and the same time as if all the commandments in the Torah are absolutely necessary to obey and as if they aren't. So, too, neither communities nor individuals can live as if Jesus both is and is not the Messiah.

Modern readers, for reasons both sound and sentimental, bristle at the strong language such difference evokes (esp. *Dial.* 38.1; 48.2; 93.4).[55] But in the ancient world vigorous, even harsh, polemic was the norm.[56] It did not necessarily signify contempt, much less a desire to persecute. Persecution there was, however, and cursing, too. It may be, says Justin to Trypho, that "now you cannot use violence against us because of those who are in power"—possibly here making reference to Hadrian's rescript—"but as often as you could, you employed force against us" (*Dial.* 16.4). Indeed, he later claims, "you curse [Jesus] and those who believe in him and, whenever it is in your power, put them to death" (*Dial.* 95.4). Christians, according to Justin, are regularly cursed by Jews in their synagogues (*Dial.* 96.2; cf. *Dial.* 16.4; 108.3; 133.6), and there are even traveling men from Jerusalem whose sole job is to spread rumors about the "godless heresy of the Christians" (*Dial.* 17.1).[57] Such realities clarify the fact that much more is at stake in the *Dialogue* than simply the rhetorical besting of a rival view.

Still, Justin insists to Trypho that "we Christians don't hate you, or those who believed the wicked rumors you spread about us" (*Dial.* 108.3). And the parting at the conclusion of the *Dialogue* could hardly be friendlier. It is true that even unto the last line Justin continues to wish for Trypho and his companions to embrace Jesus as the Christ of God, but it is also true that both Trypho and Justin acknowledge the possibility of friendship that has arisen in their attempt to reason together about the truth of God and Scripture.

> Trypho continued, "You see that it wasn't by any deliberate design that we began the discussion of these matters, but I confess that I have derived great pleasure from our association. . . . If we could meet more frequently and continue our study of the Scriptures, we would certainly profit even more by it. But since you are about to leave the city . . . do not hesitate to remember us as friends when you depart."

Justin replies:

> "As for myself," I said, "if I had stayed here, I would have liked to do this same thing every day. But since I expect to embark at once . . . I beg of you

to put your every effort into this great struggle for your own salvation, and to embrace the Christ of almighty God in preference to your teachers."

He then concludes the *Dialogue:*

> After this they left me, wishing me a safe voyage and deliverance from every disaster. And I in turn prayed for them, saying, "I can wish you no greater blessing than this, gentlemen, that realizing that wisdom is given to every person through this Way, you also may one day come to believe entirely as we do that Jesus is the Messiah of God." (*Dial.* 108.3)

Justin had not tasted the modern sap that frequently accompanies lowest-common-denominator attempts to deal with religious difference. But had he known of it, he would have found it unpalatable. Theological friendship, for him, does not come from divesting oneself of one's most basic, normative commitments. It comes, rather, from reading the same Scriptures in effort to know the same God and do his will.

It is therefore unsurprising to find Justin telling Trypho that he does not understand the things that are written "in your Scriptures, or rather not yours but ours. For we have been persuaded by them, but you, though you've read them, do not understand their deeper logic" (*Dial.* 29.2; cf. *Dial.* 82.1).[58] This "yours-or-rather-ours" encapsulates the dialectical nature of the argument Justin has with Trypho.[59] Affirmation and negation are spoken in the same breath.[60] Where late-twentieth-century scholars see in such statements a wrongful seizing of someone else's belongings, Justin himself would challenge the unstated premise of the modern view, namely, that what the Christians claim about Jesus should have no bearing on the question of how to read the Old Testament. Truth claims of this sort are just more complex, Justin might have said to his modern readers. They cannot be resolved by swinging an ideological billy stick or, in fact, by any criteria external to the traditions between which the truth about God is contested. Unless one converts to the other's way of life, dis-agreement between Justin and Trypho will continue until the coming/return of the Messiah.

So much has Justin's martyrdom become a part of his identity that many students are surprised to learn that Martyr is not his actual last name. If the writings are any indication of the man, this is really no surprise. Again and again Justin proclaims the Christians' willingness to face death for the sake of witnessing to Christ. True, Justin was the first to address systematically the wider political conditions under which such death occurred, and he argued strongly against the practice of convicting Christians. But when the time came, and his arguments had failed, he lived what he preached and went to his death confessing Christ. This was for him the Christian philosophy: not the reasoned culmination of a general wisdom simply there for the taking, but a particular lived wisdom that followed the itinerary set out by the fleshly Logos himself, Jesus of Nazareth. Precisely because Jesus not only shows the way of reason but also testifies to death's impermanence and defeat, Christians know that they will be rescued from death. We have no reason to lie about who we are, says Justin, since we do not fear death (*1 Apol.* 8.2). We can face torture and even "rejoice in the death penalty" because God will raise us up free forever of corruption, pain, and death (*Dial.* 46.7). For Justin, therefore, the shape of a true philosophical life corresponds to nothing less than a complete christological vision of humanity's current repair and eternal salvation. That he lived this conviction in addition to teaching it does not, of course, make it true per force.[61] But it does place a serious argument on the table of just the sort that Justin the philosopher would have appreciated, namely, that Christianity is truer even than death.

Part Three

7

CAN WE COMPARE?

Unlike Davidson, I hold that there are rival and alternative conceptual schemes, in some respect untranslatable into each other, and that alternative and rival conceptions of rationality are at home in different conceptual schemes.
—*Alasdair MacIntyre*

The previous six chapters raise an obvious question: how should we read them in relation to one another?[1] If we grant that the three Stoics and three Christians belong together, what are we to make of the larger Stoic/Christian relation implied in their juxtaposition?

The judgment behind this chapter is that it would be largely useless to begin yet another discussion of the Christians/Stoics under the same set of assumptions that have determined the majority of modern scholarship. Reevaluating the same evidence on the same terms may lead to something that looks like more knowledge, but in fact it would be only one more small shift of the pieces in a predetermined shape of inquiry. That shape is "cosmopolitan modernity": the complex cluster of co-commitments that makes it possible to believe in the translucifying power of scholarly reason vis-à-vis any text from any tradition, in the contribution of scholarly research on particular traditions to Knowledge in General about ancient religions/philosophies, and in the freedom of the scholar to abstain from the conflicts about which he writes.[2] Yet it is just this wider shape of inquiry that needs to be discarded if we are rightly to see what the Stoic and Christian traditions were and how to conceive their relation. In short, we must "reset" the terms of the discussion.

To that end, we turn first to the work of Alasdair MacIntyre. Not only does MacIntyre describe the intellectual conditions that best make sense of how to think about thinking in the current age, he also has developed a rich conception of "tradition" that describes better than anything else what ancient Christianity and Stoicism were.[3] Indeed, the wager here is that to miss that they were something like traditions in MacIntyre's sense is to misapprehend not only their forms of life but also the basic shape of the questions that surround how we might fruitfully think their relation. If we are to reset our thinking about ancient Christianity/Stoicism, then we ought to begin by discovering again what they were and were not—and, therefore, how to think them in relation.

ENCYCLOPEDIA, GENEALOGY, TRADITION

In his 1988 Gifford Lectures, Alasdair MacIntyre outlined three versions of inquiry that have most profoundly shaped our understanding of knowledge within the past two centuries: encyclopedia, genealogy, and tradition.[4] MacIntyre argues convincingly that these are three incommensurable, and therefore rival, ways of conceiving the work of inquiry. To opt for one is to deny the other two.[5]

Though MacIntyre's larger argument shows that only genealogy and tradition are serious options in the present, encyclopedic inquiry remains the dominant way in which scholars who study the New Testament and ancient philosophy go about their work. In order to see why the encyclopedic style of thinking prevents us from getting to the heart of the comparative question, we must first understand *in nuce* the basic shape of the intellectual terrain mapped by MacIntyre. In so doing we will be able both to locate intellectually some of the deeper difficulties in past/current work on the New Testament/ancient philosophy and—eventually—to argue for an alternative way of conceiving the Stoic/Christian relation as a conflict of traditions.

MacIntyre begins with the encyclopedic way of knowing partly because it was chronologically prior to its genealogical undoing. In truth, as with any large-scale way of organizing knowledge, the encyclopedic way of knowing was complex, but its cardinal characteristics were three. First, the late-nineteenth-century encyclopedists were committed to the notion of a single, unitary rationality. By "rationality" MacIntyre does not so much mean an explicitly worked-out philosophy of mind as he does a presupposition of the way their thought could do the work it did: for the encyclopedists, "it was a guiding presupposition of thought that substantive rationality is unitary, that there is a single, if perhaps complex, conception of what the standards and the achievements of rationality are, one which every educated person can without too much difficulty be brought to agree in acknowledging. The application of the methods and goals of this single and unitary conception to any one particular distinctive subject matter is what yields a science."[6]

"Scientific" knowledge was not the specialized domain of natural science it is today but included theology, philosophy, history, biology, and everything else. There was no such thing as the possibility of different types of knowledges, only the one Knowledge. Knowledge, or science, was "individuated" by its "subject matter" not by its "methods" (19). The encyclopedists thus took it for granted "that all rational persons conceptualize data in one and the same way" (16). In the strictest sense, therefore, nothing was unintelligible, for nothing lay outside the range of rationality thus conceived.

Second, the encyclopedists were committed to the notion of a unified world. All rational persons, it was thought, would "report the same data, the same facts" (16). The world's unity was what scientific rationality mapped as it did its work. The product of an "allegiance to the standards and methods of" a single, substantive rationality was "to be the elaboration of a comprehensive, rationally incontestable scientific understanding of the whole, in which the architectonic of the sciences matched that of the cosmos" (24). Scholarship and world were one.

Third, the encyclopedists were committed to the notion of progress. Inquiry was not starts and stops, departures and returns, but forward movement that came out of the darkness into the light of modern understanding. The encyclopedists "saw their whole mode of life, including their conceptions of rationality and of science, as part of a history of inevitable progress, judged by a standard of progress which had itself emerged from that history. . . . That the history of rationality and science might itself be a history of ruptures and discontinuities was for them an unthinkable thought" (24). Indeed, the "narrative structure of the encyclopedia is one dictated by the belief in the progress of reason" (78). Reason's discoveries, however, are not historically contingent realities but the "timeless truths" that can be formulated in timelessly true principles (78). Where the encyclopedists looked to the past, they assumed that all thinkers offered accounts "of the rational status of one and the same timeless subject matter" (28). The measuring of these accounts as better and worse depended upon the perception of progress toward the encyclopedists' conception of truth—which is to say that the past was judged in light of the present, conceived as the acme of intellectual progress.

MacIntyre's chief example of encyclopedic understanding is the ninth edition of the *Encyclopaedia Britannica* (1875–89), in which all three of the commitments just discussed are on display not only in the articles but also in the conception of the work as a whole. MacIntyre clearly sees that many of the contributors did or would disagree with each other on a wide range of things, but he argues that such disagreement was disagreement within a shared set of assumptions about the way knowledge worked; even the disagreements, that is, confirmed the larger common commitments of encyclopedic inquiry. As the original editor, Thomas Spencer Baynes, made clear, "his contributors [were] not merely to provide detailed information on every major topic but to do so within the framework of a distinctive architectonic of the sciences that had emerged in the late nineteenth century" (18). The "whole of which the subordinate sciences are parts is the encyclopedia itself" (23).

In short, to be reasonable is to be an encyclopedist. The encyclopedist's "conception is of a single framework within which knowledge is discriminated from mere belief, progress toward knowledge is mapped, and truth is understood as the relationship of *our* knowledge to *the* world, through the application of those methods whose rules are the rules of rationality as such" (42, emphasis original). Truth is thus "what it is independent of standpoint [and] can be discovered or confirmed by any adequately intelligent person, no matter what his point of view" (60). For the encyclopedist inquiry is necessarily cosmopolitan. There is nothing we cannot understand. And since understanding does not depend on us in any sort of personally significant way, there is no need to write in anything other than an impersonal sort of style—an objectifying discourse that appears as if no one in particular has written it. For, indeed, if we are all cosmopolitans, what I have written may well have been written by anyone.

As MacIntyre conclusively demonstrates, the encyclopedic version of inquiry has been defeated by its rivals. It is now only "fideism."[7] Why, therefore, "at this point in time continue to treat the standpoint of the Ninth Edition as a serious contender in the debate? After all," MacIntyre continues, "nobody now shares" the encyclopedic framework, making it "seem absurd to give to it the kind of critical attention which suggests that its claims to our intellectual and moral allegiance still deserve to be taken seriously" (170).

MacIntyre gives three reasons to justify the attention he pays to encyclopedic inquiry. First, we are now far enough away from its origins that it is possible to criticize the framework as a whole in a way that wasn't possible during its time as the operative style of inquiry.

Second, we continue to act in a large-scale way as if the encyclopedic inquiry is a live option. "Even now the organized institutions of the academic curriculum and the ways in which both enquiry and teaching are conducted in and through those institutions are structured to a significant degree *as if* we did believe much of what the major contributors to the Ninth Edition believed." Institutions and curriculum, of course, are not the same thing as the publication outlets for scholarly work—journals, monograph series, and the like—but in fact these outlets often simply reflect the assumptions of the larger university's structure. How we train is how we publish. "We often still behave as if there is . . . some underlying agreement about the academic project of just the kind in which those contributors believed." Knowledge, MacIntyre implies, is socialized in a way that contradicts what we now know about knowledge; it is time to recognize the contradiction. "The ghosts of the Ninth Edition haunt the contemporary academy. They need to be exorcised" (171).

Third, such "as if" academic practice both assumes and continues to transmit the encyclopedic "belief that every rationally defensible standpoint can engage with every other, the belief that, whatever may be thought about incommensurability in theory, in academic practice it can be safely neglected." There is nothing the university curriculum cannot encompass or absorb into itself, no text or form of life that stands outside the comprehensive capabilities of scholarly study: "The universal translatability of texts from any and every culture into the language of teacher and student is taken for granted. And so is the universality of a capacity to make what was framed in the light of the canons of one culture intelligible to those who inhabit some other quite alien culture, provided only that the latter is our own, or one very like it" (171).[8] The possibility of genuine obstacles to understanding that are endemic to the worlds of both genealogical and traditioned inquiry are completely ignored, treated as if they do not exist. The incomprehensible, the utterly strange to us and our way of knowing—these are systematically denied reality by the framework that prevents the confrontation they require.[9]

MacIntyre thus argues, in brief, that we must pay close attention to encyclopedic knowing because of the strangeness of contemporary intellectual culture. The encyclopedia lives on and continues to form structurally the way we learn and think—even though it is in fact quite dead.

Genealogical inquiry, by stark contrast, negates the encyclopedist's most fundamental commitments. Indeed, genealogy uses—historically no less than philosophically—the existence of the encyclopedic framework as the foil against which it makes itself intelligible (that on which it feasts, to use its own sort of idiom, for the joy of consumption). Where the encyclopedist presupposed unitary rationality, a unified world, and progress toward truth itself, Nietzsche, the original genealogist, saw no such things. "Reason" names for him no one "ruled" way of thinking but only the particular representations of particular interests, drives to power, distortions, and repressions. "There are no rules of rationality as such . . . there are rather [only] strategies of insight and strategies of subversion" (42). Cosmopolitanism, the genealogist argues, is an illusion: we can only take sides in the warring of various rivals (56).

Instead of reading the past as an inferior predecessor to the conception of truth in the present, the genealogist thus freely takes sides with ancient thinkers and uses them to unveil modern scholarly pretensions for what they really are. There is no progress—because there is no goal toward which to progress—only the endless recycling of moods, feelings, or sickly psychological postures. The modern pretense to objectivity, for example, is really a form of repression and of alienation from the world it claims to study: "The academic mode of utterance," so Nietzsche thought, was "an expression of merely reactive attitudes and feelings, their negative, repressed, and repressive character disguised behind a mask of fixity and objectivity" (39). It is not, however, that the genealogist takes sides with the ancients because he thinks they have a better claim to truth, since in fact Truth in the big sense does not exist (aiming at objective truth was to aim at nothing). It is rather only that he uses the ancients in the way he sees fit: to expose modern moral inquiry as just one more moment in the overall "history of those social and psychological formations in which the will to power is distorted into and concealed by the will to truth" (39). The ancients, no less than anyone else, can be useful.

The typical academic style of writing can thus be discarded for genealogical purposes. There is no objectified truth to which the research voice of impersonal truth-seeking and result-presentation corresponds. Truth is the accumulated historical weight of metaphors, rhetoric, poetry, and illusions—illusions that people have forgotten were once only illusions (35). Yet as MacIntyre notes, "it is quite difficult *not* to read *Zur Genealogie der Moral* otherwise than as one more magisterial treatise, better and more stylishly written indeed than the books of Kant . . . or of Ranke or of Harnack . . . but deploying arguments and appealing to sources in the same way, plainly constrained by the same standards of factual accuracy and no more obviously polemical against rival views" (44; emphasis in original). In other words, it looks as if the genealogist, too, is after the truth of things.

The genealogical answer to this suspicion is that the "treatise" only appears this way. As it turns out, however, "every piece of writing . . . is utterance on the move," momentary words for the occasion. Both before and after the writing of any particular piece, there is an ongoing, even circular, stream of works—and the stream itself has no truth. We simply get in and swim along. On his own terms, therefore, the genealogist isn't arguing for the truth as such but instead only showing how the use of words undoes contemporary conceptions of truth as such. But claim to have found the truth? No. Just using words, playing with them, turning them this way and that to unmask what can be unmasked. There is no finality to such play, or such unmasking, for all utterances remain open to future play, to their own future unmasking (44–45).[10]

The genealogist thus does not so much make arguments that go *toward* anything as he does take a momentary stance, pose as a critic for the time being, adopt a particular posture on a certain stage. For him, there are only masks to be worn, roles to be played, for this or that purpose—according to genealogical desire. The style can therefore be personal, even aphoristic, because the mask that is momentarily worn is particular to the role at this (and not that) moment. Foucault, for example, a master of genealogical inquiry, takes the word *author* to "name a role or function, not a person, and the use of a particular author's name discharges this function by assigning a certain status to a piece of discourse" (51). Hence can genealogical inquiry dispense with the consistency that universal rationality requires. Authors are momentary functions, texts words that play this or that role, rationality the "this kind" or "that kind" of the role the words play. If "this kind" fundamentally conflicts with "that kind"—or if we can understand "this kind" but are completely puzzled by "that kind"—so much the better.

As MacIntyre puts it, "it was a central presupposition of the major contributors to the Ninth Edition [of the *Encyclopaedia Britannica*] . . . that on questions of standards, criteria, and method all rational persons can resolve their disagreements." And it is "an equally central contention of the heirs of Nietzschean genealogy that this is not so" (170). Where "a blindness to the possibility of genuine alternative conceptual schemes is a necessary part of the encyclopaedist's point of view," an "openness to that possibility is equally necessary on the part of the genealogist" (44). They are, in short, rivals.

Which, of course, speaks *for* genealogical inquiry, as even the later editions of the *Encyclopaedia Britannica* itself attest. Already in the fifteenth edition of 1974, "heterogeneous and divergent contributions, which recognize the diversity and fragmentation of standpoints in central areas, are deeply at odds with the overall scheme, insofar as that scheme presupposes any real unity to the work, rather than merely providing some organization for a massive work of reference." What the fifteenth-edition encyclopedia embodies, as the chief editor himself acknowledges, is nothing greater than "faith in the unity of knowledge." Encyclopedic inquiry, he inadvertently admits, "has become one more fideism" (56). The transformation of the inquirer "from a participant in an encyclopedic enterprise shared by all adequately reflective and informed human beings into an engaged partisan of one such warring standpoint against its rivals is an accomplished fact" (56). Look around, MacIntyre argues, at any respectable university's intellectual shape, and what will become apparent is not only that there are incommensurable ways of inquiry on offer within virtually every department—unresolved disagreements abound—but also that there are no shared set of agreements that would be necessary to resolve the disagreements. Progress between incommensurable ways of knowing happens not. Rivals are rivals all the way down, and that it is so is the victory of genealogical inquiry.

The genealogical vanquishing of the encyclopedia does not mean, however, that every rival has been laid to rest. Indeed, in MacIntyre's view, tradition can defeat genealogy on its own terms.[11] But a tradition of inquiry is not simply one more version of pure reason's best workings; it is, rather, more like a craft, at least in five important ways.

First, a tradition of inquiry is historically deep, which is to say that it is not timeless but extends through time. Like a craft, which does not emerge out of nowhere but comes on the scene in the midst of time and is deepened and enriched through time, a tradition of inquiry takes shape only through its historically extended life. It is more, however, than a historically deep and coherent trajectory of thought, for those who engage in that trajectory "become aware of it and of its direction and in self-aware fashion attempt to engage its debates and to carry its enquiries forward."[12] That is to say, like the practitioners of a craft who are self-consciously relating to the history and current state of the craft that they practice, traditioned reasoners self-consciously engage the past and present of their tradition with an aim toward its future development. In contrast both to encyclopedic and genealogical inquiry, the narrative of traditioned inquiry "treats the past neither as mere prologue nor as something to be struggled against, but as that from which we have to learn if we are to identify and move toward our *telos* more adequately and that which we have to put to the question if we are to know which questions we ourselves should next formulate and attempt to answer" (79).

Second, like a craft in which every way to do it is not as good as every other, a tradition of inquiry has norms of and for rational success that have emerged through history as the tradition has come to identify excellence in its particular way of inquiry. "The standards of achievement within any craft are justified historically," which is to say that "just because at any particular moment the rationality of a craft is justified by its history so far, which has made it what it is in that specific time, place, and set of historical circumstances, [a craft's] rationality is inseparable from the tradition through which it was achieved." To be rational, that is, is not to follow reason's timeless principles but to participate in the tradition's particular shape of rationality as it has developed through history: "The participant in a craft is rational qua participant insofar as he or she conforms to the best standards of reason discovered so far, and the rationality in which he or she thus shares is always, therefore . . . understood as a historically situated rationality" (64–65). Rationality is thus learning a particularized skill in the midst of time.[13]

Third, learning the skills that make a tradition of inquiry cannot simply be done with "the mind." Rather, for a tradition in MacIntyre's sense, the skill of rational inquiry requires a transformation of the person in a much broader sense. In contrast to encyclopedic inquiry, in which anyone can approach any text and understand it, traditioned inquiry requires a reader who has virtues that precede the ability to interpret well. The inquirer "has to make him or herself into a particular kind of person if he or she is to move towards a knowledge of the truth" (61). Indeed, a "prerational reordering of the self has to occur before the reader can have an adequate standard by which to judge what is a good reason and what is not," that is, to know in what rationality itself consists (82). That someone would need to be wise in order to read texts well is as far from encyclopedic understanding as it is from modern natural science in which wisdom is not taken to be requisite for interpreting the "behavior" of a proton. And yet it is endemic to the notion of tradition as a craft of inquiry. There is an "understanding of [a tradition's] texts which becomes available only to the transformed self" (82). But this creates an apparent paradox: "Only insofar as we have already arrived at certain conclusions are we able to become the sort of person able to engage in such enquiry so as to reach sound conclusions" (63). How, then, does such transformation occur?

Fourth, in the same way that an apprentice learns from a teacher how to acquire the skills needed to practice a craft well, a participant in a tradition requires a teacher of the craft of inquiry. It is true, MacIntyre argues, that there is a resident, inherent potential for transformation; otherwise, we could not learn what we need to know to take part in a tradition. But not only does a teacher "help actualize" such potential in a particular direction we would not necessarily find ourselves, a teacher is also the concrete authority on what we need to learn. "We shall have to learn" from a teacher, says MacIntyre, "and initially accept on the basis of his or her authority within the community of a craft precisely what intellectual and moral habits it is which we must cultivate and acquire if we are to become . . . participants in such enquiry" (63). Learning the rationality of inquiry is not a matter of striking out on one's own but of submitting to the judgments of those who have already mastered the craft. In this way, the apprentice makes the "prior commitment" necessary to develop the habits that are prerequisite to becoming a competent member of the craft community (60–63).

Fifth, as the master/apprentice relation implies, traditioned inquiry is a "long-term cooperative activity" (150). Just as the existence of a craft presupposes a body of practitioners, so traditioned inquiry presupposes a community. There is no such thing as the solitary individual on his quest for knowledge. "Membership in a particular type of moral community . . . is a condition for genuinely rational enquiry" (60). As MacIntyre notes, "any notion that I can only think adequately by and for myself insofar as I do so in the company of others, to some of whom authority must be accorded, is quite alien to the encyclopedist, as it is indeed also to the genealogist, who cannot but see in such authority the exercise of a subjugating power which has to be resisted" (64). To have a tradition of inquiry without a community that itself embodies the tradition, however, is a contradiction in terms. Tradition means community.

MacIntyre argues that tradition was what inquiry was from Socrates to Aquinas and that a major break occurred after Aquinas.[14] "In one respect encyclopedist and genealogist . . . agree. There is on their views such a thing as the history of morality and correspondingly such a thing as the history of ethics, a history with a single subject matter and genuine continuity. As to the character of that continuity there is radical disagreement, but that one and the same history begins with Socrates and runs to the late nineteenth century is not a point of contention." MacIntyre disagrees. The history "initially generated by Socrates . . . was interrupted in the most radical way" on the path to modernity. It was in and through this interruption "that morality as understood by post-Enlightenment modernity was generated." If when we now speak of morality and ethics we mean "roughly what . . . the contributors to the Ninth Edition [*Encyclopaedia Britannica*] meant, then 'morality' is . . . a distinctively modern phenomenon" (190–91; cf. 58–59).

Lest it seem that with his focus on morality and ethics MacIntyre has left out much of what counts as inquiry, he would be quick to respond that this charge presupposes exactly the modern view of morality/ethics as something divisible from the rest of life—and thereby unwittingly testifies to the very historical break he identifies. Traditioned inquiry does of course live on the other side of the break, but its location is primarily in religious communities rather than in professional philosophy, that is, not in university departments premised on the professionalization of a discrete discipline but in the places where theological reflection presupposes the moral habituation needed to read texts with rational competence.

A tradition of inquiry, for MacIntyre, is thus a morally grained, historically situated rationality, a way of asking and answering questions that is inescapably tied to the inculcation of habits in the life of the knower and to the community that originates and stewards the craft of inquiry through time. *Tradition* in this sense is the word that best describes the forms of life that were ancient Christianity and Stoicism.

"AS IF . . ."—ENCYCLOPEDIA STILL AT WORK

MacIntyre's reading of our current situation deserves close consideration for the simple reason that he cogently describes the conditions that, first, make sense of the difficulties inherent in the majority of recent study of the Christians/

Stoics and, second, articulate the larger problems embedded in any attempt to think similarity/difference—the question of the Christian/Stoic relation. In the terms of MacIntyre's taxonomy, recent studies of the New Testament and ancient philosophy have by and large been conducted *as if* the encyclopedic style of knowing were a viable way to study ancient texts. The comparative problem has therefore systematically been obscured. For, after all, early Christianity and Roman Stoicism were not things to be entered into the encyclopedia of modern knowledge; they were traditions.

To understand the difference this mistake makes for the way we conceive each tradition and the relation between them, we must first see how the most important recent work on ancient philosophy and the New Testament has been determined by encyclopedic assumptions. This will allow us to specify the more fundamental distortions that arise from the strangeness of studying traditions as if they were something else. From there, we will be able to suggest how best to go forward in light of the fact that the relation at the heart of our study is a conflict of traditions.

An exhaustive survey of the research on early Christianity and Stoicism would doubtless turn up more than one set of normative judgments about the practice of scholarly work.[15] Still, the degree to which a common set of judgments appears is significant enough to justify describing it as a particular style of inquiry, namely, the encyclopedic. Numerous scholars did not, that is, get together, think out, and agree on how best to carry out their comparative work; rather, across both time and space they simply participate—some more consciously, some less so—in the powerful assumptions named by MacIntyre that have long shaped modern thinking about historical study.

The best way to illustrate the particular shape of this generalization is to focus briefly on two of the most outstanding scholars of the past forty years who work with encyclopedic assumptions: Abraham Malherbe and Troels Engberg-Pedersen. This will allow us to see clearly the normative claims involved in the vast majority of scholarly work, not least because the scholarship of Malherbe has had enormous influence and that of Engberg-Pedersen has provoked extensive current debate. Malherbe and Engberg-Pedersen differ on what to look for in ancient philosophy in at least one important respect (social practices on the one hand and ideas on the other), and they differ on the amount of hermeneutical reflection needed to accompany their spade work. But taken together they evidence a span of judgments about scholarly inquiry that materially informs vast numbers of books and articles on the ancient Christians/pagan philosophers. Malherbe and Engberg-Pedersen can be seen, that is, not only as prodigious individual scholars but also as "focal instances" of the encyclopedic assumptions about the work of comparison that underlie the majority of modern research on the Stoics and early Christians.

During the last quarter of the twentieth century, when it came to the question of the New Testament's relation to Greco-Roman philosophy, it would have been hard to find a more learned and influential scholar than Abraham Malherbe. In addition to publishing works on both the New Testament and classical texts, he trained a generation of scholars whose knowledge of the ancient world is deep and intellectually significant.[16]

Malherbe's published contributions are too many and varied to take all at once.[17] We shall thus focus on the substantial *Aufstieg und Niedergang der römischen Welt* (*ANRW*) article "Hellenistic Moralists and the New Testament." This article is significant for its length, its command of primary sources, and its method of sifting secondary scholarship (as well as the number of scholars who regularly refer to it). More important, however, it encapsulates and displays a range of normative judgments about the practice of scholarly inquiry. Over the course of sixty-six pages, one can discern not only the close connection to his other publications but also how Malherbe conceives comparative thought.[18] For the purposes of this chapter, three broader commitments and/or assumptions are important to note.

First, echoing the criticism that gained wide methodological consensus after Samuel Sandmels's presidential address to the Society of Biblical Literature in 1961 ("Parallelomania"), Malherbe eschews the simplistic piling up of parallels as a way to compare texts from differing traditions of thought/practice. It is true, Malherbe argues, that we can still learn much from consulting Wettstein's parallels to the New Testament, as well as Wettstein's newer incarnations. But more fundamental, continues Malherbe, is the point that words that sound alike don't always mean the same thing. Still less can we reasonably trace lines of influence from one tradition to another by means of similar-sounding words. With these points, no reasonable person could today disagree. Malherbe's argument here, that is, has to do rather more with the important but long obvious surface of things than it does with the more difficult philosophical questions that surround how we recognize similarity/difference in the first place. If the same words can mean different things on account of their different embedding in wider contexts, what are these wider contexts that allow us to discern the differing meaning of the words, and how do we see similarity/difference in light of these wider contexts? Malherbe's hermeneutical direction has not moved past the encyclopedist to ask how we relate words whose meaning is determined by the tradition in which they live to words whose meaning is determined by another tradition in which they live. His is essentially still the confident position of the encyclopedist: scholars can use parallels to relate differing "schools"—religions, philosophies, and so on—to one another under a more general umbrella of knowledge as long as the research is learnedly careful and does not overdo it.

Second, in consonance with his wider work, Malherbe holds that ancient philosophy was much broader than typical current understandings of the discipline tend to allow. In antiquity, philosophy was "psychagogy." Psychagogy "included what today is meant by spiritual exercises, psychotherapy, and psychological and pastoral counseling."[19] With such a broad range of activity, it is no wonder that psychagogy also describes many of the early Christians' attempts to guide their churches. St. Paul, for example, was a psychagogical figure: the nature of his pastoral practice, that is, is most clearly understood in light of the psychagogic practice.[20] The differences between St. Paul and the philosophers should not be overlooked, of course, but the substantively similar shape of their craft is significant for our attempt to read them both well. For Malherbe, psychagogy is thus a specific area of productive comparison between the ancient philosophers and the early Christians because it is the common practice that best describes the working-end of ancient anthropologies of repair. But to what degree difference in content means difference in thing—to whom is a spiritual exercise directed, for example? or in light of whom is it conducted?—is not given any extended thought. Regardless of the fact that we can assign only specific meaning to work such as "psychotherapy"—there are, in truth, only psychotherapies of this or that kind—Malherbe's confidence in the scholar's ability to describe a general practical similarity between practitioners with widely differing understandings of their craft is unshaken.

Third, Malherbe assumes the existence of a continuum along which both the Christians and the pagan philosophers can be placed. Both ancient Christians and philosophers "share a basic, self-orienting goal . . . a commitment to help people better themselves, but . . . differ in their own self-understandings and the consequences thereof for the ways in which they go about their shared task."[21] The "commitment to help people better themselves" is the continuum, the "self-understandings and the consequences thereof" is the difference that locates them at various points across it. J. N. Sevenster's work on the difference between Paul and Seneca is insufficient and unilluminating precisely because he saw only the points of difference and missed the continuum itself. Had he "cast the net more widely," the "differences would likely have been ameliorated."[22]

Of course, the more specific name Malherbe gives to the continuum is morality. The "moral formation of individuals as well as communities" is the task performed by the philosophers and New Testament authors alike. St. Paul, to take Malherbe's perennially important example, "followed the methods of the moral philosophers."[23] "Moral philosophers," "moral development," "moral reformation," "moral material," and so forth: all these sorts of recurrent expressions assume a wider category about which the Christian and pagan philosophers have views and in light of which their specific ways of being in the world can be described. No matter how widely the net is cast, in Malherbe's way of thinking each item that is caught will be a variant of the same basic thing—different members, one might say, of the species called "moral."

Malherbe is not given to metacritical reflection. It is thus perhaps no surprise that he offers no reasons to support the encyclopedic assumption that there is such a thing as the moral life in general. But, after all, it is this assumption of his larger project that is most obviously shared with his nineteenth-century forebears. There is some part of being human, Malherbe assumes, that is called "the moral," and by elucidating the contour of this part scholars "enrich our understanding."[24]

Malherbe is not alone, of course, in his assumption that similarity in thought or practice between the ancient pagan philosophers and early Christians can be discovered and expressed through more comprehensive categories of scholarly analysis. In fact, his is the commonplace assumption of the majority of modern comparative studies of the Stoics and the early Christians—as can be discerned through a brief examination of another way in which it is similarly at work in the most recent studies on the Stoics and the early Christians.

Because of its obvious importance and scholarly quality, the work of Troels Engberg-Pedersen has already received elaborate discussion in several academic outlets.[25] With two significant exceptions, the majority of the engagement with Engberg-Pedersen has focused on his exegetical proposals vis-à-vis St. Paul's letters rather than upon the wider conceptual commitments needed to sustain his overall project.[26] For our purposes, however, these wider commitments are what need scrutiny.

Though plenteous modern New Testament scholars will have read Bultmann's little essay "Is Exegesis Without Presuppositions Possible?" many would not know quite what to say about it. Engberg-Pedersen, however, does. All exegesis, he says, answering Bultmann's question, presupposes a philosophical account of the world. "The challenge issued by philosophical exegesis"—Engberg-Pedersen's term for his own project—"is a double one: first, that interpreters should always attempt to articulate the broader conceptual framework (worldview) within which they are operating, and second, that they (we) are under a constant obligation to try to find the best defensible framework within which to operate."[27] Engberg-Pedersen's lengthy opening chapter to *Paul and the Stoics* meets the first part of this double challenge (and, presumably, is thus the working-result of the attempt to meet the second part). But his "broader conceptual framework" is evident in his other writings as well. It is of course complex and subtle, but there are three discernible lines of thought that are both indispensable to Engberg-Pedersen's wider commitments and significantly relevant to this chapter.

First, Engberg-Pedersen holds that it is possible to investigate pure ideas. He does not think, of course, that Paul and the Stoics were ancient Hegels interested in the progressive movement of ideas or the like. But he does argue that for scholarly purposes modern academics can largely bypass ancient practice and isolate ideas for analysis. "The coherence of Paul's many ideas as ideas" is what Engberg-Pedersen claims to study.[28] In the defenses against his detractors who emphasize the social difference between the early Christians and the Stoics, Engberg-Pedersen thus doesn't so much respond to their criticisms as suggest that they missed his focus.[29] Taking "ideas as ideas" is in this case the way one should think similarity and difference.

Conceptually speaking, it is this commitment to the availability of pure ideas that underlies Engberg-Pedersen's confidence in the scholar's ability to make a "model" that fits both Paul and the Stoics. The model is not identical with Paul or the Stoics but instead is constructed as a cluster of ideas that together articulate philosophical congruence or similarity. "There is a fundamental similarity in the basic model that structures both Stoic ethics and Paul's comprehensive *parenesis* in his letters as a whole."[30]

Jonathan Z. Smith's classic point is here rejected in favor of the power of scholarly work on ideas. As all comparativists know, Smith argued that the reason things seem similar to scholars is because the comparative models they make require similarity for their intelligibility as comparative tools. Such models do not, however, actually discern similarity as much as presuppose it or, in Smith's language, invent it through the "associations" that come with the shape of memory.[31] To risk a tautology, then, the basic point of Engberg-Pedersen's model—that Paul and the Stoics understand the philosophical logic of conversion and progress in the moral life in significantly similar ways—presupposes the philosophical viability of the model itself. Such viability, however, is tied to the encyclopedic view that life is not determinative of thinking as such; it can instead be cordoned off from pure reason, the domain of ideas. In claiming to focus upon "ideas as ideas," Engberg-Pedersen repeats the encyclopedists' conviction that reason's reasons work the same way regardless of the human lives in which they are actually found. Thought is thinkable, that is, in abstraction from life.[32]

Second, Engberg-Pedersen argues for a "naturalistic" understanding of Paul's discourse. By the term *naturalistic* Engberg-Pedersen means that Paul was not writing in a revealed dialect of the Holy Spirit but in the language of men. Paul's arguments, therefore, would not have required a special gift to be understood; they would have been completely intelligible to all who encountered them. "The story (of the Christ event) might be a strange one, as Paul did not at all deny, but it was one to be accepted (or rejected) as any other account of the world. Paul's 'theologizing' stood in what we may call 'direct confrontation' with other accounts of the world, in the sense that they were logically operating at the same level. It was not secured logically beforehand in a way that would turn the dialogue into a sham."[33]

Engberg-Pedersen's concern for the integrity of "dialogue" is of course a modern one,[34] but his argument is less about that than it is the essentially rational basis of all religious/philosophical language. In principle, all claims—whether Stoic or Christian or, presumably, anything else—stand as equal claimants to rational comprehension. After evaluation, of course, they may be more or less compelling, but they all play on the same field, the level field of natural human understanding, and can in principle be understood by anyone at all. What Paul says may well be new in some significant sense, but the articulation of this newness occurs on the same rational level as does, for instance, the Stoic argument about the passions. There is no Spirit-enhanced "supernatural" discourse intelligible only to those on the inside of Christian faith: both the Christian and the Stoic claims are to be understood and accepted or rejected in the same way and on the same ground as any other claims to truth; and there is no rivalry of rationalities: the encyclopedic conception of natural, unitary rationality is explicitly promoted as the ground for relating the texts of divergent traditions.

Third, then, Engberg-Pedersen believes in the epistemological triumph of modern scholarly discourse. Scholarly analysis of "God," for example, in both Stoicism and Christianity presupposes the ability to know something that is logically distinct from the specific ways in which *God* receives its meaning in particular religious/philosophical traditions. Engberg-Pedersen speaks of a "God" that is identical neither with the Christian use of the word nor the Stoic. What then is it? It is the scholar's idea of God, or—to put it only slightly differently—the God of modern scholarly grammar, a way of speaking that implicitly claims to be more conceptually capacious, or determinative, than the specific ways of knowing endemic to the two traditions under analysis.[35]

Drawing on a distinction long made for field work in anthropology, Engberg-Pedersen justifies his way of thinking by naming it "etic." It is all fine and good, he argues, to view Paul, for example, from inside Paul's way of thinking (emic), but that simply reproduces an insider's discourse. The etic perspective, however, presents Paul's ideas through a modern idiom that is intelligible to those on the outside of Paul's view of things. Scholarly discourse, that is, is bound neither to Christian nor Stoic self-understanding but to "ordinary, human intelligibility."[36] Engberg-Pedersen goes on to suggest that theology itself should also speak in the language of ordinary, human intelligibility: "The scholarly enterprise is itself wedded to the concept of ordinary, human intelligibility. And I am saying that the theological enterprise should be, too."[37] For Engberg-Pedersen, then, scholarly language turns out to be the universally intelligible grammar that can capably translate the theological/philosophical languages of more particular traditions into its own terms.

Taking these three lines of thought together, it is relatively easy to see that they are both coherently related within and strictly necessary to the wider "conceptual framework" that structures Engberg-Pedersen's project: modern scholars can focus on ideas as ideas; these ideas are expressed in a universally intelligible "natural" language; this natural language corresponds intellectually to the etic discourse of modern scholarship; modern scholarship is itself, therefore, the universal language, the most conceptually comprehensive discourse, that which can restate, or translate, all emic expressions/claims in its own terms.

Engberg-Pedersen's consistency is admirable, though unsurprising. It is the consistency of the modern encyclopedic view of reason and the power of scholarly knowledge. What Engberg-Pedersen presents as a "natural" or "etic" way of knowing is in fact a historically developed particular epistemological claim of modernity.[38] The encyclopedia lives on.

It would not be difficult to identify similar commitments in the majority of recent comparative work on the Stoics and Christians.[39] Taken as a whole, the body of research by Malherbe and Engberg-Pedersen displays the more fundamental assumptions and intellectual parameters of an entire modern scholarly project—that of mistaking traditions for entries in an encyclopedia.

ENCYCLOPEDIC DISTORTIONS

If Malherbe and Engberg-Pedersen illustrate a way of studying traditions as if they were something else—treating them more like data in a wider, more comprehensive scheme called scholarly knowledge—it nevertheless remains for us to specify and elaborate the most damaging distortions of this type of mistake. There are three intertwined problems that, taken together, most clearly display the need to reject encyclopedic reasoning as an illuminating way of knowing the ancient texts and construing their relation.

First, the modern comparative project depends upon a philosophical mistake in which a profound abstraction is taken for a real thing and believed to provide the categorical sense in which the work of comparison can be done. As MacIntyre argues, in order to comprehend engagement of one view with another, we must posit a framework within which such engagement is intelligible as (dis)agreement over something that is already shared.[40] For the majority of those who compare ancient philosophy with the New Testament, an encyclopedically construed notion of a particular theme—"morality" or "ethics" or "views of the divine" or "the passions," for example—provides the single framework within which difference/similarity is constructed. The morality of this and that group is something we can compare; the view of "God" of this and that group is something we can compare; the understanding of "the passions" of this and that group is something we can compare. And so forth. Similarity/difference is thereby discerned in light of the category supposedly shared by the groups under comparison.

When, for example, Malherbe identifies similarity between Paul and some ancient philosophers in the views/practices of the moral life, he assumes—even as he constructs—the existence of a spectrum along which both Paul and the philosophers can be placed. The conceptual precondition for identifying similarity/difference, that is, is a framework in which similarity/difference appears as similarity/difference: the spectrum, or line, that enables specific points placed upon it to be thought in relation to one another as variants of some more fundamental thing, *morality*. This conceptual precondition is the philosophic position of the encyclopedist. Were we to find an encyclopedia of ancient morality, this position assumes, it would contain entries on Paul, Seneca, Epictetus, and the like—or perhaps, if it were topically arranged, varying topics such as anger or lust, with a wide range of different ancients as illustrations of this or that position on the topic.[41] If only Sevenster would have cast the net more broadly, says Malherbe, he would have brought in more kinds of fish.[42]

But what is morality itself, or morality in general? And where is it to be found? What is *the* moral life? Can anyone live the moral life in general? What would such a life look like?

The fact that there is no word for morality as such in any ancient or medieval language should already caution us against the assumption that we know what ancient morality in general could be. And, in fact, we do not. The reason is strikingly simple: it did not exist. No one did (or does) conceive or practice morality in general. Just as there is no such thing as religion in general except in the minds of the academics who claim to study it—it does not have beliefs, it does not have practices, it does not have adherents, and so on—there is no such thing as morality in general. Indeed, strictly speaking, we cannot even think it.

Morality as such is an abstraction that modern linguistic habits present to us as a possibility for thought; upon inspection, however, it turns out to be impossible to conceive. Try all you'd like; you'll only be able to come up with particular exemplifications of the thing you think you seek.[43]

Modern scholars who believe they are comparing similarity/difference along a spectrum called morality arbitrarily excise certain parts from more densely complicated wholes and name these parts "moral."[44] What is here obscured is the fact that the ancients did not think they were reflecting upon moral questions or developing disciplines to lead them in moral lives. They thought, instead, that they were reflecting upon and practicing how to live an entire life. It is true that they wrote much about the virtues, of course, but the virtues were exemplified within wider philosophical accounts of how to live.[45] In short, where the modern way of speaking makes one think in terms of a spectrum, or a theme, or a particular area of life along or within which ancient views can be plotted or placed, the ancients did not detach their "moral" thinking from their total lives. To the degree that we compare parts without the density of the whole, we continue to project modern abstractions onto the ancient sources and obscure the fact that what is really juxtaposed in the question of "comparison" is a full way to live.[46] "Morality" in the ancient sense is a specifically traditioned way to live a full human life.

Second, modern comparative projects are often cosmopolitan in a way that assumes the universal comprehending capacity of modern scholarship, "the confident belief that all cultural phenomena must be potentially translucent to understanding, that all texts must be capable of being translated into the language which the adherents of modernity speak to each other."[47] If we can learn the right things, we can absorb the reasoning of particular past peoples into our own forms of thought—render their terms in ours.[48]

Engberg-Pedersen's attempt to represent Pauline theology through an "etic" perspective, for example, presupposes not only the possibility of translating Christian discourse into modern scholarly language but also that no hermeneutical harm is done in the process. Just as the encyclopedist stands outside his subject matter, surveying it, classifying it, and representing it in an idiom of modern knowledge, so the etic linguist forgoes the emic reasoning of his sources and translates them into the modern idiom of "naturalistic" reason. Just as the encyclopedist assumes a superior epistemological posture from which to understand the language of another, so the etic linguist assumes an epistemological position that relegates his sources to particular instances of universal possibility. All emic reasoning, thinks he, can be expressed etically. Just as it does not occur to the European encyclopedist that, for example, "a Polynesian view of Europeans might be rationally superior to a European view of Europeans," so it does not occur to the etic linguist that the emic reasoning of his sources may eliminate *tout court* the possibility of a true etic account. Just as the encyclopedist assumes that all rivalry or incommensurability can be expressed within the framework of the encyclopedia, so the etic linguist assumes that scholarly discourse is a larger, more comprehensive grammar in which incommensurable views/practices can be expressed. Just as it does not occur to the encyclopedist that he has mistaken his type of rationality for rationality itself, so it does not occur to the etic linguist that scholarly discourse is not the language of natural reason but only one particular way of thinking about human understanding. And so on. In short, rather than a neutral discourse about things from which we have academic distance, "etic" understanding is a universal claim about the interpretative power of modern scholarship and the unitary rationality that undergirds it. Modern scholarship conducts its comparisons within a more capacious form of reasoning than particular traditions themselves exemplify. There is a larger language in which Stoicism or Christianity can be spoken without substantive loss.

Though there are multiple problems with interpretative projects of absorption,[49] for our purposes there are two errors that should clearly be seen. The first pertains to the way in which Engberg-Pedersen attempts to ground the etic perspective of modern scholarship in a notion of ordinary human intelligibility. But, as it is with morality as such, so it is with ordinary human intelligibility. We do not and cannot know what ordinary human intelligibility is. It is, of course, obvious to us that humans reason in ways that other animals, plants, rocks, liquids, and so on do not.[50] But such a difference tells us nothing about the common way in which humans themselves reason or understand reason's workings. And after all, it could not. We know only particular ways in which human beings understand things, and we know this by looking at the language they use.[51] Speaking of ordinary human intelligibility is thus simply another way of talking about an abstraction—the modern view of rationality as such—that funds encyclopedic inquiry. Modern "etic" presentations are not wedded to the notion of ordinary intelligibility; they are, rather, self-identical with the encyclopedic assertion of an abstraction: ordinary human intelligibility as a general way to absorb irreducibly particular patterns of reasoning.[52]

The second error concerns the way in which the claim to be able to render particular traditions via modern scholarly language produces a very specific kind of blindness—the kind that is unable to see that it stands not in a re-presentational relation to the sources it studies but in one of challenge and even direct contradiction. In MacIntyre's terms, either the Polynesians or the Europeans could be right, but not both. Cosmopolitan knowledge is an illusion.

Over against the encyclopedic assumptions of modern scholarly discourse, both the Christians and the Stoics say that we cannot see clearly without habituation into their specific traditions of practical thought. The Christians in particular go even farther: ordinary human language is broken, "natural" reason deeply damaged, and the cure for such brokenness and damage out of our reach. To return to blindness: repair of our defective sight is beyond our skills and even our greatest capacities. The only help for our predicament comes, as Paul might put it, from an "apocalyptic" intervention—something that is entirely outside ordinary human possibilities.

When, therefore, encyclopedic projects of absorption claim that translating their sources into etic language requires us to suspend or abandon the specific claims of the sources themselves—that, for example, we need God's help to see straight—they do not move us onto the scholarly terrain of natural reason but instead position us critically against the sources they claim to interpret. In a far-reaching and crucial respect, the encyclopedic way of knowing is a hermeneutic posture not of enlightened clarification but of contestation and negation. Modern projects of absorption are, in brief, self-deceived. Etic language is not the outside presentation of something inside (emic). It is simply a rival construal of true knowledge.

Third, modern projects of comparison frequently sever, as Thomas Pfau puts it, "theoretical inquiry from practical reason."[53] Though scholars differ on when to date the origins of such a severance, its development within modern history is indisputable.[54] As Paul Rabbow, Pierre Hadot, Robert Wilken, and many others have shown in considerable detail, theoretical discussion in ancient philosophy/theology was inseparable from the acquisition of habits of life that allowed one to think theoretically in the first place. Stoicism, for example, should not be interpreted as a body of cohering intellectual positions on various questions of perduring significance; it was, rather, a lived intellectual structure, a trajectory or style of existence in which certain kinds of thinking were made possible precisely through the spiritual and physical disciplines that made Stoicism a way of life.

So foreign to modern conceptions of knowledge is the understanding of life and thought as fundamentally inseparable that we have trouble seeing the implications of the difference.[55] For the questions I am pursuing, we can focus on only three tightly interwoven implications for the task of thinking comparatively.

The first is that studies such as Engberg-Pedersen's that are meant to present us with "ideas as ideas" commit—quite contrary to their authors' intentions and overall erudition about ancient matters—a rather gross anachronism. Neither the ancient Christians nor the ancient Stoics thought of thought in this way and, to a startling degree, would have found profoundly strange the omission of a sanctified life or practical reason as constitutive of reason's reasoning. Engberg-Pedersen thus inevitably modernizes the ancients he seeks to recover by offering the scholarly world "information" within a wider "neutral or instrumental" conception of knowledge.[56] Even Malherbe, who well understands that philosophy was more like "psychagogy" than pure thinking, does not move from this wider understanding to a critical reevaluation of its modern rejection implicit in his encyclopedic style of inquiry. He manages, instead, to present psychagogy as just another important idea in historically minded research: an illuminating parallel between ancient philosophy and Christian pastoral strategy, to be sure, but not something that cuts deep into our settled conception of reason's workings or that should cause us to rethink the modern style of inquiry.

The second implication concerns the picture of the self that is tied to the "neutral or instrumental" conception of knowledge (forming, as it were, its other side). The self who knows in the way Engberg-Pedersen wants to know is the self who emerged after Descartes and especially Locke, the "disengaged subject." The "key to this figure," as Charles Taylor puts it, "is that it gains control through disengagement."[57] Not only does the "disengaged self" create a domain that cannot touch him—placing his object of scholarly attention within a framework of objects to be investigated without prior normative commitment—he also "takes a stance" toward himself that "takes him out of his normal way of experiencing the world and ourselves." We posit a self that is beyond the experience of the world that we ourselves have, and imagine the existence of its ability to think. Our disengagement presumes, that is, an objectification of the mind—a thing capable of reasoning quite by itself—that simultaneously alienates us from ourselves. "Modern disengagement," Taylor rightly notes, "calls us to a separation from ourselves through self-objectification."[58]

Consider one of Taylor's examples from everyday life, a toothache: when I have a toothache, I can objectify myself as someone who is currently affected by the chemical processes that send signals from the site of decay to the proper place in the brain that interprets the signals as "pain"; I can think that I am not actually "feeling" the pain at the site of decay but am instead being told by the brain where the effects of decay are; or I could perhaps rehearse older or different theories of pain and think, well, no, it's not the brain that is responsible for my interpretation of pain, it is the imbalance of the body's humors; and so forth. What I cannot do, however, is *experience* my toothache *as* a chemical process. To the contrary, *I* know it in my actual life precisely and only as *toothache*. To detach from the regular way we are in the world thus "involves going outside the first-person stance and taking on board some theory, or at least some supposition, about how things work. . . . Once we disengage and no longer live in our experience, then some supposition has to be invoked to take up the interpretive slack, to supply an account in the place of the one we are forgoing."[59]

The point of Taylor's illustration is not that second-order analyses of pain, for example, are problematical, but rather that the intellectual mode, or style, of such analyses—the whole way they're done—appears sensible to us only on the basis of a prior philosophical anthropology. Taylor does not think, of course, that this anthropology is explicitly articulated every time we objectify ourselves in order to theorize about aspects of our experience.[60] It is rather that there is an anthropological picture in place that is the background against which the practice of stepping outside our lived experience in order to gain knowledge makes sense. The "taking up the interpretive slack" is the picture or philosophical anthropology that fills the space between lived experience and self-objectification so that particular (modern) ways of conceiving knowledge seem normal and, indeed, self-evidently right.

And, after all, isn't it self-evidently right that this is what serious historians should do, namely, step outside lived experience in order to gain "detachment" or "critical distance" from their sources for the sake of more accurate knowledge? "Take a stance" toward themselves that presumes the ability to objectify the mind as a thinking thing that can interpret ancient texts by itself, quite apart from the engaged way in which we know other things by living in our experience?

But, of course, this picture of the human being and how it knows seems "self-evidently right" only because of the pervading influence of a historically powerful way of conceiving the self's relation to knowledge.[61] In fact, to know in this way requires us to adopt anthropological assumptions of encyclopedic inquiry that run counter to the anthropologies of the ancient Stoic/Christian sources. In forgoing the existentially involved way in which we normally come to know things, the encyclopedist "takes up the slack" between lived experience and self-objectification by supposing the existence of a human being who—through the acquisition and skilled use of certain scholarly tools—is able to control its sources in the absence of any sort of denser life as constitutive of knowing truth.[62] But for the ancients there is no such human being: the self cannot be thus divided, for there is no objectifiable thinking faculty—the mind qua mind or soul qua soul—that can know truth apart from the much denser reality of the I that lives. I can perhaps reflect on what it might entail to know the truth of the Stoics' claims, for example, but *I* cannot *know* the truth of such claims apart from the lived I that knows them.[63]

Reading the Stoic/Christian texts in the mode of self-objectification thus requires the discarding of the very anthropological suppositions the sources claim are necessary to understand them rightly. The scholarly mode of self-objectification, that is, believes something is *humanly* possible that the texts implicitly rule out. Conceiving knowledge as that which is gained by a detached-thinking-thing—the objectified mind that knows apart from the life in which it is embedded—is yet one more way in which modern encyclopedic inquiry contravenes the traditions it seeks to absorb.[64]

The third implication follows directly from the first and the second. Reproducing the modern divorce between thought and life by presenting "information" that can be consumed by the "disengaged" reader—in a manner similar to the way one reads entries in an encyclopedia or evaluates recipes in a cookbook—obscures the fact that what we encounter in the Christian and the Stoic texts is a claim on our existence, a claim, moreover, that has its basis in a correlative claim about the way things truly are. In short, what could appear as a demand to embrace a true way of life appears instead as information to be assimilated. "Here is the true and wise way to live; you will know it by living in this way" becomes "Here is some interesting information from the past." To the extent that we sever life and knowledge and hence attempt to eliminate practical reason's role in all interpretive endeavors, we create an existential distance between us and that which we seek to know—which in this case turns out to mean that we actually *turn away and hide* from our sources in the mode of our scholarship. Precisely by displaying scholarly indifference to the truth of their claims do we fail to take the Stoics and/or the Christians seriously as *Stoics* or as *Christians* and, instead, turn them into entries within an encyclopedia. In this way we quite profoundly misinterpret them exactly through the attempt to describe them.

As these three problems demonstrate, what the most influential recent research has presented as the scholarly way to handle material from the ancient world is in fact the encyclopedic way to construe knowledge, the human being, and the force of the ancient claims. If we reject these construals as a whole and, instead, treat the three Roman Stoics and three early Christians as particular exemplifications of their traditions, we come face to face with a set of rather obvious but difficult questions: If there isn't a more comprehensive scholarly language in which to render ancient Christian/philosophical terms, how do we compare early Christianity with Stoic philosophy? In particular, if the claims most fundamental to each form of life appear to conflict, and if this conflict is based in the irreducible specificity of a lived life rather than in the alleged realm of pure reason, how would the Christians and Stoics be able to understand each other's claims? And how, further, would we be able to understand either one of their claims?

Moreover, if the scholar is not an instance of a mind at work on things that do not work on him, but is instead a person whose existential trajectory is addressed by the sources he studies, what exactly is scholarship that reckons with the truth claims of its sources? And if, in turn, such claims presuppose that we have to live them in order to grasp their meaning, how can we know we understand them without the life they apparently require?

In short, if the Roman Stoic and Christian traditions are incomprehensible within the encyclopedic version of inquiry—if we want, therefore, to dispense with the illusion of encyclopedic comprehension—how do we go forward?

We proceed in two steps: we will first juxtapose them as tradition to tradition (Chapter 8) and then consider anew the question of how we might study the traditions that they are (Chapter 9). In order to do this well, however, we need first to explain how traditions are best juxtaposed and reckon seriously with the limits to learning any alien tradition.

CONFLICT OF TRADITIONS: NARRATIVE JUXTAPOSITION

If Stoicism and Christianity are seen as traditions of inquiry, the most constructive way to conceive their relation is to think them in direct narrative juxtaposition, face to face. Traditions are of course considerably complex things, but such complexity will always be related to the narrative that makes the tradition what it is. Indeed, narrative rendering is necessarily related to the possibility of being a tradition at all: "What a tradition of inquiry has to say, both to those within and those outside it, cannot be disclosed in any other way."[65] If, like a complex craft, a tradition of inquiry becomes a tradition only in the course of history and as the participants become aware of their participation in it as participation in a history of particular beliefs, skills, practices, and so on, then narrative is that which renders the history intelligible to its participants as a history of this or that particular kind.[66]

The ability to locate one's life as a particular mode-of-being-in-the-world, that is, depends upon the story that makes a life locatable in this specific way. By working through a juxtaposition of the narratives that fund the shapes of life called Christian and Stoic, we are thus thinking relationally with that which makes it possible to be Stoic or Christian in the first place.[67]

Narrative is not, therefore, something separable from being Christian or Stoic, an independent conceptual category, say, under which we look at them; it is inseparable from "Christian" and from "Stoic." No Christian story, no possibility for the understanding "Christian" as a way to describe how my community has been and is in the world. No Stoic story, no possibility for the understanding "Stoic" as a way to describe how I am in the world.[68] In a crucial sense, to know the story is to know the thing itself.

Though the importance of narrative has gradually made its way into New Testament scholarship over the past quarter-century, scholars who work primarily on the question of early Christianity's relation to and/or participation in pagan culture—including, of course, philosophy—have not been quick to conceptualize their studies in narrative terms.[69] Their history has been done, in good encyclopedic fashion, as the history of ideas/concepts (*Begriffe*) or, in more refined cases, as the history of social practices.[70] But the sense that narrative is indispensable to an adequate understanding of either ideas or practices is largely absent.[71]

Yet we cannot understand the sense ideas or practices have apart from the stories that make them intelligible as things to think/do in the first place. Reflection and practice do not spontaneously emerge from nothing, having no wider reason for their existence, no greater context within which they mean what they mean, no larger sense-making pattern that—quite literally—makes the sense that makes sense. They are, instead, always and already embedded in much denser networks of sense-making. Charles Taylor illustrated well the necessity of these networks of sense-making when he argued for the coinherence of practices, normative judgments about the way things "ought to go," and a wide, metaphysical understanding of the world that makes normative judgments normative (rather than just one opinion among others).[72] He could have gone farther, however, and shown that even the widest metaphysical understanding of the world implies and depends upon narrative[73]—a narrative, moreover, that will inevitably include, at least by implication, origins and ends (and thus at least imply the resultant implications for the time in which we ourselves currently live).[74] And back behind narratives, we cannot go.[75] Imagine putting the question "why so?" to any account of the world you can think of, and you will have already tapped into the story that will constitute the answer that begins with "because . . ."

This is not at all to say, of course, that we should think of narrative as something that is only in the background of practices, normative judgments, metaphysical accounts of the world, and so forth. Narrative, to the contrary, is present in all layers of a tradition's particularity (even if inchoate or left unarticulated). Nor should we think of any sort of regular historical order, as if narratives must precede practice or reflective questioning. Again, to the contrary, it could easily be the case that narratives arise in light of questions pertaining to long-established practices (why do we do what we do?) or particular queries about existence, for example (why is the world here rather than not?). But as long as practices make sense and as long as "metaphysical" queries proceed beyond the mere statement of the questions themselves, narratives will be found and/or constructed and (re)told. To put it into terms more familiar to scholars of the

New Testament and early Christianity, demonstrating that Paul's letters have a "narrative substructure" simultaneously elucidates the ground of their possibility as intelligible speech. Which is but another way of saying that even in naming particular texts as Christian or Stoic, we presuppose a narrative that allows us to locate them in just this way.[76]

To understand how and why things make the sense they make, therefore, we must see something of the story that funds a tradition's particular speech. If modernity names a time in which narrative was forgotten as a way to understand divergent patterns of life, modern scholarship that treats ancient Christianity and Stoic philosophy without a consideration of narrative is a particular instance of this broader amnesia.

There is, of course, an obvious objection to the narrative way of thinking relationally, at least in this specific case: not one of the six figures treated in this book tells us directly what the Stoic and/or Christian narrative is. It is true, such an objector could say, that Luke calls his Gospel a narrative (*diēgēsis*), but that is hardly the same thing as the narrative you claim covers Paul and Justin as well. Moreover, not once in the entire corpus of surviving Stoic texts can one find the Stoic story. There are, to be sure, ample discussions of the history of Stoicism—its founders, its heroes, its past debates—as well as occasional pious hymns, such as Cleanthes's famous verses or those of Aratus in the opening of his *Phaenomena*. But such things are hardly the same as a Stoic narrative. Seneca, Epictetus, and Marcus are part of this larger history, but where is their story?

Such an objection is understandable given the way narrative has commonly been understood as a type of surface-level genre, as if one has narrative only when one can actually read it on the very top of the text. This shallow understanding, however, ignores the deeper sense in which narrative is the substructure of nonnarrative texts—making possible the particular shape of the speech in the latter's actual structure—and thus is present throughout the text even where the textual surface looks quite different.[77] And, more significant, the genre-objection ignores the fundamental philosophical point that insofar as specifically Christian and/or Stoic texts exist at all, they do so because of the narratives that make them possible to be specifically Christian and/or Stoic in the first place. If, therefore, we accept the designation Christian or Stoic, we ipso facto acknowledge the existence of the stories that make it possible for us to locate the texts in these forms of life.[78] The question, then, is not whether the Christian and Stoic texts presuppose narrative—since by naming them Christian/Stoic we have already answered that question—but, rather, how to explicate the narratives they do in fact presuppose.

SECOND FIRST LANGUAGES

If were we to think encyclopedically, we would see no difficulty here at all. The rationality of both the Stoic and the Christian texts would be the same—and the same as the way in which we ourselves reason—and we would simply need to learn the things about the ancient world that would allow us to understand them in historically informed ways. Precisely because all texts are equally comprehensible within the covers of the encyclopedia, the possibility that one or both sets of texts could depend upon patterns of reasoning that are closed to us would not even arise.

Recognizing that the texts represent traditions, however, raises exactly this possibility and considerably complicates the question of their narrative explication. If, as MacIntyre argues, rationality is tradition specific, then writing a narrative account of a tradition's self-understanding would involve learning how to reason as the tradition itself reasons—which is to say that the only truly adequate accounts are written by participants in the tradition about which they write. Participants are those who have been formed to reason in the ways that are inherent to the tradition's existence as a specific sort of rationality; outsiders simply have not been formed to reason in the way the tradition reasons.[79] How, then, can we write about a tradition in which we do not participate?

On analogy with learning another language, MacIntyre argues that the only way to learn another tradition is to learn it as a "second first language."[80] Because traditions are "languages-in-use"—their way of reasoning is inextricably tied to the concrete cultural life of the community that bears the tradition—learning a second first language cannot be done simply by matching sentences from one's second language to one's first (as if using a basic-phrase travel guide to a foreign country). Such sentence matching can only produce "tokens," discrete phrases that can work effectively within very limited circumstances to achieve a desired effect (for example, Wo sind die Toiletten? = Where is the bathroom?).[81] Producing tokens should not be confused with learning a language well enough to move fluidly within the cultural patterns that are the language's lived expression. Rather, "the learning of a language and the acquisition of cultural understanding are not two independent activities."[82] If traditions are lived languages, then, they must be "learned as second first languages or not at all."[83]

If, says MacIntyre, we are historically removed from the traditions we wish to learn, we need not despair. It "seems clear that where we have sufficient textual and other materials from a culture which no longer exists, those with the requisite linguistic and historical skills can so immerse themselves that they can become almost, *if not quite*, surrogate participants in such societies as those of fifth-century Athens or twelfth-century Iceland."[84] Through careful cultivation we can develop an "empathetic conceptual imagination" that is the condition for learning another language.[85]

Achieving fluency in one's second first language—in historically distant no less than contemporaneous traditions—is the work of disciplined imagination in yet another way: the ability to improvise. For skilled improvisation within an alien tradition presupposes that that tradition's way of reasoning has been learned. One can improvise only when one knows the patterns that allow correct spontaneity or innovation, or the "ability to go on and go further."[86] One could, for example, answer an imagined question from Lucilius in such a way that experts in the Stoic tradition could scarcely, if at all, tell a difference between the improvised question/answer and the language of Seneca himself.[87] Or when "acting in a play by Aristophanes," an actor could "introduce a piece of comic improvisation in which the best scholarship could detect no relevant difference from the original."[88] In both cases, the grammars that make the languages what they are would have been digested to the point of creating accurately ruled speech in accordance with the tradition for which one was trying to speak.

It would seem to follow, then, that those who have learned a second first language are the best translators. They are those who know how both traditions work and who therefore can put the terms of one into the terms of the other. MacIntyre argues, however, that while there may well be cases where translation of this or that can happen even between divergent traditions, a more significant marker of true traditioned learning is the ability to recognize when translation is impossible, when it's impossible to say with the words of one tradition what can be said in another (even with all the extensive interpretative glosses and paraphrases that go with the most difficult cases). Precisely because the recognition of "untranslatability presents barriers around or over which no way can be discovered," those who have learned a second first language become "inhabitants of boundary situations."[89] They do not blend conflicting traditions into a sort of Esperanto but instead exhibit conflict by means of reasoning on the edges of rival rationalities.[90] Rivalry between traditions, that is, is most profoundly recognized by the fact of untranslatability.

For MacIntyre, therefore, even though encyclopedic claims to universal textual and cultural transparency are false, learning another tradition is still possible. Such learning, however, may well entail the recognition that what is learned cannot be either learned or intelligibly framed within the tradition in which one originates. Contrary to the encyclopedists, MacIntyre thus clearly sees that serious scholarly research on past traditions does not perforce lead to better comprehension of the cosmopolitan sort; it may instead lead to the realization of ineliminable rivalry and conflict.

Even MacIntyre, however, does not seem to reckon concretely enough with the consequences of his own insights into the linguistic nature of traditions and the indispensability of initiation into a pattern of life for the shape of reason's working. As he argues, the meaning of words has a practical shape, which is to say that words are lived. But translation, then, would entail synonymy not only in conceptual patterns or imaginative conditions but in life. Indeed, lived synonymy is what conceptual translation between traditions is. Traditioned concepts are, to use Cora Diamond's characterization, existentially "thick."[91]

If reason is given its particular shape by the language that is concomitant with a tradition's life pattern, no amount of imaginative ingenuity could take the place of needing actually to live the tradition's pattern in order to learn how to reason the way the tradition reasons. Practical reason really is that connected to praxis. And yet we cannot live rival traditions at once, simultaneously. The requisite patterns or skills for participation in more than one rival tradition exclude one another in a way that is both existentially and communally dense.

This inability to live more than one tradition at a time means that in a crucial and, truth be told, rather sobering sense, even the central patterns of reasoning in one tradition—as that tradition understands them—will not be understood in another. Moreover, insofar as we do not participate in the alien tradition we seek to query, we cannot know what it is that we do not know.[92] Short of conversion, we are literally shut out of one by the life we live in another.[93] Rival rationalities are not surmountable by learning.

What then is the exercise of narrative juxtaposition in the following chapter? It is an attempt to reason Christianly about Roman Stoicism as my second first language while acknowledging that because I can do this only as an outsider, the way may in fact be closed. Said slightly differently: it is a way to extend Christian experience by engaging in a patient conflict of traditions within the only way that is existentially available. This is what comparative scholarship is that refuses to live among the dead.

If the arguments of this chapter are correct, encyclopedic thinking about ancient Christianity and pagan philosophy has to go. As difficult as it may be to jettison the grounding assumptions of the majority of scholarship in this area, there is no other choice. For far too long we have acted as if the encyclopedic way of knowing was still alive and well, producing insights and adding to the general fund of scholarly knowledge. And, correspondingly, we have neglected the profound difficulties surrounding the conflict that inevitably occurs when rival traditions encounter one another. It is time to change the way we think.

In this book, therefore, the work of comparison is best described as an exploration in the conflict of traditions—a way of conceiving the Christian/Stoic relation that takes account of the fact that difference/similarity is best construed through the narratives that provide the sense it makes to identify texts as Christian or Stoic in the first place. The construction of these narrative accounts, moreover, is not that of a distanced observer (who, after all, does not really exist). Is it, rather, an account by a Christian who reads as a Christian. Of course, my reading of the Stoics has been an effort to read with the grain of their works and to reason inside that which would let me in.[94] Precisely, however, because of the Stoic and Christian truth claims that both depend upon and implicate the shape of our lives for reason's workings, I must acknowledge that in practice I am unable to understand certain Stoic things—perhaps even central patterns of reasoning.[95] Though this inability may well surprise those who believe that all texts are more or less alike in their transparency to the scholar's mind, this is exactly what is to be expected when we take the Stoics and Christians seriously in their mutual insistence that what they have to say entails the shape and, indeed, knowing power of practical reason. Learning that we cannot adequately conceive the Stoic/Christian relation from some vantage point outside of the shapes of life that they are may indeed complicate comparative work on the ancients to a rather startling degree. But it will also be closer to the truth.

8

Traditions in Juxtaposition

> The rule with flesh and blood is that one cannot say two things simultaneously. But He who spake and the world came to be proclaimed the Ten Commandments in one utterance, something that is impossible for flesh and blood to do.
>
> —*Mekhilta d'Rabbi Yishmael*

In the previous chapter, I argued that the best way to conceive the Christian/Stoic relation is to think it in terms of narrative juxtaposition.[1] In the current chapter I thus juxtapose the narratives that enable us to locate the textual groups within the traditions for which they speak and then reflect on the most salient issues that emerge out of this juxtaposition.

TWO STORIES

Before setting forth the narratives that enable us to use "Christian" or "Stoic" for each of the six figures whose texts we have read, we need to say something brief about the act of making the stories from the texts. In the narrative constructions below I attempt, first, to make sense of the particular speech of the individual texts; second, to provide substantively plausible construals of that which ties together each textual group—what makes them part of a specific tradition; and, third, to display the intellectual worth of juxtaposition as a way to work toward a more precise understanding of the difficulties involved in the conflict of traditions.

As a kind of check on the explanatory power of the narratives I will offer, each of these aspects of the narrative-making task entails a negative corollary: if the narrative, first, makes the particular language of Paul/Luke/Justin or Seneca/

Epictetus/Marcus less rather than more intelligible, it fails; or, second, makes the textual grouping (Paul-Luke-Justin or Seneca-Epictetus-Marcus) appear artificial rather than substantively and historically rich, it fails; or, third, obscures rather than clarifies the problem of thinking the relation between different traditions, it fails.

It should go without saying, but constructing the type of narrative that makes sense of a particular textual grouping is not the same thing as providing a narrative of Christianity or of Stoicism in toto (as if that were possible within any book at all).[2] My narrative constructions, rather, articulate the substantive similarity of the texts of the three Christians on the one hand (Paul-Luke-Justin) and the three Stoics on the other (Seneca-Epictetus-Marcus). If the narrative accounts show how these texts can be located in the traditions in which we locate them—and if they help to elucidate the complexities involved in thinking the relation between two different traditions, then they are, broadly speaking, successful.

A TRADITION OF LIFE: THE STOIC STORY

Stories about the Stoic tradition's most significant figures, such as the biographies written by Diogenes Laertius, for example, were obviously known in antiquity. The history of the movement was primarily understood along the line that ran from Zeno as the founding father to his successors Cleanthes, Chrysippus—Stoicism's real architect—and beyond. By Seneca's time, of course, such a line was no longer evident in real terms, and the Athenian Stoa was no longer the hub of Stoic learning. But the sense that those who were Stoics participated in the history that began there and ran unbroken into their very own lives was alive and well.[3] Indeed, as I argued in the previous chapter, the willingness to claim the name *Stoic* presupposes a reading of their history as a specific type of reasoning life—a tradition whose shape is what Stoicism is.[4]

Seneca, Epictetus, and Marcus Aurelius constitute a historically specific substantive moment within the tradition for which they speak.[5] The task here is to display the story that makes the sense that this moment makes as a specific sort of history. What makes their counsel intelligible in the first place? Why do they speak the way they speak? What makes it make sense to them to talk in this specific way rather than another? Or, to put it yet another way, Stoic reasoning makes sense to all three—why? What makes Stoic practical reason appear right or true? The point of this section is thus not to argue that Seneca, Epictetus, or Marcus Aurelius themselves consciously reflected upon the significance of a narrative that underlay the shape of their lives. It is rather to give an account of the main lines of the story that makes their work make the sense it makes. They do not, of course, agree on everything. But exactly to the extent that we describe them as Stoics we assume that they share a common story.

The story's beginning is not a beginning in the sense that we now normally conceive of beginnings, where something that previously was not comes into existence for the first time. Strictly speaking, there is no "was not" for the Stoics. Beginnings—and endings—apply only locally or personally but not in the grander sense to what exists. All that is has been and will be. There is movement within what is and there are, perhaps, different arrangements of what is, but nothing specific comes into being that was not already potentially here in what is. Newness is but the different combination of the matter that is.[6]

And this is so even for the most dramatic case, the great conflagration. At or in or through—the right preposition is conceptually no less than historically difficult to choose—the cosmic *ekpurōsis/conflagratio,* that which is combusts. But such combustion is not toward extinction or fundamental change but toward renewal or restart. The cycle that is from combustion to combustion is just that, a cycle. There is no real or absolute beginning. The most the Roman Stoics could say is that there is a re-beginning, a restart but no start.

In stark contrast to both the modern scientific sense of evolutionary time and the Jewish or Christian sense that God precedes his creation, the Stoic story has no part without humanity. It is simply assumed that human beings are part of what the cosmic cycle produces or contains. We do not "come on the scene," nor do we go off it. As a thing, though not in its individual parts of course, we have always been here and always will be. The cosmic context in which our collective being is lived is thus eternal. Time may be marked in this or that linear way concurrently with our more limited existence (for example, "We will gather next Thursday after sunrise"), but in the big picture time is not a measurement that corresponds to progress or, for that matter, regress. It is, rather, only a local marker in the eternal pulsation that is our movement to and from the conflagration.[7]

It is true that there are finer metaphysical points to be made—such as the distinction between that which is active and passive, or the fact that everything, even a soul, is material—but the crucial matter of the larger story is the grain of that which is, the way the cosmos runs as it moves to and away from the conflagration. For it is that above all that determines the human story within its cosmic context.[8]

In the Stoic story, the name for the grain of the cosmos is "God." God is not exactly identical with the whole of the cosmos itself but is instead the determinative pattern or flow of that which is—the way in which Reason is embedded in the whole of the world and moves it toward the conflagration and away again.

Such direction from within is what the Stoics mean by "Providence." In contrast to later Deist accounts of a God/world relation, for example, the Stoic story does not take the cosmos to be running on its own according to physical laws given by God from the outside—or, in contrast to a Jewish or Christian understanding, as if Providence named active direction by a God who is distinct from the cosmos in its entirety. In the Stoic story about all that is, the cosmos has its own eternal internal resource for direction. Precisely because such direction is what reason is, the grain of the cosmos is a rational one. *God*, therefore, is the word for the ultimately rational pattern of that which is and for the way this pattern works in the never-ending cycle of fiery end-beginning.[9]

But as any time spent with the Stoic texts would soon confirm, there is also an apparent blemish to the pattern, a crookedness in the grain: Fortuna. As Seneca says, "Fortuna does not capsize us—she plunges our bows under and dashes us on the rocks" (*Ep.* 8.4). If we push this sort of language far enough, Fortuna would seem to threaten the ultimately rational order of the cosmos, turn it into a place where randomness haunts every chance to live wisely. And the story would be one not of rational direction of a rational cosmos but of a cosmos in considerable conflict, a push and pull or yin and yang or weaving and unraveling or order and chaos—all bound inseparably together to make what is.[10]

But no, the crooked grain is only an appearance, an illusion about what is. There is no real blemish or cosmic conflict. *Fortuna* is only a name for a way the world appears to us, not a name for a contradiction to divine reason. It may well be that if we take them in isolation, aspects of the world's order would remain opaque to us. We can't see the sense of a toothache or a flood, for example, or we wonder at the wreckage of a transport ship full of needed grain. But given the perspective of the whole, even things such as these would fit right in. The Stoic story of cosmological order and beauty is uncompromised by Fortuna. As Marcus says, "The works of the gods are full of Providence: the works of Fortune are not divorced from Nature or from the interweaving and binding of the threads by the guiding hand of Providence. From such guidance come all things" (*Med.* 2.3). Why, then, does Fortuna even have the potential to appear as that which cuts against the grain of order? To answer this question is to move to the second major part of the Stoic story.

Though human beings are eternally present within the cosmic cycle ordered by divine reason, they find themselves estranged from the order in which they live and, indeed, by virtue of their own reason, of which they are uniquely a part. Our nature is to be rational, to live in line with the rational grain that is the order of the world. And yet we damage ourselves by our inability to live according to our nature. We therefore become vulnerable to the world's overwhelming power, its ability indiscriminately—so it seems—to bring us things we think are good or bad, to enliven and embolden or to demoralize and deaden us, to knock on our door with tidings that change the direction of our lives or to kill us off by something as innocuous as eating a nut. Our lives become entangled in things that lie mostly or entirely beyond our control but upon which we become utterly dependent. Which is to say we become enslaved to a misperception, a sense that the world is not rational through and through but instead is our master precisely through its unmanageability. In short, we become hostages to Fortuna and are kicked around or pulled like a dog on a leash from this moment to that in fear and worry.

Even if we achieve some measure of security against the world's seeming randomness, we cannot defeat death, and it awaits us—hidden in secret behind the veil that halts human knowledge, ready to take us whenever it pleases. Death is Fortuna's final victory, the way in which the cosmos controls us by that which is beyond our knowledge and our power. Even if we try to strike first against death's power of surprise and kill ourselves before it can get to us, we cast ourselves into death's arms. Our apparent victory is reversed, and we end in a loss. What, then, shall we do?

The Stoic story of human repair tells us that the way out of fear, anxiety, and the slavery they produce—in short, Fortuna's domination—is to live in a pattern of life that teaches us what our nature is and shapes our lives accordingly. And what is that nature? It is to be rational and to be mortal. The Reason that is the grain of the cosmos is the same as human rationality, which is why it can be said that god is in us (Seneca, *Ep.* 41; Epictetus, *Disc.* 2.8.11; Marcus, *Med.* 3.5–7) and even that we walk on the plane of the gods (Seneca, *Ep.* 48.11; 59.14). Reason speaks unto reason, or, rather, reason simply is reason, and to be free of the world's potential domination is to live according to its truth, to align our reason with the order of the cosmos.

And to exercise reason with respect to our nature is to see our mortality, to admit quite frankly that death itself is proper to the human being. There is no exception; humanity is deathward in all its individual parts, for it is our nature to die. To think human being is simultaneously to think mortal thing.

And yet, within the Stoic story to speak of "exercising reason" is not to say something general—a flexing of an inherent capacity for rationality—but something rather more specific. Whatever the cause of our turn from nature into "pandemic error," our problem is not self-remedying, as if we innately know how to exercise reason well, that is, to live according to our nature.[11] To the contrary, one has to learn how to exercise. Precisely because it is a skill that must be learned, one cannot just "pick up and do" the thing called reasoning.

How, then, it is learned? The Stoic narrative of reason is a story of a skill taught by a more experienced practitioner or master. Thus students travel to Nicopolis, Lucilius seeks counsel from Seneca, and Marcus studies with Rusticus. What they see in the teacher is as important as what he says. As Epictetus says of the works of Chrysippus: "[If] I admire the mere act of exegesis, have I not become a grammarian instead of a *philosopher*? . . . Far from being proud, therefore, whenever someone says to me, 'explain Chrysippus to me,' I blush when I can't display deeds that match and harmonize with his words" (*Ench.* 49; cf. *Disc.* 1.26.8–9). Internal to the Stoic way of reasoning is the claim that its pattern is visible in a human life and not apart from it. The particulars of the exercise that is Stoic reasoning are not analytically verifiable statements but lived shapes. Or, perhaps, the statements of logic that are analytically enticing find their analysis in the course of a Stoic life. A Cato, a Musonius, a Seneca, an Epictetus—these are necessary in the strictest sense to what Stoic reasoning is taken to be. Get an *exemplum*, says Seneca to Lucilius, so that you see reason in the flesh. Call it to mind so that you know how to become what you seek (*Ep.* 11.10). According to the Stoic story, the path to nature that is reason's repair involves imitation of those who have gone before and shown the way.

As Epictetus's remark about Chrysippus presumes—and as page after page of Seneca's letters illustrate—being a Stoic was not, however, just about lived *exempla*; it also entailed the study of written work. Though Chrysippus's multitudinous books are now long lost, they were pored over in Nicopolis and everywhere else students sought to learn the truth of the Stoic tradition. Such works were not scripture in anything like the sense that we moderns understand it, but the narrative of what it meant to be a Stoic was nevertheless inseparable from the interpretation of the tradition's written word. To a significant degree, the texts were the stewards of the tradition, and commentary and discussion were its reception and mode of induction.

Reading itself, however, was not seen as a consumptive act, as we tend unreflectively to think today—where readers are the active and the books the passive parts in a literary feast. The Stoic story of human damage presumes that not even reading Stoic works can be done well without reason's repair. Unlike Augustine's story of his encounter with Paul's *Romans*, we cannot just pick up and read, but must instead be taught how to read.[12] Reading has an order to it, and this order corresponds to the repair that is necessary to make one into a good reader.[13] Which is to say that we can't be good readers until we become the kind of person who can read well.[14] If the story here tells of a seeming paradox—right reading requires reason's repair but reason's repair requires right reading—the Stoics assumed that there was time enough to work it out. Teachers and time were all one needed to repair and read, read and repair. Under the guidance of a teacher, we work on ourselves as we learn to read the tradition into which we are concurrently being inducted. Right reading, in other words, was in the living.[15]

The story of human repair—the rational life of the mortal—was of course full of specific remedies that, when properly applied, would bring us back in accord with nature. But the main story line focused upon the need for the Stoic philosopher to learn three skills above all. First was the division between what is in our control and what is not. The pain we know in life, all three Stoics say again and again, is a result of a basic confusion of exactly this kind.

We move through the world beset by "impressions."[16] The impressions are already-interpreted data of one kind or another. The perennial human problem is that we incorrectly sort the world in terms of the only two columns that matter, in our control and out of our control. Good and evil, helpful and harmful, all these types of distinctions are distinctions that make sense only in relation to what is within our control. Outside of our control, they simply do not apply. A child's sickness is utterly outside my control and is therefore neither good nor evil. Hitting the lottery jackpot is utterly out of my control and is therefore neither good nor evil. What is within my control is what I do with the impression itself. Do I allow "sick child=painful" or "much cash=beneficial" to stand, or do I interrogate its truth in light of what is within my control? If I do the latter I discover that "sickness" and "money" are "externals," and I can therefore dismiss the initial impressions as false. They are not in accordance with nature, where the nature of a human being is to be mortal and money extrinsic to its good.

We must thus make the judgments about impressions that accord with nature; so doing will allow us not only to get things into the right columns of control but also to do-think-seek the good that is ours according to nature, that is, the rational life of repair. Yet making such judgments is not something that we do without training; the Stoic story does not tell of a human being with unsullied innate ideas about what's in our control or is according to nature, nor does it tell of an individual path to right judgments that can be found independent of all traditions of inquiry. Indeed, making right judgments about impressions depends upon the acquisition of Stoic habits of life. We judge impressions well or poorly exactly to the degree that our judgments have conformed to the judgments of the Stoic life.

The second skill upon which the Stoic story focused was the elimination of the passions. Where the Aristotelians taught that passions could be moderated by reason, restrained and loosed as reason saw fit, the Stoics' story of the human being and its passions was much less optimistic. The passions were not like the common cold, which the mind/body can battle and overcome, but like malignant tumors that would grow and take over if left unexcised. Though the Stoics rejected the psychological complexity of Plato and Aristotle, as well as all mind/matter dichotomies, in the Stoic narrative about the human condition, reason is at war with the effect of the passions in such a way that no truce is possible. One or the other must win, and absent the training that the Stoics offer, the victor is assured. In the heat of the moment, as Epictetus emphasized, reason is simply no match for a pretty girl. Even love and grief were too much. Like dogs fighting over meat, says Epictetus, love divides those who initially played together; and like a raging torrent, says Seneca, grief washes away the one who grieves. Right judgments about impressions were simply impossible under the sway of the passions. Thus must reason march against them in advance—attempting to destroy the possibility of the passions' attack before they even get going—and it must do this step by step over the course of a lifetime, making wise judgments about the truth of impressions according to nature, and cultivating the virtues that would shape reason's defense.

The third skill, then, upon which the Stoic story of repair focused was the cultivation of virtue. In contrast to other ways of construing the relation of the virtues, the Stoic narrative about the human being foregrounded the fact that the virtues could gain display only in an actual human life—which is to say that in practice they were unified in the human being in whom they were being cultivated. Prudence, justice, courage, moderation—these all amounted to a unity that was a way to describe the disciplined philosophical life. Fasting, memorization, meditation, physical deprivation, copying written work, donning a beard and cloak, learning the specifically Stoic "preconceptions," and so forth, was the way to cultivate virtue and thus to aid and defend reason.[17]

Ultimately, however, in the Stoic narrative of repair, these three focal points were not fully separate things, each with its own independent logic and modus operandi. They were, rather, tightly interwoven and interdependent ways of talking about the defining contours of the philosophical life: by getting impressions sorted into the right columns we extirpate the passions and grow in virtue; by extirpating the passions we can sort impressions correctly and grow in virtue; and by growing in virtue we can sort impressions correctly and extirpate the passions. Only by developing these three skills simultaneously will we return to our nature.

If we sense a paradox here, it is only because we cannot write all three skills at once. The Stoic story says that we can, however, live them all at once. And that is, after all, the point: philosophy is a way of living in repair.

The presupposition of the possibility for living through the paradox of simultaneity is not only, however, that we have enough time to work on ourselves in mutually reinforcing ways. It is, more precisely, the fact that the human being has an "inner fortress" from which the process of self-repair can begin unhindered and to which the journey of repair returns. The Stoic story of human reparation has at its heart the claim that the human being is its own resource and the resolution of its problem. As we progress further and further in the Stoic disciplines, we discover a deeper and more profound ability to rely on ourselves.

Is, then, the Stoic story of the human problem and its solution a fundamentally "cognitive" one, as so many interpreters have thought?[18] Where therapy is conceived in exclusive ways—cognitive or emotive, for example—the Stoic story resists characterization. For in fact the narrative that underlies the Roman Stoics offers answers of both yes and no. Yes, the fundamental problem of the human being could be named as ignorance rather than, say, a broken self. And, yes, being able to analyze impressions and sort the world correctly—in short, thinking the right things about the world as we encounter it—is the way we build our acropolis and retreat behind its walls.[19]

But, no, in the Stoic story cognition is not something separable from life or from the disciplines that make for Stoic formation. Repair includes the way reason itself reasons, which is to say that thinking gets its shape through Stoic life no less than life through reason—or even that reason is reason, or becomes what it was meant to be, according to the quality of the Stoic life in which it is embedded. Correct cognition occurs through the life that is the pattern called Stoicism.

Taken as a whole, the Stoic narrative that underlies the works of Seneca, Epictetus, and Marcus Aurelius is a comprehensive narrative. It is more like an all-encompassing book than a chapter on this or that aspect of human language, or sense experience, or constitution of the world, for example. For the Stoic story tells about all that is—the world as it was, is, and will be, our place within it, what's wrong with us, how to heal and find happiness, and so on. Moreover, the comprehensiveness of the story does not correlate with a retreat from the blooming, buzzing confusion of daily life—as so many views from above tend to do—but actually goes the other way and gets down into the business of how to live moment by moment.

There was, of course, some variation within the story—different moments or side paths for the characters—but such is the nature of narrative.[20] By the time of the Roman Stoics, Stoicism was a complete narrative about human life. It offered the possibility of fortification against the world by living with the world, claiming that this "with" was the deeper truth of all things. We can live in an impregnable fortress, it said, one whose walls are constituted and built by rationally shaped therapeutic lives. Indeed, we ourselves are the impregnable fortress; this is our true nature, what we were made to be.[21]

At the heart of the Stoic story as it is expressed in Seneca, Epictetus, and Marcus there is thus a profound tension, dialectic, or, perhaps, paradox. To learn what we are and how to become what we are—rational mortals—we must be inducted into the Stoic way of being. Reason is not what we think for ourselves but a specifically traditioned communal craft. And yet to learn the Stoic craft of reason is to go into ourselves, to become solitary, self-sufficient fortresses of right judgment. There remain other Stoics—and there is the need to teach and be apprenticed—but exactly to the extent that we succeed in the Stoic life, even other Stoics are finally removed from us by the same life that initially drew us together in the common task of learning how to love wisdom.

A TRADITION OF LIFE: THE CHRISTIAN STORY

Christianity is prima facie a narrative way of life. On any account, the Gospels are foundational stories that claim to render the foundation himself, Jesus of Nazareth.[22] The Gospel of Luke, like Matthew in particular, tells of Jesus before his adulthood, but it primarily focuses on a specific slice of Jesus' life: his brief but dramatic ministry, his unjust but necessary passion, and his unexpected but glorious resurrection. Paul's letters and the Acts of the Apostles presuppose this narrative focus (less immediately in one case and more so in the other), amplify the significance of Jesus' life/death/resurrection, and extend its importance into the life of the first churches. Justin Martyr not only continues the argument about the connection between Jesus and the church but also turns the significance of Christian discipleship to the pagan world in direct engagement.

Luke was Paul's theological disciple and probable traveling companion, and Justin Martyr obviously displays strong links to them both.[23] And though these three do not tell of everything that the early Christians wanted to say, taken together they presuppose the essential features of the emerging story that enables us to name their texts as Christian. By attending to these features, we can see a historically productive way of juxtaposing traditions. At the exact time that Seneca, Epictetus, and Marcus were transmitting and extending the Stoic philosophical life, Paul, Luke, and Justin were doing something similar for Christian faith. To the moderns who would caution that the difference lay in the fact that Christianity was a brand-new tradition whereas Stoicism was an old one, all three Christians would object that such caution already betrays either a rejection or lack of understanding of the story they tell. The Christians are, after all, the continuation of Israel.[24]

In an important sense, and one to be considered momentarily, the Christian story reaches back to the founding of the world in God's creative purpose. But the epistemic claim of the story begins with the fact that Paul, Luke, and Justin all tell of Christian life as something intelligible only in light of the history of Israel as God's people. The appendage "Christ," which over time became something close to an actual name, is situated within the history that is the life of the Jews, and its Christian use is nonsensical without this history. *Christ* is not a general term that conveys superhuman ability or deity in some generic sense but the specific Israel-shaped word that describes Jesus as the awaited Messiah of his people.

Indeed, the coming of the Jewish Messiah is not so much an unwelcome message to non-Jews in the Roman world as it is entirely unintelligible to them—unless perhaps it is interpreted in categories that make it synonymous with the uprising of a Jewish king who himself is a revolutionary rival to Rome's order (this is, after all, what is implied in Pilate's question to Jesus, "are you the King of the Jews?").[25] But within the Christian story, the coming of the Messiah is the fulfillment of promises made long ago to the people whom God called through Abraham and his seed: "God has shown the mercy promised to our ancestors, and has remembered his holy covenant, the oath that he swore to our ancestor Abraham" (Luke 1:72–73). Though the irony is later resolved, the disciples on the way to Emmaus are distraught because they think that exactly this continuity—that between Israel's messianic hope and Jesus' coming—has been destroyed by Jesus' death: "we had hoped that he was the one to redeem Israel" (24:21). Paul articulates Jesus' identity and the implications thereof through a deeply dialogical engagement with scripture and assumes that who and what Jesus is, is inseparable from the Jewish Scripture that is the cradle of the Christ. To shape his churches in the life that is Christian faith, Paul teaches them to see themselves as participants in Israel's (hi)story. And Justin's entire *Dialogue with Trypho* both presupposes and argues for the continuity of Israel's life with the Messiah Jesus of Nazareth, as does the claim in the *First Apology* that the Christians are a people of old.

And yet it would be misleading to say that by "the next chapter in Israel's history" Paul, Luke, and Justin think of Christianity's dependence on Israel's history in the sense of a simple continuity in plot. The Christian story is more complicated than an easy linear progression because it tells not only of continuity but also of continuity as new beginning.

For the Christians, as for the Jews, the story did not begin with all that is but with God's creation of all that is not God. The world had a beginning. It had not always been here but was instead created by the one and only God and was distinct from him. The story that unfolds in Scripture is thus the story of God's dealings with all that is not God.

Humanity itself was one of God's creatures, a thing that was not God. Though it is impossible to know exactly how all early Christians would have read the word *day* in the opening chapters of Genesis, on any account it was clear that humanity was not coterminous with God or with the initial act of the material world's creation itself—the first day—but came on the scene as God's created image. *Adam*, the human creature itself, was the image of God in the life of the created world. Indeed, as Luke's genealogy says, Adam was the very "son of God."

Yet, as Paul put it, Adam sinned, and through this human creature's sin, all human beings have been caught up in the sin and death that entered the world. The post-Adam structure of the world, insofar as one can speak of structure rather than chaos, is the history of human life in which sin comes to dominate. As a result we—humanity qua humanity and in all its particular parts—move inescapably in patterns of self-defeating damage. Our lot is to deepen our problem not only in self-willed destruction but also—perhaps paradoxically so—in our very efforts to escape that which binds us. Our attempts to reason ourselves toward the good are frustrated not only by the fact that the world in which we reason is out of control—and therefore often unreliable in its self-presentation[26]—but also by the more sinister problem that we cannot overcome ourselves. "The good that I wish to do," says Paul in reflecting on his life apart from Christ, "I cannot." "And the evil that I wish not to do, that is just what I do" (Rom 7:19). We are ignorant, says Justin, and cannot become wise. Apart from the one and only Savior, we walk in darkness, says Luke (Acts 4:12; 26:18). No amount of self-training or discipline or goodwill can overcome the power that sin has become. Its longevity, historical texture, and accumulated weight constitute its power. In the story these three Christians know, human beings are simply not powerful enough—do not have it within their resources either interpersonally or in their collective acts—to throw off the history that is sin's immensity and make a new one in which sin does not reign.

Moreover, our bodies are destined for death and decay. Sooner or later but one and all, we are mastered by the power of death. Try to overcome death, the Christian story says, and you will see how it, too, is a power more powerful than you. Demons, unclean spirits, Beelzebul, other "gods and lords" (1 Cor 8:5)—all these, too, are more powerful than the human creature. But death is that against which we finally fight and to which we inevitably lose. Against all those both ancient and modern who would say we can become cozy with death, the Christians say otherwise. Death is the final enemy.

In the midst of a history devastated by sin,[27] the election of Israel and the giving of the Torah were to shine as a "light to the nations" by creating a people whose vocation it was to image the one and only God in the pattern of their common life. The Law was the rule of a life that would be observable as distinct from the non-Jewish world. It was holy, just, and good. And yet, like all other things in a sin-devastated world, sin seized the Law and twisted the human relation to it. The Law remained what it always was—holy, just, and good—but sin's power over the human being was the greater.

Even though sin prevented our ability to be tutored by the Law toward the Christ, however, the Law itself—in the broad sense of what it was for, what the scriptural narrative amounted to vis-à-vis God's plan for the Jewish people—continued to point to him. Jesus' life and death were according to the "law of Moses, the prophets, and the psalms" (Luke 24:44); the Scriptures "pre-proclaimed the Gospel" (Rom 1:2). Both the first coming of the Messiah and his second can be discerned in Israel's Scripture. Let me show you, says Justin to Trypho, and then cites passage after passage after passage.[28]

Yet the perception of the Law's testimony to Jesus of Nazareth in particular occurred only after his life, death, and resurrection, as the scene with Cleopas and his companion on the Emmaus road makes particularly clear. The Christians speak of God's intervention in the history of sin as an "apocalypse," a revelation that comes from God's side of the God/world distinction. The apocalypse of God in Jesus the Christ was continuous with the Law but was not, *sensu stricto*, produced within the chaotic running of a sin-devastated world—as if the line from the Torah to Jesus ran naturally from here-it-comes to here-it-is.

Indeed, in the Christian story Jesus is the second Adam, the Son of God sent forth not one day after the next but in the "fullness of time" (Gal 4:4). In the Christian telling of it, the fact that Jesus was the "son of Adam, the son of God" meant that he could restart the story, write the first chapter of human life—again. Where the First human being was tempted and failed, the Second resisted temptation and began things anew: you shall not, he says to the Tempter, tempt the Lord thy God. He who "knew no sin" was able to redo creation itself, to set on a new foundation that which human life had become. "Neither circumcision nor uncircumcision is anything—but new creation!" (Gal 6:15). "If anyone is in Christ—new creation! The old things have gone away and, behold!, new things have come!" (2 Cor 5:17).

Were one to ask what allows such remarkable claims to be made about the new possibilities for human life, the Christians would tell of Jesus as the one who was the image of God. In some contrast to modern understandings of the word *image*, they did not mean that Jesus "reflected" God as if he were a copy of some other reality. They meant instead that precisely as the human that he was—and in the "scheme" of the human life that he thus lived—he enfleshed the God who made the world (see Phil 2:5–11). The Lord of Israel has come as the Lord in the life of Jesus. When Luke speaks of the Lord of all, he means both the Lord of heaven and earth and the resurrected Jesus (Acts 4:24; 10:36; 17:24). And for Justin, God's very Word has taken flesh in Jesus; the speech of the Lord of Israel turns out to be the human life of the Nazarene.

Both the possibility and reason for this inseparability is the Holy Spirit. The dynamism of the one God was such that in the fullness of time the Father could by his Spirit send his Son in the flesh. The Holy Spirit overshadows the woman Mary, and the Son comes as Jesus.[29] In the form of God, he lives a human life. When the Christians spoke of the Power of God to make himself synonymous with the life, death, and resurrection of Jesus, they spoke of the Spirit (Luke 24 and Acts 1). The Spirit was therefore both the Spirit of God the Father and Jesus the Son.[30]

The broad pattern of theological speech in the Christian story thus includes God the Father, Jesus of Nazareth, and the Holy Spirit. To speak of one is to invoke the other two. And this, most fundamentally, is why Jesus can redo the creation and begin it anew: in his human life he is the coming of God in the flesh re-creating the world he originally made; in his human life he is the Second Adam imaging God, resisting the sin that devastated the world, and overcoming the death that has plagued the creation since the First Adam. Jesus of Nazareth is thus both the continuation of the world's story as it runs through Israel and its re-beginning. As we shall see, he is also its end. But the Christian story also tells of a meantime, a time that is between the re-beginning and the end, and is to that part that it next moves.

If Jesus re-begins the world, what does this new creation look like? The early Christians were not naïve about what is plain to see and so do not tell us that the old world is gone away once and for all.[31] The Christian story tells, to the contrary, of the new creation as an inbreaking of the new world into the old, or as the embodying and figuring forth of the new world in the midst of the old, or of the groaning of all creation for its final redemption even as it rejoices that it has been set free from the law of sin and death.

Modern analysts of the New Testament have typically seen a difference in eschatological emphasis between Paul and Luke. The latter, so it has often been said, tones down the expectation of the former that the world will soon end. Though there is some truth to the fact that one would not write the history of the church—conceptualizing it as a distinct sociological form within the flow of the world—without some sense that history continues on as before, the differences are overblown.[32] Paul, Luke, and Justin all work within a story that simultaneously says that the new creation is here now and that God is not yet finished remaking what he made. We exist in this meantime.

The name for the way by which the reality meantime is made known to the world is the church, the community whose corporate life was to witness to creation's re-beginning in Jesus Christ. Precisely because the creation has begun anew with the new Adam, the division of Jew and Gentile (that is, every not-Jew) is overcome in the community of the new creation—the body of Christ. The reuniting of Jew and Gentile in a practically dense common life is the visible proclamation that creation has begun anew. There were virtually countless and historically deep differences to be worked through, as well as some that could be retained. But in the Christian story to be baptized was to join the new creation. One God, one body, one family—Jew and Gentile, brothers and sisters in Christ.

Contrary to the individualist predilections of modernity since at least Rousseau, for the Christian story it is this community as a whole that primarily serves as the light to the nations. Individual Christians doubtless play a large role in this witness—as did both Paul and Justin themselves, for example—but the group for which they stand is the greater. As Luke tells, the word *Christian* itself came not from in-group members as a means of self-styling but from outsiders who could see something for which they needed to coin a name.

The Christians gathered together to worship God, sing hymns to Christ ("as if to a god," as Pliny would see by the beginning of the second century), eat together, redistribute possessions, learn the apostles' doctrine and discipline, and convert all to their way of life. Toward the larger pagan world across the Mediterranean, the Christians were positioned by their story in a complex relation of rejection and invitation.

The God of the Christians tolerated no rivals and prohibited idolatry; the pagan gods and all the practices that surrounded their determining presence in the lives of human beings—temples, cultic matter, house gods, magic books, and so on—were thus to be rejected. However many so-called gods and lords there may be, for us Christians, says Paul, there is only one God and one Lord. When and where the cult of the emperor would require political allegiance in the form of worship and/or sacrifice, therefore, the Christians knew they must refuse. That such a perpendicular relation to Roman political practice would potentially lead to their deaths is clearly seen, even embraced. To suffer "for the Name" is to live the story of Jesus in the flesh of one's own life and to proclaim publicly that the word *Christian* names those who worship the one and only God precisely in their devotion to Jesus Christ.

Yet the story these Christians tell does not describe such proclamation as sedition—a conscious attempt to subvert the Roman government by means of calculated resistance—but rather as invitation. Indeed, where there is no conflict between God and the idols, where there is no demand to worship or partake in idolatrous practice, the Christians resolutely affirm their worthiness as model citizens. Obey the authorities, says Paul (Rom 13:1–7); the Christians are innocent of the crime of *stasis*, says Luke (Acts 26:31 et passim); we're the best citizens you have, says Justin (*1 Apol.* 12.1; 17.1).

Such obedience, however, is always paired with the call to conversion and the claim to final truth that such conversion presupposes. "Come join us, for we know the truth" is inherent to the political vision of the Christian story and produces the tension that indelibly marks Christian existence. When and where the wider world sees governmentally obedient Christians, it will simultaneously witness the obstinate refusal to confess anyone other than Christ as Lord. When and where the wider world sees a Christian community that works within the jurisprudential norms of the land, it will simultaneously witness a community that turns such norms toward the truth of its political life. In short, the Christian story of the meantime tells of a distinction between church and world and of the different ways of knowing that are interwoven with this distinction itself.

In large part, it is these different ways of knowing that underlie Paul's pedagogical inversions vis-à-vis worldly wisdom. Reason itself cannot simply reach out and grab wisdom, as if all reason had to do was to exercise itself in the right directions. The Christian story, in fact, tells of reason's regular worldly workings not as the search for wisdom but as foolishness. True wisdom is the repair of reason by trust in the trustworthiness of the Crucified Christ—what looks to the world's way of knowing to be pure folly. The very Wisdom of God is not something general but Christ himself. To know Christ is to know the divine wisdom. For Luke the wisdom of the poets—Aratus or Cleanthes or any others—is but their own testimony to the fact that though God is indeed near, they have missed him and do not know him. And for Justin the love of wisdom is not what the Stoics or Plato teach about reason but what Christianity itself is as a way of life that follows the Crucified One.

In the Christian story, human reason is not capable of self-repair; indeed, left to its own, it will even lead us astray, mistaking foolishness for wisdom and wisdom for folly. Reason's repair occurs only through knowing God in Christ—or, rather, being known by him—and the communal norms that inculcate reason's right workings in a pattern of church life and public witness. The re-creation of reason is simultaneously the participation in the ecclesial form of life that matches the future's arrival in the present—to be a people of the meantime is to learn how to know truth and love wisdom.

Of course, devotion to Christ and the community that bears his name is only the re-beginning, the way in which the End of things is made visible in the midst of time. It is not yet the End itself.

The final chapter of the Christian story tells of "the last day," or "the day of the Lord"—the return of Christ (Acts 17:31). In Justin's language, this is the second Advent of the Messiah. It is the time when every knee will bow and every tongue will confess that Jesus is Lord. It is the time when the dead shall be raised bodily. It is the time when God will be all in all and when death shall be utterly and permanently defeated.

Against hyperspiritualists of every stripe in every age, the Christian story tells of a consummation that has not yet occurred—or at least not yet in the sense that the world's ongoing history of sin and death is plain and palpable to all. It is true that upon death we shall "live with Christ," or—in Justin's view—our souls shall be with him. But it is no less true that such postmortem presence does not communicate the fullness of the story that uses a grammar of bodies in inseparable connection to the end. Flying zombies or floating corpses or anything so ridiculous is not in view, of course, but the redeemed restoration of the material conditions of earthly existence clearly is. Death, according to the Christian story, will finally be vanquished only when its power over such conditions is no more, namely, when the bodies who have been death's victims are raised. That resurrected bodies will be transformed bodies is clear not only from Paul's extensive argumentation about exactly this question but also from Luke's portrayal of the body of the resurrected Jesus as dis/continuous with his earthly existence, and from Justin's insistence that our resurrected bodies will never die (earthly bodies always do).[33] We shall retain our specific identities that irrefragably depend upon bodily location, but such bodily continuity will be through material renewal and transformation rather than a simple repetition of earthly existence.

In the view of these three Christians, the defeat of death and bodily resurrection are not theological commitments born out of a general reflection upon the character of God or the world. They are, rather, commitments that are derived specifically from the story of Jesus' bodily resurrection. Had Jesus not been raised bodily, who knows how the Christian story would have run—or, rather, whether there would have been one at all (1 Cor 15). But in fact he had, and a fortiori so shall we: the story thus runs in the direction from him to us. Paul's argument that we shall receive spiritual bodies upon our resurrection, Luke's ordering of the church's kerygma from Jesus' resurrection to the hope of our own (see Acts 23:6; 24:15; 26:23), and Justin's insistence that the immortality of the soul is insufficiently Christian precisely because it discards our bodies, all presuppose the fundamental importance of Jesus' bodily resurrection for what we make of our end. To say it slightly differently, the way the Christian story runs to its end is unintelligible without the bodily resurrection of Jesus.

All of which is to say that for the Christians the bodily resurrection of Jesus is the beginning of the end of creation's groaning; it is that which shows us the end as it comes into the midst of time. The end itself—the thought of which lies in the realm of the hope that faith creates—is when God finishes the work of creation he has re-begun in the new creation. To be sure, there will be judgment; neither the wicked nor their works will have further sway. But the accent of the final chapter of the Christian story is not upon our just deserts but upon the culmination of the glorious, liberating work of God to set his redeemed creation free. Or to be more precise, the consummation is when the world is finally and completely taken up in the work wrought in Christ from beginning to end.

The Christian story is thus a narrative that claims to encompass all existing things. The story runs from the beginning to the end; yet the truth of beginning to end is known from a particular point within the ongoing story itself, that of Jesus of Nazareth's life, death, and resurrection. It is this point, so the story claims, that discloses the heart of the relation between God and all that is not God, namely, everything God made. For the Christians, the God of all things is tied not only to a particular history—that of the Jews—but also to a particular human being, Jesus the Christ. The human being qua human being is also tied to this particular human being. And it is this particular human being, therefore, that is the heart of the story of God and his humanity.

RIVAL TRADITIONS

Sometime in the second century or so and somewhere in the Mediterranean basin, someone wrote a fictitious correspondence between Seneca and St. Paul.[34] This correspondence is indubitably significant for the philosophical claim made by its existence: simply by the fact that its form is a series of short letters, it says that Stoics and Christians can talk to each other.[35]

Though their methods have obviously differed from this ancient text, modern scholars of comparison have thought much the same thing. Whatever the differences between the Stoics and the Christians, they can be put into mutually intelligible conversation. Scholarship on the Stoic/Christian conversation is the history of progress in understanding their mutual intelligibility and—where such things are cared about—its significance for larger questions about God, the order of the cosmos, the human being, the best-lived life, and so forth.

As I argued in the previous chapter, the indispensable assumption that underlies such comparative work—or conversation construction—is that the Stoics and Christians share fundamentally the same, similar, or at least commensurable commitments. These commitments are to some sort of reality called God or the Divine, or to a particular doctrine called Providence, or to a goal called Human Betterment, or to certain common aspects of human experience called the Passions or the Virtues, and so on.

The primary problem with such an assumption is that it is false. The stories that make Stoic/Christian commitments intelligible as Stoic/Christian commitments do not overlap or run parallel in the way that would be required for the existence of commensurable commitments or shared agreements. In fact, the stories diverge and conflict in every significant way to such an extent as to prevent the necessary conditions for commensurability even to arise. Conversation on the basis of shared substantive commitments is, quite frankly, impossible. The narratives are those of traditions in conflict.

CASES AGAINST TRANSLATION

At the beginning of Part I of this book, I wrote that the "themes" I selected from the Stoics and the Christians were those that both best captured the drift of the individual texts and facilitated the most productive way to think their relation. The danger in this way of doing things is that it could appear as if in the discussion below I have simply reproduced the position against which I have earlier argued, namely, that the Stoics and Christians can be related through scholarly abstractions (for example, the Divine) or that the Stoics and Christians share enough common commitments to make for themes that cover both types of texts in constructively similar ways. The organization, however, is not a reproduction of the position against which I have argued but is instead a focused pattern that highlights the most significant places where the incommensurability of the divergent stories exists. To put it differently, the foci are instances in which the same or similar words are used in different ways to mean different things. To describe these differences is to make the argument against the translation of one tradition into another.

Admittedly, speaking of translation is on the surface a difficult way to designate the conflict between traditions that work in the same natural languages (Greek and Latin).[36] Yet, as Alasdair MacIntyre points out, there really is no such thing as Greek-as-such (or Latin-as-such, and so on). Contrary to the impression given by a shallow consultation of a dictionary, there is only Greek as it is used by a particular linguistic community, Greek-in-use.[37] A language is "as it is used in and by a particular community living at a particular time and place with particular shared beliefs, institutions, and practices. These beliefs, institutions, and practices will be furnished expression and embodiment in a variety of linguistic expressions and idioms; the language will provide standard uses for a necessary range of expressions and idioms, the use of which will presuppose commitment to those same beliefs, institutions, and practices."[38] MacIntyre develops his argument with several compelling illustrations and repeatedly shows that the boundaries of a language-in-use are "the boundaries of some linguistic community" (373). The ability to describe well the difference between the Irish-in-use of Tory Island and the Irish-in-use of Dublin civil servants, for example, or the sociopolitical rivalry expressed through using different names for the same place (Doire Columcille in Irish or Londonderry in English), depends upon the recognition that the meaning of the Irish or English words is inseparable from the particularity of the linguistic community whose patterns of speech constitute the meaning-making grammar of the community. It is of course true that distinct communities within a common culture can overlap in their use of a particular natural language, but this is not much more significant than noting that they are part of a common culture. The critical question for this book is about the language-in-use of specific traditions.[39]

A specific tradition's language-in-use "is tied by its vocabulary and its linguistic uses to a particular set of beliefs . . . so that to reject or modify radically the beliefs will require some corresponding kind of linguistic transformation" (374). Ceasing to believe, to take an obvious example, that Israel/Jews names a people whose God is the one and only true God would require the development of a new, counterscriptural linguistic pattern surrounding the use of *Israel* and *Jew* and—should the word continue to be used—of *God*. Moreover, precisely because the tradition's language-in-use is inseparable from its "mode of life," the terms of the language will get their meaning against the background of the tradition's whole range of life. Abstracted from this background, the specific terms of a tradition's language have not a different meaning but no identifiable meaning at all. As MacIntyre says about names in particular, "the mode of life in which the name is related to its bearer . . . provides a necessary background for understanding what makes *this name* the name of *that* particular person; 'reference' is no more than a name for the unity in the diversity of use, and if the diversity of use were abstracted, what would remain would not be some pure referential relationship. Instead nothing at all would remain" (377). Abstracting the diversity of use of "Jesus" from the thick web of Christian thought and practice—to anticipate the discussion below—would not result in a purified understanding of what the name Jesus means but in the inability to understand the word *Jesus*.[40] Linguistic intelligibility thus turns out to be directly related to a particular sort of life: you need the life of the tradition to know how to use the words. Transformation of a language-in-use is therefore transformation from one particular form of life to another, even as learning to live in another form of life requires learning or developing another language-in-use.[41]

Speaking of language-in-use rather than language-as-such complicates and expands philosophically the typical understanding of "translation" to make it exactly the right vocabulary to use when thinking about the narrative juxtaposition of traditions in conflict. Indeed, MacIntyre's subtly difficult discussion opens the strange-sounding possibility that different traditions can both be speaking Greek, say, but speaking different languages. That is, when it comes to traditions, "language" does not (indeed, it cannot) simply mean Greek qua Greek but must instead mean the Greek-that-is-used-to-express-and-reflect-the-Christian-tradition-in-the-texts-of-Paul/Luke/Justin.[42] When we ask, therefore, about the translation of one tradition into another, we are not naïvely asking how, for example, Marcus's use of *akropolis* might show up in Christian discourse but the much more difficult question of how the language-in-use of one tradition sits next to the language-in-use of the other. Individual terms are always ciphers for the larger language-in-use—or, in the words of this study—the narratives that make the terms make the sense they make.

In each of the following sections, I adopt the same basic procedure: the attempt is to understand what it would entail to speak-live the terms of one tradition in the terms of the other. The use of "translation" is generous enough to allow the differences between the sections to emerge while specific enough to organize them together in a unified line of thought. This is, after all, a cumulative rather than a simply repetitive argument: the repetition from case to case makes the point that to deal with the relation of the traditions is to deal with the pattern that emerges from the cases taken together as a whole.[43]

GOD AND WORLD

In many studies the word *God* or *the Divine* is used to refer to an object that both the Christians and the Stoics write about. Malherbe, Engberg-Pedersen, Thorsteinsson, Huttunen, Balch, Vorster, and numerous others all speak in this way.[44] Such language is hardly limited to scholars who explore Stoicism and New Testament Christianity. In her otherwise illuminating book on St. Augustine, for example, Sarah Catherine Byers contrasts Seneca's view of God with that of St. Augustine.[45] Marcia Colish, too, writes of a shared "God" (or, for example, "theodicy") in her tomes that trace Stoicism's *Wirkungsgeschichte* through the early Middle Ages.[46] And Elizabeth Cochran, an expert on the works of Jonathan Edwards, argues that Edwards shares Stoic conceptions of God's moral excellence or providential work.

These examples reflect the dominant assumption about the use of the word *God* in the Stoic and Christian texts, that is, it is used in the same or similar enough ways that we can treat it as referring to the same object/subject. The Christians and the Stoics both speak about the same basic thing called God. The trouble with this assumption is that they do not.

If we pose the question of how to "translate" the Stoic use of the word *theos/deus* into Christian usage so that the Christians would say the same thing with the word *God* in their grammar that the Stoics said in theirs, we are immediately confronted with this problem: in Christian grammar, if the Stoic *theos/deus* can be rendered at all, it is best approximated not by God but by *cosmos/ktisis*. When the Stoics write of "God," it would be something like what the Christians would understand by the words *world* or *creation*.

We must say "if" and "best approximated" and "something like" because even the conception of cosmos profoundly differs: to use the word *creation* in the Christian sense is to affirm something specific about the cosmos that the Stoics would deny, that is, that the God of Israel created it. For the Stoics, the cosmos is not creation in the sense that the Christians would affirm and thus is not cosmos in the sense that the Christians use the word. Nor is the God of Israel, or the Father of Jesus Christ, or the one whose Holy Spirit makes real his identification with Jesus, the "God" that names the rational grain of the cosmos itself. In both Stoic and Christian grammar, that is, God and cosmos are inseparably and reciprocally related, but this relation and the terms that constitute it mean vastly different things within each grammatical pattern.

Indeed, when we pose the question about God in reverse—how to "translate" the Christian use of the word *theos* into Stoic usage so that the Stoics would say the same thing with the word *God* in their grammar that the Christians said in theirs—we are immediately confronted with this problem: the linguistic/conceptual resources needed to render the Christian use of *God* in Stoic grammar do not exist. There is no word for the Christian use of *God* because the thought that would entail what God means vis-à-vis the cosmos did not exist within the Stoic take on the whole of things. Moreover, there is no possible way to get the Christian sense of God as "God-as-determined-by-the-history-of-the-Jews-and-Jesus-of-Nazareth" into Stoic grammar. One might as well simply tell the entire Christian story. And, in fact, that is the point: to render God and all that this word entails is to render the narrative that makes the word *God* mean what it does to both Christians and Stoics. Were the Christian and the Stoic stories the same, the word *God* would refer to the same thing. But they are not, and the word *God* is not "translatable."

For the Stoics, to accept that the word *God* means what the Christians say it means would be to convert to the way of life that is bound to the grammar in which *God* gets its meaning (and this would entail, among other things, repentance for the idolatry practiced in ignorance). Such acceptance, that is, would be the simultaneous destruction of the Stoic take on the whole: nothing within Stoicism would make Stoic sense if *God* were to mean what the Christians say it does. The density of meaning surrounding the words *cosmos, physis, phantasia, sophia,* and so on—all this would change. In MacIntyre's way of putting it, the once-Stoics would need to learn a new language-in-use. Conversely, for Christians to accept that the word *God* means what the Stoics say it means would be to apostatize and convert to a different way of being. On the Christians' own terms, they would have become idolaters of the most basic sort, those who mistake the creation for the Creator (Rom 1:18–32).[47] In short, despite common scholarly practice, considering the word *God* in the Christian and Stoic texts does not reveal the same subject or object but an incommensurable and incompatible way of using the word.

Of the many implications of this asynonymy, we need to mention only two for the purposes of this chapter. First, the fact that *God* does not mean anything like the same thing for the Christians and the Stoics makes it all but obvious that patterns of language that are directly tied to *God* in the grammars of the different traditions will not mean the same thing. *Providence,* for example, no more names a shared conviction about a God/world relation than it does a shared sense of what that God or world is.[48] Second, precisely because of the role that *God* plays in each tradition, the patterns of language that are inextricably bound to God are constitutive of each tradition's identity as a distinctive tradition in the first place.[49] The consequence, therefore, of the fundamental difference "God" makes for the tradition's existence as a tradition is the expectation of incommensurable (and incompatible) difference elsewhere. And that is indeed what we find.

HUMAN BEING

Prima facie, when it comes to the human being, there would seem to be many substantive agreements between the three Stoics and the three Christians. After all, the human being is a more readily identifiable sort of thing than God; moreover, both the Christians and the Stoics think there is something wrong with human beings. The truth is, however, that neither group of texts displays a set of judgments about an essence of humanity—at least in the sense of what it would mean to be human irrespective of one's participation in the particular tradition for which the texts speak. Indeed, to the extent that the Stoic and Christian texts both presuppose and articulate anthropological judgments, they do so in irreducibly and robustly tradition-specific ways.

When we ask how best to render the Christian sense of *anthrōpos* in Stoic grammar, we immediately become aware of the depth of the translational problem. For the Christians, to be a human being is to be determined by the realities signified by the names Adam and Jesus of Nazareth and the history that runs from one to the other. The first name is, in fact, synonymous with the advent of the "human being" and its original waywardness. Adam's sin effects a history that marks the human being in its very humanness at the same time that it explains the origin of the human dilemma: we ourselves lie at the base of our problem and are its cause. There is no getting past ourselves, our being Adam again and again and again.

The second name is synonymous with the advent of the human being repaired. Insofar as the human being has a chance to be more than Adam again and again, it is because of the new reality given in the Second Adam, Jesus. It is in relation to him and in the community that bears his name that the human being can become a thing of repair. And insofar as the human being's repair is manifested—what repair looks like—it will take the shape of a sanctified life in public, communal witness to its origin, the Lord Jesus Christ. In short, for Christians, being human is what it is inside the narrative that is the Christian story. There is no such thing as "the human" in abstraction from the story that runs from Adam to Jesus.

Rendering the Christian account of "the human being" in Stoic grammar is thus—once again—the same thing as having to tell the Christian story Stoically. Which is rather simply to say, Christian anthropological judgments cannot be translated into Stoic terms. Were the Stoics to mean "human" in a Christian sense, they would have learned that the human is what Christians say it is and would therefore have abandoned the Stoic narrative that funds their anthropological judgments.

When we pose the question in reverse and ask how the Christians might render the Stoic sense of *anthrōpos* within a Christian grammar, we immediately confront an impossibility. Though the Stoic texts do not give an account of the origin of our propensity to disregard our nature and live contra the order of reason, they do assume that our undisciplined tendencies move us in damaging ways away from our nature.[50] And in this one might be lured into seeing promise for synonymy. But as great as it may be, due to our weakness in passion or ignorance of reason's direction, the Stoics judge our damage not to be so great as to be beyond self-repair and the future direction of self-care. As long as we learn the habits of Stoic life and build well the fortress of reason within, there is no need to receive help of any other kind than what we can offer ourselves. It is true that we learn from human exempla how Stoic lives look, but our use for them is only illustrative; we do not depend on them in any fundamental way for the possibility of self-repair and future self-care.

For Christians to mean all this when they say *anthrōpos*—and they would have to mean it all if speaking the word Stoically—would be for them to rid their speech of the necessity for Jesus himself. Paul, Luke, and Justin: they all speak of Jesus as him who was necessary for our sake, as him who alone could bring new creation, as him who repairs the damage we wrought and were incapable of rectifying, as him who saves us from ourselves and the effects of self-rule.[51] To mean *anthrōpos* Stoically would be to substitute an entire anthropology of self-correction for that of a christologically dependent humanity, which is to say that on the Christians' own terms speaking Stoically about humanity eliminates the reason for Christianity itself.

In short, the judgments that make for what the human being is in each tradition are incommensurable. Neither the Christians nor the Stoics, moreover, can render the other's sense of *anthrōpos* within their own traditions without dissolving and/or abandoning the distinctive commitments that make their traditions traditions in the first place. When it comes to the human being, the Stoics and the Christians stand face to face in conflict.

JESUS OF NAZARETH

It is an obvious but often overlooked point in the comparison of Stoicism with early Christianity that the sticking point of any claims to similarity is Jesus of Nazareth. But it is only by ignoring or somehow attempting to minimize the fact that Christianity's existence is directly dependent upon—indeed, utterly inconceivable without—Jesus of Nazareth that one can posit shared philosophical agreement between wide or deeply important patterns of speech.

When we, once again, pose our fundamental question and ask how within Stoic grammar we might render Jesus of Nazareth and all that he signifies within Christian grammar, we can easily see the impossibility of any remotely similar rendering. As MacIntyre notes, names are often in need of paraphrase or glosses to explain how they might be rendered in contexts other than their originating linguistic community. No amount of extensive interpretative glosses—for *anthrōpos* or *anēr* or *sophos*, for example—could sufficiently explain the name Jesus of Nazareth.[52] It is true, of course, that Jesus was taken to be an exemplum of sorts for the early Christians, but claiming that a generalized notion of exemplum could provide a point of shared philosophical understanding about Jesus on the one hand and a Sage (or philosopher-teacher) on the other obscures the mistaken sense that the Stoics can say "Jesus" with the word *exemplum*. It is not otherwise with the notion of "founder," as if Zeno (or textually speaking, Chrysippus) could stand somehow for "Founder of the Movement" in some materially similar way to Jesus as "Founder of the Movement." The word *founder* would mean such drastically different things in each case that it would dispel the illusion that we were talking about the same sort of thing.[53]

For the Christians, of course, knowing the reality signified by the word *God* depends upon knowing Jesus; knowing that creation has been made new depends upon knowing Jesus; knowing wisdom is knowing Jesus; being a part of a community of repair is being "in Christ Jesus"; preaching and missionizing is "in the name of Jesus"; overcoming death is being raised from the dead like Jesus; the consummation of all creation will result in bending the knee to the Lord Jesus; and so on. The Stoic sense of *exemplum* says none of this, and yet all of this—and much, much more—is essential to what the Christian texts mean when they speak of "Jesus."

Once again, as in the case of *God* and the *human being*, rendering *Jesus* intelligibly entails nothing less than the narrative that makes the sense that Christian faith makes. Getting *Jesus* over into Stoic language would require the ability to tell the Christian story in Stoic terms, which is to say that it cannot be done. There is no chapter in the story or sequence thereof, or concept or cluster thereof, or term or cluster thereof, or anything else within Stoicism that can receive the meaning of Jesus for Christians. Likewise, there is no Stoic word that, when put into Christian discourse, captures enough of what *Jesus* means to make for substantive agreements.

DEATH

It would be hard to argue against the fact that both the Stoics and the Christians think we will die. Only the most deluded could avoid this realization while living in a world full of death. Yet what is death? Is it not exactly this that is debated down through the ages when we debate anything else at all about being human? Upon closer reflection the Stoics and Christians turn out to construe death in light of their larger stories about what it is to be in the world at all. Death, like the notions of intention and action, is intelligible only in light of a wider account of what is going on when we die.

When we ask, then, how to say what Christian "death" is with Stoic grammar (or vice versa), we are asking the same thing as how to translate the interlocking use of curse, sin, power, enemy, soul, resurrection of the body, judgment, eternal life, and more—and all that goes with them, and more—into a pattern that says death is natural, part of the cycle of the whole, not to be feared by rationally directed persons, incapable of being overcome, preferable to weakness even if it means suicide, and so forth. As difficult as it may be for those who think that we can talk about the fact of death apart from an interpretation of what it means to die, the Christian and the Stoic texts are not at all saying the same thing when they say we die. When they talk about death, they are simultaneously talking about the full breadth of their take on the whole of things.[54] Which is to say, of course, that we are asking yet again about how to tell the broader Christian story in Stoic terms and how to render Roman Stoicism Christianly. When put this way, the impossibility of such a task is obvious and little more needs to be said. Their takes on death are as incommensurable and incompatible as their uses of the word *God*.

POLITICS/SOCIETY/COMMUNITY

It is difficult, of course, to think of politics in the ancient world, since the ancients did not distinguish between politics and things such as religion or family life. The dichotomies that have become ours in the late-modern West were not theirs. When we ask them what we think of as political questions, their replies immediately range beyond the shape of our modern questions and into the full breadth of ancient life. To be political in this or that way was also to be religious in this or that way and to be a husband or a father—or a wife or a mother (think only of Agrippina!)—or a master or a slave in this or that way, and much else besides.

When we therefore ask what it would be to speak Christian politics in the language of Stoicism, we are asking yet again about the wider range of things that make up Christian/Stoic life in the first place. The differences we would discover in politics would thus be exactly the difference between the Christians and Stoics. For the Christians, to be political is to participate in community that follows the Christ, which is to say that Paul, Luke, and Justin all presuppose a distinction between the church and the world. The Christian community is itself a particular sort of politics, over and above any specific spiritual disposition or individual growth in holiness (or lack thereof). The publicly identifiable community does see itself as participating in new creation, and in that sense the church is the world as it ought to be (and is always invited to be). But there is no grand political goal for society at large. Indeed, the primary political grammar is that of witness, a way of speaking that inevitably presupposes the difference between those who have heard and those who need to hear.[55] Even though the Christians aim to be good citizens, their true citizenship is located in the place where Jesus' Lordship is confessed and recognized, that is, in heaven and on earth in the church. It is true that the Christians might find themselves engaged with non-Christians in any number of common "political" pursuits or obligations (for example, paying taxes—rendering to Caesar what is his). But such common endeavors can never be severed from devotion to the Lord Jesus, as if the ancient Christians could create a separate sphere of common political action and call it politics or ethics—a realm where the navigation was conducted by pilots of the common good or some type of generalized "ethicist." Even in common activities or tasks, the grammar of Christian politics remains that of witness. And when and where Christian citizenship conflicts with the duties of citizens of an earthly empire—or any of its smaller versions on down to the customs of a rural village—the former always trumps. Jesus is Lord above all lords is the shape of Christian political life.

Precisely because there is no such thing as Christian politics without Jesus, to say what the Christian shape of politics is with Stoic language would be to transform it into Christian discourse. The possibility of translation is directly dependent upon the possibility of transforming "Jesus is Lord" into something else, either something specifically Stoic or some generalized notion of ethics or the common good that the Stoics also share quite apart from their specific sort of Stoic politics—which is to say, it is an impossibility. If anything, to Stoic eyes Christian politics would appear most like that of a strange secret society or the Epicureans (or at least the charges typically leveled against them).[56] More likely, however, Christian politics would simply appear odious and obstinate to the Stoics, as it did, for example, to Marcus Aurelius.

Because the Stoics were known for cultivating detachment, they were often accused of neglecting the duties of citizenship. Such a charge is of course nothing less than absolutely bizarre vis-à-vis Seneca and Marcus, but Epictetus is careful to deflect it. Though the telos of Stoic philosophy was in fact the building and maintaining of the individual's inner fortress—isolated from all that is external to its rationally directed happiness—the politics of the Roman Stoics was one of thorough involvement in all civic matters. To the degree that there could be considerable conflict between a Stoic and the apparent duties of civic life (Cato was always revered), such conflict was rooted in the practical wisdom of the individual Stoic rather than in a sociologically distinct community that set itself against specific political practices. Seneca was ordered to commit suicide because of his (alleged) role in the Pisonian conspiracy—not because a community called "Stoics" were themselves a political problem and he was identified as one of their members. The Stoic story does not tell of fundamental distinction between the politics of this world and that of another. The political distinction, rather, that corresponds to the word *Stoic* is between the individual's disposition and the practices of the ignorant. As Marcus's *Meditations* show, the Stoic story contains no hint that the world's politics are misguided as a whole—and therefore in need of redemption and transformation—but instead positions those cast into civic roles inside their inner fortress in detachment from things over which they have no control and enjoins them to act as a Stoic would.[57]

The impossibility of speaking Christianly in Stoic political terms should be apparent. On the surface, of course, it may seem that the Christians could say something similar to the Stoics, namely, be Christian in whatever civic role you find yourself. But, more deeply, to tell the story of political life in anything less than christologically shaped communal terms is to speak in ways that have left Christian discourse behind. Even Justin's appeal to "justice" shows that the wider politics that make the word mean what it does for Christians are inextricably bound to following Jesus Christ and differ profoundly from those who see such following as madness (cf. Acts 26:24–25). None of this is to say that Christians and Stoics cannot find themselves engaged in common political pursuits, but it is to say that they will not do so because of substantively shared agreements about the shape of political life.[58]

Taken cumulatively, these five cases resist the long-held and prevalent position that the Christians and Stoics share the sort of agreements that are necessary for substantive conceptual translation. These five cases also resist, therefore, the long-held and prevalent position that the isolation of similar words or phrases from each corpus of texts provides a common philosophical grammar that reveals the synonymy of the common terms. The five cases also resist, therefore, the long-held and prevalent position that generalizing abstractions are the best way to conceive the relation of different traditions.

The argument they make together is instead that we must deal with the density of word meaning inside the narratives that shape the traditions in which the words receive their meaning in the first place—and that, further, when we do this we discover that in every case the synonymy required for shared substantive agreements presupposes the possibility that the Christian story can be the Stoic and the Stoic can be the Christian. Saying the same thing when they say "God" or "human being" or "Jesus Christ" or "death" or "politics" involves the telling of the same story. And this, they manifestly do not do. The Christians and the Stoics are not, in the profoundest and most difficult philosophical sense, saying the same thing.[59] They face each other with different and competing stories about all that is. And no amount of scholarly labor can erase this most basic juxtaposition. They are, permanently and irreducibly, traditions in conflict.

THE CASE FOR DIS-AGREEMENT: LIFE AS A WAY OF KNOWING—PHILOSOPHY

But for all that, the juxtaposition is more difficult than conflict *simpliciter*. Donald Davidson, Jeffrey Stout, and others have long held that in order to have an argument there must be enough agreement for the word *argument* to describe what you're having. Argument presupposes some sort of agreement; otherwise, you are simply talking past each other.

While there are multiple ways in which traditions in conflict do not share enough agreements to have an argument, there is one highly significant way in which the Christians and the Stoics do in fact agree enough to allow an argument. They agree that living is the way that one comes to know the truth of the world; and they agree that one cannot come to know this truth apart from living in the pattern of life in which the truth is learned. But they disagree over what kind of life one has to live to learn the truth.

For the Stoics, the truth of the world is learned by living the life that is the Stoic dogmata in practice. Precisely because the truth of the Stoic way of life is learned in the living, one cannot become convinced of its truth ahead of time—without the time it takes to live the life one must live to learn the truth of the teaching. One trusts to the Stoic way of life and learns the truth of the world through the practice that is becoming a Stoic.

For the Christians, the truth of the world is learned by living the life that is faith in the Lord Jesus Christ, which of course presupposes a prior practical trust in the Christian way of life. One joins the community called Christians in trust and learns the truth of the world through the time it takes to practice what being a Christian is.

Each tradition argues both that the truth of all things is that which it teaches and that one has to live the tradition to know this truth. They are existentially exclusive claims of the same, universalizing sort. Their disagreement is thus located precisely at the point on which they agree. And their agreement is found precisely at the point at which they most seriously diverge. As Rudolf Bultmann once wrote in a slightly different context, the tie that binds them together (*Anknünpfung*) simultaneously entails a contradiction (*Widerspruch*).[60] Where there is the first, there is the second. And yet the second cannot occur without the first. Agreement and contradiction are one and the same.[61]

The question immediately arises, what kind of argument is this? Thought often proceeds by way of negation, as Hegel so clearly saw, but in this case the negation is not part of a movement toward a larger unity. Instead, in contrast to Hegelian dialectic, the conflict that is the argument between these traditions is irresolvable—at least before the conversion that would bring one inside the distinctive rationality that enables one to resolve the problems encountered before conversion.

It is true that some might want to avoid the claim about postconversion clarity and say that rational arguments are, by definition, resolvable. Most married couples would immediately know that this is false to human experience. But it is false in a more precise sense as well. Existentially thick conflicts of the sort that traditions of life embody are not capable of rational settlement ahead of the life one has to live to learn what the rationality is one needs to think with in the first place.[62] Not only do Christianity and Stoicism not share enough in common to resolve their fundamental disagreement over the truth of all things—they cannot argue the other to defeat because the arguments they make presuppose the practical rationality of their respective tradition—both traditions also locate the most important evidence for the truth of their arguments in the lives of their practitioners.

Which is to say two very important and closely interrelated things: first, the argument between the Christians and the Stoics is foremost an argument of display. The focus on the wider public's ability to perceive the distinctive life-shape of the Stoics or the Christians differs, of course, but the substantive character of the argument does not: the lives of the Christians or Stoics witness—or don't—to the truth of their tradition. Their claim is not "We can argue anyone to defeat on shared rational grounds" but instead, "Here you see the truth of all things in the shape of human life."

Second, exactly because it is an argument of display, their argument is also one of existential provocation, or, differently said, a call to conversion. Only the Christians engaged in mission in any serious sense of the term,[63] but provocation and call are built into the style of existence that is each tradition's claim in motion/practice. Both traditions say with the shape of their lives: "Come and have your life turned to the truth of all things! Here it is and nowhere else!"

The argument at the heart of this conflict of traditions is thus finally about a true kind of life. It is therefore irresolvable in the normal sense of rational resolvability not only because resolution presupposes a conversion to a way of life—in light of which (and only in light of which) one sees retrospectively the inadequacy of previous claims to truth—but also because human lives cannot demonstrate their rational superiority apart from the time it takes to live them. It is only at death that one knows what sort of life has been lived.

Insofar as the traditions themselves extend beyond the death of any of their particular members, the quality of their argument through time will depend on the congruence between the claims to truth and the lives of their practitioners through the history that constitutes the shape of the tradition itself. Though not capable of rational defeat on independent grounds, the Stoic and Christian traditions are thus nevertheless open to profound criticism—both from within and without—and hypocrisy is a charge often leveled at the first hint of false witness or incongruous display.[64] But in an important sense, the criticism of hypocrisy only underlines the point that for these traditions truth is a way of life.

In this chapter I have argued that the juxtaposition of the stories that make the sense that the Christian and Stoic texts make illuminates five interrelated aspects of their relation.

First, the Christian and Stoic stories are the requisite sense-makers of the particular terms within them so much so that adequate translation of words such as *God* from one tradition into the other requires the retelling of the story in which the words originally received their meaning.

Second, because the stories are incommensurable and incompatible, the retelling of one story in the terms of the other is simply impossible—they are traditions in conflict.

Third, the two traditions nevertheless agree on the crucial point that in order to know the truth of all things, one has to participate in the particular tradition for and from which the texts speak; knowing the truth of all things is done only through the life one lives in the Stoic or Christian tradition and not prior to or apart from it.

Fourth, this agreement is simultaneously a disagreement of the profoundest sort, one that is incapable of resolution apart from actually living inside one tradition or the other—the traditions stand irresolvably in existential no less than narrative rivalry.

Fifth, because the irresolvability is the counterpart to the type of claim the traditions make—that of universal truth and its discovery by means of traditioned life—it points inescapably to the fact that an encounter with either tradition demands a choice about how to live. Precisely because we cannot live more than one life, encountering the claim "Come and have your life turned to the truth of all things! Here is it and nowhere else!" results in a practical "yes" or "no" that by its lived response accepts or rejects the claim itself.

Bernard Williams once astutely observed that we should not be surprised at disagreement itself but at the fact that we frequently find disagreement surprising. There is really no reason, said Williams, to find disagreement surprising. It is simply a regular feature of our world and no more surprising than agreement or even strange mixes between the two. Williams went on to say that the real issue at stake in disagreement is "whether a question has to be resolved about what life is going to be lived."[65]

As with much of his writing, Williams's point here has the effect of clarifying the importance of an obvious but often overlooked truth. Disagreements are everywhere; they abound in virtually every layer of the extraordinary density that is human life. What matters are the disagreements that open onto different ways of living the one and only life from birth to death that a human being has to live. If we decide A, we live in this way, but if B we live in that (or C, or D, or E, and so on and on almost ad infinitum). How do we know we have lived the right life and not wasted the only chance we get?[66]

In the next and final chapter I will explore the consequences of studying the sort of disagreement that matters. For, after all, that is what we have been doing and what a proper study of the Christians and Stoics really is.

9

The Argument of Rival Traditions

The great challenge of this century . . . is
understanding the other.
—*Charles Taylor*

There are multiple ways to think about the Christians and the Stoics.[1] This book has been written under the conviction that the most coherent and compelling way is to think them as rival traditions of life. If that is correct, we are faced with several significant questions about the implications of their rivalry for the way we study the ancient world and navigate the issue of truth that such study implies. In this final chapter, then, I directly address the most significant and stickiest questions raised by the previous eight chapters.

CONFLICT OF TRADITIONS: TRANSLATION

In the preceding chapter I argued that "translation" is the most enlightening way to speak about the relation of rival traditions and, further, that the Christian and Stoic traditions cannot be translated. The strongest objection to this argument is not that Christians have in fact tried to use this or that aspect of Stoic tradition for constructive purposes but instead that translation, no matter how difficult, is always possible.

Jeffrey Stout remains the most articulate proponent of a powerful version of this argument. Though in *Ethics After Babel* he pursues many interesting paths, his central point for our purposes is that there is no compelling reason to doubt the possibility of translation—and, on down the road, shared moral judgment and right action—between profoundly different schemes of life.[2] Stout does not think, however, that such translation is achieved by developing a "universal moral language in which all differences can be stated and resolved" (2). He clearly sees, in fact, that the nineteenth-century way of knowing is nothing like a philosophically viable way to think and thus rejects the encyclopedic assumption that we can speak "moral Esperanto."[3] How, then, does Stout avoid the charge that he speaks out of both sides of his mouth, that is, that he admits fundamental difference between moral schemes, rejects encyclopedic ways of knowing, and—still—affirms the possibility of mutually intelligible shared moral judgments?

Stout's answer would be at least as subtle and sophisticated as his written work more generally, but three arguments from *Ethics After Babel* sufficiently indicate the line of his thought. First, Stout rejects the idea that there ever was such a thing as a unity of moral judgment from which we somehow departed (in the main, a criticism of MacIntyre's *After Virtue*). As far as human beings go, Stout observes, we have no reason to think that disagreements are anything other than the way it has always been. The history of human engagement, therefore, has been a history of navigating difference. We have done this both poorly and well, of course, but Stout's point is simply that we have in fact done it. History shows that translation between different schemes for human life is not only possible but a fact of our complex and historically entangled existence. There are individuals who achieved remarkable feats of translation (Thomas Aquinas, for example), but there are also larger cultural shifts that can be read as the historically long and complicated process of translation ("the secularization of moral discourse," for example). Otto Neurath's famous boat provides the image for Stout's reading of the reality of human difference: the boat is forever afloat but "can never be brought into dry dock for complete overhaul." It can, however, "be repaired, plank by plank, while remaining at sea. The process of criticism and revision—of plank repair, if you will—is carried out on board, at sea."[4] We are at sea in difference, the image implies, and the only way we have ever dealt well with life is to work at this difference as a passenger would work on a boat permanently afloat.[5]

Second, as the image of repairing Neurath's boat suggests, the human situation of difference is not hopelessly static, incapable of new configurations, a prison. The boat, rather, is entirely open to hard work and real change. It cannot be "hauled into dry dock," but it can do quite a lot: it can "travel the open seas, trade with foreign places, and send parties ashore in search of virgin timber. Its crew can take unimagined treasures on board, plunder shipwrecks for usable gear, and invent an engine to pull weight once pulled by oar" (59). Stout's extension of Neurath's image argues for ongoing, remarkable change and growth over time through the creative labor that re-forms the boat into a new set of working arrangements. We need not always use oars to get us through the water.

Stout's use of Neurath's boat illustrates his commitment to translation through what he calls "hermeneutical enrichment." True, he says, it could easily appear that translation between different traditions was or is impossible. But such impossibility often betrays a historically curtailed view of the way language actually works. Relating two natural languages well enough to be able to say that "so and so" in one language basically means "such and such in the other" often takes considerable, historically elongated effort—one that is replete with false starts and needed stops, transliterations, annotations, commentaries, bridge dialects (pidgin), new linguistic patterns (creole), and the like.[6] Translation, for Stout, is not a now-or-never endeavor.

Taking the Wittgensteinian point that being able to use a word correctly within established patterns of usage is having the concept (of justice, say),[7] Stout thus develops his criticism of the advocates of untranslatability by arguing, first, that they presuppose a timeless situation in which traditions face each other in exactly the same way for all time, and, second, that time allows the hermeneutical innovation necessary for translation between traditions that initially seem untranslatable.

Untranslatability may be overcome by hermeneutical innovation. If, at a given time, a proposition expressible in one language, L1, is not expressible in another, L2, this need not be so at some later time. L2, after all, can develop hermeneutically. Inexpressibility cannot seal us off permanently from those whose concepts differ from ours unless we treat languages as static systems not subject to hermeneutical enrichment. Natural languages actually in use are not static systems. That is why cultures are not, simply by virtue of conceptual diversity, hermeneutically sealed. Nothing in the nature of conceptual diversity itself prevents one culture from developing the means for expressing an alien culture's moral propositions or grasping their truth (64–65). Language, he says, has "the capacity for hermeneutical enrichment" (218).

As Stout acknowledges, his argument about hermeneutical enrichment is not only a position on the way natural languages have worked. (Though it is difficult, it is not in fact impossible to conceive of natural languages that could not be translated.)[8] Stout is also philosophically committed to Davidsonian convictions about the limits of disagreement. Disagreement, says Stout, is limited precisely to the extent that we recognize it as disagreement at all. Absent a larger background of agreement, difference would show up as unintelligibility, not disagreement: "Our disagreements . . . to be intelligible, require a background of truths taken for granted" (59, cf. 19–21, 43, et passim). To say "that another society has a moral language is to say that it has views on at least some of the topics we denominate as moral" (69). It is this larger background of agreement that makes disagreement disagreement and simultaneously affords the promise of translation. Hermeneutical enrichment is a real possibility exactly to the extent that disagreement is parasitic upon a deeper agreement and does not—indeed, it apparently cannot—"go all the way down" (20). We inevitably understand *something* of those with whom we disagree. Articulating this something, finding its linguistic shape and expounding it, discloses the agreement and simultaneously points the way toward the mutually intelligible judgments that are translation in action.[9]

Third, translation between different schemes for life need work only as well as our present dilemmas require. Stout is a pragmatist, after all, and uninterested in metaphysical truth (there is no comfort here anyway, he says) or whether a translation of one tradition's notion of justice into another's is perfectly correct down to the letter. Such theoretically heavy worries only obscure the fact that we can get on well enough without them. What matters is what the present need calls for. Translation for the sake of current need can do quite well "with whatever is at hand" by creatively including, excluding, and reconfiguring all past and present sources that have possible relevance to the pressing problems. "Bricolage," the name for the processes of "inclusion, exclusion, and reconfiguration," is a way of using the inherent possibility of translation to "arrange and rearrange fragments of moral language in relation to each other and to the whole"—namely, the purpose for which one engages in bricolage to begin with (74–78). Bricolage is not a particular method; it is instead the work of an odd-jobber, who draws "on a collection of assorted odds and ends available for use and kept on hand on the chance they might someday prove useful" (74). Like the odd-jobber, the *bricoleur* "starts off by taking stock of problems that need solving and available conceptual resources for solving them." There follows the "taking apart, putting together, reordering, weighting, weeding out, and filling in" that itself is the work of bricolage (75). To reflect morally on what we need is to use this and that, translating as we go.

In short, if we can use words from other traditions well enough to meet our currently pressing needs, we have adequately translated them into our language (see 80–81 et passim). Stout's pragmatism is thus the philosophical correlate to his sense that time is on our side. It may well be that there is "no single best response" to a given dilemma, or that there is a "tie for first place" (47). Not to worry, new information may easily come forward over time to help us know how to break the tie. And where it does not, we can infer that there is no best way to go. In either case, the task for the present remains the same: competent judges simply judge the best they can.[10] To the degree that the competent use words/concepts from other traditions, they perform the act of translation.

Reading Stout helps to clarify both the importance and the difficulty of the issues involved in describing the conflict of traditions of life as a question of translation. To put it as starkly as possible, if Stout is right, the conflict of traditions is only as deep as their agreement—which is to say that it isn't really a conflict at all. Rival traditions are rivals only to the degree that they have yet to work out their differences in light of their shared agreements or have not yet encountered a master bricoleur or cultural shift that brings them together in whatever creative or interesting combinations could occur to satisfy the needs of the present.[11] Stout's argument would thus point to a serious substantive mistake in construing the relation between Christians and Stoics as one of rivals in juxtaposition. What I should have done instead would be to scour the sources for possibilities of deeper agreement, looking to see where the potential for translation lay.[12] Stout would tell me, in short, that I have misdescribed the nature of the conflict; indeed, that I have misunderstood philosophically what conflict itself entails.

Stout's argument is, I think, as compelling an argument as could be made while still being wrong. It is vastly superior, for example, to the fossil-like thinking of today's encyclopedists, and there is much in it that every thinker ought to admire. Moreover, bricolage as a description not only of current intellectual effort but also of late postmodern experience more generally has a rather rich ring of truth to it: in the aftermath of modernity's demise, we sense that we're all just cobbling with fragments of this and that as best we can. But Stout's argument is nevertheless seriously misleading in several significant ways that, when taken cumulatively, point to the inadequacy of his pragmatist account of the rivalry between traditions.

First is the question of truth. Stout does not bypass the question of truth. Indeed, he carries on extensively about how he understands statements such as "the earth isn't flat" and "slavery is wrong" to be true (the latter in an ethically binding sense; 21–32). But all the same, he does the pragmatist shuffle and tries to sidestep the implications of the rather basic question, "What if the truth claims of particular traditions such as Christianity and Stoicism are true?" How would translation work then?

Stout's logic assumes that the pragmatist can overwhelm this question, push it away or into the background, by pointing to the vast body of "platitudes" that ancient Christians and Stoics would have shared and (almost) taken for granted (say, that the path of wisdom does not regularly and inescapably involve indiscriminate and widespread killing of *peregrini* for their lack of Roman citizenship).[13] These platitudes form the conceptual base of the work of translation (they show the agreement underlying the disagreement), and given the right conditions can be the ethical background—the "overlapping consensus"—against which the Christians and Stoics "muddle through" the world together without the need to kill each other or, presumably, demand conversion.[14] In Stout's view it is impossible to lay bare all the platitudes on which traditions that coexist in any given culture already agree. But they are there, and without them we could neither see our disagreements with each other nor resist tearing "at each other's throats."[15]

No amount of pragmatist rhetorical flourish about the significance of platitudes, however, can push the question of truth far enough away. Stout certainly makes an elegant appeal: "Don't we in fact muddle through much of the time, quite reasonably, by appealing to areas of agreement with fellow citizens, by practicing immanent criticism on our opponents or on ourselves, by coming to terms with unfamiliar vocabularies in conversation, by using our creative powers, by confronting the moral imagination with instances of injustice and suffering, and by, in countless other ways, exploiting a culture too rich and complicated to be confined to a canon?" (217). But such appeals miss the point of the very type of claims the ancient Christians and Stoics would have made.

For while it is indubitably true that Christianity and Stoicism do have particular views about particular things—they make statements they want to be taken as truth claims about this matter or that—in the big picture they are not so much making individual statements to be taken as true or false, as justified or not, case by case, as they are summoning people to a different pattern of being in the world. To put it differently, the type of claims the early Christians and ancient Stoics made were comprehensive truth claims—readings of the world and styles of existence that were to be taken whole or not at all.[16] This sort of claim is not the type that can be examined bit by bit, statement by statement, but the type that is either taken or left. One was either in or out.

This is not to say there were no "platitudes" upon which Christians and Stoics could have agreed were someone to point them out. But it is to say that Stout's way of looking at things misses the fact that whatever overlapping consensus could have been found through platitudes would not have included the things that were most important to the traditions themselves—those matters that together constitute their traditions as specific traditions. Agreement upon platitudes, therefore, could not possibly be the basis for a translation of one tradition into another.[17] Not only would such agreement altogether miss the tradition-constituting "thick concepts" of each tradition, it would also fail to answer the main question the traditions pose: are they true?

Were Stout (or an ancient historian of a Stoutian stripe) to object that humans can live together well and agree on very important things without ever answering this question—that answering the question is not constitutive of a society's moral dimensions—one could reply that this is simply the pragmatist attempt to change the subject. Or it is the effort to overwrite the Christian/Stoic claim to truth with a will to power based in the insistence that this type of truth doesn't matter for what matters: getting along well together as best we can ("well" and "best" being construed according to the one offering the direction). Or, rather simply, it is the rejection of the Christian/Stoic claims in favor of another version of truth, Stout's particular brand of pragmatism as a way to cope with the conflict of traditions.

More deeply still, the statements involved in the Christian and the Stoic claims to truth cannot be divorced from the lives in which their truth comes to be known. True or false is learned—and therefore judged—by the pattern of life one lives. As Wittgenstein once put it about Christian truth: "Christianity is not based on a historical truth; rather, it offers us a (historical) narrative and says: now believe! But not, believe this narrative with the belief appropriate to a historical narrative; rather: believe, through thick and thin, which you can do only as a result of a life. *Here you have a narrative, don't take the same attitude to it as you take to other historical narratives!* Make a quite different place in your life for it." Or, as he also says, "This message (the Gospels) is seized on by men believingly (that is, lovingly)."[18]

As Wittgenstein's remarks suggest, Stout's argument for translation is inadequate not so much because the Christians and Stoics couldn't find some platitudes on which to agree but because Stout's logic ignores what truth most deeply entails for Christians and Stoics. Seizing on a way of life believingly, lovingly, through thick and thin cannot be reduced to "my position on issue X or Y is . . . Let's try to work together on X where we agree and work harder—have more conversation—to understand each other on Y."[19] In the Christian and Stoic sense of true, you have to make a decision *for* one and *not for* the other *with the life you live.* And since you cannot know ahead of time whether the life you will live is true or not, the judgment of true or false vis-à-vis the sort of claims Christians and Stoics make occurs precisely through the total course of the life you live. Who you are as you live your life is the true/false judgment you make.

Translation between rival traditions, therefore, is not simply about the pliability of natural languages, their possibility for hermeneutical enrichment and augmentation through time. It is in fact more fundamentally about the (in)compatibility between different overall styles of human existence and the reality that we can live only one life. If two claimants to the truth of all things are incompatible in one human life—its pattern or style of existence can be one or the other but not both—they cannot be translated. No amount of linguistic innovation, augmentation, or enrichment could make it possible to live rival traditions in one life at the same time. In this precise and extraordinarily significant sense, the disagreement does go all the way down.[20]

CONFLICT OF TRADITIONS: LIFE

If the truth of traditions is in the first instance something that is lived, and the question of translation centers upon the relation of different forms of life, we might well wonder how to think further about the juxtaposition of rival traditions. If the disagreement between the three Christians and the three Stoics goes all the way down—and it does in the all-important existential sense that you could not have lived the claims of both traditions at once; and if understanding the truth is itself a product of afterthought—a *Nachdenken* according to the life you live in the tradition that shapes what reason itself is and comes to be—how might we describe the relational possibilities of juxtapositional rivalry?

In my judgment, there are two candidates worth serious consideration. Over against all types of proposals that suggest that the best way to relate rival traditions is to eliminate tradition-specific language/convictions and look for shared judgments about the common good, both candidates acknowledge the utter—and, frankly, obvious—indispensability of tradition-specific reasoning for the difficulty of relating rivals.[21]

The first candidate is a traditioned variation of Stout's version of bricolage. A specific tradition of life such as Christianity or Stoicism would reject Stout's pragmatism—which, despite Stout's avoidance of this fact, *is* a claim to be the truest way to be in the world—but retain the practice of bricolage as the way to deal with other traditions. Each tradition learns how to use the words of the other and creatively employs these words within its own tradition to fashion a broader discourse that responds to pressing needs. Conceived in this way, bricolage is a sort of tradition's education on the road toward greater moral discernment, a way of learning from another tradition what your tradition could not (yet) say, a manner of gaining otherwise unavailable insight by extending and enriching the linguistic—and therefore conceptual—resources you have at your disposal.

At a glance, this sort of bricolage appears simply to name what in fact has occurred in the history of Christianity's engagement with Stoicism. Engberg-Pedersen on St. Paul; Colish on Sts. Ambrose, Jerome, and others; Byers on St. Augustine; Cochran on Jonathan Edwards—all these and numerous others have articulated the case for "Christian bricolage."[22] Christians throughout antiquity, the Renaissance, the Enlightenment, and so on have "explore[d] selected ideas from Stoic thought in a manner that detaches them from broader Stoic commitments" and used such ideas to shape Christian thought where it seemed fruitful.[23]

Despite the sophistication of these studies and the historically deep conviction that Stoic ideas can be appropriated by Christians, the relation of rival traditions is much more challenging than the description bricolage allows. There are several difficulties, but we can focus here on only two primary problems.

First, there is the enormous and—one would have thought by now obvious—difficulty that words do not mean the same things in different grammatical contexts. Stout draws from Wittgenstein to say that using a word in established patterns is having the concept (of *dikaiosunē/iustus,* say) and that when we can use the word-patterns of an alien tradition we have translated and taken their concepts into our tradition. But the more basic Wittgensteinian grammatical point vis-à-vis the translation of conflicting traditions is that words take their meaning from the "language games"—the established patterns—in which they are used.[24] When the game changes, so does the meaning of the words.

Wittgenstein characteristically makes this philosophical linguistic argument with unforgettable imagery. He says, for example, with reference to the use, and therefore meaning, of words: "It is like looking into the cabin of a locomotive. There are handles there, all looking more or less alike. (This stands to reason, since they are all supposed to be handled.) But one is the handle of a crank, which can be moved continuously (it regulates the opening of a valve); another is the handle of a switch, which has only two operative positions: it is either off or on; a third is the handle of a brake-lever, the harder one pulls on it, the harder the braking; a fourth, the handle of a pump: it has an effect only so long as it is moved to and fro."[25] Wittgenstein's point, of course, is that it is only by knowing that you are looking inside a locomotive that you know what these variously shaped "handles" are. Locomotive cabin is the "game" in which these handles are cranks or brake-levers or pumps. Absent the cabin, the handles could be "anything or nothing."[26]

Stout seems to think of "established patterns of usage" as a small or smallish linguistic area—chunks, really, or, to use Wittgenstein's image, handles whose meaning is discernible by looking at them in isolation rather than at the cabin in which they are placed. Over time these patterns can be seen, learned, and replicated apart from the wider context in which the patterns appear in the first place. By contrast, the Christian and Stoic patterns of usage mean what they mean within a vastly complex and broad context of meaning. The game here is not really a chunk of patterns but the entire context of what constitutes the tradition's language as the language of a specific tradition. For the Christians, for example, the language game is the biblical narrative (Old Testament and then, for Justin, the new writings) and its interpretation in Christian discourse/practice (which itself is of course interwoven with biblical language). "Established patterns," as was illustrated in the previous chapter with respect to God, human being, death, and so forth, turns out to mean more or less the entire Christian narrative that makes the sense the words make as Christian words in the first place.

Thus do advocates of traditioned bricolage who speak of "shared insights" into "God" between the Stoics and the Christians, for example, entirely obscure the fact that the established patterns of usage require different meanings of the word *God*. Or to say it slightly differently, the referent of the word *God* for the Christians and the Stoics is ignored. When modern scholars speak of God as some object or subject that Stoics and Christians share, a subtle but crucial interpretative slippage has occurred in which scholars substitute the words of their established patterns of usage—the way God functions in the modern scholarly language game—for the more determinative grammar of the Christians/Stoics. As I argued in a slightly different context, "The category of a general 'G/god' is neither the God about whom the author of Hebrews spoke nor that of the pagan philosophers: it is an abstraction that we can conceive only because of the extraction of particular words and their subsequent reembedding in a different grammar (the academic theorizing of religion)."[27] Were we to encounter the famous phrase from Paul's Areopagus speech "in [God] we live and move and have our being" in a Stoic text, the "God" of whom the text speaks would not be the God of the established patterns of the Lukan corpus but something altogether different.[28] Not all handles are cranks.

On this understanding, one tradition's use of another tradition's words looks dramatically less like the sort of bricolage that depends upon and develops conceptual translation and more like what Justin says to Trypho: you do not understand the true meaning of the words of your tradition (see discussion in Chapter 6). Their true meaning shows up once they are placed within the hermeneutical patterns of our words.[29] Which is to say that the same words mean different things; they have undergone hermeneutical transformation and are played differently according to the Christian game. A bricologian may well use words from any tradition to make what an intellectual cobbler would want to make, but the words he uses will mean something different once he uses them. "Christian bricolage" is the name not for how Christians draw untrammeled insight from other traditions but for how they change the meaning of words they find elsewhere by situating them within Christian grammar.

Or to put it differently, the traditioned bricologian seems to have a strange bedfellow: the old-school natural theologian who sees the Christian meaning of words in words he sees as Christian, regardless of where he finds them.[30] Both the bricologian and the natural theologian see words they like, detach them from their original grammatical hosts, and use them to say things they want to say—all *within* the hermeneutical framework that already determines the meaning of their extractions. Seeing in the words meanings that they like means no more (and also no less) than seeing in the words meanings that they already like—or, to switch the metaphor, the words sound to them like words they need precisely because the words make their sound within the ears they use to listen. That is, for bricolage to be a practice of gathering insight as a way to enlarge one's own tradition, its inexpungible assumption that words have meaning "as such," or that the truth words speak is spoken "per se" and not according to the wider grammar in which the words are embedded must be valid.[31] But it is not, and to recognize that the meaning of words changes with the change in the wider grammar in which they occur is simultaneously to see that the reembedding of words from one interpretative framework into another is not the translation and appropriation of insights but transformation or transfiguration.[32] As Wittgenstein might have said, "See how high the seas of language run here!"[33] And yet they run higher still as we turn to the second problem with thinking of tradition-specific bricolage as a constructive way to deal with rival traditions.

So, second, the grammar of a tradition is not only the rules that make the concepts. It is also a grammar of life.[34] When Stout says that "nothing in the nature of *conceptual diversity* itself prevents one culture from developing the means for expressing an alien culture's moral propositions or grasping their truth," he betrays the residue of modern conceptions of thought in his own thinking about translation.[35] If conceptions are what Hegel thought they were—thought thinking itself and the like—perhaps Stout could be correct. But concepts, at least in the most important sense of tradition-constituting concepts, are lived, embodied, enfleshed. "Words are deeds," said Wittgenstein. The point was not only J. L. Austin's later one about the way words do things; it was also that language is lived.[36] As the exposition of their texts in the first six chapters of this book shows, neither the ancient Christians nor the Roman Stoics would have been able to separate word meaning from living, something we call "concepts" from something else we call "practice" or, more simply, life. How to relate "moral propositions" or discover "insights" is not the primary problem we face when thinking about the feasibility of traditioned bricolage as a way to relate rival traditions. The primary problem, rather, is the fact that the grammar that gives the meaning of the words is simultaneously a way of life.

Instead of bricolage, therefore, we need an account that takes seriously the incompatibility of word-meaning in rival ways of life. We thus turn for our second candidate to Alasdair MacIntyre's account of an "epistemological crisis." Epistemological crisis better describes the way in which untranslatable rivals can be related precisely because it is more committed to the internal justification and coherence of a tradition as tradition and avoids conceiving the relation between rivals as one that can be thought through analyzing bits and pieces of this or that concept or conceptual cluster (for example, Providence, the passions, and so on). We must deal with traditions as traditions, says MacIntyre, and not simply as materials with which the cobbler does his work. As we will see, however, even MacIntyre's account is finally insufficient.

For MacIntyre, an epistemological crisis occurs when the schemata used to interpret social life on any or all of its levels break down and are shown to be inadequate, or when philosophical or scientific interpretative schemata falter and can no longer account for the problems they face. As an example of the former, MacIntyre says, "Consider first the situation of ordinary agents"—his term, along with "plain persons," for nonphilosophers—"who are thrown into such crises. Someone who has believed that he was highly valued by his employers and colleagues is suddenly fired; someone proposed for membership of a club whose members were all, so he believed, close friends is blackballed." For such a person "the relationship of *seems* to *is* becomes crucial. . . . What they took to be evidence pointing unambiguously in one direction now turns out to have been equally susceptible of rival interpretations."[37] "Ordinary agents" can also experience an epistemological crisis vis-à-vis an entire cultural web of interpretative schemata and "as a result come to recognize the possibility of systematically different possibilities of interpretation, of the existence of alternative and rival schemata which yield mutually incompatible accounts of what is going on around [them]" (4). In such cases, even though the ordinary agent may not put it to himself in this way, the criteria of both truth and understanding must be reworked (5).[38]

As an example of a philosophical/scientific epistemological crisis, MacIntyre shows how Galileo responded to a tradition of scientific inquiry that had "lapsed into incoherence" (12, 18). There was the conflict between the Ptolemaic and Copernican astronomies, the inconsistency of Ptolemaic theory with Platonic and Aristotelian astronomy and physics, the contradiction of these matters by two hundred years of findings by university scientists, and instrumentalist philosophical theory. By the time Galileo began his serious work, the epistemological crisis was in full swing, and there was no way to move scientific inquiry forward on the inherited basis of contradictory fragments that made current knowledge. The relationship of *seems* to *is* was capable of too many rival interpretations and no compelling solutions.

In both types of epistemological crisis, the resolution of the crisis must entail "the construction of a new narrative which enables the agent [and philosopher] to understand both how he or she could intelligibly have held his or her original beliefs and how he or she could have been so drastically misled by them." Crisis resolution does not, in MacIntyre's view, entail the loss of the ability to understand the original beliefs. To the contrary, resolution enables a better understanding of the original beliefs precisely because the new narrative accounts for their status both as things-once-worth-thinking and as things-no-longer-capable-of-being-reasonably-thought. "The narrative in terms of which he or she at first understood and ordered experiences is itself now made into the subject of an enlarged narrative. The agent [and philosopher] has come to understand how the criteria of truth and understanding must be reformulated" (5; cf. 11). The understanding of how understanding works has changed, and the shift in truth is not a change in the opinion of what counts as true within the same way of thinking ("A" and then "not A" where A stands for a particular proposition) but a change in how we know what's true and not ("A" and "not A" is not the right way to think about truth). "The old mythological empiricist view of Galileo saw him as appealing to the facts against Ptolemy and Aristotle," says MacIntyre. But "what he actually did was to give a new account of what an appeal to the facts had to be" (10). Galileo was able not only to show how we thought what we thought—and why it was both right and wrong—but also to show how we needed to rearrange what scientific thinking itself was in order to move scientific inquiry forward. His achievement, however, was not possible simply by better logic-chopping but was instead the result of casting the various aspects of late-medieval science "into a coherent narrative," one that enabled them all to share a set of common standards. In light of Galileo's work, it became "retrospectively possible" to understand why his theory was successful: "The criterion of a successful theory is that it enables us to understand its predecessors in a newly intelligible way. It, at one and the same time, enables us to understand precisely why its predecessors have to be rejected or modified and also why, without and before its illumination, past theory could have remained credible. It introduces new standards for evaluating the past. It recasts the narrative which constitutes the continuous reconstruction of the scientific tradition" (11). Galileo, that is, told the story of scientific questioning and discovery in a way that allowed the tradition of inquiry to go on.

But this sort of an example, it may be noticed, is an example of a crisis *within* a particular tradition of inquiry and was meant to counter the explanations of those such as Polyani and Kuhn, who argued that transitions in the history of science from one mode of knowing to another were more like "conversion experiences" than like the progressive movement of rational inquiry.[39] But what if two traditions of inquiry stand against each other face to face? Would not the change from one to the other be more like a conversion?

MacIntyre would reply that the dynamics surrounding an epistemological crisis within a tradition are analogous to those that can occur when traditions conflict: one tradition, that is, can put the other into epistemological crisis, and can be the occasion for the sort of realization of an incoherence *within* that leads to a move outside. Though of course the impetus of the crisis could be conceptual in the more refined sense of the academic philosopher or scientist, it does not have to happen that way. It could be, for example, that a second-century Roman discovers that Christians will care for the sick and dying in the midst of the plague while Galen and his troupe flee from the ravages of death to their villas in the hills. In this case, Christian nursing practice could begin a crisis.[40] Following this discovery, however, rational investigation would disclose inadequacies of the Roman's home tradition that could not be remedied with the resources endemic to that tradition. Had he the time and aptitude, the Roman would then try to learn the Christian tradition as a second first language and would thereby discover new resources for the inadequacies that surfaced during the crisis. The subsequent narrative provided by the Christian tradition would then make sense of both the reasonableness of his former tradition's belief about sickness and death and its inadequacy in the face of Christian care for the dying during the plague.[41] Of course, in MacIntyre's view, after learning a second first language, one may not in fact be able to translate the first tradition into the second or vice versa—they remain incompatible—but one learns how the second accounts for the problems of incoherence in the first and moves on out of the first and into the second.

MacIntyre's account of how one moves from one tradition to another is intended not only to describe the intellectual conditions of change but also to uphold the work of reason in the transition from one tradition to another. To think that conversion is what best describes the move occasioned by an epistemological crisis is to say that "there is no rational continuity between the situation at the time immediately preceding the crisis and any situation following it." There is only a break, a great gulf separating the two traditions across which reason cannot leap. "To such a crisis the language of evangelical conversion would indeed be appropriate. We might indeed begin to speak with the voice of Pascal, lamenting that the highest achievement of reason is to learn what reason cannot achieve" (17).

Pascal's famous position on the limits of reason can be fended off, however, because "it can never be the case that everything is put in question simultaneously. That would indeed lead to large and unintelligible lacunas not only in the history of practices, such as those of the natural sciences, but also in the personal biographies of scientists" (17).[42] As the evocation of Pascal is meant to convey, the continuity between different traditions does not reside in the particular (type of) thoughts—which can be radically discontinuous—but in the fact that reason itself does the work of thinking in any and every tradition. Both the pre- and post- of an epistemological crisis are the work of reason. Pascal's voice is discarded, that is, because reason persists as the same sort of working tool regardless of where it works. In short, provided that we undergo the disciplines needed to acquire a second first language, epistemological crises can be the bridge across which reason travels from one tradition to another. Despite his rejection of universal, encyclopedic rationality, MacIntyre presumes that in the end we can in fact think ourselves out of one tradition and into another.

MacIntyre's account of an epistemological crisis works well to describe certain types of important transitions in the life of a "plain person" or within an ongoing tradition of inquiry. It may also work, in my judgment, to describe the sort of transition from one type of Greco-Roman philosophy to another.[43] Martha Nussbaum's imaginative depiction of Nikidion's journey through several Hellenistic philosophies is in fact a picture of just such a philosophical itinerary; epistemological crises of varying intensity and complexity lead her from one school to the next.[44] But when we turn to the relation between the ancient Christians and Roman Stoics, the situation is markedly more complex. Three of the complicating issues deserve particular attention. They take us to the question that is at the heart of this book.

First, the Christian sources are uniformly clear that the move into the Christian tradition is made possible by the God and Father of Jesus Christ and is not something that can be achieved by human effort of mind or will. It is, rather, a setting free. As Paul would describe it, God's work is a liberation from bondage to sin; without this liberation no amount of clear thought could lead to an embrace of the Christian faith. Jesus Christ is not the conclusion of a process of critical reasoning—no matter how incoherent another tradition has become—but the living person who sets the human free from that from which it absolutely and categorically cannot free itself. For Luke, the name of the sort of knowledge Christian knowledge is for pagans is "apocalypse," a revealing of the truth from God's side of the Creator/creature distinction (see Luke 2:32). The best pagan thought ends, so Luke thinks, in ignorance of God (Acts 17). Justin's version of the claim that Christian knowledge is received by the work of God is phrased in terms of illumination: "No one," says the old man to Justin, "can perceive or understand these [Christian] truths unless he has been enlightened by God and his Christ" (*Dial.* 7.3). Subsequent to liberation and illumination, of course, Christians can reason about things in ways that were previously unavailable. But no amount of retrospective reasoning about the incoherence or incompleteness of a former way of life can make it appear that human beings can think themselves into the Christian tradition without falsifying the sources' claim that it is the God of Abraham, Isaac, and Jacob, and of Jesus Christ who creates the possibility for retrospective reasoning in the first place. What we learn retrospectively is how whatever form of life we inhabited was something from which we needed "deliverance" (paganism) or something that needed "fulfillment" (Judaism). The need for deliverance and fulfillment, according to the Christian texts, is a post-hoc conclusion of enlightened and educated reason. Conversion, therefore, is a better name than MacIntyre allows for the move to the Christian tradition because it preserves the texts' claim that Christianity remains strange or opaque—or even odious—to those who have not been set free and therefore think in darkness.[45]

To call the move into the Christian tradition "conversion," however, is not to say that it is nonrational. Retrospective reason is reason no less than any other sort; or, to be more precise, it is the reason of a tradition that says one has to learn the tradition to reason. Pascal did not, of course, cast things in terms of "traditions" in MacIntyre's sense, but Pascal nevertheless explicated better the anthropology of Christian knowledge: the human being is not the sort of thing that can think its way to the inside of the Christian tradition; it is the sort of thing that needs to be set free to learn to think about the God who set it free. In the Christian case, tradition already implies conversion.

Second, in the specific instance of the conflict between the Christians and the Stoics, it is extremely difficult—impossible, one might say—to see how either tradition could be the answer to conflict or incoherence within the other. Contrary to those who accuse MacIntyre of conceptualizing tradition in too pure a fashion—a monolithic block of agreement, unsullied by conceptual and practical divergence—he explicitly argues that traditions are necessarily constituted by conflict over what the tradition itself actually is. Being a Christian or a Stoic is as much to be involved in a continuous argument over what it means to be a Christian or Stoic as it is to be distinct from outsiders.[46] But no amount of conflict within Christian tradition can lead to Stoicism as the particular answer to Christian conflict, and vice versa.

Even leaving aside the difficulties of translation, if we conduct a thought experiment at the places where each tradition might profitably say something the other tradition needs to know to keep or develop its coherence, we still cannot see any line that runs from a lack in one to fulfillment in the other (or, in reverse, from fulfillment to diagnosis of lack), from incoherence in one to coherence in the other (or in reverse), from problem in one to solution in the other (or in reverse). The greatest lacuna in Stoicism is the absence of an account of the origin of the human problem. The Stoics assume our task is to reduce our estrangement from our nature, but they give no reason for this estrangement as a feature of human existence, the condition under which all humans come to be and must exist. They talk much about our ability to return to nature and not at all about why the human being qua human being is estranged from its nature in the first place. There are symptoms (passions, for example) but no disease, effects but no cause. In light of the Christian narrative, one might say that the Stoics do not have an account of the human problem that does the work the Fall does for Christians.

The greatest lacuna in Christian discourse is the absence of a word for the world's completely inscrutable power vis-à-vis the helplessness and frailty of human beings in the face of such power. There are many words for the varying problems humans face (sins, demons, and so on) and there is an affirmation of the living God's providential direction of the world toward its final end. But there is no word that captures the way that the world is experienced as an unorderable, untamable, and innumerable set of forces that can make or break human life in its everyday dimensions. In light of the Stoic narrative, one might say that the Christians do not describe the world's fallenness in a way that takes sufficient account of what Seneca calls Fortuna.[47]

Still, not even at these points does one tradition solve the problems of the other or complete it by offering something its rival lacks. Not only are the "Fall" and "Fortuna" rich, contextually embedded, and tradition-specific ways of naming our situation and the world in which we live—and therefore incapable of translation into the terms of a rival tradition without the rest of that which makes them intelligible—they are also only very small slices of the larger form of life in which they find their home.

The contrast with Judaism is instructive. Many Jews in the couple of centuries surrounding the birth of Jesus of Nazareth hoped for the coming of the Messiah. There were several claimants and ongoing conflict about whose claim was true and whose wasn't—which is another way of saying that many Jews saw their tradition as needing to be extended or even completed in a certain way. The Christians, of course, argued that their tradition was the correct completion. Jews who did not take Jesus of Nazareth to be the Messiah argued that it was not. Whether Christianity is in fact the correct extension or completion of the Jewish tradition is obviously an argument that will not be settled until the end of human life, but it is nevertheless the sort of argument between traditions that makes excellent sense as an argument about completion (namely, the resolution of an epistemological crisis).[48]

The rivalry in traditions between the Stoics and the Christians makes no such sense. They are not in conflict with each other because of internal breakdown, epistemological crises, or incompleteness but because they offer genuinely rival ways to be in the world. The alternative they present is an existential either/or.[49]

Third, then, as I wrote in Chapter 7, MacIntyre argues that learning another tradition as a second first language is a feat of "philosophical and moral" imagination—and that insofar as we learn another tradition we can "on occasion" question our home tradition in light of the newly learned one, on the one hand, or, on the other, show in the new tradition's own terms how our home tradition solves the other's (heretofore) intractable problems. Says MacIntyre, "Through the exercise of philosophical and moral imagination someone may on occasion be able to learn what it would be to think, feel, and act from the standpoint of some alternative and rival standpoint, acquiring in so doing an ability to understand her or his own tradition in the perspective afforded by that rival." "The analogy here," he continues, "is with the ability of the anthropologist to learn not only how to inhabit an alternative and very different culture, but also how to view her or his own culture from that alien perspective." MacIntyre grants that such a task is extremely difficult, can happen only occasionally, and may still result in disagreement "even between highly intelligent people." But it is nevertheless possible "through the exercise of philosophical and moral imagination" to acquire the "conceptual resources" needed to "transcend" the limits of a tradition and demonstrate the rational superiority of one tradition over the other. Of course, it may happen that one never does acquire the ability to transcend "on occasion" the "limitations and constraints of [one's] particular moral standpoint"—and the possibility for critical engagement with a rival thus remains unrealized. But this practical lack of acquisition should not "lead us to suppose that there are not adequate resources available for the rational resolution" of the conflict between traditions.[50]

Doubtless we need imagination to engage another tradition. The trouble is that imagination is not a faculty or ability that exists independent of the way we reason—which is to say, in keeping with the Stoics and Christians, the lives we live. MacIntyre speaks of imagination as if it were a special capacity that would allow us to overcome the difficulties that would otherwise stick with us. But there is no magical quality to imagination that somehow enables it to leap over the existential barrier erected by traditions that claim they must be lived to be learned. Invoking imagination does not, that is, enable us to reason from within lives that we do not live. Like reason—if imagination is at all to be differentiated from reason in the first place—imagination is formed through the tradition we inhabit. Anthropologists and their philosophical modern and ancient analogues are close observers to be sure, but insofar as they could through their imagination learn to reason like a Stoic or a Christian, they would have become one.

And here we come to the crux of this book. It is precisely the place where the ancients put it to us moderns in a way that makes us uneasy or even squirm. They would give us a pill that neither Stout nor MacIntyre, Malherbe nor Engberg-Pedersen, Levering nor Cochran, can swallow. It is, frankly, just that difficult for us to believe that if we will not enter a way of life, the door to understanding is shut upon us. Such a claim entails views of reason and the inseparability of thinking and living that cut so sharply and deeply against our inherited presuppositions of what understanding is that it is hard to take the claim seriously. We resort to talking about the independent truth of mathematics, or retreat to the language of insights, or point out that no tradition grew ex nihilo (and therefore none is completely pure), or construct incredibly esoteric models of this or that sort, or suggest that as long as we can get along well enough with one another nothing else much matters, or hold out for occasional rational resolution of rivalry by the imagination of the highly intelligent. But all this—and much, much more—is one great avoiding of the central problem put by the six figures whose texts we expounded: Stoicism and Christianity are claims to the truth of life, and knowing the things they teach requires a life that is true.

To put it this way is to suggest that the study of rival traditions of what a true life is is simultaneously an exploration of the existential limits of reason and of the summoning—or kerygmatic—nature of this sort of a tradition's language. If the claim is that we have to live in a certain way of life in order to learn how to reason truly about the truth of all things, then we can never know ahead of that life whether the claim is true or not. We simply dive in—or don't. MacIntyre frequently worries about Kierkegaard's leap of faith—what MacIntyre calls "criterionless choice"—as the basis of the judgments we make about the claims of rival traditions. We must be able to evaluate rationally, MacIntyre thinks, that on which we are to make judgments. If we must use language of conversion, it is a reasoned conversion of which we must speak.[51] But as the ancient Christians and Roman Stoics would see it, Kierkegaard was closer to the truth: no matter how many criteria we find for living in one way or another, we cannot make them add up to a judgment about a true life before we live it. "Come join!" is not the same as "Test and confirm!" In this crucial sense perhaps, the choice can be called criterionless. There is really no place on which to stand that could secure us against the need to live one way or another in faith. And so we leap—or don't.[52]

Which is to say that Pascal was finally right. We cannot know ahead of the lives we live that the truth to which we devote ourselves is the truth worth devoting ourselves to. So we wager our lives, one way or the other. The tradition of life that is Stoicism is a certain kind of historically dense and elongated wager; and so is Christianity.[53] If our being is in becoming, then the wagers we make are on the patterns of life that make who we are. Our being is caught up in them, and we are what we become. Traditions of life, therefore, are not as much series of moral propositions or candidates for modern reason's scrutiny as they are summonses to certain kinds of becoming. We cannot be what we are summoned to become without the time it takes to train the being in becoming. And that is to say—yet again—that we cannot know the truth before we take the existential plunge and try to live it within the time that is the one and only life we have to live.[54]

This book is thus one long and exegetically thick statement that any intellectually serious attempt to engage rival traditions of life will inevitably disclose the existential limitations of comparative inquiry and of the human being *qua* human being—and disclose further, therefore, the fact that the languages of traditions of life are inescapably grammars of truth and summons, calls to live according to their truth. It is an argument that rejects the assumption that humanistic scholarship can render all forms of life transparent and that human thought is more alike than the difference of the traditions that make lives different. To study a rival tradition is to encounter difference of the profoundest and possibly most opaque sort—the result of exquisite existential trajectories that have not been yours. To ignore this difference or suppress it with a claim about the possibilities of universal understanding is not to be more scholarly or philosophically rigorous.[55] It is rather to be at once hopelessly out of date and voguishly cosmopolitan—and, ultimately, to fail to recognize how deeply difference really cuts. Talk really is, after all, as deep as life.

APPENDIX: OBJECTIONS AND REPLIES

This book's argument is academically surprising because it suggests that the central problem in understanding a rival religious/philosophical tradition is not a lack of knowledge but the fact that rivalry is rooted in different lives. An inexpungible existential wager—and possibility of conversion—is at the heart of all rivalry between traditions. No amount of further study or clearer thinking can overcome lived difference on the question of final truth when the living is necessary to the knowing of the truth.[1]

If the implications of this argument are clearly grasped, many protests will doubtless arise. Working through some of the more important objections and replies should show the pattern of the judgments needed to make the book's argument.[2]

Objection 1. Your argument flies in face of the crucial epistemological assumption that funds the vast majority of religious studies programs and humanistic scholarship more generally. The assumption—crudely stated—is that all things, no matter how strange or how distant, can be understood. The "faith that such understanding is, in principle, possible is a normative assumption as well as a hopeful one. . . . It is implicit in the work of all scholars in the humanities." It belongs to the "daily business [of the humanities scholar] to make strange goings-on—the historically or culturally distant traces of human activities—more familiar."[3] Given certain levels of learnedness, the scholarly gaze can penetrate even the most opaque forms of life.

Response. Yes, the argument of this book does entail the rejection of the dominant way of thinking about our knowledge of lived difference of traditions of life. The notion that in principle we can understand all strangeness and/or difference is a residue of modernist, encyclopedic conceptions of knowledge, no matter how it is repackaged as the basis of "humanistic" practice or the anthropologist's work or how avant-garde its adherents believe it to be. It directly contravenes the claims of the traditions it seeks to study and is therefore a way to deny the connection on which the ancients insisted, namely, the unity between intellection and life.

Objection 2. Your argument flies in face of legions of New Testament studies that show this or that line of influence or similarity in thought between Stoic and Christian traditions. Abraham Malherbe, Troels Engberg-Pedersen, and others have demonstrated how much the New Testament writings draw on the philosophical or "moral" assumptions of their time.

Response. Yes and no. Yes, the argument of this book presumes that many of these studies not only have been committed to an epistemologically broken view of how we learn what traditions of life had to teach but also have worked with a philosophically deficient understanding of the way words mean—and therefore with a naïveté about the consequences that different grammars of meaning have for the construal of similarity and difference. Grammars of meaning are lived. Insofar as this is recognized, the conclusions of the studies of influence/similarity will have to be rethought.

But, no, the argument takes for granted that there were many things in wider Greco-Roman culture that were simply assumed by both pagan philosophers and early Christians.[4] They lived in roughly the same place and time, after all, and could not help but share some assumptions about this or that; it would be nothing short of stunning if they did not. Such shared assumptions are not, however, as significant as they have been said to be. The most significant assumptions and convictions of each tradition—tradition comprising assumptions and convictions—are precisely those that keep them apart.

Objection 3. Your argument is historically thin because it does not include enough pagan philosophers. Making claims about rival traditions on the basis of three Stoics and three Christians is claiming too much on the basis of too little. Displaying the early Christian relation to Greco-Roman philosophy requires a much wider textual base.

Response. No, the argument of this book rejects the assumption that creating a philosophical smorgasbord against which to read early Christian texts is historically more illuminating than juxtaposing close readings of the work of particular philosophical and Christian figures. "Smorgasbord comparison" abstracts from the traditions that make the sense that "philosophy" makes in any particular case and creates a new context for the interpretation of philosophy, that is, the philosophical smorgasbord itself. The historically rich textual explications of particular philosophical traditions are exchanged for the hermeneutical power of scholarly mélange.[5] Philosophy becomes anthology and resembles a collection of important intellectuals' "views on things" rather than historically elongated, distinctive, and mutually exclusive claims to a true way of life. This is modern encyclopedic epistemology at work. It is not historical thinking. Stoic philosophy was a tradition. To think historically about its relation to anything else at all, we must treat it as the thing it was.

Objection 4. Your argument that Roman Stoicism and early Christianity are incommensurable traditions of life flies in face of history. Christians have always preserved, read, and used Stoic texts. They have been able to take "insights" or "concepts" from the Stoics—as they have other philosophies—and discard the Stoicism.

Response. No and yes. No, the argument of this book has no stake in denying the history of Christian engagement with Stoic texts. It is a long and rich history, as I stated above.

But, yes, I do redescribe what the Christians have been doing. Their engagement has not been conceptual translation or (dis)agreement in some independent realm called philosophy. Rather, the Christians have been treasure hunting. The treasures they find are the words in the Stoic texts, not the Stoic "thoughts" that are somehow independent from the Stoic grammar in which thoughts have their shape and meaning—and that can somehow be transported from one grammar to the other without a change in meaning. I am committed, that is, to the view that we cannot think about language in the same way after Wittgenstein. There is no such thing as a word-meaning or language "as such." I realize that this is a distinctive (and debatable) position about the way philosophical progress works in the history of human reflection and that it entails the judgment that we currently think better about ancient Christian practice of philosophical dialogue than we did before Wittgenstein. But these are, I think, the most defensible positions and the ones I thus take in this book.

Objection 5. Your argument flies in the face of the distinction between philosophy and theology. We can know true things philosophically that are independent of the theological guidance of reason or confessional conviction.

Response. Yes, the argument of this book rejects this distinction. It is a relatively modern invention that is entirely foreign to the earliest Christians and to the pagan philosophers.[6] No more evidence is needed to locate this division on the modern(ish) side of things than to remember the ancient understanding of the word *philosophy* itself: loving wisdom for a wise way of life. Only after Descartes has the word come to mean thinkable thought in abstraction from the disciplined life that is the guide of thought.[7] Thus not only does the distinction between philosophy and theology often depend upon indefensible views of the way language works—taking words to mean the same things regardless of where they are found—it is also a division that explicitly severs what the ancients tried to keep together: the unity of thought and life.[8]

Objection 6. Your argument flies in the face of contemporary ethics of conversation. The necessary presupposition to getting along without violence is that we can understand one another's traditions by means of conversation. An ethics of conversation takes into account the unity of the human species through language and works from the conviction that understanding is possible if we take the time to talk to one another.[9] Working together against evil of one sort or another depends upon the ability to understand different traditions.

Response. Yes, the argument of this book rejects the position that traditions of life are inherently transparent or can be understood through conversation alone. Instead, it argues that the grammars of traditions that claim truth in the way the Stoics and Christians do are inherently invitational or kerygmatic. The invitation to enter is simultaneously the condition of true understanding; invitation, that is, names the fact that conversion is the inevitable goal of all traditional speech toward outsiders. This does not mean that ad hoc commensurability in life is ruled out.[10] (In fact, we do not need a theory to tell us how to work together with others against things we both see as evil. The best way to work together is simply to work together.) But it does mean that we cannot bypass life with talk.

Objection 7. Your argument about incommensurable traditions of life is extreme. We understand people from other traditions of life all the time. Your argument contravenes so much of how we normally think about different traditions that it is impossible—or nearly so—to take seriously. In fact, it borders on the ridiculous.

Response. Yes, the argument is extreme given the current canons of cosmopolitan liberal theory on the one hand, and the long history of encyclopedic conceptions of knowledge within the scholarly practice of history on the other. Since, however, there is no compelling reason to endorse cosmopolitan liberalism—and many reasons not to—and since encyclopedic assumptions about knowledge are the wrong assumptions to have, what seems extreme may seem that way only because of the presupposed background against which this book is being read. In any event, finding an argument extreme is not tantamount to finding it incorrect.

If the argument *is* extreme, however, it is principally because it takes the Stoic tradition so seriously. The Stoics are not treated, that is, as supplemental to Christianity or as a grab-bag from which Christians can take out what they like, but as a genuine rival, an alternative tradition in its own right about the truth of all things. At the very least, this is to take them at their word. And that, in fact, is the sine qua non of the attempt to study otherness.

Objection 8. Your argument about the otherness of traditions of life means that we are stuck where we are and—more significantly, perhaps—destined to commit violence on our fellow human beings. If I am "this" and you are "that" and true understanding is not to be had unless I become that or you this, we will eventually decide to kill one another. Much violence—not all, but much—is rooted in the types of difference that separate strong traditions.

Response. Yes and no. Yes, the argument of this book rejects the conception of both the human being and traditions of life that would allow us to picture ourselves as able to move noetically between traditions without living different lives. In this significant sense we are stuck in the traditions in which we live. I understand this as the biblical—specifically Pauline—anthropology that correlates with the claim that God saves us from his side of the God/creature distinction. Conversion from one tradition to another is possible, but it is a turning of a life. Apart from such turning, it is impossible to see how we are anything other than completely embedded in the finitude that makes different traditions of life impossible to live at one and the same time.

But, no, we are not thereby destined to violence. It is admittedly hard to see how we would not kill each other if we are stuck in difference with no normative reason not to kill and notice that other traditions imply that the lives we live are false. Moreover, contra liberalism, pragmatism, and so on—in all their forms—there is no general answer that will keep us from killing each other or appear convincing enough to suppress the Nietzschean question that should come to mind: why not kill each other? If I'm stronger than you and your difference from me bothers me, why shouldn't I kill you? The Nietzschean mood would simply sweep aside the pleas and reasons of a Stout, the Democrats, or the liberals as cowardice or meddling. Say what you wish, if I'm stronger, I win, and you matter not. Christians, at least—and here I speak out of the specific tradition of life in which I live—have normative reasons from God's work in Jesus Christ and from the New Testament itself not to kill, no matter what difference we encounter. The early church knew this well, but we cannot claim to have remembered it faithfully through our history. Still, the direction is there and the difference that is Christian difference should be marked by the witness that is the refusal to kill.

Notes

INTRODUCTION

1. Of course, *choose* might be too strong a word: we can slip or slide or fall into a certain type of life, or just drift along. But even here we are living out an answer—an existentially grained and perhaps verbally unarticulated answer, but an answer nevertheless—that comes from the shape of the life that is lived.
2. Much of the angst that reverberates from the projects of "comparative religion" is the unarticulated recognition of this intersection. The risk we take in exploring rival traditions of how to live is the same risk we take in the paths of our own lives. If we can get different traditions to agree, our anxiety is reduced because the choice is not so existentially sharp.
3. Stout, "Commitments and Traditions in the Study of Religious Ethics," 23–56, is right that *tradition* is a word that—without proper description—can cause much mischief (49–50). As will become clear throughout the book, I draw from Alasdair MacIntyre to understand what tradition is as it properly describes Christianity, and from Wittgenstein and a range of work in the history of Christianity (for example, Robert Wilken) and ancient philosophy (Paul Rabbow, Pierre Hadot, and others) to augment MacIntyre's understanding with a richer conception of "life."
4. Barnes, *Logic and the Imperial Stoa.*
5. Of course, where their texts can be helpfully illuminated by other preserved evidence—the fragments of Musonius, or Cicero's works, or Plutarch's themes, or invective, and so on—this other evidence will not be discarded.
6. One might legitimately wonder why I have limited my focus to these six figures in particular. Shouldn't I have extended it to include other ancient philosophies and philosophers, or at the very least to other Stoics or other Christians? The answer to this question is complex because it goes to the heart of how I think about the relation of rival traditions. I will address it briefly here and then again in the Appendix. It is true that I had originally conceived of the book as an exploration of early Christianity vis-à-vis Greco-Roman philosophy more generally—a kind of extension of the point in *World Upside Down* about Christianity's unsettling interface with larger cultural patterns

(see especially the treatment of the Areopagus speech in Acts 17). But I quickly became convinced that the problems of learning other traditions were so philosophically difficult that I couldn't really treat all the figures I wanted to discuss within an intellectually convincing framework. So Plutarch, for example, is out, but so, too, is Dio Chrysostom, who may have a more rightful place here. (Christopher Gill treats him as a Stoic of sorts in his article, "Stoic Writers of the Imperial Era," in *The Cambridge History of Greek and Roman Thought*, but Gill also says Dio is philosophically "eclectic" and "elusive"; Gill focuses on Dio's speeches that have some Stoic-sounding material. My own reading of Dio's Kingship discourses, for example, suggests that *eclectic* is the best description; it's not at all clear that Dio is part of the Stoic tradition.) To put it simply, if ancient philosophies were traditions of life, we need to pick a tradition to study as a tradition. Like many people I have been reading the Roman Stoics off and on since college. I remember well the trip to a local bookstore in the second semester of my freshman year when my father bought us a copy of Marcus Aurelius's *Meditations*. But like other people I was reading them within the framework of encyclopedic inquiry. Not until graduate school did I really begin to understand what the ancient philosophers were up to, and I have been puzzling over how in the world I could learn from them since. Explaining the Christians is easier: Paul and Luke cover almost the entire New Testament, and Justin is the first post–New Testament Christian to talk about philosophy. After Justin, the next truly significant Christian figure for philosophy is Clement of Alexandria. Though Stoicism is important for Clement, the most important philosophy is revived Platonism, which by Clement's time had started to become the dominant philosophy. After Clement comes Origen, and Origen scholarship is a field in itself.

7. Sellars, *Art of Living*. As Sellars points out, however, Sextus thought his own way of doing philosophy would transform lives and therefore actually upheld the underlying point he has in common with the majority of ancient philosophy, Stoics included—even if he differs from the way the Stoics think life is transformed (103).
8. Nussbaum, *Therapy of Desire*, 337.
9. Sellars, *Art of Living*, 127.
10. This is perhaps an unpopular position. But the truth is that fragments get the meaning they have in relation to wider understandings of how to fit them in—that is, their Stoic meaning will derive from their placement within a wider sense of Stoicism. Anthologies are interpretatively problematical for ancient philosophy for the same reason that encyclopedias or certain types of museums are for the phenomena they present. See Chapter 7, note 9 on Foucault.
11. Cicero, of course, is enormously important in the history of reception among Christians. Think only of the attempt during Erasmus's day to make all Latin like Cicero's (Erasmus rejects this attempt). But as useful as Cicero is as a source, he does not actually articulate a strong, normative philosophical position. Officially, he is a Skeptic, but he frequently sounds Stoic. The *Tusculan Disputations* do have a lovely hymn to philosophia as the *dux vitae*, but the conviction this hymn articulates is something that Cicero holds in common with the Stoics.
12. The "wager" and "leap" show up most famously, of course, in Pascal and Kierkegaard.

13. A. A. Long, "Stoicism in the Philosophical Tradition," in *The Cambridge Companion to the Stoics:* "In recent decades, ancient Stoicism has become a mainstream scholarly interest" (365–66). This is in contrast to earlier periods of history: "No secular texts were more widely read during the Renaissance than Cicero's *On Duties* (*De officiis*), the Letters and Dialogues of Seneca, and the Manual of Epictetus" (365). Engberg-Pedersen, "The Relationship with Others": "The scholarly exercise of comparing and contrasting Paul and Stoicism is no more than at its very beginning" (60).
14. It was not missing in the ancient world. St. Augustine, for example, knew this well.
15. Stout, *Ethics After Babel,* xi.
16. This is hardly to say we should ignore critical scholarship—I have read it until I'm blue in the face—but it is to say that scholarly reflection on the primary sources often becomes the tail that wags the dog. In the expository chapters of this book recent scholarship is primarily refracted through my readings of the texts. Obviously, when it came to the Stoic tradition in particular, I had much to learn, and I've developed dependencies and favorites—scholars/thinkers who help me best to clarify my reading of the primary sources: Pohlenz, Long, Inwood, White, Frede, Sedley, Rist, Gill, Nussbaum, Hadot, Sellars, Bobzien. There are others, but these are those who come immediately to mind. Ultimately, however, there is simply no substitute for immersion in the primary sources.
17. My ad hoc use of imaginary students to engage the six authors treated in this book also reveals my commitment to a Collingwood-like view of questions/answers as a way to think historically. Karl Barth's prefaces to his commentary on Romans also stress the importance of the question-answer dialectic for serious interpretation.
18. As will become clear through the course of the argument, the "as if" in this sentence is philosophically crucial when it comes to the Stoics. See the discussion of MacIntyre's "second first languages" in Chapters 7 and 8.
19. Indeed, I try to avoid second-order-like comments whenever possible and instead let the question-answer dialectic do the hermeneutical work. The attempt is to write in a way that historically conditions the imaginative language of the dialogue. For example, in the first six chapters I occasionally use "someone might say" to begin an objection of this or that kind. This phrase is not simply an advantageous way to make a transition; it is also a standard rhetorical/literary device from the ancient world (*tis*). See, for example, *1 Apol.* 7.1, "someone will say" (*tis erei*); or Luke's Gospel, which also uses *tis* in a rhetorically strategic manner.
20. A word about translations: I almost always write something similar to the Loeb texts for Seneca, Epictetus, and Marcus because these are the most easily available editions for those who wish to read them alongside my chapters and consult the Latin or Greek. I wrote with constant consultation of other editions and translations, of course (for the *Meditations* of Marcus Aurelius, for example, A. S. L. Farquharson's standard two-volume critical edition and commentary; but also the German edition *Kaiser Marc Aurel: Wege zu sich selbst,* edited by Willy Theiler, which has commentary on text transmission and other matters). But the Loeb editions are as close to the base as it gets. For Paul and Luke, I use the Nestle-Aland *Novum Testamentum Graece*, 27th ed., rev./New Revised Standard Version, and for Justin, the new translation edition of Denis

Minns and Paul Parvis (*Apologies*) and Thomas Halton's revised translation of Thomas B. Falls (of *Dialogue with Trypho*)—along with Bobichon's magisterial edition in French. In all cases I adjust as I see fit based on both interpretive and philological considerations. Because it would be extraordinarily tedious and distracting, I do not always provide justification for my translations. Again, scholars who know the texts well in Greek or Latin and the debates that surround sticky passages will be able to see why I render certain phrases the way I do. To take only one example: 1 Cor 15:42–50 uses the word *psychē* in a way that is notoriously difficult to render in English without reproducing in Paul's mouth some of the Corinthian dichotomies against which Paul is actually arguing in this section of the letter. I have not gone into detail about this difficulty but have instead simply translated in a way to draw out what Paul is saying without creating a problem in English. The trained New Testament scholar will see, of course, that I prefer "natural body" as a translation of *psychē* and its compounds because that is what best keeps both the parallelism of the Greek and the substance of Paul's argument.

21. Hadot, *Inner Citadel*, x. One sentence later, he says, "Our era is captivating for all kinds of reasons: too often, however, from the philosophical and literary point of view, it could be defined as the era of misinterpretation, if not of the pun: people can, it seems, say anything about anything. . . . I want my reader to make contact with the text itself, which is superior to any commentary."
22. That is why we begin the body of the book with the texts. A slightly different way to put this larger point is that I am contesting two different sorts of readers at once: the first is the historicist, for lack of a better term, who knows every nook and cranny of the ancient texts (and the languages in which they were written) but, to be blunt, does not, as a whole, know how to think about the way they are thinking; the second is the retriever, again for lack of a better term, who thinks constructively and with sophistication about using ancient wisdom for contemporary questions but, to be blunt, does not know the ancient texts or the relevant historical scholarship that surrounds them.
23. See Bernard Williams's essay on Collingwood in *The Sense of the Past* for an interesting exploration on the importance of getting our questions right for understanding the past. Obviously there are exceptions to my description of the field as one mired in minutiae. But quarter after quarter after quarter, the journals confirm it.

1. SENECA

1. Veyne, *Seneca*, vii.
2. Lucilius was of the Equestrian rank (*Ep.* 54.2) and was, at the time of Seneca's writing, governor of Sicily. It has been argued that he should be seen as a fictive addressee (Griffin, *Seneca: A Philosopher in Politics*). This thesis has been persuasive to many (see, e.g., Inwood, *Reading Seneca*, 346). But I see no reason to oppose literary achievement with personal reality. Lucilius could easily be a Stoic neophyte and the letters simultaneously polished literary products. Pliny's letters to Trajan were written with publication in view (and are polished), yet both are obviously real people. The question of fictive addressee exists also in the New Testament: Luke and Theophilus.

3. Nussbaum, *Therapy of Desire*, 340: "one long rich *exemplum* of what the Stoic way of life has to offer . . . an open-ended and highly complex story of two concrete lives," in her discussion of how crucial a role exempla play in Stoic philosophical care. Richard Sorabji, "Is Stoic Philosophy as Helpful as Psychotherapy?" suggests that "it would be possible to read Seneca's *Letters* as containing, on the subject of emotions, no more than random tips, often about particular situations, if one did not bear in mind the analysis of emotions that he gives in his treatise *On Anger*" (205). Sorabji makes this point in his discussion of the importance of learning Stoic "analysis" as a necessary prerequisite to the effectiveness of their "techniques" over the long haul (a point about which he is doubtless correct). In one sense the discussion of Seneca in this chapter acknowledges the truth of Sorabji's remark: I do interpret his letters in conversation with his topical treatises—as well as his satire and tragedy—though this conversation has taken place behind the scenes, as it were. That is, what I as interpreter think about when reading Seneca's *Epistles* includes the full range of his works, but what I present to the reader is Seneca's counsel to Lucilius and not a free-ranging conversation with the Senecan corpus. In another way, however, I think Sorabji is right only to the degree that we lack the historical imagination required to engage Seneca's counsel to Lucilius (and others that appear in the *Epistles*) as counsel that makes sense. Techniques are never analysis-free, context-free, or free-floating recommendations: they always have a larger, though often entirely implicit, analytical background against which they derive their sense and force. This is true even when the recommendations are "banal" or commonsense (contra Bernard Williams in his response to Sorabji). For the most engaging reading of Seneca's moral essays, see Nussbaum on *De ira* (*Therapy of Desire*, 402–38); her reading of Seneca's *Medea* is equally engaging (439–83).
4. Veyne, *Seneca*, viii.
5. The Stoics were ancient materialists in the sense that everything was material. This included the soul (contra Platonists, for example).
6. See Ernest Becker's still remarkable book *The Denial of Death*.
7. One may wonder, of course, what Seneca makes of actual physical pain. He has much to say that downplays the significance of pain. The underlying point seems to be that nature has made us such that pain is "either endurable or short" (*Ep.* 78.7; cf. 24.14, where Seneca says of pain, "You are slight if I can bear you and short if I cannot").
8. For a remarkable book on the *ars moriendi* tradition, see Verhey, *The Christian Art of Dying: Learning from Jesus*.
9. Seneca goes on to talk about himself as one of these great men. "I can promise you, Lucilius, I shall find favor among later generations"; moreover, he continues just before citing Virgil, "I can take with me names that will endure as long as mine" (*Ep.* 21.5). The fact that we are still reading Seneca should give us much pause before we think him arrogant. Perhaps he was simply a good appraiser of deep talent: we read Virgil, too. Rightly appraising talent is actually closer to humility than it is to arrogance, though broadcasting one's talent does rather offend good taste.
10. Seneca frequently cites Epicurus in these letters. Seneca's basic position on using Epicurus or other philosophers to support his own advice is clear: "Any truth, I maintain, is my own property" (*Ep.* 12.11).

11. Next, says Seneca, revealing the importance of his own wealth, is to free oneself from the fear of poverty (*Ep.* 80.6).
12. Seneca says no general arguments can be made about the propriety of suicide (*Ep.* 69.11). But by this he merely means that if we kill ourselves we should do it for the right reasons. We should not, for example, commit suicide out of weakness or fear of suffering in itself or out of despair or admission that Fortuna has won or the like.
13. Seneca speaks frequently on freedom and death. His argument elsewhere is the importance of suicide in light of Fortuna's assault, but the underlying point is the same (e.g., *De prov.* 6.7–9).
14. For a brilliant exploration of modern medicine's attempt to bring death within its power, see McKenny, *To Relieve the Human Condition.*
15. See, e.g., *Ep.* 9.15: the highest good "arises entirely within itself. If the good seeks any portion of itself from without, it begins to be subject to the play of Fortune."
16. Lucilius also evidently wrote: "The good that has been given can be taken away" (*Ep.* 8.10). As he often does, Seneca counsels Lucilius not only by deepening the latter's understanding of the topic about which Seneca writes but also by reminding him of things he already knows.
17. Not that he thinks the present is always pleasant; indeed, *Ep.* 13.7 shows that he knows otherwise.
18. If we asked how we would actually know what this kind of posture looks like, Seneca would reply that we know it through human exempla (cf. *De prov.* 3.4: Mucius, Fabricus, Rutilius, Regulus, Socrates, Cato, etc.). We draw on the shape of their lives and deaths to show how a virtuous soul conquers Fortuna.
19. "Nature is a tricky term in Seneca" (Veyne, *Seneca*, 41). Virtue is equally complex in Seneca. Take, for example, these two remarks: "Virtue is according to Nature; vice is opposed to it and hostile" (*Ep.* 50.8). "Virtue is nothing else than right reason. All virtues are reasons" (*Ep.* 66.32). But as a whole virtue is to be in accordance with our nature, that is, to be rational.
20. Cf. *Ep.* 44.5: "The soul may rise superior to Fortuna out of any earlier condition." Seneca is here talking about birth, rank, and the like. None of these "externals" fundamentally conditions the soul so that it cannot rise above Fortuna.
21. In particular, *Ep.* 90.27–29 illustrates well how Seneca sees wisdom in relation to the wide variety of gods (traditional deities, lares, genii, and the like): wisdom shows these gods to be "initiation rites" into the deeper truth of the divine aspect of the universe as a whole (the "vast temple of all the gods").
22. *Superstitio* was a particularly derogatory term in the Greco-Roman world. Augustine preserves parts of a work by Seneca that was lost (*City of God*, book VI). The work's title: *On Superstition.*
23. A particularly interesting passage in this regard is *Ep.* 95.50: "The first way to pay cult to the gods is to believe in them; the next to acknowledge their majesty . . . also to know that they are the supreme commanders in the universe, controlling all things by their power and acting as guardians of the human race, even though they are sometimes unmindful of the individual. They neither give nor have evil; but they do chasten and restrain certain persons, and impose penalties, and sometimes punish by bestowing that

which seems good outwardly. Would you win over the gods? Then be a good man. Whoever imitates them is worshiping them sufficiently." Here Seneca clearly speaks about the gods in personal terms; indeed, he says that our imitation of them is their right worship (paying cult in the right, rather than superstitious, way). Yet because of his larger thought it seems clear that we should read "imitating the gods" as a way to say "living according to Nature." Thus "winning over the gods" means, in more strictly philosophical terms, enjoying the good/happy life that comes from living according to Nature.

24. This is also, I think, the best way to understand statements about God's work in the eternal cycle of what is (e.g., *Ep.* 71.14: "The whole universe about us go[es] by turns, that whatever has been put together is broken up again, that whatever has been broken up is put together again, and that the eternal craftsmanship of God, who controls all things, is working at this task." That is, *God* here is not the word for a personal presence who works upon this cycle from without, but is instead the word for the ordering principle inherent within.
25. The dualism is not Manichean in the sense of two ultimate realities, for the Stoics do believe in unity of all things. But there is, one might say, an experiential dualism—in the sense of two very basic or fundamental realities in one cosmos.
26. Readers of Seneca's wider corpus may wonder why I do not treat Fate (*fatum*) directly. The simple answer is one of economy, both intellectual and spatial. There is not space to do it, and intellectually speaking Fate fits well within the broad outlines of Seneca's theological language given above. His best statement on Fate is, I think, *De prov.* 5.8: "What is the part of a good man? To offer himself to Fate. It is a great consolation that it is together with the universe we are swept along; whatever it is that has ordained us so to live, so to die, by the same necessity also binds the gods. One unchangeable course bears along the affairs of men and gods alike. Although the great creator [*conditor*] and ruler [*rector*] of the universe himself wrote the decrees of Fate, yet he follows them. He obeys forever, he decreed but once"—or perhaps *De prov.* 5.7: "I am not God's slave but his follower . . . because I know that everything proceeds according to law that is fixed and enacted for all time. Fate guides us, and it was settled at the first hour of birth what length of time remains for each." Fate is not a distinct entity, or even exactly synonymous with God, but is instead something like the direction of the whole of things. Of course, "direction" is both right and wrong: the cosmos is eternal and cyclical; it is going somewhere only in the sense of going toward conflagration again and again and again. But it is not going somewhere in the sense of an overarching purpose of cosmos, a telos toward which it aims. Stoics from Chrysippus on were, of course, well known for their tight link between fate and a kind of universal determinism.
27. In my view, the richest book on this question as a whole is still Nussbaum, *Therapy of Desire.*
28. See, e.g., *Ep.* 23. Nussbaum treats *De ira* and *Medea.* The pattern is also evident in the *Epistles.* See, e.g., *Ep.* 98.11, where Seneca instructs Lucilius in our duty to remember that which we have lost as a way to cope with the loss itself. Seneca's guidance here could only be called risky by stricter Stoic standards.
29. This does not mean that Seneca thinks the soul cannot be immortal or that the body can be. Because the soul is corporeal, some Stoics worried that if the body was crushed,

the soul would be, too. Seneca rejects this possibility and says that there is always a place in the body through which the immortal soul can escape (*Ep.* 57). See Troels Engberg-Pedersen's *Cosmology and Self in the Apostle Paul,* which makes much of the Stoics' view of the body. See also the insightful response by John Barclay in *JSNT.*

30. Seneca, *Ep.* 99. As Gummere (Loeb) notes, the identification of Marullus as Iunius Marullus depends upon a remark in Tacitus, *Annals* 14.48. It may not be right, but it's as good a guess as we can make.
31. "I have not observed the usual form of condolence, for I did not believe he should be handled gently" (*Ep.* 99.1). Here I am not going through the letter in order but simply taking the central points as a whole.
32. Cf. *Ep.* 63, where Seneca admits to weeping at the loss of a friend but says he should have known better.
33. This is the anthropological reason Seneca can stop and correct himself to say: we can pursue pleasure not only in the midst of grief but also "by means of" grief (*Ep.* 99.26).
34. By Stoic definition, when someone is in considerable existential pain, it is because he has made a bad judgment. There is nothing that can get to the wise man unless he lets it.
35. This raises a question about "location" of the passions. Nussbaum says that Seneca believes in two parts of the soul and that passions are in the rational part because they are judgments and subject to treatment by means of correct(ive) judgments. This is surely one part of the truth. But Seneca is more complex because he says that there are two irrational parts of the soul. Nussbaum is at times too strong when she says that emotions are cognitive judgments (*simpliciter*): for example, Seneca says that the shock of loss hits even the wise man and brings him to tears. But the outworking of the passions indubitably involves cognitive judgments.
36. It is unclear how Seneca would think this argument could work inside larger Stoic thought. Presumably the same logic would apply to the sorrow at a wayward adult child as it would to a death of young child, that is, it is not something that can ultimately upset the wise man. If so, Seneca's argument is pointless (because subject to his own critique).
37. Seneca could make an analogous point about anger, for example. For the way in which the control of anger, the need for "righteous anger," and normative notions of justice intersect, see Nussbaum's treatment of Seneca's discussion of the murderous kings (*Therapy of Desire,* 432–38).
38. *Coinhere* is an attempt to capture the inseparability in the phrase: *cohaerunt inter se philosophia virtusque.*
39. The entirety of this letter is a withering response to the philosophers whom Seneca considers to be engaged in pointless intellectual chatter. For the importance of this kind of philosophizing in the imperial Stoa, see Barnes, *Logic in the Imperial Stoa.*
40. Cf. *Ep.* 108.4, where Seneca talks about those who "lounge" in the philosopher's hall but have not come to learn the law of life. Such people are "squatters," not really engaged in philosophical pursuit.
41. Seneca goes on to talk about using this master as someone against whom Lucilius should measure the other persons he chooses as exempla. The underlying point is thereby strengthened: Seneca counsels Lucilius to pattern his life according to the

example of those who live the philosophy they know. In *Ep.* 123.6, Seneca recognizes that we always live according to exempla of one kind of another. It is a false question, therefore, to ask whether we shall have exempla or not. The question, rather, is about which exempla we shall live by; Seneca's point in *Ep.* 123.6 is that much of human worry and sorrow comes from living according to conventional, unexamined (and harmful) exempla. His advice to Lucilius to choose an exemplum thus also has a considerable critical edge: there is much unlearning to be done along the path of philosophical education.

42. This notion has seen much treatment: Rabbow's book began it, then Pierre Hadot et al.
43. Cf. *Ep.* 53.8: "Devote yourself wholly to philosophy. You are worthy of her; she is worthy of you; greet one another with a loving embrace. Say farewell to all other interests with courage and frankness. Do not study philosophy merely during your spare time."
44. Seneca then immediately exegetes these two central findings as follows: the Sage has "made life conform to universal principles; and he has taught us not merely to know the gods but to follow them, and to welcome the gifts of chance precisely as if they were divine commands. He has forbidden us to give heed to false opinions, and has weighed the value of each thing by a true standard of appraisal. He has condemned those pleasures with which remorse is intermingled, and has praised those goods which will always satisfy; and he has published the truth abroad that he is most happy who has no need of happiness and that he is most powerful who has power over himself" (*Ep.* 90.34).
45. Indeed, the Sage can even be superior to a god: "The Sage's life spreads out to him over as large a surface as does all eternity to a god. There is one point in which the Sage has an advantage over a god. For a god is freed from terrors by the bounty of nature, the Sage by his own bounty" (*Ep.* 53.11).
46. For Seneca's arguments on whether the Sages need one another, see *Ep.* 109. His answer is: at bottom, no, but it can nevertheless be a good; a friendship of the virtues helps reinforce virtue, etc.
47. Seneca, *Ep.* 14.14 continues, "without incurring the displeasure of those in power. The Sage will not upset the customs of the people, nor will he invite the attention of the public by any novel ways of living." Both of these aspects—incurring the displeasure of those in power, and living in novel ways that the public sees as worth attention—are obvious points of contrast with early Christianity.

2. EPICTETUS

1. Long, *Epictetus*, 77–78, takes "How is that possible?" to be the words spoken by Epictetus's questioner (the father who could not bear to remain at home while his beloved daughter was sick).
2. Millar, "Epictetus and the Imperial Court," 141–48.
3. The phrase is Long's (*Epictetus*, 43). Long calls them "dialectical lessons," and this they are (they are not treatises). The trouble, of course, is that many of the sayings have no real *Sitz im Leben:* we therefore must make it up. This is analogous to form-criticism within New Testament studies and includes all the same pitfalls.

4. Here I strongly disagree with Long. Long disparages the *Manual* as "potted" excerpts, doctrine, and so forth (*Epictetus*, 9 et passim) and declines to treat it as part of his book. Long's book is one of the best I have read, but I find this choice odd on historical grounds. The *Manual* is no less Epictetus than the *Discourses*. And for much of Western history, the *Manual* has been the better known. In what is otherwise a powerful synthetic account of Epictetus, it appears that Long is not saying much more than "I don't like the *Manual*," or "I don't like the Epictetus of the *Manual* as much as I like the Epictetus of the *Discourses*"—this is little more than personal preference.
5. Also like Seneca's *Letters*, Epictetus's *Discourses* by and large presuppose some basic philosophical education on the part of his disciples (see Long, *Epictetus*, 90). We are listening, that is, to a discussion among insiders, though of course there are exceptions (for example, when Epictetus responds to a question from a visitor). The *Discourses* do not begin from scratch but with the assumption that the listeners are those who already desire to be transformed (that is, students in Nicopolis).
6. As far as is possible, we are trying to read Epictetus "on his own terms" (a problematic phrase to be sure, but a useful one in this context). That is, we're not going to go through exactly the same themes or in the same order we did with Seneca—that would be, of course, treating Epictetus on Seneca's terms (the order Seneca's thought suggests for Epictetus). Obviously there will some overlap; they are both Stoics after all! But the attempt is to see each for what he says. We also have some fragments of Epictetus's teaching. They are preserved mostly in the texts of Stobaeus (also a few elsewhere, as in Marcus Aurelius's *Meditations*). It has proven difficult to know which fragments are authentic and which are not. It is also somewhat difficult to know how to interpret them since they lack a context. We will mention them only where they cohere with a broadly recognizable aspect of the two primary remaining texts (Frag. 16 says that repeating and applying the same "principles" every day is the way to become a philosopher: this same basic thing is said over and over in the *Discourses*).
7. Long's language for this is "personalist." This is acceptable but it hides the *almost* affective—he is a Stoic—quality of the language. Personalist is what academics analyzing Epictetus's language call it. It is hard to suppress the suspicion that Epictetus himself would prefer something warmer. Still, God is not a person for Epictetus any more than for any other Stoic.
8. It is true, of course, that the exhortation to sing is rooted in his conception of what the human being actually is, and could thus be interpreted as a way to call his students to employ their reason rightly by engaging their "natural" religious sensibilities (hymns exercise our reason by directing it toward philosophical truth). But such demythologizing would risk obscuring the rather obvious fact that for Epictetus song, praise, prayer, and so forth represent the right posture in relation to "God."
9. Epictetus's repeated use of *mē genoito* to answer his own questions is significant. It indicates, as it does in Paul's letters, a vigorous rejection of the thought.
10. Epictetus's play here of course is on the *divi filius/huios theou* title of Caesar and his heirs.
11. Or, what is essentially the same, intelligence (*gnōmē*, *Disc.* 1.3.3). Elsewhere when speaking of the part of God in us, Epictetus speaks of *prohairesis* (see discussion following

in the section on "Human Being"). Not exactly reason—but much of this amounts to same thing.

12. Long has a concise treatment of "god within you" passages in *Epictetus*, 165–68.
13. Epictetus does speak of "the gods" (plural), but this should not be taken to refer to specific enumerable entities that compete with God (singular) for the top of the ladder. It's simply the way he talks—like any pagan does. But he basically means the same thing by both expressions. See *Disc.* 1.9.11–13, where he speaks interchangeably of "kinship with the gods" (*theoi*) and "kinship with God" (*theos*).
14. Human beings are not to be only the "spectators of God's works but also their interpreters." All the citations in these sentences are from *Disc.* 1.6.1–20.
15. As we saw with Seneca, there is an important sense in which God and Nature are synonymous also for Epictetus. He can speak, for example, of the "law of God and Nature" (*Disc.* 1.29.19).
16. Long, *Epictetus*, 148, prefers "universal mind" but then in n. 5 on same page unwittingly articulates the reason why we should not speak this way. And Long and others also speak of panentheism, but this is a problem for reasons I mention above.
17. *Disc.* 1.27.15–21. Epictetus is here mocking the Pyrrhonic and Academic skeptics whose claims to challenge everything the senses teach are obviously overwrought (cf. *Disc.* 1.5.6).
18. Epictetus does assume there is a space between "us" and the world we experience—and that this space is large enough that we can hold the world at bay for a long enough time to decide what to make of it. All of his philosophical positions intersect at the point of how humans experience the world; in this way he is a kind of empiricist (but certainly not in modern sense).
19. Misreading their nature leads us to misidentify the place of their belonging: we think of them as ours, but they are really given to us and may be taken back (*Ench.* 11.1).
20. The general-principles classification is also how Epictetus prevents contradictions in the preconceptions: he says several times that contradictions can't exist (*Disc.* 1.22.1, 2.26.1, et passim), and many of his examples used to show that we need to learn preconception sorting schemas depend on contradiction for their argumentative force. Surely, we might think, there are ambiguous cases. Epictetus would agree. If things are uncertain, withhold judgment; indeed, the soul does this naturally: it assents to the true, dissents from the false, and withholds judgment in a case of uncertainty (*Disc.* 3.3.1–2).
21. As far as we know, Epictetus did not endorse the anamnetic epistemology of Plato's *Meno*, but there's a certain sort of similarity—at least in the sense that Epictetus thinks we can discover what we were born with. Obviously Epictetus doesn't need the Platonic myth, but there's an epistemological similarity in the importance of recollection.
22. This is another reason why Epictetus can say there are no contradictions in preconceptions. He is not looking at general reasoning ability but at the practice of a certain kind of rationality. Indeed, Epictetus is quite sophisticated in noting that there are different concepts of rationality itself (*Disc.* 1.2.1–11). With this insight he anticipates, in his own way, much late-modern discussion about the unity of rationality, "foundations," and so forth.

23. This is said to a young male visitor who is a student of rhetoric and a dandy.
24. This is true in terms both of content and of form: content (what he actually teaches) and form (elenctic—Socratic rhetorical style).
25. Epictetus gives a different threefold division in *Ench.* 52. It is hard to know how to reconcile the division of *Ench.* 52 with that of the *Discourses.* In general, I take the division in the *Discourses* to be Epictetus's "real" position for the simple reason that he refers to it multiple times. In this I am in agreement with Hadot, *Inner Citadel,* 82–98, and Long, *Epictetus,* 112–18. Long follows Hadot in seeing Epictetus's divisions in terms of the classical Stoic distinction among physics, ethics, and logic: the first division is physics, the second is ethics, and the third is logic. This is doubtless correct, as long as one remembers that physics was a topic broad enough to include the passions.
26. Epictetus also shows that we often mistake self-interest for "love": the famous example is the man who leaves home allegedly out of love because his daughter is sick. He argues that he cannot watch her suffer because he loves her so much. Epictetus does a marvelous job of exposing the self-interest that lies at the base of this father's actions (*Disc.* 1.11.1; cf. 2.22.15–16).
27. Cf. *Disc.* 1.18.19, where Epictetus says it is permissible to groan if one is in pain (earache, headache, or the like), as long as one does not groan inwardly (*esōthen*). Normally, as I mentioned in the Introduction, I simply adjust the Loeb translation without remark. Here, however, a remark is actually needed: by translating *symperipheresthai* "to sympathize," the Loeb edition contradicts Epictetus's point. His point is that the philosopher should *not* sympathize with the sufferer but should "accommodate" himself to the sufferer's blight in what is only a surface display of co-suffering. The philosopher does not actually "feel with"—that is, suffer with—the afflicted. He only appears to ("inwardly," *esōthen*).
28. In an age without so much as ibuprofen, the second part of Epictetus's statement makes sense. In our modern way of thinking, however, we usually associate hospitals with relief from pain, illness, and so forth rather than with the infliction thereof. This is right in some ways, of course, though it should also be said that for anyone who has ever spent much time in or around hospitals, Epictetus's statement will not sound as odd as it might to otherwise healthy moderns.
29. Pierre Hadot, of course, makes this point particularly well (see in his chapter on Epictetus in *Inner Citadel*).
30. It is not entirely clear to me whether I have demythologized Epictetus here. He may mean "God" in his sense (in *Disc.* 4.1.103, Epictetus uses "Another" in a similar way and from the immediate context this "Another" clearly means God); on the other hand, he explicitly tells the student to act "as if" another is watching, and his larger thought would preclude the idea that there is Another in the sense of One who could watch.
31. There is a certain kind of similarity to contemporary neuroscientific work; see Damasio's *Descartes' Error*—though of course Damasio is explicitly talking about the passions, which Epictetus wants to eliminate. But neither one believes in pure reason.
32. "Moral purpose," "volition," "self" are among the most common options on offer. The translation problem is primarily because our anthropology has changed and the

traditional words we use now—*self, inner self, soul, will,* and so on—do not really capture all of what Epictetus wants to say with *prohairesis.* Another important word in Epictetus, as in ancient Stoic philosophy more generally and Marcus Aurelius in particular, is *hēgemonikon* (governing faculty). Long, *Epictetus,* 211–12, is right not to see the two terms as synonyms (despite *Disc.* 1.15.2). For Epictetus, *prohairesis* is clearly the more important.

33. I use *faculty* in this sentence because *prohairesis* is itself singular (Epictetus never speaks of *prohaireseis*). But once again, Long is perceptive. *Prohairesis* is not equivalent to "soul" in body/soul dualism. It is more the "capacities and dispositions" than any one "thing" in particular. Epictetus does speak in dualistic ways (see *Disc.* 1.9.11, 1.29.16, 2.13.23–27), but we would be mistaken were we to treat the *prohairesis* as one side *simpliciter* of the dualism. This is why it is puzzling that Long also calls *prohairesis* the "self." Whatever we could mean by "self" in the late-modern world, it would almost inevitably include the body within its ambit (cf. Taylor's *Sources*). Even if we don't mean by "self" some specifiable "thing" but more of a set of skills or practices learned and used through time, we assume those skills include the body. For Epictetus, *prohairesis* does not include the body; it is not the body, or derivative from the body. It cannot, therefore, be what we mean by self. (And in Greek, of course, there is no word for "self" by itself, only reflexive pronouns.) Neither for Epictetus is the *prohairesis* the soul (*psyche*). Nor is it the mind (*nous*). Nor is it the will (*boule*). It involves all of these things, but *prohairesis* itself is its own kind of—what to put here in the blank is exactly the problem—"capacities" or "faculty" or "anthropological space" or something like this needs to be said. As far as I know, Epictetus's position is unique in ancient philosophy.
34. See *Disc.* 3.8.1–6, where Epictetus gives several bullet-point examples of things that fall within the realm of our *prohairesis* and things that do not (death of a son, condemnation by Caesar, shipwreck do not; our responses to these things do)—and argues that where we make this distinction in practical life, there we make progress.
35. When asked what exactly the king (that is, emperor) has authority over and what he doesn't, Epictetus is unequivocal: "Take my paltry body, take my property, take my reputation, take those who are around me"—these all belong to the emperor. But where the emperor says, "I want to control your judgments, too," Epictetus replies, "And who has given you this authority? How can you have the power to overcome another's judgment?" "By bringing fear upon him," the king answers, "I will be victorious." Wrong, says Epictetus. "Nothing can overcome a person's *prohairesis*"—and therefore lead to a change of mind—except the "*prohairesis* itself" (*Disc.* 1.29.10–13). Epictetus missed John Locke by about sixteen hundred years, but he would have nevertheless recognized a deep similarity to Locke's argument against coercive "conversion." No matter what you do to someone, you ultimately cannot force him to believe something he simply doesn't believe. There is not a direct relationship between body and mind/soul/*prohairesis* such that hurting the body produces faith where there is none, or belief in something as true which one knows to be false.
36. The Loeb takes "No, nor have children" to be Epictetus. This works only if we presuppose him to be very sarcastic when making this statement (which he may well be). It

may make better sense, however, to take the speaker simply to be continuing the Epicurean line (as Epictetus himself presents it). Also, "political formation of the young men" translates *ephēboi*—the young Athenian men aged eighteen through twenty who were taught citizenship in school.

37. It is tempting to talk about this difference in terms of "disposition." The trouble is that we do not have access to their dispositions and have no reliable way of determining the exact contours of a disposition in the first place. So we simply name the difference as a difference.

3. MARCUS AURELIUS

1. Hadot, *Inner Citadel*, vii.
2. The highly problematic source *Historia Augusta* puts Marcus's decision to wear the philosopher's cloak at age twelve. But we do not know this, and there is no indication from (what remains of) his correspondence with Fronto that he was already serious about philosophy. Haines notes that the town of Tyras in Scythia stamped *Verissimus* on coins (Loeb, 267, n. 7).
3. Scholars have adopted both views on both points (pre- and postscripta; Marcus and someone else).
4. For this reason, readers of the *Meditations* are always in danger of overdetermining Marcus's sayings by means of an interpretive context that we import from somewhere far beyond the *Meditations* themselves. Yet there is no other choice than to provide a context for understanding—that is how the thing we call "understanding" actually works. The task required to read the *Meditations* well, therefore, is to supply the right kind of interpretive context in which to fit Marcus's sayings, the framework that persuasively suggests their natural hermeneutical home. This is one reason why the *Meditations* continue to be read by so many people in different walks of life: it is easy to insert a saying of Marcus's into our own context and assign it the meaning it would have only in our context (which, of course, makes it seem immediately relevant to us).
5. Hadot, *Inner Citadel*, ix.
6. Hadot has argued that each book of the *Meditations* has at least some degree of internal thematic coherence. His term for this coherence emphasizes its literary expression: "interwoven composition" (Hadot, *Inner Citadel*, 264–73).
7. Hadot, *Inner Citadel*, 44 et passim.
8. To take only two examples from book V: Marcus writes what could be said by anyone anywhere anytime: "to crave impossibilities is lunacy" (5.17); and "Neither tragedian nor harlot" (5.28) with no surrounding interpretive context whatsoever. What this means to him is anyone's guess.
9. Admittedly, for those who do not understand the existential work the *Meditations* represent, the frequent repetition can make for frustrating reading. But once the purpose of repetition is understood, it becomes easy to see that repetition is the way Marcus practices the disciplines that are his philosophical work. The advantage for interpreters of Marcus, of course, is that such frequent repetition means that we are not facing something new on every page.

10. Thus can one see that the Stoic tradition is the background against which I read Marcus's sayings.
11. Rist, "Are You a Stoic?" suggests that Stoicism was dead by Marcus Aurelius's time. Read Marcus, says Rist, and one can know why Platonism soon revived. Rist's work is often illuminating, but this argument is highly problematical. The point of Stoicism is not to be original—as it is in the modern university—but to embody the heart of their philosophic tradition. The revival of Platonism, or the turn from Stoicism to Platonism, is a classically interesting question, but it cannot be answered by accusing Marcus of a lack of philosophical verve. He's after not "originality" but a healing way of life.
12. One of the clearest passages in the *Meditations* that illustrates the typical Stoic conviction that even the soul is a material thing is 4.21. Here Marcus wonders where all the room in the air can be for the souls of those who die. If the soul outlives the body, he wonders, how can all the souls fit into the air? Wouldn't there be too many, wouldn't it get crowded? It is true, of course, that his solution displays Stoic cosmology at work, but more fundamentally it is constructed on the analogy with the decomposition of the body: so many have died, yet decomposition ensures that there's still enough room for those who have not yet died. So, too, with the soul: periodically the souls that outlive their bodies are dispersed, dissolved into fire, and taken back into the seminal reason of the whole. In 6.24 the emphasis is upon the fact that the distinction between Alexander the Great and his muleteer will be erased by death and the subsequent "reuptake" into "the same reasonable seeds" of the cosmos (*eis tous autous tou kosmou spermatikous logous*). Obviously the difference could not be erased were they to continue on as "Alexander" and whoever his muleteer was.
13. Or, as he reminds himself in a common-coin analogy with sunlight: "There is one light of the sun, even though it is divided by walls, mountains, and countless other things; there is one common substance, even though it is divided into myriads of individual bodies; there is one soul, even though it is divided into myriads of natures and individual outlines; there is one intelligent soul, and even it seems to be divided" (12.30). Had Marcus been around much later to hear William James describe the world as a "blooming, buzzing confusion," he would have known what James meant. James himself was, of course, against monism—of which pantheism could be seen as a certain sort—and was more interested in the dimensions of the world best named by the prefix *poly-*. Still, the point is not so much that Marcus and James are philosophically compatible as it is that Marcus understands that "poly-" is how the world can first present itself. Marcus, unlike James, does not, however, think that "poly-" is the world's deepest reality.
14. Marcus frequently speaks of cycles, plural (for example, 5.32), but the point is not fundamentally different from what is conveyed with the use of the singular cycle. The main statement is about the world's eternality and self-renewal through change.
15. The participle *tō dioikounti* is somewhat difficult to translate because it requires us to make a judgment about how to make explicit the unexpressed thing in which Marcus's courage is put. Based on his language about Providence elsewhere, it is hard to translate with any sort of personalist rendering (for example, "take courage in the One who orders"). I chose *principle* for the reason that it makes best sense out of how Marcus actually speaks about Providence throughout his *Meditations*.

16. The *ekeithen* there has to refer to the guiding action of Providence, not to "the other world" (Farquharson) or "from there" in general (Loeb).
17. By "the practices that cultivate its excellence" (*ta orgia tēs toutou aretēs*), Marcus refers to what Hadot has identified as the three disciplines. See the discussion above.
18. We know from Marcus's correspondence with Fronto, for example, that both he and Faustina were much troubled by the illness of their little daughter Domitia, who was sickly and then died (Fronto, 4.11); see Birley, *Marcus Aurelius*, 105. They lost other children as well.
19. Marcus speaks less about the damaging potential of the passions than one might expect. See, in particular, 2.10; 4.3.3; 5.26; 5.36; 6.51; 7.29; 7.55.2 et passim.
20. Marcus does say that some sensations are natural and not to be resisted (5.26). Presumably we know which ones fall into this category through Stoically shaped reflection on what is natural to begin with (for example, hunger).
21. "Remember, Nature gives you authority over impressions" (8.29, *exousia*).
22. The Stoic view of *pneuma* (spirit) is complex. Here in 2.2 Marcus calls it *anemos* (wind, air) and identifies it with the breath that is repeatedly exhaled and inhaled. It can also be seen as that which infuses all things (one also has to think in this sense of the Stoic's view of *pyr*/fire). Marcus does not have a "worked out" or consistent tripartite anthropology. In 3.16, for example, he offers a slightly different division: the body (*sōma*), the soul (*psyche*), and the mind (*nous*). In 12.3 it is the body (*sōma*), the spirit (*pneuma*), and the mind (*nous*). And in 6.32 he says to himself: I am body (*sōma*) and soul (*psyche*). He continues in such a way that it becomes clear that, in this note at least, "soul" is equivalent to "mind" (*dianoia*). The larger point to grasp is that in the *Meditations hēgemonikon* works best as a kind of umbrella term under which to put the terms Marcus uses to characterize the life of reason (*nous, dianoia, psyche, logos, hē logikē technē*), even if he does not use these anthropological terms with rigorous consistency (in particular, for example, his use of *psyche* in 3.16 to speak about the part of us that is subject to *hormai*—desires, impulses—is difficult to reconcile with his use of *psyche* in 6.32 as an equivalent to *dianoia*).
23. Marcus begins this note by admonishing himself to honor his *tēn hypolēptikēn dynamin*, which can be rendered "the power to form opinions," that is, the *hēgemonikon*.
24. Here Marcus uses *logos* and *hē logikē technē*, but the material point is obviously about the self-sufficiency of reason's operation from within the inner citadel. On Marcus's anthropological grammar, see n. 22.
25. Among many possible jottings, see 7.11, for example, where to live by the *logos* is to live *kata physin*.
26. Cf. *Med.* 9.11: "If it's possible show the wrongdoer a better way" (*metadidaske*).
27. Marcus is obviously talking about his own life (war and fame and being in a foreign land).
28. In accordance with his language elsewhere (see in particular the sections on gods and judgments), I have translated *ton endon daimona* as "Reason within you." Obviously, it could be rendered "your inward genius" or "your inward god" and so forth. But these amount to the same thing: the inward reason that is our participation in the divine element that suffuses the cosmos. Cf. 6.30 (don't be Caesarified; strive to be how philosophy makes you to be); 12.1 et passim.

29. What Marcus literally says is: "All this is most unprofessional" (*idiōtikōtaton*). But for Marcus, to be unprofessional or unskilled is precisely to be unphilosophic. Cf. 7.2 for the language of "renewal" or "new life" (*anabiōnai*), or 8.2 for the language of entering into "another life" (*eis bion heteron*).
30. Turning inward does not mean becoming existentially reduced, however, since we can travel the cosmos in our own mind (see 11.1).
31. On *technē* as the art or craft of a Stoically shaped human life, see, e.g., 8.26 or 11.5.
32. Marcus's initial question is deceptively hard to translate given the vast changes in the meaning of the word *self* and its associated anthropologies (see Taylor, *Sources of the Self*). *Tis autos* could be rendered "What am I?" "What is 'yourself'?" "Who is the 'self'?" and so on.
33. Marcus admits that all the philosophies in the world still leave a lot unanswered (5.10). What is enough is to know how to get on with living.
34. Cf. *Med.* 5.30: "The mind of the whole is communal" (*koinōnikos*).
35. Or, in terms of competing citizenships, Marcus says that he is a citizen of both Rome and the world (6.44). When these conflict the former trumps the latter (cf. 3.5). His comment on the Christians is well known (11.3).
36. Cf. *Med.* 9.27, on the gods as the makers of other humans. Marcus reminds himself of the positive side of our common reason: we can love (*philein*) other humans because of their reason (7.22). Of course, Marcus would mean "love" in the Stoic sense (a nonvulnerable, innerly secure love that is seen primarily in acts of justice).
37. To injure or forsake even one of our neighbors, says Marcus, is to cut ourselves off from the rest: "A branch that is cut off from its neighbor branch cannot help but be cut off from the whole plant. Likewise, a man severed from one man has been torn away from the community of all" (11.8).
38. In most of his notes "Marcus' individuality can scarcely be discerned" (Hadot, *Inner Citadel*, 29). One place where you can sense his individuality, however, is Marcus's grasp of the transitory condition of human existence.

4. ST. PAUL

1. We say "wrote" but in most cases we mean "dictated." Paul, like many other ancients, used an amanuensis (Rom 16:22 names him Tertius). All reasonable scholars accept the Pauline authorship of Romans, 1 and 2 Corinthians, Galatians, Philippians, 1 Thessalonians, and Philemon. From there, scholarly opinion is divided over the direct Pauline authorship of the rest of the letters ascribed to Paul. I see no convincing reasons why Colossians and Ephesians could not be by Paul (though Ephesians would not originally have been intended for Ephesus). There are also letters that are clearly pseudonymous (for example, 3 Corinthians or his correspondence with Seneca), and lost letters (for example, the letter to the Corinthians that was composed before 1 Corinthians).
2. See "An Essay for the Understanding of St Paul's Epistles, by Consulting St Paul Himself," 103–16, in Locke, A *Paraphrase and Notes on the Epistles of St Paul*. The language "word on target" comes from Beker, *Paul the Apostle*.

3. See Childs, *The Church's Guide for Reading Paul*, and Scherbenske, *Canonizing Paul.*
4. See, for example, Sanders, Beker, and Hays.
5. By treating God before Jesus Christ, I do not intend to suggest that (a) Paul's view of God can be seen in isolation from his view of Jesus, or (b) that somehow Paul's view of God is more fundamental or basic than his view of Jesus Christ, as if the latter were superimposed upon the former (contra Dunn's image of "levels" in *Theology of Paul*). Indeed, as will become clear, learning to speak with Paul about "God" will involve learning how to speak simultaneously of Jesus and the Spirit. On this point, see, e.g., Watson, "The Triune Divine Identity," 99–124. My only hesitation about Watson's article is his occasional practice of speaking as if Paul himself thought in terms of the inseparability of being and act ("Paul's understanding" and the like). It is better to speak of the theological and philosophical implications of attending to Pauline grammar. That is, by following Paul today, one is required to speak in the way Watson does, but Paul himself would have thought within the noetic boundaries that reflect the finitude or historicity of all human thought. The way Watson puts things about the unity of being and act was not available to Paul. Karl Barth, Robert Jenson, John Zizioulas, et al. had yet to put pen to paper.
6. When he wrote his letter to the Romans, Paul had not yet visited the Christian community there. His somewhat full presentation of his teaching, therefore, makes a certain kind of sense: he wanted them to know what he considered the Gospel to be. Why exactly he wrote Romans is a subject of considerable scholarly debate; there is no consensus.
7. It is true, of course, that Paul can speak with the Corinthians of lesser numinous beings as "gods," but these are pagan spirits or "demons" and not other options on offer for the identity of God. Both "henotheism" and "monotheism" are abstractions. The terms presuppose a common "God," but it is exactly the meaning of the word *God* that is at issue. *Theoi* with reference to other numinous beings can be found in the Greek OT.
8. Pauline scholars worry about where Paul's theology begins, what's most fundamental, and so forth. But the different elements that make up something as complex as "Pauline theology" are too intertwined to discern where he "begins." It's all present, all the time. Francis Watson's article that criticizes James Dunn (*JSNT* 2000) for Dunn's talk of levels is right. Paul's different ways of speaking about God evidence not different levels but different moments in speech; the overall pattern is too integrated to slice into different levels.
9. This obviously does not mean that for Paul God is humanity writ large. It means rather that one cannot give the meaning of the word *God* for Paul apart from the life of the Jews. God's self-revelation is that bound up with particular names and histories.
10. Of course in the Greek version of Exodus 3:14 YHWH is exegeted as *ho ōn*—"the one who is," or "the being"—but this is the translator's elaboration of YHWH. Elsewhere in the Septuagint YHWH is almost uniformly rendered as *kyrios*. The debate surrounding the pre-Christian Greek OT rendering of YHWH is complex, but in this case it is clear that Paul was reading *kyrios* because his argument depends hermeneutically on *kyrios* in the Septuagint (LXX).

11. There is extensive literature on Spirit, for example, Gordon Fee's classic big work, *God's Empowering Presence*. The best short article is that of Friedrich Wilhelm Horn, "Kyrios und Pneuma bei Paulus," in *Paulinische Christologie*, 59–75.
12. There is a complex exegetical debate about how best to read the Spirit language in 2 Cor 3:17–18, but it makes the best sense of the argument at this point in 2 Corinthians to coordinate 3:17–18 with 3:3 (see, e.g., Horn, "Kyrios und Pneuma," 66–67).
13. This was a charge that was levied against the Christians in the early days. On the christological redefinition of the Shema in 1 Cor 8:6, see esp. Wright, *Climax of the Covenant*.
14. For a sense of the importance of singularity of Israel's Lord—that the Lord is the "only Lord"—see the use of *monos kyrios* in Exod 22:20; Deut 6:13; 10:20; 32:12; Judge 10:16 et passim.
15. Of course, if one thinks 2 Cor 10–13 precedes 2 Cor 1–9, then this is not the last recorded communication. I'm following the manuscript tradition here.
16. The triadic statement of 1 Cor 12:4–6 displays an obvious parallelism: "There are varieties of gifts, but the same Spirit (*to auto pneuma*); and there are varieties of service, but the same Lord (*ho autos kyrios*); and there are varieties of working, but the same God (*ho autos theos*) works all of them in all."
17. This is not to say that Paul's letters do not make use of a narrative about Jesus, for in fact they do. Of course, inasmuch as understanding human identity requires narrative, Paul had little choice about this. On the "narrative substructure" of Paul's letters, see the essays in Longenecker, *Narrative Dynamics in Paul*. Michael Gorman's little book *Reading Paul* succinctly shows the main points in the plot.
18. And Paul himself reflected long and hard on this passage (see, e.g., Rom 9–11, 1 Cor 10:7). See Barclay, "'I Will Have Mercy on Whom I Have Mercy,'" 82–106.
19. On the image language in Paul's letters, see Rowe, "New Testament Iconography?"
20. My translation here is an attempt to get across the significance of *schema*; it is not just "form" but more like "pattern of the thing in question."
21. On "sin," see pages 97–99.
22. Of course, as a Jew Paul simply took it for granted that the shape of pagan lives more generally also testified to this brokenness (see, e.g., Gal 2:15, "we who are Jews by nature and not Gentile sinners").
23. Law is an extremely complex topic in Pauline theology. In my judgment the best article is still Hays, "Three Dramatic Roles: The Law in Romans 3–4," now in *The Conversion of the Imagination*. The question may be raised about the Gentiles: the Gentiles were not given the Law; how were they supposed to do it? Well, in the Pauline epistles Law also means the whole sweep of Scripture, which as it turns out indicts the entire human community (e.g., Rom 1–3).
24. This is the real strength of Wright's *The Resurrection of the Son of God*—the grammar of resurrection is a grammar of bodies.
25. My translation here departs from the standard translations. The use of *psychē* in 1 Cor 15:44–46 has long caused problems for Paul's interpreters. It is clear from the logic of his argument against the Corinthians that Paul does not endorse a body and soul dichotomy. Indeed, this dichotomy would severely undermine his counterpoints to

the Corinthian skepticism. Nor does he wish to establish a soul and spirit dichotomy. Nor does he wish to establish a physical and spiritual dichotomy. His most basic contrast is between the body with which we make our way through the world from birth to death (the "natural body") and the body we receive after our deaths upon our resurrection (the "spiritual body"). Over against the tendencies to reintroduce with "soul" or "physical" one of the dichotomies against which Paul is arguing, I am attempting to maintain the material contrast through the English translation.

26. The LXX renders the same Hebrew word (*adam*) differently in Gen 1 and 2 (*adam* in Gen 1 is humanity as such; *adam* in Gen 2 is the male person). In contrast to modern source theorists, Paul reads Genesis 1 and 2 together as one narrative. Adam was a figure of considerable theological importance in the Second Temple period more generally.
27. Obviously he would have known about Jew and Gentile from his own life! The point is not that he "discovered" this difference in Scripture but rather that it is a difference grounded in Scripture and history and about which Paul had to think a great deal.
28. Cf. Rom 10:4, where *telos* should be taken as "goal" or "purpose": "Christ is the *telos* of the Torah."
29. Becker, *Denial of Death*, xvii. For those who are looking at the headings and wondering why I frame humanity with the first and last parts of the Christian story—where is redemption?—I would point out that I treated Jesus first (in the previous section). The middle is, epistemically speaking, the center of the thing, the point from which we look at the others. So the order is: Jesus, then creation and sin, and death and eschatology. Jesus, that is, is the true human. He shows us how to treat humanity in light of the first and last parts of the story.
30. Some scholars in the twentieth century (e.g., Käsemann, Jewett) tried to establish a particular content for each of these terms, or looked to the *Umwelt* to explain why Paul speaks this way (e.g., to Philo for the use of "inner and outer" language). Their arguments were not finally compelling. If Paul has a consistent tripartite anthropology, he does not tell us enough about it for us to say much. He can speak with dexterity about the complexity of the human constitution, but he doesn't develop things anthropologically, and at the end of the day he is committed to a unified view of person. The body is essential to being reasonable, for example (see Rom 12:1: "Present your bodies . . . which is your *logikos* [reasonable] worship").
31. Belief in resurrection of the dead was one of the defining features of Pharisaic Judaism in Paul's time (see Acts 23:6–10, for example). See Feldmeier and Spieckermann, *God of the Living*, for the significance of this way of speaking about God and the biblical view of the Living God over against death.
32. As far as I can tell, Paul does not really address the question of what happens to those who died before Jesus. My hunch is that he would answer along similar lines: they are "with" God. As far as we can tell from Paul's correspondence, the Christians in Thessalonica were the first really to worry over the fact that people were dying before the last day.
33. *Pistis/pisteuein:* faith/believe/trust/obey with whole life, and so on. Unfortunately, in English we have to make choices that are not required in Greek. In Greek one just

reads *pistis* and understands the whole of the range. On the different senses of faith in Paul, see Wright, "Faith, Virtue, Justification, and the Journey to Freedom," in *The Word Leaps the Gap*, 472–97, which is concise and clear.

34. See Campbell, "Romans 1:17—A Crux Interpretum for the Πίστις Χριστοῦ Debate," 277–85.
35. As Richard Hays has made clear multiple times, the "faithfulness of Christ" is a synecdoche for this whole complex of things.
36. Hays, *Echoes of Scripture in the Letters of Paul*, is the definitive statement. See also his response to his critics, "On the Rebound," in *Paul and the Scriptures of Israel*, ed. Craig A. Evans and James A. Sanders (Sheffield: JSOT Press, 1992).
37. In Greek "nations" is "Gentiles," non-Jews. On the importance of the Old Testament in 1 Cor 10, see Hays, "The Conversion of the Imagination," in *The Conversion of the Imagination.*
38. See Barclay's incisive essay "Why the Roman Empire Was Insignificant to Paul," in *Pauline Churches and Diaspora Jews.* Especially important is the end, where Barclay writes about Paul's way of going at things "diagonally."
39. Hart, *Atheist Delusions*, 177–82, has a rich interpretation of this sermon.
40. This has long been recognized as a complex passage. For an illuminating treatment that takes hunger to be a central problem in these feasts, see Henderson "'If Anyone Hungers . . . ,'" 195–208.
41. Locke, "The Preface: An Essay for the Understanding of St Paul's Epistles by Consulting St Paul Himself," in *A Paraphrase and Notes on the Epistles of St Paul*, 104.

5. ST. LUKE

1. Acts is the most importance source for all understandings of early church development. To be sure, Paul's letters give us snapshots of Christian communities, but without Acts we have no idea even how to begin to put the story together. Regardless of what one thinks about its reliability in the details large and small, Acts is the foundational narrative for all subsequent accounts of the Christian church's existence.
2. I use "biographies" to mean two things: (a) the ancient sense of a narrative that is not meant to cover the whole life of a person or to concentrate exclusively on establishing the "facts," but rather to display the overall character of a man or something of his most significant moments as they reveal his character; and (b) an agreement with Charles Talbert, Richard Burridge, et al. on the genre to which the Gospels are best likened.
3. The earliest manuscript is the papyrus known as Papyrus Bodmer XIV (P^{75}). It is dated between AD 175 and 225. Despite the modern vogue to question all authorial ascriptions, the best evidence, as Joseph Fitzmyer argues, shows that it makes credible historical sense to assume that "Luke" is the right attribution—and that this "Luke" is the Luke that the ancients uniformly spoke of. If the Gospel is by someone else, then we know nothing about its author. That is of course possible, though in my view not probable.
4. The so-called "we" sections are Acts 16:10–17; 20:5–15; 21:1–18; 27:1–28:16.
5. The Muratorian Fragment and a prologue external to Luke's Gospel.

6. The alleged medical language in Luke and Acts has been shown to exist more widely in ancient Greek. Moreover, Galen himself commented that he wrote about medical matters so that the *hoi polloi* could understand him.
7. Theophilus was probably the financier (patron) of the Lukan corpus, though some have thought him a fictive addressee.
8. The hermeneutical trick is therefore to make sure one's extractions and resettings presuppose the specific Lukan narrative for their intelligibility (even as they are generated from the narrative itself).
9. Dahl, "The Story of Abraham in Luke-Acts."
10. On Luke's use of the passage from Malachi, see Laurentin, *Structure et Théologie de Luc I–II*.
11. Claudius's expulsion of Jews from Rome (Acts 18:2) is part of the "your blood be on your heads," but the narrative content is nevertheless something like this: I'm leaving! (but really I'm only moving next door); I'm leaving! (but really I'm going to hang around for eighteen months first).
12. This leads to the sense of Christian life as a "school" or "sect" within Judaism, a *hairesis* (the lawyer Tertullus uses this word in 24:5, and it is found in the mouth of Roman Jews in 28:23).
13. Talbert, *Luke and the Gnostics*.
14. NT scholars often think that Luke has "softened" Mark's cry of dereliction. Perhaps. But this depends on (a) understanding Jesus' cry in Mark without its intertextual potential in which the end of Psalm 22 would be heard to express Jesus' faith, and (b) a romanticization of his "into thy hands I commit my spirit" in Luke. We do not know the exact tone here—Luke does not say "and Jesus said in a loud and miserable-sounding voice" or "in a loud but strangely joyful voice"—but he is being crucified.
15. Luke 24:46 is a citation of Ps 31:5. The intertextual potential here has long been recognized and is very important. Those who know the psalm will also hear in Jesus' cry the psalm's end in faith and vindication. Narratively speaking, the centurion's remark that Jesus is *dikaios* works as a provisional answer to the prayer of Psalm 31.
16. As a result—on down the road—"being" here gets an entirely different "structure" than in Greek philosophy. See especially the first chapters of John Zizioulas's now-classic work, *Being as Communion*.
17. Rowe, *Early Narrative Christology*, 98–105.
18. See Shepherd, *The Narrative Function of the Holy Spirit as a Character in Luke-Acts*.
19. Alone among the Gospel authors, Luke writes of Jesus as "the Lord" during his earthly ministry. "When the Lord," writes Luke, "saw [the widow]" (Luke 7:13). Surprising as it is to learn that only Luke writes in this way, once learned, this unique stylistic feature is impossible to forget. Neither Matthew nor Mark nor John has anything similar, but Luke writes of Jesus as the Lord at least thirteen times. It is the *Leitwort* of the Gospel as a whole; see Rowe, *Early Narrative Christology*.
20. Luke 1:39–56 is a transitional interlude.
21. The opening lines that describe John's vocation take on a new significance, as there, too, the resonance can be heard.
22. I say "somewhat" backward because it is true that the narrative meaning of Christ is not something created ex nihilo. *Messiah* will inevitably share in the meaning generated

by the term's history of use, however much the narrative use differs from what has come before. It is therefore appropriate to see how the word was used before its use in the New Testament.

23. The stranger is of course Jesus himself, but the two disciples do not learn this until later in the story. The scene is thus supremely ironic. Let anyone who thinks the New Testament has no humor read this scene carefully.
24. Fitzmyer is a classic example of a learned scholar whose understanding of Luke's sense of the Old Testament is completely wooden. More precisely, what scholars such as Fitzmyer have done is to substitute a modern proof-texting hermeneutic for an ancient one. Moderns ask, "Where does it say that in the Bible?"; the ancients ask, "Where doesn't it say that in the Bible?"
25. Luke's use of the Old Testament relies much more on atmospheric resonance and analogical similarities with key figures from Israel's history (Moses, Elijah, Elisha) than it does on finding particular phrases or words that "fulfill" what needs to be fulfilled.
26. On this important verse, see Rowe, "Acts 2:36 and the Continuity of Lukan Christology."
27. This transformation in the meaning of Messiah is exactly the transformation in understanding undergone by the disciples as they move from events of the Gospel into the Acts of the Apostles. In the Gospel they cling to the expectation that Jesus' deliverance will be an immediately political one (this is, for example, why they still have swords in the garden at his arrest). But by Acts they no longer understand *Messiah* in this way but instead as a term that corresponds to the creation of communities of Jews and Gentiles.
28. See John Carroll's essay "The God of Israel and the Salvation of the Nations," in *The Forgotten God*. Carroll recognizes that "theocentric" cannot be meant in a way that excludes the importance of Jesus.
29. Luke 2:49: the translation of Jesus' words here has always been difficult.
30. Cf. Luke 3:23 where the Lukan parenthesis "as it was supposed" also comments on this question: "Jesus was about thirty years old when he began his ministry, being the son (as it was supposed) of Joseph, the son of Eli, the son of Matthat."
31. The "Promise" is the Holy Spirit that is poured out at Pentecost (Acts 2).
32. Cf. the genealogy in which Jesus' lineage is traced back through Adam to "son of God." On the significance of this genealogy, see the discussion on pages 131–132.
33. As many modern commentators note, the parable may better be called the parable of the lost son. It is the third and final parable about the finding of something that was lost; each parable increases the value of what was lost (one lost sheep out of one hundred sheep, one lost coin out of ten coins, one lost son out of two sons).
34. There has been a debate over the phrase "come to himself": does it mean that the son has fully repented? Or that he simply realizes his father is a sap? The Lukan text does not resolve this question.
35. Nouwen's meditation still is basically the best on how to reflect on the different characters in this story.
36. Some English translations (ET) read, "Son, you are always with me." The Greek, however, is *teknon* (child); moreover, "always with me" does not get across the considerable pathos in this remark.

37. Cf. Luke 1:78, which speaks of God's tender mercy.
38. Obviously in narrative terms this parable is the third one told to the Pharisees and scribes because of their grumbling against Jesus for eating with tax collectors and sinners (Luke 15:1–3). But this does not settle matters for the readers of the Gospel, who are able to hear contemporaneous developments and/or perennial human problems in the story line.
39. For example, Joel 3:1–5 (ET 2:28–32) in Acts 2:17–21 and Ps 15:8–11 (ET Ps 16) in Acts 2:25–28.
40. See Luke 10:21; and Luke 3:16; cf. Acts 1:5; 2:38; 11:16; and Acts 1:2; and Luke 4:1, 14; and Luke 4:18; cf. Acts 10:38.
41. Cf. Schapp, *In Geschichten Verstrickt: Zum Sein von Mensch und Ding*. Luke does not thematize history any more than he does anthropology, of course, but it is safe to say that he would not endorse a Troeltschian sense of general history. Luke's is a very particular history, the one that is bound up with a specific man, Jesus from Nazareth. And yet were we to ask Luke, he would doubtless affirm that this particular history is universal history in a more important sense—the sense that means it is relevant to all human beings. With respect to traditional anthropological terms, he does use the word *psychē* (soul), but for the most part it is interchangeable with "life": Luke 10:27 cites the Shema from Deut 6 (heart, soul, strength, understanding/mind); Luke 12:20 (on this very night the rich man's soul is required—*soul* here means life, as it also does in "do not be anxious about your soul . . . for the soul is more than food" [Luke 12:22–23], and "whosoever seeks to gain his soul will lose it" [Luke 17:33]). See also Acts 15:26; 20:24; and 27:10, 22. In Acts 2:41 soul means person (three thousand souls were added that day to the church; cf. 27:37). In Acts 14:2 *soul* means something more like "feelings" or "mind"—Jews stirred up Gentiles against brothers; see also 15:24. And in Acts 20:10 *soul* means "life" as in "life force" or perhaps simply "breath" (Eutychus's "*psychē* is still in him").
42. In Luke's story this declaration causes a problem: "Who can forgive sins but God alone?" (5:21). The scribes and Pharisees (reasonably, given their assumptions about who Jesus is) say Jesus' declaration is blasphemy. The theological logic that underlies this scene is presented in the sections on Jesus and God.
43. Sin cannot, for example, exhaustively explain tragedy. In Luke 13:1–5 Jesus negates the idea that the "Galileans whose blood Pilate mingled with their sacrifices" were "worse sinners than all the others." The victims of the collapsing tower of Siloam, he also says, "were not worse debtors than all others."
44. Cf. the important claims about the historical nature of sin made in Anderson, *Sin: A History*. Anderson's work discloses not only that our conceptions of sin change throughout time but also that it is impossible to speak of sin in abstraction from its particularized history.
45. On the history of this passage's interpretation, see briefly, Anderson, *Sin*, 111–13.
46. "Only God can forgive" or cancel the debt. On the canceling of debts as a central theological motif around the time that Luke was written, see Nathan Eubank's work on Matthew's Gospel: *Wages of Cross-Bearing and Debt of Sin*.
47. Luke is here exegeting Ps 2. "Why did the Gentiles rage, and the peoples [i.e., Israel] imagine vain things?"

48. Sanders spoke of this as "covenantal nomism." Only Protestants of a certain stripe would understand the "blameless" statement about Zechariah and Elizabeth to mean "no sin." It really means in a Jewish context: doing what the law says to do about sin, etc. People sinned; they did what the Law said to do about it; they were then blameless before the law.
49. The naming at the baptism fulfills Gabriel's promise in Luke 1:32, 35.
50. As mentioned in Chapter 4, note 26, Adam was a theologically important figure in the Second Temple period.
51. New Testament scholars will note here that I do not accept the common view that apocalyptic (Paul) and salvation history (Luke) are of necessity opposed. Indeed, I see no conceptual reasons at all why they cannot be held together. Of course Luke thinks Jesus is an apocalypse; and of course Paul cannot conceive of God's apocalyptic action apart from the history of Israel.
52. This is in contrast to Paul. Luke does, however, offer the most extensive narrative depiction of the resurrected Jesus in the New Testament. If we were to ask Paul what a spiritual body actually looked like—how to think about its continuity and discontinuity with the natural body—he might well have pointed to the end of Luke's Gospel: Jesus is quite obviously himself as he was on earth, and yet he is quite obviously different from the way he was on earth.
53. Alfred Loisy is the one most often noted for expressing it this way (in *The Gospel and the Church*). But the sentiment is widespread and has connections to broader intellectual trends. The Weberian notion of the way charisma works, for example, has been influential, particularly when connected with anti-institutional sentiment. The founder of a religion has charisma, thought Weber, but his followers do not (or at least not to the degree the founder does). Absent charismatic leadership, routinizable forms of life move in, and an institution takes the place of charisma. The inevitable result is deterioration.
54. This is in no way intended to minimize the significance of Paul's "body of Christ" theology, which is substantively very similar to Luke's. In fact, one might say that Acts is a kind of narrative "body of Christ" theology. Still, Paul did not talk much about the life of Jesus.
55. There has long been an (irresolvable) argument about a dating discrepancy here with Josephus, *Ant.* 20.97–104. Josephus puts Theudas after Judas.
56. Acts 5:17 has often been translated "filled with jealousy." This is incorrect. The word here means "zealous," not "jealous" in the modern sense. That is, the leaders are very worried about the consequences of what is going on, not jealous of the Christian success.
57. Luke tells us that the Jews came from Antioch and Iconium and persuaded the crowds. The interesting question is how they did this. To answer along the lines that the text of Acts would have us to answer, we need to look at the rest of story and ask what the accusers say elsewhere in similar situations. The answer is obvious: the Jewish accusers say (either directly or through those whom they recruit) that the missionaries "advocate customs which it is not lawful for us Romans to accept or practice" (Acts 16:21), or "are acting against the decrees of Caesar, saying there is another King, Jesus" (17:7), or

"persuade people to worship God contrary to the law" (18:13), or cause seditious revolt (24:5, *stasis*), and so on. In short, the accusations point explicitly to the politics of the early Christian movement vis-à-vis the Roman Empire, which—when closely inspected—turns out to be the question of the early Christians and the political currents of the Greco-Roman world.

58. Luke plays on the term *deisidaimonia*, which can mean at once both "exceptionally religious/pious" and "exceptionally superstitious."
59. The clearest indication of this is the crucial Jerusalem council in Acts 15, where the political negotiations presume a complex authority structure.
60. This does mean that there are no goods to be discovered in Roman culture or that there is no overlap between the church and world in significant ways. As I wrote in *World Upside Down*, "Luke's reading of the world's predicament does not include a flatfooted negation of all that pagan culture could possibly offer, as if the narrative of Acts split cleanly all of reality into two monolithic blocks: the Christian community (good) and pagan culture (bad). . . . Luke's language of darkness and ignorance," that is, "does not . . . emerge from a more fundamental theological and narrative grammar that would entail an in-principle dismissal of the possibility of goods within pagan culture. . . . Indeed, on Luke's terms, one should expect to find them" (171).

6. ST. JUSTIN MARTYR

1. The epigraph is from "The Martyrdom of the Holy Martyrs Justin, Chariton, Charito, Evelpistus, Hierax, Paeon, and Liberian," 2, 4 (rec. B), in Musurillo, *The Acts of the Christian Martyrs*, 49, 51. Of the three recensions, recension B is the best known. Though it is clear that recension C is a literarily developed version of Justin's trial, it is difficult to decide whether the full version of A or of B is more accurate. On the material cited here, they are substantially the same.
2. Only one full manuscript (*Parisinus graecus* 450, dated to 1364) constitutes the whole of the tradition we have of Justin's texts (there are quotations in other works, of course, but not texts). This is a sober reminder of how lucky we are to have things from the ancient world. Justin's influence also led to the circulation of some pseudonymous compositions and spuriously attributed works, though these works have not exercised much sway in Justin's reception history.
3. Justin also makes this point when he insists that God the Father of all has no given name (*1 Apol.* 61.11; *2 Apol.* 5.1). Justin takes it for granted that names are things given, and since nothing exists that could name God (this thing would then itself be more God than God), God has no name. Readers familiar with the story in Exodus of Moses and the burning bush might wonder how Justin could say that God has no name. Justin's answer would be that it was not God the Father who spoke to Moses from the burning bush but was instead an angel, which for Justin is frequently another word for the Logos. It was the Logos, or Jesus Christ, who spoke to Moses (see *Dial.* 59–61; 127.4; 128.1; *1 Apol.* 62.3–4; 63.7–13).
4. Justin's texts are many of those that become important in the history of christological exegesis (Gen 1: "Let us make"; Gen 19: oaks at Mamre; Gen 18: Sodom and Gomorrah;

Gen 28: Jacob's ladder; Exod 3: fiery bush; Ps 110:1: the Lord said to my Lord; Prov 8: wisdom—and so forth).

5. Cf. Justin Martyr, *Dial.* 36.2: "Permit me to quote the following prophecies to show that the Holy Spirit *by parable* called Christ 'God,' and 'Lord of hosts,' and 'of Jacob.'"
6. This is my translation of some rather sticky Greek (especially the anarthrous *archē*—echoing Gen 1:1), but Justin's point is to put the *Logos* on the uncreated side of Creator/creation. Italicizing *before* and putting in *very* (neither of which, strictly speaking, is in Greek) is my way of trying to capture this emphasis. On the historical shape of the doctrine of creation from nothing (*creatio ex nihilo*), see the concise article by J. C. O'Neill, "How Early Is the Doctrine of *Creatio ex Nihilo*?" O'Neill cogently argues that this doctrine was firmly in place before the New Testament.
7. Of course this analogy works etymologically (*Logos*=word).
8. God of God, as the creedal formulations later put it. Whether Justin would have used *very*—as in very God from very God—is an interesting question, but not one we can satisfactorily answer here. My hunch is that had he had access to the arguments that produced the "very" language, he would have been happy to use it.
9. Justin has long been called subordinationist; this is not quite right. Clearly Jesus is included in the grammar of God and clearly there is differentiation or order within God's life.
10. In one place at least, Justin does also say it was the *Logos* that spoke from the days of old (*1 Apol.* 36.1). Naturally, this makes good etymological sense.
11. *1 Apol.* 6.2 is interesting for the way in which Justin appears to include "the company of the other good angels" in the list of those whom Christians "venerate and worship" and "honor in reason and in truth": the true God and Father, his Son Jesus, the company of the other good angels who follow the Son and are like him, and the prophetic Spirit. Given the totality of his writings, and what we know of early Christian theology and practice, it is unlikely that Justin means that Christians worship good angels in the same, strong sense of worship that he would apply to God himself. It seems more likely that the room found between the two words (*seb.* and *proskyn.*) points toward Justin's affirmation of the Christians' reverence for the good angels. The sentence in *1 Apol.* 6.2 is also interesting for the fact that the word *other* apparently requires the understanding that the Son is here called an angel ("other good angels"). But this is easily enough resolved by reading the *Dialogue* where it is clear that Justin understands the Son to bear the title *angel*—which for him is taken in its more basic sense of "messenger," as in the Old Testament; see *Dial.* 127.4, where he's said to be called an "angel" because "of his serving the Father's will" (cf. also *Dial.* 61.1).
12. Justin's word for memoirs (*apomnēmoneumata*) indicates a genre that included, among others, Xenophon's famous work on Socrates (*Apomnēmoneumata of Socrates*). The early Christian Papias had also called the Gospels memoirs.
13. The word I have translated as "suffer as we do" is *homoiopathēs*. It is difficult to know exactly how best to render this word in English. The problem is that *pathos* has such a long history as a topic of debate in both philosophy and theology (whether pathos is good or bad, whether God's pathos is analogically similar to humanity's or not, and so on). Falls and Halton translate "has feelings like our own," but the modern sense of *feelings* is not what Justin would have meant with his gesture to the passions. Justin's

point is that Jesus is capable of undergoing what humans undergo (suffering in that sense).

14. As Skarsaune, *Proof from Prophecy*, 33–34, notes, Justin may here reflect a contemporary translation of *almah* as *neanis* (young woman). There is, of course, later evidence for *neanis* in the Greek translations Aquila, Symmachus, and Theodotion.
15. Justin probably depends on the story about the origin of the Septuagint told in the *Letter of Aristeas* (cf., e.g., *1 Apol.* 31). His citation is slightly closer to the version of Isa 7:14 found in Matthew 1:23 than the (reconstructed) LXX itself. This may be because Justin is citing Matthew, or because he is using a testimony source (Skarsaune), or because he is citing from memory (and remembers the Matthean version), or because he cites from a text—as may have Matthew—that was current during their time but was not "original" LXX, and so forth. We cannot choose among these options based on the available evidence.
16. See Skarsaune, *Proof from Prophecy*, esp. 202–3, on how the interpolated verse Isa 8:4 exercises hermeneutical control in the attempt to show that Isa 7:14 cannot be speaking of Hezekiah. Justin says the Isa 8:4 verse shows that only someone who had power over demons even as a baby—only Jesus—can really be the subject of Isa 7:10–17.
17. Justin makes the same argument for other myths that have similar-sounding parts to the story of Jesus; demons modeled these myths on Christ (*Dial.* 66–79). Justin claims that the Old Testament and the Jesus story historically antecede these other myths, but he is not making the modern argument of literary/oral dependence (since demons are involved).
18. Justin's phrase here is clever (*ouk anthrōpos ex anthrōpou*). Trypho accuses Justin of speaking in the language of paradox.
19. The argument at this juncture is also about whether or not Elijah has come. Both Trypho and Justin take it for granted that the coming of Elijah adjoins the coming of the Messiah (the former must anoint the latter). Justin cites the book of Malachi—though he mistakenly calls it Zechariah—as the text that underlies their common belief.
20. That Justin is aware of the repetitive feel of the *Dialogue* is a testimony to the fact that he willingly subordinates literary beauty to (what he thinks is) argumentative advantage (see *Dial.* 128.2).
21. The Greek in *1 Apol.* 5.4 could also be rendered "acquired physical form and became human" (Minns and Parvis). There is no *physis* root, though, which moves us away from "physical" form. It is really more like transformed or formed as a human and became (born, as *genomenou* in Rom 1:3, for example) a human.
22. Cf. Boyarin, "The Crucifixion of the Memra: How the Logos Became Christian," in his *Border Lines*.
23. Justin probably gets his argument from Paul (on this verse, see Gal 3:10). Justin does admit that some do better and some worse, that Jews are far better than Gentiles, and so on. But these differences do not amount to the transcendence of sin.
24. Justin goes on to say that the Jews cursed Christ by crucifying him—enacted Deut 21:23—and that the Gentiles enact the Jewish curse by killing Christians. This "cursing" is bound up with the Birkhat-ha-minim question (*Dial.* 96).

25. On mystery, see Lang's Duke University dissertation, "Mystery and the Making of a Christian Historical Consciousness."
26. See, e.g., Justin Martyr, *Dial.* 100.2, where Justin says clearly that "all that he has learned from the Scriptures" about Jesus has been "revealed by his grace." When one needs revelation and grace to understand, one is well beyond a simple process of present-assent.
27. Cf. *Dial.* 7.2, where the old man (Christian) says with respect to the apostolic writings, "Whoever reads them with the proper faith will profit greatly," implying that one needs the proper faith to profit from the writings. And in 7.3 he says that to understand the things he speaks of one has to be enlightened by God and his Christ.
28. Against Trypho on the one side and Marcionites on the other.
29. On the character of this ending as resurrection, see the discussion in this chapter under "Human Being."
30. It is possible that the "old man" is supposed to represent an appearance of Christ. See Hofer, "The Old Man as Christ in Justin's 'Dialogue with Trypho,'" 1–21.
31. There is a word play on *logos:* Justin actually says he is there to do "philology" (not what moderns mean by the word but more like the internal dialogue of reason with itself); the old man takes the etymology and uses it as objection (Justin is a lover of words).
32. The word translated "prudence" is *phronēsis,* which has a long history in philosophical discourse. It can mean a range of things, but *prudence* is best here; it means something like virtue that comes from straight thinking and good judgment.
33. The term translated "happiness" is *eudaimonia,* the classic word in Greek philosophy that means existential peace, virtue, management of emotion, and so on, all wrapped up in one total package.
34. Halton's translation here is good. "Method" is not quite right (the Greek is literally: from what shall one derive profit/benefit?). But Justin means tradition/source of help/method. Bobichon translates "to which teacher should one have recourse and where shall one search for help?"
35. Might one say: philosophers have the right telos (truth and piety, *1 Apol.* 3; cf. *Dial.* 2.7), but the wrong method (*Dial.* 7.1)?
36. In Justin's logic, the philosophers did not always comprehend what they were reading—Plato, for example, could not see the prefiguration of Christ's Cross (*1 Apol.* 60.5)—but they were able to see truth. Still, the truth that they saw was the truth they learned from Moses and the prophets.
37. Justin's "genetic" argument is in part why he can confidently say that those who lived in line with Logos before Christ were Christians no matter what they were called (*1 Apol.* 46.3). They were living according to Christ and derived their "accordance" from their dependence upon Old Testament prophecies. Again, Justin's is not an argument about a generic logos, but an argument that claims that truth has a particular historical order.
38. Many folks have made a mountain of Justin's *one* comment about this in his entire writings (*2 Apol.* 13). Zack Phillips, a doctoral student at Duke, has written a very smart paper in one of my seminars that carefully investigates Justin's use of the word Logos.

Phillips concludes that the Logos is "not a general cognitive capacity to reason [to the truth about God] . . . but the specific enlightening activity of Christ." See, e.g., *1 Apol.* 14.1–3, where to be persuaded by the Logos is to learn a transforming pattern of life. All of this makes much more complex a statement like "God persuades and leads to faith through the rational powers which he bestowed" (*1 Apol.* 10.4)—especially since this statement occurs in the context of Justin's account of the Fall.

39. There are those think otherwise and believe that we pass into unconsciousness after death, but they are wrong and show a hatred for humanity (*1 Apol.* 57.3).

40. In *2 Apol.* 10.1, Justin does say that the "whole rational principle became the Christ, who was made visible for our sake, body, logos, and soul." It is not clear, however, that Justin here means to speak of a tripartite anthropology as much as he means to say that the Logos was present in the body and soul of Jesus. See Minns and Parvis, *Justin, Philosopher and Martyr: Apologies*, 309, n. 2, which strikes the right balance.

41. See Rowe, *World Upside Down*, 126–35. Still, even from Justin's writings one can see that at the highest official level Rome is not yet too worried about the Christians. In describing the whole affair with Urbicus, Ptolemy, etc., in *2 Apol.* 2.7, Justin mentions that the emperor granted Ptolemy's wife the petition she made to have a longer time before having to answer the charge of being Christian. This longer time was to get her affairs in order, think about what she needed to say, and so forth. That is, she was not considered an immediate threat. Obviously, when Christians showed up in the higher echelons, they usually received better treatment than the run-of-the-mill converts, who were at the mercy of local magistrates/governors. Status/economics were always relevant to persecution in particular cases.

42. Trypho is surprised that Christians suffer but do not do Torah (*Dial.* 19.1).

43. And we won't even ask you to punish those who accuse us, that is, we won't seek reprisal (*1 Apol.* 7.5). Roman law was clear on this point: they could seek reprisal.

44. Whether this is Justin's literary device or something he has actually heard or encountered is not clear (it uses his *alla phēsei tis*).

45. Cf. *1 Apol.* 4.1, where Justin says that those who deny Christ (upon arrest and trial) are likely not living a Christian life anyway. These folks give true Christians a bad name (see also *1 Apol.* 16.8).

46. We moderns think atheism is a theological charge—and of course it is, though it means something different from and more specific than our modern sense of *atheist*—but it is really a specifically political charge. It means denial of Roman gods. It is a dangerous charge. Cf. Frend, *Martyrdom*, 240: "Atheism was the most damning charge against the Christians" (in Asia ca. 150s and beyond).

47. Especially important is *Dial.* 46.7, where Justin says explicitly that Christians suffer severe punishments because "we refuse to sacrifice to those whom we formerly worshiped." The former practice obviously applied to Gentiles, since Jews would not have worshiped the emperor or the gods.

48. *Dial.* 39.5–6, where, alluding to Gen 1–3, he tells Trypho the Romans are influenced by the Serpent.

49. Frend, *Martyrdom*, 238, is right that this is not an isolated claim: "Mild administration [on the part of Roman officials] would not lead to any abatement of the Christian's

claims to the allegiance of the world on a basis wholly at variance with that represented by Antonine Rome. If the law stood in the way, then the law was the inspiration of demons. This was not an isolated claim. It was to be repeated just as forcefully by Origen on the eve of the Decian persecution."

50. Of contemporary works that raise the question of confession/denial that the early Christians faced, none is more powerful than Endō's novel *Silence*. When Justin says to Trypho that Christians would and should "endure all things rather than deny Christ even with a word," he displays a material difference from Endō's novel (*Dial.* 131.2). In Endō's novel, it is Christ himself who speaks the words "trample, trample" as a way to enable a priest's (alleged?) apostasy to save those who are being tortured. Endō's novel is a profound attempt to think through the question of confession/denial by questioning how deep Christ's suffering *pro nobis* really runs—and, in particular, whether it runs deep enough to allow Christians to free other Christians from torture "with a word" and a simple action.
51. The most interesting recent round of debate comes from Daniel Boyarin's provocative claim that Justin "invented" Judaism. Boyarin's claim is based on a wide range of reconsiderations of both primary evidence and theoretical reflection. For responses to Boyarin, see, for example, Marcus, "Birkat Ha-Minim Revisited." I think Boyarin—probably better than any other current scholar—helps us to remember that the forms of life we describe as "Christianity" and "Judaism" were in antiquity far more intertwined and inseparable than we (scholars) are accustomed to thinking and than they later became. The nodal points of Boyarin's historical arguments are the Council of Yavneh, the development of rabbinic Judaism, and the Birkat ha-minim. My judgment is more in line with the arguments of Marcus. But Boyarin indubitably raises the right questions to get us thinking more clearly. (It is important to note that on page 435 of his article in *Church History*, Boyarin says Justin first attests to—but surely doesn't invent—the claim to be Verus Israel and that this kind of thing is the catalyst for nonliturgically formalized cursing of Gentile Christians.)
52. It will persist until the last day, that is, until the two traditions of reading the Old Testament learn from God's consummation of creation who has been right about the way these texts speak of God.
53. To what degree we should call the (later named) New Testament texts that Justin is reading "Scripture" is of course a debated question. They are clearly authoritative for him. But the Scripture that he shares with Trypho is (for the most part) what Christians now call the Old Testament.
54. Though his remark about Justin's "dislike" of Judaism is imprecise at best, Frend puts concisely the political significance of Justin and Trypho's agreement vis-à-vis Rome: "Despite [Justin's] dislike of Judaism he does not praise the Imperial government. Indeed, the solidarity of Christians with Jews on this issue is striking in an age which produced Marcion" (*Martyrdom*, 238).
55. In our time, it is difficult to be polemical about others' beliefs. We can be horrid in political races, attack a person's character, family, personal appearance, decisions made as an adolescent, and everything else. But we can't say "your religious beliefs are wrong" without incurring the wrath of the "offended." But the ancient world was

nothing like this, and vigorous polemic was the norm. It was given, and it was taken—and it was expected.

56. If Justin's polemic strikes us as harsher than Trypho's, that is probably because (a) Justin wrote the *Dialogue* and is trying to "win" the argument; (b) Christians were persecuted in Justin's day; and (c) we have a post-Holocaust awareness of how such language could sound to Jews.
57. Justin's remarks about the Jewish treatment of Christians have been much studied. See the work of Judith Lieu, among others. Whether or not the "cursing in the synagogues" in particular is to be identified with the famous Birkat ha-minim is a subject of considerable and unresolved debate (for: Joel Marcus; against: Daniel Boyarin). The point above does not depend on resolving this debate.
58. "Deeper logic" is my term for *nous* here. Some have rendered *nous* as "spirit"—which is grammatically and theologically acceptable—but it obscures the play on "understand" in this line ("you don't *noein* their *nous*").
59. This is the same dynamic that is at work in the claim that Christians are the true Israel: this is significant because Justin is not simply saying, as Marcion did around the same time, that the Christians are some other thing entirely and have nothing to do with Israel. Justin is more subtle than Marcion. By using the word *Israel,* Justin lays claim to continuity, and by using the word *true,* Justin characterizes the real question at the heart of the discontinuity with the Jews who do not accept Jesus as the Messiah (*Dial.* 11.5; 123.7).
60. This is an affirmation with an immediate negation, but a negation that depends on a first affirmation.
61. Justin does say that he is trying to persuade those who love the truth (*1 Apol.* 12.11; cf. *1 Apol.* 12.5–6).

7. CAN WE COMPARE?

1. The epigraph is from an interview of Alasdair MacIntyre with Giovanna Borradori in MacIntyre and Knight, *The MacIntyre Reader,* 265.
2. MacIntyre, *Whose Justice?* 327.
3. MacIntyre's notion of tradition is in most of what he writes, especially since he believes that he cannot think apart from the tradition of which he is a part. There are those, of course, who do not find MacIntyre persuasive. There are two things to say about that: (a) my use of him has no stake in holding that he is right about every little thing; the argument is that he is right about the big picture; (b) there is no criticism I know of that pertains to his big picture that has done anything at all to put even a question mark beside it. Even Stout, e.g., basically takes the taxonomic/epistemological point for granted when he argues that democracy itself is a tradition.
4. Published as Alasdair MacIntyre, *Three Rival Versions of Moral Enquiry: Encyclopedia, Genealogy, and Tradition.* They are "rival" because they are incommensurable and do not even share standards that would allow them to find one way to be superior to the other (lack has to be shown from within). They are "moral" because they take positions on whether you have to be a certain kind of person to engage in inquiry.

5. Cf. MacIntyre, *Whose Justice?* 368: "The multiplicity of traditions does not afford a multiplicity of perspectives among which we can move, but a multiplicity of antagonistic commitments, between which only conflict, rational or non-rational, is possible."
6. MacIntyre, *Three Rival Versions*, 14. Page numbers cited subsequently in the text are from this work.
7. MacIntyre, *Three Rival Versions*, 56. Cf. MacIntyre, *Whose Justice?* 368.
8. Though we will discuss MacIntyre's use of *translatability* in the coming chapters, it requires brief elaboration for the time being: he means something like the entire ordering grammar of a language as it was actively used in a whole context of a particular shape of life (language-in-use), not a static set of signs/symbols that can be decoded if you have the right lexica, etc.; or: the entire way you'd have to be immersed in the lived-ness of a language to know how to speak it fluently, i.e., use it well within the myriad of things that go into "life." It is true that, in comparison with the conception of rationality at the end of the nineteenth century, the current conception is "weak" rather than "strong," but that does not lessen the substantive point of similarity (MacIntyre, *Three Rival Versions*, 172). By "weak" MacIntyre means a rationality that is "compatible with the coexistence of widely divergent points of view, each unable, at least by those generally accepted standards, to provide conclusive refutation of its rivals" (172).
9. For the most startling description of strangeness I know, see Foucault's citation (of Borges's citation) of "a certain Chinese encyclopedia," in Foucault, *On the Order of Things: An Archaeology of the Human Sciences*, xv–xvi.
10. The genealogical narrative has two strands: (a) the history "of that which the genealogists aspire to undermine," and (b) the history "of the genealogists' own project and of the evasions and stratagems without which the genealogist would inevitably fall back into just those modes which he or she is concerned to repudiate and to expose" (MacIntyre, *Three Rival Versions*, 79).
11. The unity of the self that is presupposed in genealogical critique undoes genealogical claims about the absence of a true "self" (we only wear masks, and so on). See especially MacIntyre's comments on the apologists for Paul de Man (*Three Rival Versions*, 210–13).
12. MacIntyre, *Whose Justice?* 326. MacIntyre's notion of tradition takes definitive shape in *After Virtue* and is present in all his work; but here for the sake of convenience most citations will continue to be from *Three Rival Versions*.
13. Innovation regularly occurs, of course, but it is always achieved through—not apart from or against—the skill acquired by the inquirer. In this way it is also like a craft, which continues to develop newer and better ways of practice/results without changing the craft. There are innovations within furniture making, for example, but the innovations that occur in this craft are not on the basis of and do not lead to skills needed for the craft of auto mechanics (furniture making is MacIntyre's example).
14. MacIntyre does not, of course, think the "break" was immediate or quick. It was, rather, complex and "extended." But it was a break nevertheless.
15. I would like to think I have done such a survey, but surely works have escaped me somewhere. Still, my judgment is based on a sense of the broadest reading I was capable

of—whether this reading was broad enough or not will have to be decided by others. Dale Martin, for example, obviously focuses on the ancient world in a way that differs from Malherbe and Engberg-Pedersen. And John Barclay's response to Engberg-Pedersen presupposes that Barclay thinks differently, too. And there are others. But what I am talking about in this chapter is the manifestly dominant tendency in book after book and article after article.

16. These scholars are now full professors and have trained many others. For a sample of Malherbe's influence see his Festschrift: Fitzgerald, Olbricht, and White, *Early Christianity and Classical Culture*. This is only the tip of the iceberg.
17. His essays have now been published in two volumes: *Light from the Gentiles: Hellenistic Philosophy and Early Christianity: Collected Essays, 1959–2012*, 2 vols., ed. Carl R. Holladay, John T. Fitzgerald, Gregory E. Sterling, and James W. Thompson (Leiden: Brill, 2014). These volumes were published after I wrote this chapter (I therefore retain the original *ANRW* page numbering for "Hellenistic Moralists," though it can be easily coordinated with the republished version). I read as much of Malherbe's work as I could find, but one remarkable article in these volumes that I had not seen is "Heracles."
18. Not all judgments are explicit: some are carried inside the actual work, as it were (the assumptions that are there for the work to work the way it does). Reading through the essays in *Light from the Gentiles* confirms the structuring importance of these judgments for Malherbe's scholarly career. As the editors correctly put it, the *ANRW* article "provides a unique window into two decades of Abe's scholarly development" (xxi). The story of this article is itself interesting (see xxi–xxii and Malherbe's note to his friends appended to the republication of his article in *Light from the Gentiles*, 675).
19. Malherbe, "Hellenistic Moralists and the New Testament," 301.
20. See esp. Malherbe, *Paul and the Thessalonians: The Philosophic Tradition of Pastoral Care*.
21. Malherbe, "Hellenistic Moralists and the New Testament," 300.
22. Malherbe, "Hellenistic Moralists and the New Testament," 277, 300. Malherbe likes the "wide net" metaphor, and uses it elsewhere.
23. Malherbe, "Hellenistic Moralists and the New Testament," 303.
24. Malherbe, "Hellenistic Moralists and the New Testament," 300 (Sevenster, e.g., does not "enrich our understanding" of Paul).
25. His program is evidenced in his various essays and two large books on St. Paul and the Stoics. In addition to the essay at the beginning of *Paul and the Stoics*, Engberg-Pedersen's responses to his critics constitute the clearest and most explicit articulation of the commitments that underlie his larger project.
26. The exceptions are the incisive responses in *JSNT* by Martyn, "De-Apocalypticizing Paul," 61–102; and Barclay, "Stoic Physics and the Christ-Event," 406–14.
27. Engberg-Pedersen, *Cosmology and Self*, 2.
28. Engberg-Pedersen, *Paul and the Stoics*, 3.
29. See his responses in the *Journal for the Study of the New Testament* and, to some degree, in *Zeitschrift für die neutestamentliche Wissenchaft und die Kunde der älteren Kirche* to Philip Esler.

30. Engberg-Pedersen, *Paul and the Stoics*, 301 et passim.
31. Smith, "In Comparison a Magic Dwells"; Smith says "invent" because of the principle of "association" (the way in which memory works to put things in relation to one another, whether such things have a real relation or not). "Association" as a way humans think has much occupied us since Hume.
32. For a remarkably stimulating discussion of the opposite view, see Jonathan Tran's brief discussion of Heidegger's view of death (*The Vietnam War and Theologies of Memory*, 65–67, esp. 66). Tran shows how it is impossible to divorce being from becoming, which is a serious point against the view that we can focus on ideas alone. Focusing on ideas alone requires a knowing subject who knows things in his own being without becoming, and this is impossible (Tran's discussion of Heidegger's critique of Kant's pure knowing, which is also very helpful, emphasizes that Kant posits an a priori knowing ego that then has objects in its being-known—and this, it turns out, is both impossible and related to an avoidance of death).
33. Engberg-Pedersen, *Paul and the Stoics*, 304.
34. Habermas comes to mind, but there are others.
35. The word *God* is of course only one of many possible examples. The point would hold for the scholarly use of words such as *moral progress* (*prokopē*) or even the more modern use of the word *self*: for Engberg-Pedersen, this way of talking is conceptually general enough to encompass the divergent uses of these terms/ideas in Stoicism and Christianity.
36. Engberg-Pedersen, "Paul's Body: A Response to Barclay and Levison," 433–43. Engberg-Pedersen has liked the emic/etic terminology for a long time. For a confusing attempt to join them together—which would make what perspective?—see his introduction to *Paul Beyond the Judaism/Hellenism Divide*, 11–13.
37. Engberg-Pedersen, "Paul's Body: A Response to Barclay and Levison," 442. Engberg-Pedersen says that Barclay is emic (inside Paul) and he himself is etic (outside Paul)—and then goes on to say theology should also be like this: it should elucidate the inside from the outside perspective and should be wed to outside perspective (such as scholarly discourse). Theology is finally then religious language on the same plane as scholarly language.
38. It has deep roots, however, in the Stoic theory of logos, nature, and so on. The Stoics are the first cosmopolitans. Engberg-Pedersen has also been deeply influenced by the Stoics themselves.
39. Though Engberg-Pedersen is correct that "the scholarly exercise of comparing and contrasting Paul and Stoicism is no more than at its very beginning," there is nevertheless an abundance of essays that engage this or that aspect of their relation ("The Relationship with Others: Similarities and Differences Between Paul and Stoicism," 60). See also, for example, the essays in Dunderberg, Engberg-Pedersen, and Rasimus, *Stoicism in Early Christianity*; Thorsteinsson's book on Paul, *Roman Christianity and Roman Stoicism*; the essay on the Passions in John Fitzgerald's book, *Passions and Moral Progress in Greco-Roman Thought*. And so on.
40. To return to Jonathan Smith's terms, it is not that similarity and difference are simply discovered—out there, as it were, to see for anyone who took the trouble to look. They

are instead "invented" (Smith, "In Comparison a Magic Dwells"). I think this language is ultimately too strong, but it makes a conceptual point that is true to the comparative question: that comparison is always already comparison within some wider hermeneutical frame. Smith is often cited but his point seldom taken on board.

41. Plutarch's *Moralia*, for example, are not this at all, nor are Diogenes' *Lives*—even though both sorts of works aim to illustrate particular positions on character, virtue, life, and so on.
42. For Malherbe the wider net is usually the "Hellenistic moralists."
43. Strictly speaking, morality as such/in general cannot be thought. (It is the same with action, as MacIntyre argued in *After Virtue*, and with intention, as Elizabeth Anscomb argued in *Intention:* an intelligible action is a more fundamental concept than action per se; intelligible intention is a more fundamental concept than intention in general.) Incidentally, some of these matters are as interesting and old as Plato and Aristotle. You can't think "duck" in general but only particular sorts of ducks. And yet we know what a "duck" is and is not. Why? Plato: it participates in the form "Duck"; Aristotle: we discern the similarities of the particulars and abstract to make "Duck": either way, we don't *know* what Duck is and can't think it. We can sort of "chase" it through ducks, but not think it.
44. Often these are passions on the one side and virtues on the other.
45. See C. Kavin Rowe, "The Art of Retrieval: Stoicism?" esp. 716 on "general virtue." The point applies also to the passions. What, for example, is anger (*ira*) as such? One cannot answer this question.
46. Scholars of morality reproduce the distinctly modern side of the rupture between morality as a largely independent category of thought/practice and the rest of life. The very fact that we can speak of morality as such testifies to a profound change in our conception of how human life is to be understood. By continuing to employ modern morality grammar for ancient life, scholars inevitably "modernize" the ancient philosophers and thereby further obfuscate the problem of comparison.
47. MacIntyre, *Whose Justice?* 327.
48. In a sense, of course, this is hardly surprising. We cannot think apart from the lives we live, which is to say that the historicity of human understanding is constitutive of whatever understanding could itself mean. If we are to read the ancients at all, we will inevitably understand them in our own terms. There are, however, different ways of displaying the historicity of understanding—different interpretative projects, in other words, that render their objects more or less clearly, and more or less in line with the grammar of the sources. In the case of comparison between the New Testament and ancient philosophy, what has been billed as a particular form of scholarly discourse is in fact a hermeneutically overwhelming project of encyclopedic absorption.
49. In areas of politics, for example.
50. See MacIntyre, *Dependent Rational Animals,* for a positive account of the human creature who reasons. See MacIntyre, *Whose Justice?* for an account that complicates how we know what rationality actually is; in particular, pages 326–403 are critically important to the argument above.

51. Could an aborigine understand Engberg-Pedersen's reasoning? Presumably so, Engberg-Pedersen would answer, if he were trained in a way that would allow him to understand it. But just here we see that it's not ordinary human intelligibility that Engberg-Pedersen is talking about but something more like the capacity to understand given this or that formation. This or that formation is the crucial point. What is the capacity? We cannot say without utter redundancy or tautology (for example, capacity = reason). Of course, the entire question becomes even more complicated when we try to sort out what "reason" is vis-à-vis mentally ill or mentally handicapped people. Particular views of reasoning capacity are often tied to a notion of what it means to be human in a way that winds up presenting the ill or handicapped as deficient in a manner that compromises their humanity.
52. One might wonder how to relate these claims to "ordinary language" philosophy (for example, Stanley Cavell). I think it's something like this: Cavell is not positing the existence of some universal language that is based in a universal type of rationality—so the term *ordinary* does mean ordinary in that sense—but is instead talking about language as it is ordinarily used and the way that ordinary language is rooted in, for example, the constraints of life (ninety-foot basepaths on a baseball field rather than nine thousand feet, and so on). "Ordinary" means something like the way language that is regularly used or lived displays philosophical knowledge of human life, which is quite different from the sort of use of ordinary that we see in Engberg-Pedersen.
53. Pfau, *Minding the Modern*, 3. Compare his entire discussion of modernity's "reaction against the mere suggestion that to *know* might depend on the cultivation of moral and intellectual virtues such as patience, good sense, moderation, and studiousness" (13, emphasis in original). Pfau shows, among a great many other important things, that the humanities as a whole participate in the modern tendency to divorce the shape of one's life from what one is able to know. In this they forsake their only purpose in the university—hence the desperate and pathetic attempts of many universities to justify the money spent on the humanities by claiming that the humanities (somehow) really do serve society.
54. Pfau, for example, dates it to Duns Scotus and the nominalists. Pierre Hadot dates it even earlier. The figure of Descartes is often in play, but in relation to this question even the interpretation of his project is debated. Bernard Williams's classic book talks about Descartes in terms of "pure enquiry," but Hadot reads Descartes's *Meditations* as active spiritual exercises (which would not be pure inquiry). As evidence of the split that came to be, no one is clearer than Hegel. See his *Lectures on the History of Philosophy 1825–26*: "In what sense do we wish to treat the history of philosophy, namely, the history of free, concrete thought, or of reason? Nothing counts as reason that is not the result of thinking. *Thought that is free is thought that relates itself to itself. . . . Thought alone has significance on its own account*" (1:209–10; Oxford critical edition, 48; emphasis added).
55. Obviously, the modern divisions are closely related to the developments in natural science, but that is a topic for another time.
56. Pfau, *Minding the Modern*, 91 et passim. Malherbe obviously understands the importance of "psychagogy" but then somehow presents his material as "information" all the same.

57. Taylor, *Sources of the Self,* 160. Taylor's own term for this picture of the self is the "punctual self."
58. Taylor, *Sources of the Self,* 161–76. Cf. Simon Haines's description of the same self: "universalizing, featureless, dimensionless, rational isolated self" (Haines, "Deepening the Self," 21–38).
59. Taylor, *Sources of the Self,* esp. 161–63.
60. Certain kinds of scientific knowledge, for example, may require such objectification, but scientists themselves need not be aware of the philosophical anthropology that accompanies the shape of their work. Indeed, unless they have somewhere acquired a philosophical education, many excellent scientists would doubtless not even know what Taylor is talking about.
61. Taylor, *Sources of the Self,* 164: "The option for an epistemology which privileges disengagement and control isn't self-evidently right. It requires certain assumptions."
62. When we approach texts as if *our* reading them is not part of the way we "live in our experience," we have stepped outside our lives and into the role of "mind"—a thinking thing that interprets texts by itself—and this stepping outside creates the need to "take up the slack," to say how and why this sort of move is possible and good and right when it comes to ancient texts of the kind we're talking about. Think only of the different kinds of reading: we don't read urgent messages outside our lived experience, of course, and these ancient texts are more like urgent messages (about life) than anything else.
63. This is a very tricky phrase: it calls to mind the tension in Karl Popper's old point about the impossibility of anticipating true innovation (we cannot anticipate the invention of the wheel, for example, for in the very anticipation itself we would have already invented it). The word for the objectified self in the sense we are talking about is usually "scholar." Even Epictetus's teaching on the *prohairesis* does not imply that it can make judgments apart from the shape of the life in which judgments take place. Indeed, part of Epictetus's point is that the *prohairesis* won't work correctly unless it is disciplined.
64. The picture of self, that is, depends on the self-objectification of a mind that knows. But there is no such mind.
65. MacIntyre, *Whose Justice?* 11.
66. I say "the narrative": this does not exclude the complexity of a narrative that makes us want to say "narratives." I resist using the plural, however, because it seems to me obvious that if there is a form of life that is recognizable as a tradition it will have enough of a story line to be seen as such. That there is debate over this story line, that there are multiple and perhaps competing accounts of its main points or central tenets/practices, that there are those within its ambit who seek to get free of it, and so on—all this is simply taken for granted.
67. MacIntyre, *After Virtue,* esp. 190–209. We should not imagine, that is, that we are situating two things in relation to some more fundamental basis—such as the abstraction "morality" or specific epistemological principles.
68. The indispensability of narrative for the location of life is true for communities no less than individuals. David Kelsey, for example, shows well how "narrative identities" are

the way we get at the "unsubstitutable concreteness" of a particular human life (*Eccentric Existence*, 2.614 et passim), but particular communities are also "unsubstitutably concrete" insofar as we are able to locate them at all. If we ask, how do we know where to locate them—as Christians, say—we will wind up with narrative.

69. Sometimes biblical scholars think of narrative primarily in terms of "genre"—over against poetry or letter or something of that sort. This is understandable, but it misses the more significant fact that we can't even know the meaning of words like *Israel* (and so on) without the stories that tell us who Israel was/is.

70. As Hans Frei amply demonstrated more than forty years ago, the loss of the awareness of narrative as a constitutive feature of human understanding was made possible by particular developments in modern hermeneutics (*Eclipse of Biblical Narrative*). To put it all too simply, history was reconceptualized as an area of inquiry distinct from story. *Eclipse* is such an important book that it is worth every cent of the struggle with the prose.

71. A significant exception is a portion of Wayne Meeks, *The Origins of Christian Morality*. In chapters 10–11, Meeks uses story as a way to understand the formation of early Christianity's moral imagination. Of critical importance is his observation of the difference between the Christian story's comprehensive sweep—with beginning, middle, and end—and the more limited scope of the narratives in the pagan world (though it should be noted that even those narratives imply things about the beginning and end, even if their temporal index differs from that of the Christian narrative). Meeks has read some of MacIntyre (and Hauerwas), but he nevertheless misses the chance to make narrative a more fundamentally important way to describe Christian difference/newness precisely because he misses the point that intelligibility of the sort that is bound up with the interpretation of ancient texts is dependent upon narratives. Still, after more than twenty years, Meeks's chapters have much to commend them, and it is a puzzlement why they have not had more methodological effect on those who think about Christianity and the Greco-Roman world. In a different sphere: in some important ways, this absence of a sense of the importance of narrative is what makes the Polynesian taboo unintelligible to the European encyclopedists (MacIntyre's example). It's not only that they don't understand the "morality" of the Polynesians; it's that they don't know the narrative that would make such morality make sense to the Polynesians.

72. Taylor, *A Secular Age*. His chief example is a demonstration in a democracy. For an attempt to think about the New Testament with Taylor's taxonomy see Rowe, *World Upside Down*. On the issue of "contextualization" for meaning, see also Taylor's chapter "Language Not Mysterious?" in *Dilemmas and Connections*, 39–55. Taylor speaks of the modern tradition as Descartes, etc., and calls their atomism a "tunnel" from which we are finally beginning to emerge.

73. See the essays in Jones and Hauerwas, *Why Narrative?* This is not to say that the narratives are on the surface; they are often inchoate or left unarticulated. But they are still there. Even those who want to move away from narrative have to tell a story about why/how we can leave narrative behind. I am not making an "essence claim" about human experience (see Stephen Crites's "homemade phenomenology" in "The Narrative Quality of Experience") but only saying that this is how things work.

74. Even if one were to say that this or that narrative did not have an account of the beginning/end, it would still imply "takes" on the beginning/end; agnosticism about beginnings/endings simply means that you do not know what your take is, not that you do not have one. A good Socratic questioner could easily enough dig up some basic convictions about the beginning and the end. In any event, Stoics and Christians do have takes on the beginning/end.
75. Incidentally, this is why those moderns who retained a notion of the importance of "myth"—in the broad sense of a founding discourse for a particular tradition—worked more closely with the grain of human understanding than those who thought all things explicable in natural scientific terms (NB, even the natural sciences have narratives by which they both operate and understand their own development). So, too, Plato's understanding of poetry belies a sense that when it comes to origins we cannot do without stories.
76. The difficulty we sometimes have with locating texts in this or that tradition—how Stoic is Seneca? how Academic is Cicero? and so on—is really a difficulty over knowing how well this or that text fits within the narrative we presuppose to describe the traditions in which we seek to place the texts.
77. See Richard Hays's discussion of the surface structure of the argument vis-à-vis the implied narrative in Paul's letter to the Galatians (*The Faith of Jesus Christ*).
78. Conversely, the debate about what philosophy someone adheres to, or where to locate his texts philosophically, is a debate about which stories enable us to locate them.
79. A maker of excellent furniture would still have to learn how to smith. . . . The knowledge of hammer and anvil are not the same knowledge as that of saw and chisel.
80. MacIntyre, *Whose Justice?* 374 et passim. MacIntyre also speaks of "overhearing" another tradition (350). In the next two chapters of the book, we will discuss MacIntyre's view of how well one can really learn another tradition.
81. The study of "parallels" is an example of sentence matching. Engberg-Pedersen's "model" has lots of sentence matching.
82. MacIntyre, *Whose Justice?* 382: "Learning its language and being initiated into [a] community's tradition . . . is one and the same initiation."
83. MacIntyre, *Whose Justice?* 375.
84. MacIntyre, *Whose Justice?* 374. Emphasis added. As we will see, the "if not quite" is as important as the rest of the entire sentence.
85. MacIntyre, *Whose Justice?* 395 (cf. 166–67).
86. MacIntyre, *Whose Justice?* 382–83.
87. One could test one's skill, for example, by forging a "Senecan" fragment.
88. MacIntyre, *Whose Justice?* 375.
89. MacIntyre, *Three Rival Versions,* 114.
90. For use of Esperanto see the discussion of Stout, *Ethics After Babel,* in Chapter 9.
91. Cf. Diamond on "thick concepts," in "Losing Your Concepts," 255–77. The importance of "thick" goes back to Geertz and Ryle.
92. Knowing what we do not know presupposes that we know it; strict ignorance means that we really don't know. The most important insight of Martha Nussbaum's *Therapy of Desire* is precisely that her character Nikidion has to live the different traditions to

know which one she wants to choose. Of course, Nussbaum's Nikidion looks suspiciously like the "liberal self" and is in this way problematical for Nussbaum's overall project. But it is dead right about the need to live to learn.

93. Another way to put this would be to say that the "if not quite" in MacIntyre's statement—"those with the requisite linguistic and historical skills can so immerse themselves that they can become almost, *if not quite*, surrogate participants in such societies as those of fifth-century Athens"—has as much weight as a human life itself. MacIntyre's confidence in the ability of one tradition to overcome rationally another tradition is a correlative of his confidence in philosophy/natural reason as a part of the philosophy/theology division. We shall return to this matter in Chapter 9. (One could mention the way MacIntyre characterizes Aquinas's solution to Augustine or Aristotle. MacIntyre says, of course, that Aquinas overcomes the choice by uniting them and thereby extends the Christian tradition. But this way of talking about it still overlooks the fact that Aquinas was not living as an Aristotelian. His life was lived through the Christian worship and devotional pattern, not in the Lyceum or Lyceum-like disciplines.)
94. For example, insofar as I've been able to learn from them, I've learned that my tradition doesn't have a word for the world that their word *Fortuna* expresses.
95. The significance of this fact will be treated in Chapter 9.

8. TRADITIONS IN JUXTAPOSITION

1. The epigraph is from *Mekhilta d'Rabbi Yishmael* (J. Z. Lauterbach translation, Judah Goldin adaptation, 197–99). R. Yishmael goes on to say that God can also listen to more than one voice at a time—indeed can hear the whole world at once.
2. I will, however, use the words *Christian(ity)* and *Stoic(ism)* as shorthand for the-Christianity-of-Paul-Luke-Justin and the-Stoicism-of-Seneca-Epictetus-Marcus. Anything else is simply too cumbersome and distracting.
3. This would be true even from the outsiders' perspective: in his *Philosophies for Sale,* e.g., Lucian of Samosata uses the name Chrysippus to speak for the Stoic positions. The Loeb helpfully, I think, translates *Chrysippus* as "Stoic."
4. Still, a history of Stoicism is not the same thing as the story that makes the history possible as a distinct and particular history. Yet they are obviously related.
5. This is evident in the term scholars give to them, the "Roman Stoics." Others are included in this designation—most significantly, Musonius Rufus and occasionally Dio Chrysostom (Gill), but by and large we mean the texts of the Big Three when we speak of what we know about Roman Stoicism.
6. Stoics believe that everything is material (including souls). It is unclear in the history of Stoicism whether they spoke of one recurring cycle where everything would be the same, or a recurring cycle with the same material but different combinations of it, or cycles within some larger cycle, and so on (see, for example, the essay on cosmology in *Cambridge Companion*). For our authors it amounts to much the same thing. Whether or not the same world will come round again—another Seneca, another Marcus—is not finally settled, or at least it is not finally ruled out. But their comments on death suggest that they do not expect to exist again as themselves. This is why Long's point in

his essay on *Conflagratio* is difficult to swallow in relation to the texts of the Roman Stoics. It just doesn't seem like Seneca, Epictetus, or Marcus expect to exist again in the same way. See also the following note.

7. As I already mentioned, it is a matter of some debate—within both Stoicism and its modern interpreters—which exact construal of "recurrence" we should adopt. See especially A. A. Long, "The Stoics on World-Conflagration and Everlasting Occurrence," who argues that everlasting recurrence means that the cosmos repeats itself in all its self-identical particulars. Socrates, for example, will return as Socrates and will do the same things Socrates did "last time" and "the next time." Long's clarity is—as always—admirable, and his thesis may work for Chrysippus and older Stoic "orthodoxy," but it does not square with Seneca or Marcus (despite the fact that Long cites Marcus, *Med.* 2.14; 11.1–2). Much of the discussion is bound up with how one interprets Stoic commitments to cosmic "determinism." The degree to which particular things recur is prima facie related in a rather strict sense to the degree that things are (pre)determined. Michael J. White, "Stoic Natural Philosophy (Physics and Cosmology)," 142–44, argues that the Stoics are front-runners of "soft determinism," which would obviously be incompatible with the type of recurrence for which Long argues.
8. Determinism is a major part of the Stoic tradition, but exactly what is meant by it turns out to be rather complex. In one important sense all Stoics are determinists: the whole cosmos runs the way it runs. There is no "open" future. The cosmos is simply going to go along to or away from the conflagration. As a whole, however, it would true to say that the language of the Roman Stoics is hard to reconcile with the strictest form of determinism.
9. The rational order may evoke praise or something like prayer—though the word here is conceptually difficult to use—but such reactions are but comments on the sublimity or excellence of reason.
10. Much, perhaps, like the dualism of later Manicheans (though without their distinction between good and evil).
11. The phrase "pandemic error" is from Tad Brennan, "Stoic Moral Psychology," 258. Brennan uses it to talk about how widespread error is among human species (answers the question, are there many who are in error?), but it also works to describe the range and depth of our particular errors.
12. Of course this is unfair to Augustine himself (who obviously thinks he needs to be taught to know how to read well). I am primarily thinking of the way the scene in the *Confessions* can be used.
13. Of recent commentators, Pierre Hadot has shown this with particular clarity. Diogenes Laertius lists dozens of works of various Stoics. He also mentions an introductory textbook, as it were.
14. It is possible to become a good enough reader to read safely outside the Stoic tradition. Seneca can "go into the enemy's camp"—that is, read Epicurus—but always as a "scout" and not as a "deserter."
15. Learning the intellectual finery of a Chrysippus, for example, was inseparable from the Stoic pattern of life that made such finery intelligible as that which you needed to learn.

16. Brennan, "Stoic Moral Psychology," 261, n. 8, gives a philosophically astute analysis of the Stoic sense of impressions. In some ways, his analysis works less well for the language of the Roman Stoics than it does for some earlier fragments—or for the comments of Diogenes Laertius and Plutarch, for example—but in one crucial respect his discussion is especially illuminating. In contrast to what was later meant by impressions, Brennan clearly explains how for the Stoics impressions are not just sensory data; they are instead interpreted data—a "psychic entity" even—that correlate with one's body of working concepts (or, in Epictetus's language, one's preconceptions).
17. Brennan, one of the most lively contemporary writers on Stoicism, gets it wrong here when he thinks the memory work Epictetus gives is somehow noncognitive or only a "catechetical pushup" in the sense of not really reasoning ("Stoic Moral Psychology," 278–79).
18. Most elegantly, perhaps, Nussbaum. See also Brennan's comment on pushups.
19. Indeed, even conceiving of "impressions" as the way we are in the world—at least as the Stoics conceive of impressions—is a kind of cognitive read of the whole thing.
20. That is, it allows for multiple developments within an overarching unity.
21. What we were "made for" in a loose sense of "made."
22. Inasmuch as a human life can be depicted only through narrative means, the Gospel form is philosophically necessary to the claims about Jesus' life made by the early Christians.
23. On Luke as Paul's theological disciple, see briefly the appendix on Luke/Paul/John in Rowe, *Early Narrative Christology*, and the treatment of Acts 17 in Rowe, *World Upside Down* (contra Vielhauer and legions like him); on Luke as Paul's probable traveling companion see Fitzmyer, *Luke* (though this point is not necessary for argument here); on Justin and Luke, see Susan Wendel's *Scriptural Interpretation and Community Self-Definition in Luke-Acts and the Writings of Justin Martyr.* There is some argument about whether or not Justin knew Paul's letters, since he does not directly cite them. See T. J. Lang's Duke dissertation, "Mystery and the Making of a Christian Historical Consciousness," the most recent summary of the research on this question. Lang rightly concludes that Justin did know Paul's letters.
24. Ancient argument was often trying to say "we're the oldest" (we're not new). This is partly why the charge against Athens in Acts 17 that Paul is introducing something "new" *has bite in antiquity*. That this is opposite of our contemporary culture's emphasis on novelty hardly needs to be said.
25. The reason I say "perhaps" is that it is not clear to me that Pilate would know to ask this on his own. It is more readily understandable as the question he knows to ask in light of his contact with the Jewish authorities (they describe to him how exactly Jesus is a threat to the order required at Passover and help him know what to ask in order to convict and execute Jesus).
26. Against those who think that the nonhuman world is undamaged and fundamentally there for the observer (theoretically construed as one who can see clearly) to see in its empirical truth Romans 8 could not be clearer: all creation is damaged. I do not know how a flower or a tree or a cloud or a worm is unreliable in its self-presentation, but there is a rather deep sense in which Christians are committed to saying such possibilities exist.

27. See Paul J. Griffiths on "devastated time" in *Decreation.*
28. Trypho doesn't see it, of course, but the point is that the very fact of the argument shows the commitment to the Law's role in testifying to the Christ.
29. This is scripturally shaped theology. Like the Jews before them, the early Christians took the Scriptures of Israel to speak of the living God in dynamic ways. God was not a monad in the scriptural story but Wisdom and Word and Spirit.
30. For those who wonder about such things, this is why Barth's defense of the *filioque* clause is so compelling theologically. But the clause does not have to be in the Constantinopolitan creed because of historical (it was added later) and ecumenical reasons.
31. The story does not have a chapter called "what we wish were the case but know is not."
32. A lot of the discussion over differing eschatologies within the New Testament is making mountains out of molehills. Most early Christians knew both that the world was continuing on as before and that Jesus was going to return. Between these two basic affirmations there was room for differing emphasis—depending on local context, subject under discussion, a writer's temperament, and virtually countless other matters.
33. Justin himself, however, might draw attention to the biblical stories of Enoch and Elijah.
34. Most of the dating, authorship, or provenance questions are guesswork. This sentence—sometime, somewhere, someone—is intended to reflect that fact. Both Jerome and Augustine know of the document.
35. Eusebius's *Ecclesiastical History* tells of a picture of St. Paul in philosopher's garb—material evidence of this type of thinking. The letters between Paul and Seneca actually say remarkably little in the way of substantive discussion.
36. *Translation,* after all, is the word we normally use to speak of the relation between different natural languages.
37. MacIntyre, *Whose Justice?* 373 et passim. Good dictionaries, such as the *Oxford English Dictionary* (OED) for English or the *Thesaurus linguae graecae* (*TLG*) for Greek, show the historical depth of how a word is actually used and why, therefore, it has the associations for us that it does. Philosophically speaking, what the historical depth also shows, however, is that there is no such thing as the word-as-such. The meaning is the word-in-use. Cf. Wittgenstein, *Culture and Value,* 22e, where he notes that language can fool us into thinking everything looks the same. The dictionary, above all, is where such trickery happens: "the power language has to make everything look the same, which is most glaringly [or: crassly] evident in the dictionary." Orthography is only minimally complicated: while it is true that one has to know the Hebrew letters, for example, to know that the language one is reading is in fact Hebrew, knowing the Hebrew letters does not mean one knows the meaning of what one is reading. That meaning will depend upon the specific use of the words.
38. MacIntyre, *Whose Justice?* 373. Page numbers cited subsequently in the text are from this work.
39. Because distinct communities often share linguistic patterns with the larger culture of which they are a part, MacIntyre resorts to speaking of a "primary linguistic community" as a way to talk about how language-in-use can describe both a community's distinctive pattern of usage and its shared usage with the wider society.

40. If one were to object that Jesus was a common name, MacIntyre's logic would simply have us reply: yes, of course. But the point is that you cannot understand any use of the name Jesus—the way this particular name specifies that particular person—apart from the linguistic community in which it makes sense to use this name to specify that person. The point thus holds even for common names.
41. As I say elsewhere, "words are deeds," which in this case is simply to say that the meaning of a tradition's words is lived within the particularity of the tradition itself (*Culture and Value*, 46e). Wittgensteinian thought would also caution us, however, against turning "word meaning=use" into a general theory that would cover all words at all times in all places. See *Philosophical Investigations*, 43: "For a *large* class of cases of the employment of the word 'meaning'—though not for *all*—this word can be explained in this way: the meaning of a word is its use in the language" (emphasis in original).
42. Seneca's choice to write in Latin is interesting for a variety of reasons, not least of which is the Ciceronian-like statement that serious philosophy can be done in Latin. See MacIntyre, *Whose Justice?* 372, for a brief but accurate philosophical description of Cicero's linguistic task (which would, *mutatis mutandis*, apply to Seneca).
43. Isolating this or that issue does not do enough work with the traditions as traditions. If rivalry between traditions is most profoundly recognized by the fact of untranslatability, this rivalry can nevertheless be discerned only through larger patterns of untranslatability.
44. Because this way of speaking is both frequent and widespread, substantiation is virtually pointless. One can read through the essays in *Greeks, Romans, and Christians* (the Festschrift for Malherbe) or Dunderberg et al., *Stoicism in Early Christianity* to get the flavor.
45. Byers, *Perception, Sensibility, and Moral Motivation in Augustine*, esp. 158–59.
46. This is evident in any number of places in Colish's two volumes (*The Stoic Tradition from Antiquity to the Early Middle Ages*), but see, e.g., esp. 2.153–59, or 2.293.
47. Which turns out to mean that *eidōlon/eikōn/simulacrum* in the more spiritualized sense is the best rendering of the Stoic use of *God* in Christian terms (not images per se, but the way we confuse aspects of the creation with the reality of God).
48. I choose *Providence* because this word is often taken to imply that the Christians and Stoics believe something similar about God's general direction of the cosmos. Both the Christians and the Stoics, it is assumed, believe in Providence. One is tempted to say—and here I give in—that one who has read Seneca's treatise *On Providence* and who knows something about the way the early Christians conceived of God's relation to the world cannot possibly believe there is much in the way of synonymy *unless* one already thinks the God whose Providence they describe is the same God. But there is no reason to think this and every reason not to think it. See briefly, Rowe, "Art of Retrieval," 713–14.
49. Cf. Rowe, *World Upside Down*, esp. 17–18.
50. As far as I can tell, no Stoic text offers an explanation for *why* we emerge in the world in some degree of estrangement from our nature. Many passages in multiple texts assume that we are, for example, ignorant of what we need to do, but they do not tell us why we are ignorant in the first place. What is the human condition that makes us ignorant or

subject to passions such that we tend in these damaging directions and must have Stoicism as a reparative solution to our problem? If it is our nature to be rational, why do we depart from our nature—not in this or that instance that could be explained by ignorance or the passions, but at all? This is a question that receives no answer.

51. Recall that for the Pauline Christians one is either a slave to sin or a slave to Christ.
52. See MacIntyre's discussion of names in *Whose Justice?*, esp. 376–79.
53. Or at least *founder* would become so general as to apply to anyone who stood at the origin of any distinct tradition. This does not get us far at all down the road of knowing similarity. In fact, it obscures all the significant difference (which must be thought if similarity is to be seen).
54. For example, the Stoics and Christians do not mean the same thing by *matter* or *spirit* or *soul* and so would not mean the same thing by *body*—even a description such as "bodily death," therefore, does not help us to get the Stoics and Christians closer together.
55. In recent times, Karl Barth is the theologian of witness. See Hauerwas on Barth in *With the Grain of the Universe.*
56. And, of course, the association of the Christians with the Epicureans was not unknown (for example, Lucian in *Alexander the False Prophet*).
57. For a book that explores political deviance in the Roman Empire, Ramsay MacMullen's *Enemies of Roman Order* is still the place to start—despite MacIntyre's legitimately critical review, "Ancient Politics and Modern Issues," 425–30.
58. Common pursuits will be entirely contingent and ad hoc, not based in substantive narrative similarity. On "hospitality" as the practice necessary to sustain ad hoc common political pursuits, see my colleague Luke Bretherton's *Hospitality as Holiness.*
59. In MacIntyre's terms, their languages-in-use cannot be translated.
60. Bultmann, "Anknüpfung und Widerspruch: Zur Frage nach der Anknüpfung der neutestamentlichen Verkündigung an die natürliche Theologie der Stoa, die hellenistischen Mysterienreligionen und die Gnosis," 401–18.
61. Because of the discursive nature of thought in writing, it is impossible not to present these things as one and then the other, but really they occur simultaneously.
62. Encyclopedic rationality once again proves to be in the background of those who think we can resolve arguments between traditions without conversion to one or the other.
63. Rowe, *World Upside Down*, 116–26.
64. Think of Paul's criticism of Peter in Galatians. One can live an untrue life.
65. Williams, *Ethics and the Limits of Philosophy*, esp. chaps. 8 and 9 (quotation from page 160).
66. Both the Christians and the Stoics answer that we cannot know ahead of the choice to live in a certain way that we have chosen not to waste the only life we can live. We learn through the living of our one life whether or not we have chosen well. If, after being inducted into the tradition that shapes our lives, we discover that we have chosen poorly, it may well be too late. And, truth be told, you don't ever really know. Death will reveal the wisdom of the choice (or not, but Christians hope so). Such is the human lot. Creatureliness really is that deep.

9. THE ARGUMENT OF RIVAL TRADITIONS

1. The epigraph is from Taylor, "Understanding the Other," 24.
2. *Ethics After Babel* originally spawned much discussion, leading to a new edition in 2001. Page numbers cited subsequently in the text are from this work. The book itself is better than the discussion of it. In general, Stout's work is among the richest reading in contemporary religion, ethics, and politics. *Democracy and Tradition* and *Blessed Are the Organized*, for example, are not only exemplary for the rigor of the arguments but delightfully well written.
3. "Esperanto," says Stout, drawing on a derisively accurate way to describe encyclopedic thought, "becomes the language of morals, it rules the deep structure of morality as such" (*Ethics After Babel*, 5).
4. Stout, *Ethics After Babel*, 57. The image of the boat occurs first in Plutarch's *Life of Theseus* (vol. 1 of *Vitae*).
5. The image works for Stout in two more specific ways: (a) pragmatic: we work at what is needed; (b) creative: when it comes to what is needed, we are not bound to a plodding sort of work but may in fact be remarkably creative in what we do. Stout uses this image in a self-written "objection" to his project as a way to allow him to say more about his overall recommendations for moral discernment and practice.
6. Stout uses the word *language* to describe what "moral creole" is, but his larger point would be better served by speaking of linguistic patterns rather than of language. He quite clearly means the former, as is evidenced by his example of the grammar surrounding "human rights."
7. See, e.g., Wittgenstein, *Philosophical Investigations*, 208.
8. This would further depend, of course, on what one means by *natural*. Extending the thought experiment to make the point: who knows what (say) Martians might speak? For Christians, if there are Martians, they are God's creatures. But we do not know that we could ever understand them or they us. Stout is not a modernist, but he remains cosmopolitan.
9. The most insightful brief criticism of Davidson known to me is Taylor, "Understanding the Other," 24–38, esp. 33–35.
10. Throughout his book, Stout assumes definitions of "reason" and "competency" that are not suitably defended. That all reasonable people surely are against this or that is a recurrent form of his argument; for example, we are all against worshiping great basketball players (*Ethics After Babel*, 51). Well, given a certain culture, a certain way of thinking of reason, and so on, we may be against this or that; in practice, of course, it does not look like many Americans are against worshiping professional athletes. Stout's sort of pragmatism is seductive precisely because it is one giant *avoiding* of the hardest questions. One is tempted to think that we don't have to answer the hardest questions with the living of our lives.
11. This is not to say that such things do not happen, of course. Even MacIntyre acknowledges the combination and intertwining of traditions: "It can happen that two traditions, hitherto independent and even antagonistic, can come to recognize certain possibilities of fundamental agreement and reconstitute themselves as a single, more complex debate" (MacIntyre, *Whose Justice?* 12).

12. This is one way to understand Engberg-Pedersen's model-making.
13. By "platitude" Stout does not mean "insignificant moral achievement" but merely something taken for granted that lies in the background of our moral reasoning (*Ethics After Babel*, 210–19). Some of the platitudes he names are vast moral achievements, for example, "We all agree that nuclear destruction would be bad" (214)—though even here rhetoric abounds (surely we do not *all* agree about nuclear destruction; many would presumably be glad to see others destroyed by nukes were there to be no ramifications upon the destroyers). The example I give of Christian/Stoic agreement is a random one, but it would open out onto a whole range of questions about citizenship, about violence, and so on.
14. Stout, *Ethics After Babel*, 214–16. Presumably there must be the "right conditions" for platitudes to do massive moral work: in our time, for example, the development of democratic institutions and processes are the right conditions for the sort of platitudes Stout likes. What "right" conditions existed for democratic institutions and practices to develop is a historically and conceptually more complex question.
15. Stout, *Ethics After Babel*, 215. Stout's focus, of course, is on the present, but he maintains that it applies to earlier societies as well (e.g., 217)—as well he should, given his rejection of an original moral unity.
16. As Long said about Stoicism: "Although Stoicism in antiquity was pillaged by eclectics, in the eyes of its greatest exegete Chrysippus, it was an all-or-nothing system" ("Stoicism in the Philosophical Tradition," 367). Long goes on to say that Cicero is correct when he states on behalf of the Stoics that "Stoic philosophy is coherent through and through—a system such that to remove one letter would be to destroy the whole account. Although Stoicism does not have Spinoza's geometrical rigor, its rationalist ambition was similar to his. No modern philosopher, as far as I know, has ever taken this Stoic claim to complete coherence seriously, but I believe it is the key to the original system and to much of its appeal" (368). Cf. Veyne, *Seneca*, 45: "In a sort of forward retreat, Stoicism reasons by all or nothing."
17. Justin's *Apology* could be read as attempting to identify points of overlapping consensus with Roman (legal) culture, some of which would obviously include matters with which Stoics could easily agree. The trick, however, is that Justin also claims that these are not the heart of the matter, that the pagans are blinded by demons, and so on. In short, focusing on overlapping consensus or "platitudes" in Stout's sense tends to overlook the crucial fact that the same is often not the same, that is, the same words can often mean entirely different things. *Philosophia* itself is a crucial example. See my discussion of Justin's use of this word in Chapter 6.
18. Wittgenstein, *Culture and Value*, 32e (emphasis in original).
19. There is perhaps nothing so modern academic and university-like in Stout's book than this: we can solve our problems by talking more. An analogy: speak (say) Chinese to me all day long; I still won't understand you. Stout might reply: live in China, or listen to Chinese for years, and you will. I reply: but the whole time you're still living your life. And at the end you may understand that you've been hearing nothing contentwise but worthless prattle the whole time . . . Then you've wasted your life. In short: we cannot get out of our existential pickle. Sometimes disagreements are not about

this or that particular decision or issue but about the whole background that will come to form, in Stout's terms, the platitudes you wind up sharing. Stout says we do not need a "third thing" (for example, a hermeneutical theory) to translate between traditions that disagree. But it turns out that his pragmatism is itself a third thing and requires the rejection of Christian truth (and Stoic). It thins down things to particular statements about particular issues or background agreement on moral platitudes rather than keeping the whole of life in view.

20. Cf. Wittgenstein, *Culture and Value*, 62e: "One keeps forgetting to go right down to the foundations. One doesn't put the question marks *deep* enough down" (emphasis in original). This is contra Stout, *Ethics After Babel*, 19 et passim, who says that pushing disagreement down too far tends to cause it to disappear by becoming merely verbal. His example of the words *clocks* and *cars* actually works against his thesis. The situation he describes is exactly what is the case when one looks, for example, at the use of the word *God:* the patterns of usage that give the word its meaning are so different that it calls into question whether we are actually talking about the same word.
21. One should observe what is not here: seek the common good. This sort of language is exactly what modern liberalism tempts you to believe in without ever wondering about how you could know what goods you have in common. For all his sophistication, Stout mostly reproduces this sort of problem in a pragmatist vein. He assumes you share the right kinds of goods to pursue and, if not, you can simply talk it out—give and defend your reasons—and vote on it when you cannot come to consensus. Richard Rorty, of course, thought that "religion" ought to get out of public argument (Rorty did eventually moderate this view, but his earlier position is representative of a wide swath of current thinkers). I also reject the idea that developing some sort of "third language" is intellectually viable; it is, to be sure, profoundly disrespectful of the traditions it seeks to speak for, but that would not make it wrong. What makes it incoherent is that it cannot represent the traditions it claims to speak for without simultaneously assuming that their truth claims are false.
22. Cochran, "Consent."
23. Cochran, "Bricolage," 723. The arguments of these (and like) scholars are of course more careful and subtle than simply suggesting that Christians have taken Stoic ideas about this or that. Byers, for example, argues that Augustine developed parts of his thought through the rejection of particular Stoic claims. The character of bricolage as these scholars describe it is thus often a combination of acceptance and rejection rather than acceptance *simpliciter.*
24. Wittgenstein, *Philosophical Investigations,* 8, 12, 18, 20, 22, et passim.
25. Wittgenstein, *Philosophical Investigations,* 12; cf. 6.
26. Wittgenstein, *Philosophical Investigations,* 6.
27. Rowe, "God, Greek Philosophy, and the Bible," 73.
28. Cf. Rowe, "God, Greek Philosophy, and the Bible," 72. Interpreters such as Levering ("God and Greek Philosophy") treat handles as if they look the same in all locomotive cabins, or go only in locomotive cabins, or are all cranks or brake-levers, and so on.
29. See Rowe, "The Grammar of Life," 31–50, for a close exposition of how this works in a particular case.

30. The phrasing here says exactly what I mean.
31. Levering, "God and Greek Philosophy," 179–82. Stout would presumably deny that this is his position (he says he is a Wittgensteinian). But his actual argument requires this assumption about words.
32. Admittedly this position requires me to say something like this about the early Christians who thought they were using "Greek philosophical insights" (Levering): they did not know what they were doing hermeneutically to the words they were using. This would have to include the giants: Origen, Augustine, and so on. This position does come with a concurrent conviction that we have learned things from Wittgenstein that change how we think about word meaning and behind which we cannot now go. That is, it is not the case that Augustine was less intelligent than his late-modern readers—he was vastly more so—but it is the case that the view of language articulated by Wittgenstein was unavailable to him (and is superior to his view).
33. Wittgenstein, *Philosophical Investigations*, 194.
34. A point Stout well knows and makes much of in his outstanding book *Democracy and Tradition.*
35. Stout, *Ethics After Babel*, 65 (emphasis added). Stout does know well the point that grammar and life go together, as he demonstrates in *Democracy and Tradition* (and parts of *Ethics After Babel*, too, of course). But here he forgets it.
36. Wittgenstein, *Culture and Value*, 46.
37. MacIntyre, "Epistemological Crises," 3. Page numbers cited subsequently in the text refer to this work.
38. Rowe, *World Upside Down*, explores epistemological crises of ancient pagans as they confront the Christian mission in places such as Lystra, Ephesus, and Philippi. Stephen Fowl, "Could Horace Talk with the Hebrews?" 1–20, attempts to "split the difference" between Stout and MacIntyre. Fowl's article is astute, as one would of course expect, but he ultimately does not split the difference on the central point and sides with Stout on the question of translation. This, I think, is because the difference between Stout and MacIntyre cannot be split. Fowl also does not take translation to be a question of the lived meaning of words but focuses primarily on natural languages (Aramaic, Hebrew, and Latin). Fowl's ecclesiological points are well formulated and well taken, but I do not think that they depend on his argument about Stout and MacIntyre.
39. MacIntyre, "Epistemological Crises," 15–23. Kuhn has of course responded to his critics, as MacIntyre notes.
40. See Rodney Stark's account of Christian nursing and medical practice during the plague of Galen in *The Rise of Christianity*.
41. In the case of our Roman, he would declare himself a Christian because Christianity provides the view of the human being that sustains the care of the sick because he believes that death has been defeated by the resurrection of Jesus Christ. If you're afraid of death, you can't care for the sick during the plague. Christianity is not afraid of death.
42. Elsewhere, MacIntyre rejects Pascalian thinking for a different reason: admitting the limits of reason as they apply to the move from one rival tradition to another appears to

put us in the position of having to make a "criterionless choice," much as Kierkegaard's leap of faith seems to presuppose. See MacIntyre, "Once More on Kierkegaard," 341, 343. Cf. his remarks in "Moral Relativism; Truth and Justification," 1: 72–73. MacIntyre is also worried about fallibalism, but we do not need to discuss those worries here.

43. Stout's bricolage does *not* work well for this sort of transition because Stout assumes that you are basically making your own thing. Ancient philosophy was an induction into a pattern of practical reasoning through disciplines that were themselves the tradition called Stoicism, Epicureanism, and so forth. In other words, Hadot (for example) shows why Stout is insufficient.

44. Nussbaum, *Therapy of Desire*. Of course, if we are to believe Diogenes Laertius (*Vitae* 10.7), Nikidion was a real person, though "Little Victory" may have been her nickname. One might want to argue that the ancient Greco-Roman philosophers shared agreements to the degree that we should not say that they were undergoing an epistemological crisis when they changed from one philosophy to another. Admittedly, this is a complex question. There were enough differences among the schools to suggest both that, on the one hand, there weren't enough agreements, and one would have had to move from, for example, the Stoa to the Lyceum to change traditions—and that, on the other hand, repeated agreement between traditions was apparently taken for granted by some philosophers (as seen, for example, in Cicero's *De natura deorum*). Obviously, the styles of the Academy and the Lyceum were more similar to each other than Cynicism was to either one (moving to Cynicism from a more mainstream philosophical tradition would require an epistemological crisis). In short, ancient philosophical traditions changed through time, and the question about epistemological crisis would require considerable refinement for each tradition at each step of the way.

45. MacIntyre himself came to see this, of course (see, e.g., "Once More on Kierkegaard," 350–55), but he still talks about it in terms that accord with his acceptance of the distinction between philosophy and theology or nature and grace; see, e.g., the interview in *The MacIntyre Reader*, 265–66. MacIntyre gives a retrospective account of his entrance into Christianity that (a) radically underestimates the fact that it is retrospective, and (b) is overintellectualized. According to the New Testament, one could not give a narrative of conversion in rational and intellectual terms alone. A more provocative way to put the New Testament's point against MacIntyre is this: being a Thomist doesn't make you a Christian. Or: if you're a Christian and a Thomist it is because God has set you free to see Thomism as something like the best way to articulate what you take Christianity to imply about this and that.

46. E.g., MacIntyre, "Epistemological Crises," 11–12. He names Jew, American, historian; they all have "epistemological debate as a necessary feature of their conflicts."

47. For a theologically and existentially rich response to the fickleness of fortune, see the discussion of Gregory Nazianzus's treatment of lepers in Hauerwas, *The State of the University*, 187–201.

48. At this point, we do well to remember that the argument about completion is not simply the Christian take on things. All the earliest Christians were Jews: they were arguing for the extension or fulfillment of their *own* tradition as the community of those people who gathered around the Jewish Messiah Jesus.

49. The revival of speculative Platonism certainly displaced Stoicism from the center of ancient pagan philosophy, but it was not because the Stoic tradition had lapsed into incoherence and the Platonist one provided the solution. Christianity, as one scarcely needs to say, did not break down.
50. MacIntyre, "Moral Relativism," 72–73. Though he may not admit it, MacIntyre's argument appears to be based on Christian conceptions of rational truth—rational demonstration of superiority is possible—as some of his critics have noticed. See, e.g., Bernard Williams's review of MacIntyre, *Whose Justice?* Since I do not believe in the division between philosophy and theology, I find this unsurprising—it is as it should be for a Christian. Williams obviously does not think this is a good way to do philosophy. But his dislike only shows that the disagreement is the sort of disagreement that I'm describing. The shortest, best treatment of "reason" that says much of what I think, too, is Alan Torrance's essay "*Auditio Fidei.*"
51. See, especially, MacIntyre, "Once More on Kierkegaard."
52. MacIntyre says that we cannot have both him and Kierkegaard. I would rather say that if we have MacIntyre on traditions, we need Kierkegaard to deal with the problems MacIntyre raises. Put another way, nature is too strong a category for MacIntyre. He is trying to solve the problem he creates by his description of traditions without resorting to explicitly theological descriptions of change/conversion. He wants to stay in nature/philosophy, but that is why he can't really solve the problem he creates for himself. If MacIntyre would discard the divisions between nature/grace and philosophy/theology, he could finally learn from Pascal and Kierkegaard that the way he describes traditions requires a robust theological account of conversion/reason.
53. Pascal's wager fragment (*Pensées*, 680) is well known and has received much commentary. Perhaps as an indication of its importance—its existential weight, as it were—Pascal kept this note in his pocket.
54. There is no way to escape the fact that we have to live before we can think life out. There are various attempts to deny this—some of them rationalist, some of them pragmatist, some of them Thomist—but the time it took to conceive the denials already betrayed the deniers: they were living as they thought. We leap existentially well before we learn what the reasons are for our leap and even how to reason in the ways that would teach us why we have leapt the way we have.
55. Pascal, *Pensées*, 177, "What the Stoics propose is so difficult and worthless." This sort of reaction to the Stoic claims is closer to the sort of thing that they would appreciate—and humanly deeper—than "I understand them." For those who have forgotten or do not know, Pascal was aware of the complexities of knowing "the other" and of the sort of silliness that can accompany different versions of truth. See his sarcastic comments, for example, on jurisprudence and truth in *Pensées*, 94: "Three degrees of latitude overthrow jurisprudence. A meridian determines truth. . . . Truth lies on this side of the Pyrenees, error on the other." To be sure, his remarks about Islam, Muhammad, and the Koran are not what twenty-first-century Western scholars would wish for, but for the seventeenth century they are remarkably subtle in their understanding of the differences between strong religious traditions.

APPENDIX

1. Lest we forget, the position that tries to reject final truth altogether is but one more version of what final truth is.
2. Stout does something similar in *Ethics After Babel;* I did it, too, in *Early Narrative Christology.* But anticipating objections and offering replies is obviously an old, old practice. Think of Descartes or Hobbes (Objection by Hobbes, though not mentioned by name, and Reply by Descartes—both written by Descartes) or on back to Plato himself. Indeed, objection and reply is at the heart of all dialectical reasoning.
3. Stout, "Commitments and Traditions," 35. Stout's article is illuminating for many different reasons, but it avoids the central question of whether certain kinds of rationality are tradition-dependent. Stout rejects the idea that Christians are inherently better at understanding their tradition than non-Christians. This he calls the epistemology of "it takes one to know one" (drawing from Henry Levinson). But besides the counterclaim that all strange things are intelligible to humanistic reason, Stout says only, "Judging by the performance of some Christians in my courses on Christian ethics, being Christian does not always help, and sometimes even hinders the process [of understanding Christian ethical discourse]" (34–35). For a more constructive way to think of "religious studies," see David Ford's proposals in *The Future of Christian Theology.*
4. See comments on Stout's platitudes in Chapter 9.
5. There are striking similarities to Foucault's description of the modern museum as a heterotopia in "Of Other Spaces." There is a sense in which the creation of the scholarly smorgasbord attempts to do away with the time that it takes to live the philosophical claims. Of course, the creators of scholarly smorgasbord would presumably deny this and say that their smorgasbords are explicitly targeted at specific times in history. But this denial would simply miss the point.
6. I know that by "modern invention" I say something contestable. I do not, however, think that it is wrong. Even in Aquinas, it seems that natural reason does not correspond to a theologically independent sphere of human knowledge called "philosophy." On this point vis-à-vis Aquinas in particular, see Hauerwas, *With the Grain of the Universe.*
7. Descartes's precise place in this development is debated. Pierre Hadot takes the *Meditations* to continue the ancient philosophical tradition of spiritual exercises—and thus reads them in opposition to modern understandings of philosophy—but Bernard Williams argues that Descartes's philosophy was "pure enquiry." My reading of Descartes's texts is that they can be used to support both the Hadot and Williams lines. This is in part why Descartes is neither preserver nor founder but something more like a transitional figure: Descartes clearly speaks of natural reason/philosophy as something that is distinct from theology (in, e.g., his "Letter of Dedication" to the faculty at Paris), but what he means by "natural reason/philosophy" is not what we would mean today.
8. Wilken's crucial essay "Alexandria" shows how virtue is connected to insight, which is implicitly a rejection of the way of thinking that could lead to the distinction between philosophy and theology. See also Wilken's chapter on Clement of Alexandria in *The Spirit of Early Christian Thought.*

9. See, for example, the brief but very illuminating discussion between Jürgen Habermas and Joseph Ratzinger (Pope Benedict XVI), *The Dialectics of Secularization.* Jeffrey Stout's view of the practice of democracy presupposes something like a conversational ethic, too. His emphasis upon the giving and taking of reasons is often described in terms of conversation/discussion/debate, and so on. See especially Stout's *Democracy and Tradition.*
10. See Bretherton, *Hospitality as Holiness.*

Select Bibliography

Anderson, Gary A. *Sin: A History*. New Haven: Yale University Press, 2009.

Anscombe, G. E. M. *Intention*. Ithaca, N.Y.: Cornell University Press, 1957.

Augustine. *Concerning the City of God Against the Pagans*. Trans. Henry Scowcroft Bettenson. Harmondsworth, Middlesex: Penguin, 1984.

Balch, David L., Everett Ferguson, and Wayne A. Meeks. *Greeks, Romans, and Christians: Essays in Honor of Abraham J. Malherbe*. Minneapolis: Fortress, 1990.

Barclay, John M. G. "'I Will Have Mercy on Whom I Have Mercy': The Golden Calf and Divine Mercy in Romans 9–11 and Second Temple Judaism." *Early Christianity* 1 (2010): 82–106.

———. *Pauline Churches and Diaspora Jews*. Wissenschaftliche Untersuchungen zum Neuen Testament 275. Tübingen: Mohr Siebeck, 2011.

———. "Stoic Physics and the Christ-Event: A Review of Troels Engberg-Pedersen, *Cosmology and Self in the Apostle Paul: The Material Spirit*." *Journal for the Study of the New Testament* 33 (2011): 406–14.

Barnes, Jonathan. *Logic and the Imperial Stoa*. Philosophia Antiqua 75. New York: Brill, 1997.

Becker, Ernest. *The Denial of Death*. New York: Free Press, 1973.

Beker, Johan Christiaan. *Paul the Apostle: The Triumph of God in Life and Thought*. Philadelphia: Fortress, 1980.

Benedict XVI and Jürgen Habermas. *The Dialectics of Secularization: On Reason and Religion*. San Francisco: Ignatius, 2006.

Birley, Anthony. *Marcus Aurelius: A Biography*. New Haven: Yale University Press, 1987.

Bobzien, Susanne. *Determinism and Freedom in Stoic Philosophy*. New York: Oxford University Press, 1998.

Boyarin, Daniel. *Border Lines: The Partition of Judaeo-Christianity*. Divinations. Philadelphia: University of Pennsylvania Press, 2004.

———. "Justin Martyr Invents Judaism." *Church History* 70 (2001): 427–61.

Brennan, Tad. "Stoic Moral Psychology." Pages 257–94 in Inwood, *The Cambridge Companion to the Stoics*.

Bretherton, Luke. *Hospitality as Holiness: Christian Witness amid Moral Diversity*. Burlington, Vt.: Ashgate, 2006.

Bultmann, Rudolf Karl. "Anknüpfung und Widerspruch: Zur Frage nach der Anknüpfung der neutestamentlichen Verkündigung an die natürliche Theologie der Stoa, die hellenistischen Mysterienreligionen und die Gnosis." *Theologische Zeitschrift* 2 (1946): 401–18.

Burridge, Richard A. *What Are the Gospels? A Comparison with Graeco-Roman Biography*. Grand Rapids, Mich.: Eerdmans, 2004.

Byers, Sarah Catherine. *Perception, Sensibility, and Moral Motivation in Augustine: A Stoic-Platonic Synthesis*. New York: Cambridge University Press, 2012.

Campbell, Douglas A. "Romans 1:17—A Crux Interpretum for the Πίστις Χριστοῦ Debate." *Journal of Biblical Literature* 113 (1994): 265–85.

Carroll, John. "The God of Israel and the Salvation of the Nations: The Gospel and Luke and the Acts of the Apostles." Pages 91–106 in *The Forgotten God: Perspectives in Biblical Theology: Essays in Honor of Paul J. Achtemeier on the Occasion of His Seventy-Fifth Birthday*. Ed. A. Andrew Das and Frank J. Matera. Louisville, Ky.: Westminster John Knox, 2002.

Chapman, Stephen B. *The Law and the Prophets: A Study in Old Testament Canon Formation*. Forschungen zum Alten Testament 27. Tübingen: Mohr Siebeck, 2000.

Childs, Brevard S. *The Church's Guide for Reading Paul: The Canonical Shaping of the Pauline Corpus*. Grand Rapids, Mich.: Eerdmans, 2008.

Cochran, Elizabeth Agnew. "Bricolage and the Purity of Traditions: Engaging the Stoics for Contemporary Christian Ethics." *Journal of Religious Ethics* 40 (2012): 720–29.

———. "Consent, Conversion, and Moral Formation: Stoic Elements in Jonathan Edwards's Ethics." *Journal of Religious Ethics* 39 (2011): 623–50.

Colish, Marcia L. *The Stoic Tradition from Antiquity to the Early Middle Ages*. New York: Brill, 1990.

Crites, Stephen. "The Narrative Quality of Experience." *Journal of the American Academy of Religion* 39 (1971): 291–311.

Dahl, Nils Alstrup. *Jesus in the Memory of the Early Church*. Minneapolis: Augsburg, 1976.

———. "The Story of Abraham in Luke-Acts." Pages 139–58 in *Studies in Luke-Acts*. Ed. Leander Keck and J. Louis Martyn. Philadelphia: Fortress, 1966.

Damasio, Antonio R. *Descartes' Error: Emotion, Reason, and the Human Brain*. New York: Avon, 1998.

Descartes, René. *Meditations on First Philosophy: With Selections from the Objections and Replies*. Trans. Mike Moriarty. Oxford: Oxford University Press, 2008.

Diamond, Cora. "Losing Your Concepts." *Ethics* 98 (1988): 255–77.

Dunderberg, Ismo, Troels Engberg-Pedersen, and Tuomas Rasimus, eds. *Stoicism in Early Christianity*. Grand Rapids, Mich.: Baker, 2010.

Dunn, James D. G. *The Theology of Paul the Apostle*. Grand Rapids, Mich.: Eerdmans, 1998.

Endō, Shūsaku. *Silence*. New York: Taplinger, 1980.

Engberg-Pedersen, Troels. *Cosmology and Self in the Apostle Paul: The Material Spirit*. New York: Oxford University Press, 2010.

——. *Paul and the Stoics*. Louisville, Ky.: Westminster John Knox, 2000.

——, ed. *Paul Beyond the Judaism/Hellenism Divide*. Louisville, Ky.: Westminster John Knox, 2001.

——. "Paul's Body: A Response to Barclay and Levison." *Journal for the Study of the New Testament* 33 (2011): 433–43.

——. "The Relationship with Others: Similarities and Differences Between Paul and Stoicism." *Zeitschrift für die neutestamentliche Wissenchaft und die Kunde der älteren Kirche* 96 (2005): 35–60.

Esler, Philip F. "Paul and Stoicism: Romans 12 as a Test Case." *New Testament Studies* 50 (2004): 106–24.

Eubank, Nathan. *Wages of Cross-Bearing and Debt of Sin: The Economy of Heaven in Matthew's Gospel*. Beihefte zur Zeitschrift für die neutestamentliche Wissenschaft und die Kunde der älteren Kirche 196. Berlin: de Gruyter, 2013.

Farquharson, A. S. L. *The Meditations of the Emperor Marcus Antoninus*. 2 vols. Oxford: Clarendon, 1944.

Fee, Gordon D. *God's Empowering Presence: The Holy Spirit in the Letters of Paul*. Peabody, Mass.: Hendrickson, 1994.

Feldmeier, Reinhard, and Hermann Spieckermann. *God of the Living: A Biblical Theology*. Waco, Tex.: Baylor University Press, 2011.

Fitzgerald, John T. *Passions and Moral Progress in Greco-Roman Thought*. New York: Routledge, 2008.

Fitzgerald, John T., Thomas H. Olbricht, and L. Michael White, eds. *Early Christianity and Classical Culture: Comparative Studies in Honor of Abraham J. Malherbe*. Supplements to Novum Testamentum 110. Leiden: Brill, 2003.

Fitzmyer, Joseph. *The Acts of the Apostles: A New Translation with Introduction and Commentary*. Anchor Bible 31. New York: Doubleday, 1998.

——. *The Gospel According to Luke: Introduction, Translation, and Notes*. Anchor Bible 28–28A. Garden City, N.Y.: Doubleday, 1981–85.

Ford, David. *The Future of Christian Theology*. Blackwell Manifestos. Oxford: Wiley-Blackwell, 2011.

Foster, Paul, and Sara Parvis. *Justin Martyr and His Worlds*. Minneapolis: Fortress, 2007.

Foucault, Michel. "Of Other Spaces: Utopias and Heterotopias." Pages 350–55 in *Rethinking Architecture: A Reader in Cultural Theory*. Ed. Neil Leach. New York: Routledge, 1997.

——. *The Order of Things: An Archaeology of the Human Sciences*. New York: Pantheon, 1971.

Fowl, Stephen E. "Could Horace Talk with the Hebrews? Translatability and Moral Disagreement in MacIntyre and Stout." *Journal of Religious Ethics* 19 (1991): 1–20.

Frei, Hans W. *The Eclipse of Biblical Narrative: A Study in Eighteenth and Nineteenth Century Hermeneutics*. New Haven: Yale University Press, 1974.

Frend, W. H. C. *Martyrdom and Persecution in the Early Church: A Study of a Conflict from the Maccabees to Donatus*. New York: New York University Press, 1967.

Geertz, Clifford. *The Interpretation of Cultures: Selected Essays*. New York: Basic, 2000.

Gill, Christopher. "Stoic Writers of the Imperial Era." Pages 597–615 in Rowe and Schofield, *The Cambridge History of Greek and Roman Political Thought*.

———. *The Structured Self in Hellenistic and Roman Thought*. Oxford: Oxford University Press, 2006.

Gorman, Michael J. *Reading Paul*. Eugene, Ore.: Cascade, 2008.

Griffin, Miriam T. *Seneca: A Philosopher in Politics*. Oxford: Clarendon, 1976.

Griffiths, Paul J. *Decreation: The Last Things of All Creatures*. Waco, Tex.: Baylor University Press, 2014.

Hadot, Ilsetraut. *Seneca und die griechisch-römische Tradition der Seelenleitung*. Berlin: de Gruyter, 1969.

Hadot, Pierre. *The Inner Citadel: The Meditations of Marcus Aurelius*. Cambridge: Harvard University Press, 1998.

———. *Philosophy as a Way of Life: Spiritual Exercises from Socrates to Foucault*. Ed. Arnold Davidson. Trans. Michael Chase. New York: Blackwell, 1995.

———. *The Present Alone Is Our Happiness: Conversations with Jeannie Carlier and Arnold I. Davidson*. Trans. Marc Djaballah. Stanford: Stanford University Press, 2009.

———. *What Is Ancient Philosophy?* Cambridge: Harvard University Press, 2002.

Haines, Simon. "Deepening the Self." Pages 1–38 in *Renegotiating Ethics in Literature, Philosophy, and Theory*. Ed. Jane Adamson, Richard Freadman, and David Parker. Cambridge: Cambridge University Press, 1998.

Hart, David Bentley. *Atheist Delusions: The Christian Revolution and Its Fashionable Enemies*. New Haven: Yale University Press, 2009.

Hauerwas, Stanley. *The State of the University: Academic Knowledges and the Knowledge of God*. Illuminations—Theory and Religion. Oxford: Blackwell, 2007.

———. *With the Grain of the Universe: The Church's Witness and Natural Theology*. Grand Rapids, Mich.: Brazos, 2001.

Hauerwas, Stanley, and L. Gregory Jones, eds. *Why Narrative? Readings in Narrative Theology*. Eugene, Ore.: Wipf and Stock, 1997.

Hays, Richard B. *The Conversion of the Imagination: Paul as Interpreter of Israel's Scripture*. Grand Rapids, Mich.: Eerdmans, 2005.

———. *Echoes of Scripture in the Letters of Paul*. New Haven: Yale University Press, 1989.

———. *The Faith of Jesus Christ: The Narrative Substructure of Galatians* 3:1–4:11. 2nd ed. Grand Rapids, Mich.: Eerdmans, 2002.

Hegel, Georg Wilhelm Friedrich. *Lectures on the History of Philosophy, 1825–26*. Vol. 1, *Introduction and Oriental Philosophy*. Trans. Robert F. Brown. Oxford: Clarendon, 2009.

Henderson, Suzanne Watts. "'If Anyone Hungers . . .': An Integrated Reading of 1 Corinthians 11:17–34." *New Testament Studies* 48 (2002): 195–208.

Hofer, Andrew. "The Old Man as Christ in Justin's 'Dialogue with Trypho.'" *Vigiliae christianae* 57 (2003): 1–21.

Horn, Friedrich Wilhelm. "Kyrios und Pneuma bei Paulus." Pages 59–75 in *Paulinische Christologie: Exegetische Beiträge; Hans Hübner Zum 70. Geburtstag*. Ed. Udo Schnelle and Thomas Söding. Göttingen: Vandenhoeck and Ruprecht, 2000.

Inwood, Brad, ed. *The Cambridge Companion to the Stoics*. New York: Cambridge University Press, 2003.

———. *Reading Seneca: Stoic Philosophy at Rome*. Oxford: Clarendon, 2005.

James, William. *The Principles of Psychology*. New York: Classics of Medicine Library, 1997.

Jülicher, Adolf. *Die Gleichnisreden Jesu*. Darmstadt: Wissenschaftliche Buchgesellschaft, 1963.

Justin Martyr and Philippe Bobichon. *Justin Martyr, Dialogue Avec Le Tryphon: Édition Critique*. Fribourg: Academic Press, 2003.

Justin Martyr, Thomas P. Halton, and Michael Slusser. *Dialogue with Trypho*. Selections from the Fathers of the Church 3. Washington, D.C.: Catholic University of America Press, 2003.

Justin Martyr, Denis Minns, and P. M. Parvis. *Justin, Philosopher and Martyr: Apologies*. Oxford Early Christian Texts. New York: Oxford University Press, 2009.

Kelsey, David H. *Eccentric Existence: A Theological Anthropology*. Louisville, Ky.: Westminster John Knox, 2009.

Lang, Timothy. "Mystery and the Making of a Christian Historical Consciousness: From Paul to the Second Century." Ph.D. diss., Duke University, 2014.

Laurentin, René. *Structure et Theólogie de Luc I–II*. Études Bibliques. Paris: Gabalda, 1957.

Lauterbach, Jacob Zallel. *Mekhilta d'Rabbi Yishmael*. Library of Jewish Classics. Philadelphia: Jewish Publication Society of America, 1976.

Levering, Matthew. "God and Greek Philosophy in Contemporary Biblical Scholarship." *Journal of Theological Interpretation* 4 (2010): 169–85.

Locke, John. *A Paraphrase and Notes on the Epistles of St Paul to the Galatians, 1 and 2 Corinthians, Romans, Ephesians*. Ed. Arthur William Wainwright. Oxford: Clarendon, 1987.

Loisy, Alfred. *The Gospel and the Church*. Buffalo, N.Y.: Prometheus, 1988.

Long, A. A. *Epictetus: A Stoic and Socratic Guide to Life*. Oxford: Clarendon, 2002.

———. *From Epicurus to Epictetus*. Oxford: Oxford University Press, 2006.

———. "Stoicism in the Philosophical Tradition: Spinoza, Lipsius, Butler." Pages 365–92 in Inwood, *The Cambridge Companion to the Stoics*.

———. "The Stoics on World-Conflagration and Everlasting Occurrence." *Southern Journal of Philosophy* (1985): 13–38. Rpt. in *From Epicurus to Epictetus*.

Longenecker, Bruce W., ed. *Narrative Dynamics in Paul: A Critical Assessment*. Louisville, Ky.: Westminster John Knox, 2002.

MacIntyre, Alasdair. *After Virtue: A Study in Moral Theory*. 3rd ed. Notre Dame, Ind.: University of Notre Dame Press, 2007.

———. "Ancient Politics and Modern Issues." *Arion* 2 (1973): 425–30.

———. *Dependent Rational Animals: Why Human Beings Need the Virtues*. Chicago: Open Court, 1999.

———. "Epistemological Crises." Pages 3–23 in *The Tasks of Philosophy*, vol. 1, *Selected Essays*.

———. "Moral Relativism; Truth and Justification." Pages 52–73 in *The Tasks of Philosophy*, vol. 1, *Selected Essays*.

———. "Once More on Kierkegaard." Pages 339–56 in *Kierkegaard After MacIntyre: Essays on Freedom, Narrative, and Virtue*. Ed. John J. Davenport and Anthony Rudd. Chicago: Open Court, 2001.

——. *The Tasks of Philosophy*. Vol. 1, *Selected Essays*. New York: Cambridge University Press, 2006.

——. *Three Rival Versions of Moral Enquiry: Encyclopedia, Genealogy, and Tradition*. Notre Dame, Ind.: University of Notre Dame Press, 1990.

——. *Whose Justice? Which Rationality?* Notre Dame, Ind.: University of Notre Dame Press, 1988.

MacIntyre, Alasdair, and Kelvin Knight. *The MacIntyre Reader*. Notre Dame, Ind.: University of Notre Dame Press, 1998.

MacMullen, Ramsay. *Enemies of the Roman Order: Treason, Unrest, and Alienation in the Empire*. Cambridge: Harvard University Press, 1966.

Malherbe, Abraham. "Hellenistic Moralists and the New Testament." In *Aufstieg und Niedergang der römischen Welt: Geschichte und Kultur Roms im Spiegel der neueren Forschung*, part 2, *Principat*. 26.1. Ed. Hildegard Temporini and Wolfgang Haase. New York: de Gruyter, 1992.

——. *Light from the Gentiles: Hellenistic Philosophy and Early Christianity: Collected Essays, 1959–2012*. Ed. Carl R. Holladay, John T. Fitzgerald, Gregory E. Sterling, and James W. Thompson. Leiden: Brill, 2014.

——. *Paul and the Thessalonians: The Philosophic Tradition of Pastoral Care*. Philadelphia: Fortress, 1987.

Marcus, Joel. "Birkat Ha-Minim Revisited." *New Testament Studies* 55 (2009): 523–51.

Martin, Dale. *Inventing Superstition: From the Hippocratics to the Christians*. Cambridge: Harvard University Press, 2004.

——. *Slavery as Salvation: The Metaphor of Slavery in Pauline Christianity*. New Haven: Yale University Press, 1990.

Martyn, J. Louis. "De-Apocalypticizing Paul: An Essay Focused on Paul and the Stoics by Troels Engberg-Pedersen." *Journal for the Study of the New Testament* 24 (2002): 61–102.

McKenny, Gerald P. *To Relieve the Human Condition: Bioethics, Technology, and the Body*. Albany: State University of New York Press, 1997.

Meeks, Wayne A. *The Origins of Christian Morality: The First Two Centuries*. New Haven: Yale University Press, 1993.

Millar, Fergus. "Epictetus and the Imperial Court." *Journal of Roman Studies* 55 (1965): 141–48.

Musurillo, Herbert, ed. *The Acts of the Christian Martyrs*. Oxford Early Christian Texts. Oxford: Clarendon, 1972.

Nouwen, Henri J. M. *The Return of the Prodigal Son: A Story of Homecoming*. New York: Doubleday, 1992.

Nussbaum, Martha Craven. *The Therapy of Desire: Theory and Practice in Hellenistic Ethics*. Princeton: Princeton University Press, 1994.

O'Neill, J. C. "How Early Is the Doctrine of Creatio Ex Nihilo?" *Journal of Theological Studies* 53 (2002): 449–65.

Pascal, Blaise. *Pensées and Other Writings*. Ed. Anthony Levi. Trans. Honor Levi. Oxford World's Classics. Oxford: Oxford University Press, 2008.

Percy, Walker. *The Message in the Bottle: How Queer Man Is, How Queer Language Is, and What One Has to Do with the Other*. New York: Farrar, Straus and Giroux, 1975.

Pfau, Thomas. *Minding the Modern: Human Agency, Intellectual Traditions, and Responsible Knowledge*. Notre Dame, Ind.: University of Notre Dame Press, 2013.

Pohlenz, Max. *Die Stoa: Geschichte einer geistigen Bewegung*. 4th ed. Göttingen: Vandenhoeck and Ruprecht, 1970.

Rabbow, Paul. *Seelenführung: Methodik der Exerzitien in der Antike*. Munich: Kösel-Verlag, 1954.

Reydams-Schils, Gretchen. *The Roman Stoics: Self, Responsibility, and Affection*. Chicago: University of Chicago Press, 2005.

Rist, John M. "Are You a Stoic? The Case of Marcus Aurelius." Pages 23–45 in *Jewish and Christian Self-Definition*, vol. 3, *Self-Definition in the Greco-Roman World*. Ed. Ben F. Meyer and E. P. Sanders. Philadelphia: Fortress, 1982.

———. *Man, Soul, and Body: Essays in Ancient Thought from Plato to Dionysius*. Collected Study Series C549. Brookfield, Vt.: Variorum, 1996.

Rowe, C. J., and Malcolm Schofield, eds. *The Cambridge History of Greek and Roman Political Thought*. New York: Cambridge University Press, 2000.

Rowe, C. Kavin. "Acts 2:36 and the Continuity of Lukan Christology." *New Testament Studies* 53 (2007): 37–56.

———. "The Art of Retrieval: Stoicism?" *Journal of Religious Ethics* 40 (2012): 706–19.

———. *Early Narrative Christology: The Lord in the Gospel of Luke*. Beihefte zur Zeitschrift für die neutestamentliche Wissenschaft und die Kunde der älteren Kirche 139. Berlin: de Gruyter, 2006.

———. "God, Greek Philosophy, and the Bible: A Response to Matthew Levering." *Journal of Theological Interpretation* 5 (2011): 69–80.

———. "The Grammar of Life: The Areopagus Speech and Pagan Tradition." *New Testament Studies* 57 (2011): 31–50.

———. "New Testament Iconography?" Pages 289–312 in *Picturing the New Testament: Studies in Ancient Visual Images*. Ed. Annette Weissenrieder, Friederike Wendt, and Petra von Gemünden. Wissenschaftliche Untersuchungen zum Neuen Testament 193. Series 2. Tübingen: Mohr Siebeck, 2005.

———. A Review of N. T. Wright, *The Resurrection of the Son of God: Christian Origins and the Question of God* 3. *Nova et Vetera* 3 (2005): 411–14.

———. *World Upside Down: Reading Acts in the Graeco-Roman Age*. New York: Oxford University Press, 2009.

Ryle, Gilbert. *Collected Papers*. Vol. 2, *Collected Essays, 1929–1968*. New York: Routledge, 2009.

Sanders, E. P. *Paul and Palestinian Judaism: A Comparison of Patterns of Religion*. Philadelphia: Fortress, 1977.

Sandmel, Samuel. "Parallelomania." *Journal of Biblical Literature* 81 (1962): 1–13.

Schapp, Wilhelm. *In Geschichten verstrickt: Zum Sein von Mensch und Ding*. 4th ed. Frankfurt am Main: Vittorio Klostermann, 2004.

Scherbenske, Eric W. *Canonizing Paul: Ancient Editorial Practice and the Corpus Paulinum*. New York: Oxford University Press, 2013.

Sellars, John. *The Art of Living: The Stoics on the Nature and Function of Philosophy*. Ashgate New Critical Thinking in Philosophy. Burlington, Vt.: Ashgate, 2003.

Sevenster, Jan Nicolaas. *Paul and Seneca*. Supplements to *Novum Testamentum* 4. Leiden: Brill, 1961.

Shepherd, William H. *The Narrative Function of the Holy Spirit as a Character in Luke-Acts*. Society of Biblical Literature Dissertation Series 147. Atlanta: Scholars Press, 1994.

Skarsaune, Oskar. *The Proof from Prophecy: A Study in Justin Martyr's Proof-Text Tradition: Text-Type, Provenance, Theological Profile*. Supplements to *Novum Testamentum* 56. Leiden: Brill, 1987.

Smith, Jonathan Z. "In Comparison a Magic Dwells." Pages 19–35 in *Imagining Religion: From Babylon to Jonestown*. Chicago: University of Chicago Press, 1982.

Sorabji, Richard. "Is Stoic Philosophy as Helpful as Psychotherapy?" Pages 197–209 in *Aristotle and After*. Bulletin of the Institute of Classical Studies Supplement 68. Ed. Richard Sorabji. London: Institute for Advanced Classical Studies, 1997.

Stark, Rodney. *The Rise of Christianity: How the Obscure, Marginal Jesus Movement Became the Dominant Religious Force in the Western World in a Few Centuries*. San Francisco: HarperSanFrancisco, 1997.

Stout, Jeffrey. *Blessed Are the Organized: Grassroots Democracy in America*. Princeton: Princeton University Press, 2010.

———. "Commitments and Traditions in the Study of Religious Ethics." *Journal of Religious Ethics* 25 (1997): 23–56.

———. *Democracy and Tradition*. Princeton: Princeton University Press, 2004.

———. *Ethics After Babel: The Languages of Morals and Their Discontents*. Boston: Beacon, 1988.

Talbert, Charles H. *Luke and the Gnostics: An Examination of Lucan Purpose*. Nashville, Abingdon, 1966.

———. *What Is a Gospel? The Genre of the Canonical Gospels*. Philadelphia: Fortress, 1977.

Taylor, Charles. A *Secular Age*. Cambridge: Belknap Press of Harvard University Press, 2007.

———. *Sources of the Self: The Making of the Modern Identity*. Cambridge: Harvard University Press, 1988.

———. "Understanding the Other: A Gadamerian View on Conceptual Schemes." Pages 24–38 in *Dilemmas and Connections: Selected Essays*. Cambridge: Belknap Press of Harvard University Press, 2011.

Theiler, Willy. *Kaiser Marc Aurel Wege zu sich selbst*. Die Bibliothek der alten Welt, Römische Reihe. Zürich: Artemis-Verlag, 1951.

Thorsteinsson, Runar M. *Roman Christianity and Roman Stoicism: A Comparative Study of Ancient Morality*. Oxford: Oxford University Press, 2010.

Tolstoy, Leo. *War and Peace*. Trans. Richard Pevear and Larissa Volokhonsky. New York: Knopf, 2007.

Torrance, Alan. "*Auditio Fidei*: Where and How Does God Speak? Faith, Reason, and the Question of Criteria." Pages 27–52 in *Reason and the Reasons of Faith*. Ed. Paul Griffiths and Reinhard Hütter. New York: T. and T. Clark International, 2005.

Tran, Jonathan. *The Vietnam War and Theologies of Memory: Time and Eternity in the Far Country*. Malden, Mass.: Wiley-Blackwell, 2010.

Verhey, Allen. *The Christian Art of Dying: Learning from Jesus.* Grand Rapids, Mich.: Eerdmans, 2011.

Veyne, Paul. *Seneca: The Life of a Stoic.* New York: Routledge, 2003.

Vielhauer, Philipp. "On the 'Paulinism' of Acts." Pages 33–50 in *Studies in Luke-Acts: Essays Presented in Honor of Paul Schubert.* Ed. Leander E. Keck and J. Louis Martyn. Nashville: Abingdon, 1966.

Watson, Francis. "The Triune Divine Identity: Reflections on Pauline God-Language, in Disagreement with J. D. G. Dunn." *Journal for the Study of the New Testament* 23 (2001): 99–124.

Wendel, Susan J. *Scriptural Interpretation and Community Self-Definition in Luke-Acts and the Writings of Justin Martyr.* Supplements to *Novum Testamentum* 139. Leiden: Brill, 2011.

White, Michael J. "Stoic Natural Philosophy (Physics and Cosmology)." Pages 124–52 in Inwood, *The Cambridge Companion to the Stoics.*

Wilken, Robert. "Alexandria: A School for Training in Virtue." Pages 15–30 in *Schools of Thought in the Christian Tradition.* Ed. Patrick Henry. Philadelphia: Fortress, 1984.

——. *The Spirit of Early Christian Thought: Seeking the Face of God.* New Haven: Yale University Press, 2003.

Williams, Bernard. *Descartes: The Project of Pure Enquiry.* New York: Routledge, 2005.

——. *Ethics and the Limits of Philosophy.* Cambridge: Harvard University Press, 1985.

——. "Modernity." *London Review of Books*, January 5, 1989.

——. "Stoic Philosophy and the Emotions: Reply to Richard Sorabji." Pages 211–13 in *Aristotle and After.* Bulletin of the Institute of Classical Studies Supplement 68. Ed. Richard Sorabji. London: Institute for Advanced Classical Studies, 1997.

Williams, Bernard, and Myles Burnyeat. *The Sense of the Past: Essays in the History of Philosophy.* Princeton: Princeton University Press, 2006.

Wittgenstein, Ludwig. *Culture and Value.* Ed. G. H. von Wright. Trans. Peter Winch. Chicago: University of Chicago Press, 1980.

——. *Philosophical Investigations.* Trans. G. E. M. Anscombe, P. M. S Hacker, and Joachim Schulte. Malden, Mass.: Wiley-Blackwell, 2009.

Wright, N. T. *The Climax of the Covenant: Christ and the Law in Pauline Theology.* Minneapolis: Fortress, 1992.

——. "Faith, Virtue, Justification, and the Journey to Freedom." Pages 472–97 in *The Word Leaps the Gap: Essays on Scripture and Theology in Honor of Richard B. Hays.* Ed. A. Katherine Grieb, C. Kavin Rowe, and J. Ross Wagner. Grand Rapids, Mich.: Eerdmans, 2008.

——. *The Resurrection of the Son of God.* Christian Origins and the Question of God 3. Minneapolis: Fortress, 2003.

Zizioulas, John D. *Being as Communion: Studies in Personhood and the Church.* Contemporary Greek Theologians 4. Crestwood, N.Y: St. Vladimir's Seminary Press, 1997.

Index